Transforming Global Healthcare

The Role of AI and IoT in Modern Medical Systems

Editors

Anindya Nag
Lecturer, Department of Computer Science & Engineering
Northern University of Business and Technology Khulna
Khulna-9100, Bangladesh

Md. Mehedi Hassan
UniSA STEM, University of South Australia
Mawson Lakes, Australia

Dr. Riya Sil
Associate Professor, Department of Computer Science & Engineering, Brainware University, Kolkata, India

Dr. Asif Karim
Lecturer, Information Technology
Faculty of Science and Technology
Charles Darwin University, Australia

CRC Press
Taylor & Francis Group
Boca Raton London New York

CRC Press is an imprint of the
Taylor & Francis Group, an **informa** business
A SCIENCE PUBLISHERS BOOK

First edition published 2026
by CRC Press
2385 NW Executive Center Drive, Suite 320, Boca Raton FL 33431

and by CRC Press
4 Park Square, Milton Park, Abingdon, Oxon, OX14 4RN

CRC Press is an imprint of Taylor & Francis Group, LLC

Library of Congress Cataloging-in-Publication Data (applied for)

ISBN: 978-1-041-02620-4 (hbk)
ISBN: 978-1-041-06393-3 (pbk)
ISBN: 978-1-003-63521-5 (ebk)

DOI: 10.1201/9781003635215

Typeset in Times New Roman
by Prime Publishing Services

Preface

This book, Transforming Global Healthcare: The Role of AI and IoT in Modern Medical Systems, investigates the use of artificial intelligence, knowledge management, and sustainable practices in healthcare. The content of the chapters of this book are as follows:

Chapter 1 examines healthcare disparities worldwide, highlighting the differences in access, infrastructure, and results between high- and low-income nations. It also looks at how globalization, innovation, and technology affect health systems, pointing out both advancements and enduring difficulties.

Chapter 2 highlights the fact that using an Active Learning-based strategy not only accelerates model convergence but also mitigates the risk of overfitting, ensuring a more generalized and robust classification system. The significance of this work extends beyond pneumonia detection, as Active Learning holds substantial potential for broader applications in medical imaging, including segmentation and disease staging. By optimizing resource utilization and minimizing data annotation costs while maintaining diagnostic accuracy, Active Learning emerges as a transformative approach in machine learning-driven medical diagnostics.

Chapter 3 provides a comprehensive review of the existing research to evaluate the diagnostic applicability of automatic microaneurysm detection and the delineation of preliminary diabetic retinopathy identification.

Chapter 4 presents a novel hybrid deep learning framework, ESOA-HDNN, for accurate skin cancer diagnosis. By integrating a two-channel CNN, Bi-RNN, and Egret Swarm Optimization, the model achieves high diagnostic accuracy and sensitivity, surpassing conventional approaches.

In Chapter 5, a new AI framework, MicrobiomeNet-X, is introduced. This framework is intended to reveal the intricate relationships between obesity and type 2 diabetes by analyzing the intestinal microbiome. It emphasizes clinical trial outcomes and advanced ensemble learning techniques that exhibit substantial enhancements in metabolic health and cost savings.

Chapter 6 explores how Intelligent Decision Support Systems (IDSS) are transforming healthcare by improving diagnostic accuracy, optimizing treatment plans, and facilitating overall clinical decision-making. These systems use artificial intelligence (AI), machine learning (ML), and big data analytics to process massive volumes of medical data, providing real-time insights and personalized suggestions. Recent advances in IDSS have used deep learning techniques, natural language processing (NLP), and cloud computing to provide more precise and scalable solutions.

Chapter 7 follows by analyzing the potential impact of integrating AI and networking on enhancing patient outcomes, improving precision in diagnosis, increasing the efficacy of treatments, and increasing accessibility to healthcare in general. Further issues covered are interoperability, security, and data privacy, along with possible fixes, to guarantee the success and adoption of AI-powered smart healthcare systems. In the long run, this AI and networking convergence has the potential to enhance healthcare in the future by making it more patient-centred, scalable, and efficient.

Chapter 8 introduces a complete QRAIN-HEAL architecture that integrates NIST-standard lattice-based cryptography (Kyber-Falcon hybrid) with a Heterogeneous Ensemble Deep Learning model to enhance security and efficiency in healthcare IoT. It showcases quantum-resistant encryption, elucidates anomaly detection through transformers, employs 3D CapsNets and pSNNs, and attains ultra-low latency, energy efficiency, and bias mitigation across embedded and cloud platforms.

Chapter 9 sets forth with a wearable gadget that can detect and track stress and sadness by continuous monitoring of physiological data, made possible by the Internet of Things. While a companion smartphone app provides soothing music during episodes of severe depression, processed data is uploaded to the cloud, allowing for real-time notifications to caregivers and doctors.

In Chapter 10 we examine how the convergence of IoT and Big Data is revolutionizing public health through real-time surveillance, predictive analytics, and personalized care. We highlight applications in disease monitoring, chronic illness management, and smart city health initiatives while addressing challenges in privacy, security, and ethical data use.

Chapter 11 presents specific examples of IoT use in remote care tracking and disease forecasting, and individual therapeutic approaches, together with explorations of security problems and privacy risks, and ethical concerns. This chapter also invests attention into both environmental and sustainable factors of digital healthcare systems by presenting strategies to lower medical waste output while maximizing energy usage efficiency. Such framework comparisons help identify both their positive aspects and their drawbacks. The analysis explores global trends together with future outlooks to help healthcare professionals empower Big Data and IoT implementation, which leads to better patient results and improved data safety, as well as sustainable public health measures.

Chapter 12 investigates the potential of blockchain architectures to secure, decentralize, and simplify healthcare data administration by establishing tamper-proof, permissioned ledgers. This approach addresses privacy concerns, interoperability gaps, and breaches. It examines the integration of blockchain with AI and IoT to enhance efficiency, while also addressing challenges in scalability, cost, and regulation. Additionally, it examines use cases in EHRs, patient identity, and drug supply monitoring.

Chapter 13 compares anomaly-based and signature-based approaches as well as different clustering algorithms to assess the NSL-KDD dataset's efficacy for healthcare-focused IDS. It draws attention to NSL-KDD's shortcomings in identifying contemporary, healthcare-specific attack vectors and promotes the creation of a customized dataset to improve regulatory compliance and real-time threat monitoring.

Chapter 14 discusses the role of blockchain in healthcare security, encompassing how blockchain safeguards electronic health records, ensures that clinical conference papers and pharmaceutical clinical study data are not tampered with, secures pharmaceutical supply chains, and streamlines the processing of insurance claims, among others. An architecture is also suggested to decentralize control over information flow with the inclusion of patients' generated data.

In Chapter 15 we present an integrated cybersecurity framework for Healthcare 5.0, which amalgamates lightweight cryptography, AI-driven anomaly detection, and blockchain audit trails, enhanced by federated learning and quantum-safe techniques. The simulation on realistic datasets illustrates the attainment of solid security with little latency and excellent usability, informing future standardized procedures for scaled healthcare systems.

Chapter 16 emphasizes that the advancement of electronic technologies in healthcare has improved patient care but has also presented considerable cybersecurity issues. It underscores the necessity for a holistic strategy that integrates new technologies, regulatory adherence, and ethical considerations to protect sensitive patient information.

Concluding in Chapter 17 we examine sustainable practices in healthcare, emphasizing the sector's environmental effect and the necessity for eco-friendly measures, including circular economy, green human resource management (GHRM), and green leadership. We highlight international case studies and prospective pathways concerning technology, policy, and research to synchronize healthcare with sustainability objectives.

The authors hope that by producing this book, they may assist and educate people in their area.

Anindya Nag
Md. Mehedi Hassan
Riya Sil
Asif Karim

Contents

1 | Global Healthcare System and Industry Evaluation

Snigdha Madhab Ghosh[1], Amit Roy[1*] and Ashish Kattamuri[2]

[1] Department of Computer Science & Engineering – Artificial Intelligence, Brainware University, India

[2] Proofpoint, Inc., Sunnyvale, California, USA

Global health systems are complex interconnected networks of diverse stakeholders including governments, the private sector, non-governmental organizations, health care providers, etc. This assessment examines the structure, accessibility, and performance of health systems across the region, analysing significant variations in health service delivery, outcomes, and equity. The research this chapter focuses on disparities between high-income and low-income countries, exploring issues such as unequal distribution of resources, inadequate infrastructure, and challenges caused by cultural, economic and political factors. These differences often lead to disparate health outcomes, with vulnerable populations in underserved areas having limited access to essential services and life-saving interventions. The healthcare industry that covers pharmaceuticals, biotechnology, medical devices, and healthcare plays an important role in training in the world healthcare environment. This evaluation is explored as innovation, technical results and investment contribute to progress in the medical field. Digital medical tools, telemedicine, artificial intelligence and precision medicine have revolutionized the industry, offering new solutions for diagnosis, treatment and prevention. However, the rapid pace of technological change also raises concerns about accessibility, affordability and ethical considerations, particularly in developing regions where resources are limited, with the promotion of medical resources, technology, and information, globalization had a greater effect on the health sector. Vaccinations, treatment methods, and the creation promoted by international alliance and cooperation. But globalization also compounds issues such as the spread of infectious diseases,

*Corresponding author: amr.cse@brainwareuniversity.ac.in

DOI: 10.1201/9781003635215-1

health disparities, and moral dilemmas over cross-border clinical trials and intellectual property rights.

1. Introduction

The global healthcare system is a vast and intricate network of medical services, facilities, professionals, policies, and technological advancements all aimed at improving human health and well-being. Healthcare systems across the globe play a pivotal role in enhancing the quality of life and ensuring the well-being of populations. These systems encompass a wide range of services, including preventive care, diagnostic services, treatment, and rehabilitation, delivered through public and private sectors [1]. Evaluating the global healthcare industry involves analysing various factors such as accessibility, affordability, quality of care, healthcare infrastructure, government policies, and technological integration. With the ongoing advancement of medical sciences, the healthcare industry is vital in tackling public health challenges, managing diseases, and improving overall quality of life. Healthcare systems around the world vary significantly in structure and efficiency due to factors such as economic status, cultural norms, government involvement, and contributions from the private sector. Developed nations like the United States, Canada, the United Kingdom, and Germany have well-established healthcare systems with advanced medical technologies, specialized healthcare providers, and structured insurance models. However, disparities still exist in these countries related to healthcare access, costs, and service delivery efficiency. In contrast, developing and underdeveloped nations often face challenges such as inadequate healthcare infrastructure, limited medical personnel, restricted access to essential medications, and financial constraints, resulting in suboptimal healthcare outcomes. To sum up, evaluating the global healthcare system and industry necessitates a thorough examination of various elements, such as accessibility, cost-effectiveness, care quality, infrastructure, regulations, and technological innovations. Although notable strides have been made in enhancing healthcare services around the globe, there are still challenges like escalating healthcare expenses, shortages in the workforce, the burden of chronic illness and the risk posed by pandemics. This chapter provides a comprehensive overview of future trends [2] in global health services.

Accessibility is one of the most important factors in the assessment of the global healthcare sector. For many countries, universal healthcare access is still a top priority, but attaining it calls for large financial outlays, legislative changes, and effective healthcare delivery systems. To offer healthcare services to its citizens, many nations have used a variety of strategies, including hybrid structures, single-payer systems, and multi-payer insurance models. Some countries, like the United States, rely on a combination of public and private insurance alternatives, while others, like Canada and the United Kingdom, provide universal healthcare that is paid for by taxes. Geographical obstacles, economic discrepancies, and governmental regulations that either help or impede the delivery of healthcare are frequently the causes of accessibility disparities [3].

Another important factor to consider while assessing the healthcare sector is affordability. Prescription medications, medical treatments, insurance premiums, and healthcare services are growing increasingly expensive around the world. High medical expenditures cause financial hardship for countless individuals and families, contributing to healthcare inequities. Affordability is a big concern in underdeveloped countries, as numerous populations cannot afford even the most basic medical treatment. International aid, health insurance plans, and government subsidies are crucial in closing the affordability gap and guaranteeing that underserved groups receive necessary medical treatment [4].

A key factor in determining how well healthcare systems work is the quality of care provided. Modern medical facilities, patient-centered care, evidence-based therapies, and prompt access to qualified medical personnel are all components of high-quality healthcare. To guarantee high-quality healthcare services, many developed nations have put strict laws, accreditation requirements, and ongoing monitoring systems into place [5]. Even in wealthy countries, however, there are differences in the quality of healthcare, which are frequently caused by socioeconomic status, urban-rural divides, and the accessibility of healthcare providers. Due to a lack of funding, antiquated medical technology, and insufficient healthcare expertise, the quality of care is often degraded in low-income nations [6].

Government rules and policies have a significant impact on how the healthcare sector is shaped. Funding distribution, medical practice regulation, medication approvals, insurance models, and public health programs are all governed by healthcare policy. Better health outcomes, reduced mortality rates, and efficient disease control methods are typically found in nations with well-structured healthcare policies. To combat the COVID-19 pandemic, countries adopted emergency response plans, vaccination distribution initiatives, and public health awareness campaigns, underscoring the significance of government involvement in healthcare [7].

The global healthcare industry has seen a considerable transformation due to technological improvements. Healthcare delivery and patient outcomes have been completely transformed by innovations like wearable health gadgets, robotic surgery, telemedicine, artificial intelligence (AI), and electronic health records (EHRs). Medical operations are becoming more accurate and efficient thanks to AI-driven diagnostics, predictive analytics, and automated medical systems. Particularly in rural locations, telemedicine has helped close the distance between patients and medical professionals by facilitating online consultations and online medical support. Early disease identification has been made easier, hospital admissions have decreased, and patient monitoring has improved as a result of technology integration in healthcare [8]. The effectiveness and sustainability of the global healthcare sector are also impacted by a number of issues. The growing prevalence of chronic illnesses including diabetes, heart disease, and cancer is one of the main worries. These illnesses raise the overall cost of healthcare because they necessitate specialized therapies, long-term medical care, and lifestyle changes. Furthermore, the aging of the population in many nations is a problem for healthcare systems since older people need geriatric experts, long-term care facilities, and more frequent medical attention [9].

Lack of workers in the healthcare sector is another urgent problem. There is a shortage of qualified medical personnel in several areas, including physicians, nurses, and medical technicians. Workforce shortages are caused by a number of factors, including excessive educational expenses, insufficient training programs, and the movement of healthcare professionals to nations with higher wages. Lack of workers in the healthcare sector is another urgent problem. There is a shortage of qualified medical personnel in several areas, including physicians, nurses, and medical technicians. Workforce shortages are caused by a number of factors, including excessive educational expenses, insufficient training programs, and the movement of healthcare professionals to nations with higher wages. Investments in medical education, incentives for medical professionals, and better working conditions to retain qualified staff are all necessary to address this issue [10].

The threat posed by infectious illnesses and pandemics is another significant obstacle facing the global healthcare sector. The COVID-19 pandemic highlighted the need for strong public health infrastructure, emergency planning, and international collaboration by exposing the weaknesses of healthcare systems around the world. To fight future pandemics and emerging infectious diseases, efficient disease surveillance, quick response systems, and international cooperation are crucial [11].

Notwithstanding these obstacles, there are plenty of chances for expansion and advancement in the worldwide healthcare sector. Precision healthcare solutions and enhanced therapies are being made possible by investments in genetics, customized medicine, and biotechnology. Access to healthcare is becoming easier because of the growth of telehealth services and mobile health apps, especially in underprivileged areas. Additionally, international programs and alliances like the World Health Organization (WHO) and non-governmental organizations (NGOs) are still vital in enhancing healthcare delivery and tackling health inequalities across the globe [12].

To sum up, evaluating the global healthcare system and industry necessitates a thorough examination of various elements, such as accessibility, cost-effectiveness, care quality, infrastructure, regulations, and technological innovations. Although notable strides have been made in enhancing healthcare services around the globe, there are still challenges like escalating healthcare expenses, shortages in the workforce, the burden of chronic illness and the risk posed by pandemics. It is essential for governments, healthcare institutions and tech innovators to work together to build sustainable, fair and efficient healthcare frameworks that prioritize patient welfare and global health safety. The future of healthcare relies on ongoing advancements, policy changes and inclusive healthcare strategies that guarantee medical services are available to everyone irrespective of their socio-economic background or geographical position. This chapter provides a comprehensive overview of future trends in global health services.

The Global Landscape of Healthcare Systems

Healthcare Models, globally these healthcare systems can be classified into four primary models. Though the healthcare models vary country to country based on weather pattern, general immunity of public and financial capabilities of masses. The Beveridge Model is funded and provided by the government, such as the United Kingdom's National Health Service (NHS). It emphasizes universal coverage and equitable access [13]. The Bismarck Model is funded through employer and employee contributions, as seen in Germany and Japan. It relies on regulated private providers and insurance schemes. The National Health Insurance Model, combines elements of the Beveridge and Bismarck models, as in Canada. The government acts as a single payer, ensuring universal coverage. An Out-of-Pocket Model exists predominantly in low-income countries, where individuals pay directly for healthcare services, often resulting in disparities in access.

Key Stakeholders in Global Healthcare

Healthcare systems involve a diverse set of stakeholders, including governments and policymakers, healthcare providers (hospitals, clinics, and practitioners), pharmaceutical and biotechnology industries, non-governmental organizations (NGOs), patients and advocacy groups, and determinants of health. The effectiveness of a healthcare system is determined by a number of factors, including GDP allocation to healthcare, insurance coverage, and affordability. Social determinants include education, work, housing, and nutrition. Technological advancements Integration of artificial intelligence, telemedicine, and electronic health records. Epidemiological shifts affect disease burden, including noncommunicable diseases (NCDs) and infectious diseases. Evaluation metrics for Healthcare Systems, evaluating healthcare systems requires a multidimensional approach that considers efficiency, equity, and outcomes [14]. Key metrics include the provision of healthcare services to a diverse population. Geographical and financial accessibility, quality of care, and patient outcomes (such as survival rates and quality-adjusted life years). Safety, effectiveness, and patient satisfaction. Cost efficiency equals the value for money spent. Administrative expenses and resource use. Health outcomes include life expectancy, infant mortality, and disease prevalence. Vaccination rates are one example of a public health indicator. Equity in healthcare and disparities in healthcare access and outcomes are being tracked across a number of population categories. Detecting service gaps and addressing social determinants of health. Global Healthcare Challenges, urban and rural locations have different levels of access. Disparities between socioeconomic groups and races. Drug and medical technology expenses are on the rise and aging populations lead to greater healthcare demands. Workforce Shortages: Many places lack a sufficient number of skilled healthcare personnel. Burnout rates are high, as is skilled worker migration. Emerging global health hazards include pandemics (such as COVID-19), climate change, and its effects on health. Antibiotic resistance and the emergence of superbugs. Care fragmentation occurs when providers and systems do not work together effectively, creating gaps in the continuity of care. [15].

Technological Divide

Access to high-quality healthcare is restricted by the unequal adoption of health technologies in poor nations, which is still a major problem. Widespread adoption is hindered by different elements including high costs, a lack of digital literacy, and poor infrastructure. Additionally, the efficacy of digital health solutions is hampered by unstable power supplies and internet access. Integration of AI-driven diagnostics, telemedicine, and electronic health records is challenging in many areas. Progress is further slowed by regulatory obstacles and opposition to change. Government action, international cooperation, and customized solutions are needed to address these issues and provide fair access. Closing the technological barrier is necessary for improving global healthcare outcomes [16]. AI and Machine Learning: Enhancing diagnosis, planning of treatment, and operational efficiency. Wearable technology encourages preventive care and patient engagement. Blockchain enhances data security, interoperability, and transparency [8]. Personalized medicine tailors therapies to individuals' genetic profiles. Progress in genetics and biotechnology. Precision medicine efforts aim to improve therapeutic outcomes. Value-based healthcare shifts the focus from volume to value. Focus on patient outcomes and cost-effectiveness. The implementation of accountable care organizations (ACOs) and bundled payment methods. Global collaborations are partnerships between states, NGOs, and the corporate sector to address global health issues. Examples include WHO projects, Gavi (the Vaccine Alliance), and Global Fund programs. Pharmaceutical innovation involves the creation of vaccines and enhanced therapeutics for chronic and infectious diseases. Research into rare diseases and orphan pharmaceuticals [9].

This chapter will cover various case studies and localities.

(i) **United States:** With its state-of-the-art research facilities, innovative therapies, and cutting-edge technologies, the United States leads the world in medical innovation. Progress in healthcare is fuelled by developments in precision medicine, biotechnology, and AI-driven diagnostics. But problems still exist, such as the high expense of healthcare, which puts a strain on both individuals and families. Disparities in access to high-quality treatment depending on socioeconomic class and location continue to be a major problem. Furthermore, many people lack access to proper care due to coverage gaps caused by the insurance system's complexity. Expanded access, cost control, and legislative changes are necessary to address these issues and provide universal access to quality healthcare [17].

(ii) Scandinavian Countries: Scandinavian countries, such as Sweden, Norway, and Denmark, are well known for their universal healthcare programs, which guarantee all residents fair and high-quality access. Preventive care, patient-centred services, and state-of-the-art medical infrastructure are given top priority in their healthcare strategies. However, aging populations, growing healthcare demands, and rising long-term care expenses present sustainability challenges. It's still difficult to manage resource allocation and maintain efficiency. In order to guarantee long-term sustainability without sacrificing the quality of care, policymakers concentrate on creative solutions, workforce growth, and digital health integration [18].

(iii) India: Advances in medical technology, more private sector investment, and the growing use of telemedicine are all contributing to India's fast-growing healthcare sector. Digital health solutions are increasing accessibility, overcoming gaps, and offering remote consultations. Significant obstacles still exist, though, such as the glaring disparity in healthcare between urban and rural areas, where the former lacks both qualified medical personnel and high-quality medical facilities. The infrastructure and provision of healthcare services are restricted by insufficient public funding. To achieve equal healthcare across the country, government investment must be strengthened, access to healthcare must be expanded in rural areas, and technology must be utilized.

(iv) China: China has a vast public health system that includes sophisticated medical research, government-sponsored healthcare programs, and vast hospital networks. A variety of therapeutic options are made possible by the merging of traditional Chinese medicine with contemporary healthcare. However, high patient loads frequently overwhelm urban healthcare facilities, resulting in resource strain and lengthy wait times. Due to a lack of facilities and fewer medical experts, access to healthcare is uneven in rural areas. Improving rural healthcare investment, expanding digital health, and changing policies to ensure fair access are all necessary to meet these problems.

(v) Sub-Saharan Africa: This continent has robust community-based healthcare systems, with local healthcare providers playing a vital role in providing necessary services. To increase vaccination rates and disease prevention measures, NGOs and international organizations actively assist healthcare initiatives. Significant obstacles, however, exist in the area, such as a lack of funding and medical resources, high rates of tuberculosis, HIV/AIDS, and malaria, and a lacklustre healthcare system. Hospitals, qualified personnel, and necessary medications are scarce in many remote locations. For long-term improvement, infrastructure development, workforce training, and healthcare funding must all be strengthened.

In section 2, the authors have provided a detailed discussion on digital transformation and telemedicine. Section 3 consists of the future directions in global healthcare. Section 4 provides the need for digital health in global collaboration. The healthcare industry report is included in section 5. The global healthcare services market overview is discussed in Section 6, followed by the conclusion in Section 7.

2. Digital Transformation and Telemedicine

The incorporation of digital health technologies, such as artificial intelligence (AI), telemedicine, wearable health devices, and electronic health records, is transforming healthcare delivery. Telemedicine has greatly enhanced access, particularly in isolated and underserved areas. As reported by the World Health Organization (WHO), digital health can improve the efficiency and effectiveness of healthcare systems in all countries [1]. AI and machine learning algorithms are more frequently being utilized for predictive diagnostics, image analysis, and even treatment suggestions. Wearable devices, such as fitness trackers and smartwatches, facilitate real-time monitoring of patient vitals, promoting preventive care and early intervention.

Personalized and Precision Medicine

Future healthcare approaches are moving away from a "one-size-fits-all" model towards precision medicine adapted to specific genetic profiles and lifestyle elements. Progress in genomics and biotechnology enables the creation of personalized treatments that enhance patient results and minimize negative effects. The National Institutes of Health (NIH) emphasizes precision medicine as a key component in tackling intricate diseases such as cancer and Alzheimer's [2].

Strengthening Global Health Security

The COVID-19 pandemic exposed vulnerabilities in global health systems and underscored the need for coordinated international response mechanisms. Future directions focus on improving pandemic preparedness through stronger disease surveillance, faster vaccine development, and robust public health infrastructure. The Global Health Security Agenda (GHSA) plays a key role in promoting international collaboration to prevent, detect, and respond to infectious disease threats [3].

Climate Change and Environmental Health

Climate change greatly affects health results, leading to the expansion of vector-borne illnesses, respiratory issues, and food scarcity. Upcoming healthcare needs to include climate resilience by developing adaptive systems and encouraging environmental sustainability. The WHO highlights the critical need to weave climate factors into health policy to safeguard at-risk communities [4].

Equity and Universal Health Coverage (UHC)

Inequities in access to healthcare continue to be a significant obstacle. Upcoming international healthcare initiatives should prioritize the attainment of Universal Health Coverage (UHC), guaranteeing that everyone can access the necessary health services without experiencing financial difficulties. UHC is a fundamental objective of the United Nations' Sustainable Development Goals (SDG 3), seeking to lessen the differences in health services among low, middle, and high-income nations [5].

3. Future Directions in Global Healthcare

Universal Health Coverage (UHC) achieves fair access through policy changes and investments, strengthening basic healthcare systems to serve as the cornerstone for universal health coverage and adapting healthcare systems to climate change implications and implementing environmentally friendly approaches in healthcare delivery [6]. Improving pandemic preparedness and response mechanisms while strengthening surveillance and rapid response frameworks including investigating public-private partnerships and novel funding mechanisms and Utilizing health bonds and micro-insurance programs. This also includes addressing worker shortages through worldwide training initiatives, encouraging collaboration among academic institutions worldwide ensuring global access to telehealth and digital solutions, and bridging the digital gap to prevent healthcare inequities [7].

Industrialisation Lifecycle

Emerging trends across industries point to common characteristics of industrialization, including shifts in production and service delivery from artisanal, ground-up approaches to industry models that are increasingly aggregated, standardized, professionalized, and tech-powered. Most industries went through this lifecycle in the 20th century. In most instances, healthcare delivery is still in its early stages of development, with characteristics similar to the foundational and catalytic eras that many other sectors experienced a century ago. In the early phases, industry may be fragmented and have limited size. Multiple participants, with little consolidation and localization without scale. External factors contribute to an extended pre-industrialization period [8]. External enablers lay the framework for market development. Transportation and technological advancements are two examples of enablers. This includes the emergence and rapid growth of regionally dominant players, as well as the fundamentals and key components of the industry. Innovation, expansion, and capital aggregation all contribute to rapid growth including large-scale consolidation of the phase of expansion into new geographies. An excellent human health care system produces optimal phased results. Thus, the global system factor materializes the function, new environment, and viable research. Therefore, nature's consequences generate the session [9].

India's Impact on Global Health

With more than 1.4 billion people, India has the largest population in the world and one of the largest diasporas. In 2022, almost 18 million Indians were living abroad, according to the UN World Migration Report. India's diaspora reflects the nation's rich and diverse cultural heritage and provides an invaluable bridge between home and host societies [10].

India is a major force in the field of international health and medicine. According to the NIH World Report, some of the world's largest medical research funders, including the NIH, the European Commission, the Institute Pasteur, and the Japan Agency for Biomedical Research and Development, have funded over 4,300 health research studies in India since 2016. Between 2022 and 2023, Fogarty oversaw more than 30 research across the country on various topics, including women's health, environmental exposures, mental health, and vision. AYUSH manages India's traditions of Ayurveda, yoga, and other holistic health practices, giving the country a distinct position in the global health landscape. The combination of these practices, along with conventional Western medicine, has started to gain a larger influence in India and beyond. AYUSH released official guidelines for remedies to treat mild to moderate COVID-19 in 2021 [11–12]. By working with global organisations and taking part in global health initiatives, India and its diaspora continue to practice health diplomacy as their influence grows abroad. Figure 1 provides the growth of the Global Healthcare Services Market.

World Health Day

World Health Day is observed annually on April 7th to commemorate the establishment of the World Health Organization (WHO). Each year, this day highlights various aspects crucial to the health and well-being of humanity. World Health Day's theme in 2023 is 'Health for All', which recognizes the various healthcare requirements of people and communities around the globe. This theme recognises different public health initiatives and global progress in providing healthcare to the most vulnerable and underprivileged members of society. The healthcare sector has experienced substantial expansion worldwide, with the industry's value increasing from $ 8.5 trillion in 2018 to $ 12 trillion in 2022. India's overall healthcare industry is estimated to be around $ 372 billion in 2022, with a compound annual growth rate (CAGR) of 22 percent [13].

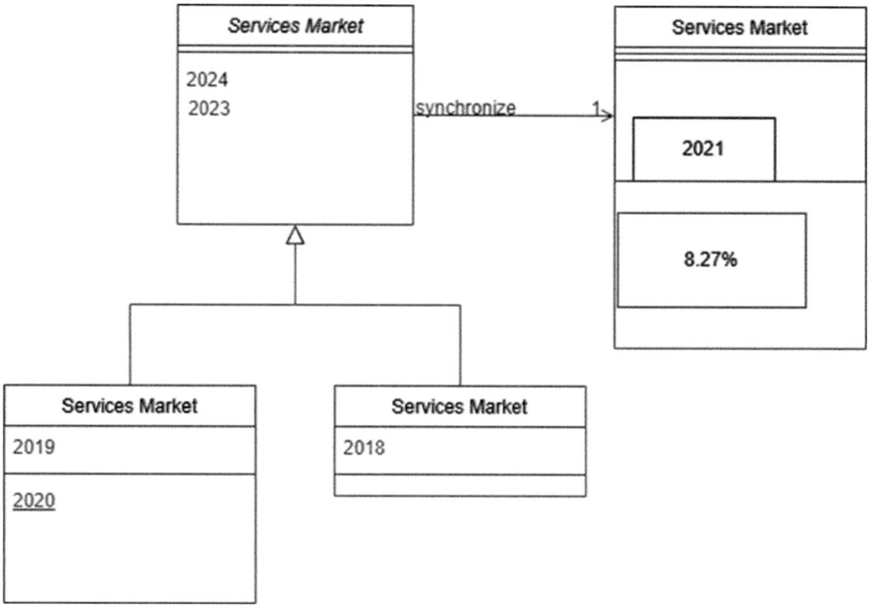

Figure 1: Global Healthcare Services Market.

4. Digital Health needs Global Collaboration

The healthcare challenges of today, rising costs, unequal access, poor outcomes and the growing burden of chronic diseases, demand collective action. The global digital health revolution requires more than technological breakthroughs; it requires effective collaboration and system-level alignment. For instance, the effectiveness of AI in healthcare depends on strong interconnectivity across diverse data sources, which enables scalable, trustworthy, and equitable algorithms. Duplication of digital platforms and tools across countries wastes resources and delays progress in addressing universal health challenges. Private-sector innovation faces obstacles without foundational digital public infrastructure, policy alignment, and sustainable financing. Localized innovations often fail to scale globally due to the lack of frameworks for cross-border knowledge exchange and harmonized standards [14]. Figure 2 shows the Different Global Healthcare Segmentation.

5. Healthcare Industry Report

Healthcare has become one of India's largest sectors, both in terms of revenue and employment. Healthcare comprises hospitals, medical devices, clinical trials, outsourcing, telemedicine, medical tourism, health insurance, and medical equipment. The Indian healthcare sector is growing at a brisk pace due to its

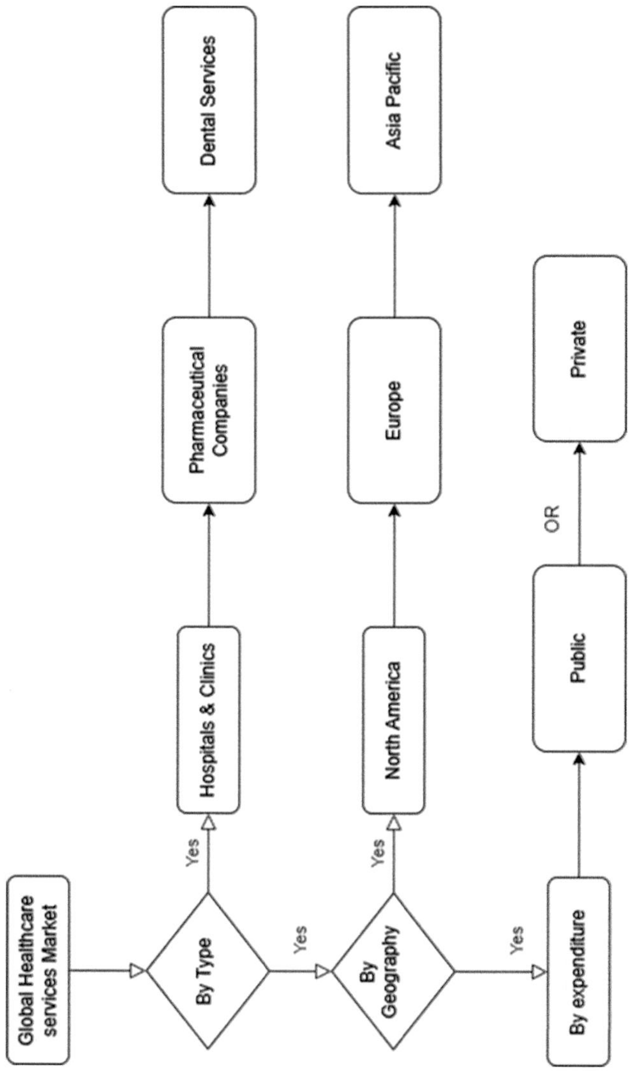

Figure 2: Different Global Healthcare Segmentation.

strengthening coverage, services, and increasing expenditure by public as well as private players [7].

India's healthcare delivery system is categorised into two major components, public and private. The government, i.e., the public healthcare system, comprises limited secondary and tertiary care institutions in key cities and focuses on providing basic healthcare facilities in the form of Primary Healthcare Centres (PHCs) in rural areas. The private sector provides the majority of secondary, tertiary, and quaternary care institutions with a major concentration in metros, tier-I, and tier-II cities. India's competitive advantage lies in its large pool of well-trained medical professionals. India is also cost-competitive compared to its peers in Asia and Western countries. The cost of surgery in India is about one-tenth of that in the US or Western Europe. The low cost of medical services has resulted in a rise in the country's medical tourism, attracting patients from across the world. Moreover, India has emerged as a hub for R&D activities for international players due to its relatively low cost of clinical research [15].

Given India's enormous population and size, public health is given a lot of importance by the Indian government. Health spending has been allotted INR 88,956 cr in the Union Budget 2023–24, a 2.71 percent rise over the previous year. Controlling and eliminating the deadly consequences of tuberculosis (TB) in accordance with WHO's "End TB Strategy" has been a primary emphasis of India's public health strategy. WHO has set a goal to lower new cases of TB by 80% and fatalities by 90% between 2015 and 2030. Approximately 9% of the world's TB incidence rate dropped between 2015 and 2019. In India, heightened efforts to combat tuberculosis also resulted in a 24 percent decrease in cases between 2015 and 2019.

1. **Ayushman Bharat Digital Mission:** India's healthcare system, a mix of public and private providers, faces challenges in resource allocation and access, particularly in rural areas, but is working towards a more integrated and digitized system through initiatives like the Ayushman Bharat Digital Mission.
2. **Healthcare Services Market:** The healthcare services market size is forecast to increase by USD 6,263.7 billion at a CAGR of 8.73% between 2023 and 2028.

Several trends are shaping the industry's growth. The elderly population's expansion is driving the demand for long-term care services, including medical devices and consumables. Economic growth and lifestyle changes are leading to an increase in healthcare spending, particularly on medical devices and consumables [16]. Hospitals are adopting bundled payments and digital tools to improve efficiency and reduce costs. Cross-industry partnerships are emerging, allowing for innovation in the development of novel drugs and treatments.

The rise of telemedicine in the healthcare sector is revolutionizing patient care, enabling remote monitoring and access to medical services. These trends present both opportunities and challenges for market participants. While the increasing demand for healthcare services offers growth potential, rising costs and regulatory requirements pose significant hurdles [17–21]. To remain competitive, companies must stay abreast of these trends and adapt to the evolving market landscape. Table 1 provides statistics on the healthcare market.

Table 1: Annual Per Capita Healthcare Expenditure in Selected Countries (Source: OECD International Health Expenditure Data-2022)

Country	Per capita expenditure
United States	$12,197
Switzerland	$7,582
Germany	$7,518
Belgium	$6,022
Sweden	$6,228
Austria	$6,690
France	$6,106
United Kingdom	$5,467

6. Global Healthcare Services Market Overview

The increase in the number of elderly people, faster economic growth, technological advancements, changes in lifestyles, and enhanced ability to survive and the standard of living is expected to contribute to the growth of the Healthcare Services Market [22]. Increasing the assertion of bundled payments, utilizing digital tools, rising cross-industry and cross-company partnerships, concentrating on the development of novel drugs, and obtaining hybrid imaging techniques are all major trends in the Healthcare Services Market [23]. The costs of medical facilities have increased dramatically over the past few decades. Sophisticated testing techniques have prepared the path for initial and enhanced disease detection, as well as research into the treatment of terminal diseases like cancer. The Healthcare Services Market is forecast to expand due to rising affordability and a rise in awareness, which is already obvious in many countries as it significantly contributes to GDP growth. Several developed countries have introduced health insurance plans in response to rising healthcare costs. Healthcare insurance is by far the most crucial component of the healthcare industry in North America. Its growing popularity among many consumers and the general public is expected to boost demand in the coming years [24]. Furthermore, healthcare services contribute significantly to the overall earnings of the healthcare industry [25].

7. Conclusion

The global healthcare system and industry evolution point towards a future of increased standardization, personalization, and technological integration, aiming for better outcomes and addressing inequities, while also facing challenges like workforce shortages and climate change. The global healthcare system has undergone a profound transformation over the past century, driven by technological innovation, policy reforms, demographic shifts, and the growing burden of chronic diseases. From reactive, hospital-based care to a more proactive, patient-centered approach, the industry continues to evolve toward value-based models emphasizing prevention, accessibility, and efficiency. Digital health tools, artificial intelligence, and data-driven decision-making are redefining how care is delivered and managed across borders. Remarkable advancements and challenges remain—such as unequal access, rising costs, workforce shortages, and the need for resilient public health systems, especially in the face of global threats like pandemics and climate change. Moving forward, a collaborative and inclusive approach—integrating innovation, policy, and equity—will be essential to shaping a sustainable, adaptable, and universally accessible healthcare future. The modern era has brought unprecedented transformation to healthcare systems around the world. Driven by advancements in science and technology, shifting demographics, and evolving patient expectations, healthcare in modern times has transitioned from a reactive, disease-focused model to a more proactive, personalized, and integrated approach.

References

1. World Health Organization Maximizing Positive Synergies Collaborative Group. (2009). An assessment of interactions between global health initiatives and country health systems. *The Lancet*, 373(9681), 2137–2169.
2. Sawyer, T., Gray, M. M., Umoren, R., and Umoren, R. A. (2022). The global healthcare simulation economy: A scoping review. *Cureus*, 14(2).
3. Jarrett, P. G. (2006). An analysis of international health care logistics: The benefits and implications of implementing just-in-time systems in the health care industry. *Leadership in Health Services*, 19(1), 1–10.
4. Dang, H. S., Nguyen, T. M. T., Wang, C. N., Day, J. D., and Dang, T. M. H. (2020). Grey system theory in the study of medical tourism industry and its economic impact. *International Journal of Environmental Research and Public Health*, 17(3), 961.
5. Unger, J. P., Morales, I., and De Paepe, P. (2020). Objectives, methods, and results in critical health systems and policy research: Evaluating the healthcare market. *BMC Health Services Research*, 20, 1–13.
6. Umar, M., Mata, M. N., Abbas, A., Martins, J. M., Dantas, R. M., and Mata, P. N. (2021). Performance evaluation of the Chinese healthcare system. *International Journal of Environmental Research and Public Health*, 18(10), 5193.

7. Attaran, M. (2022). Blockchain technology in healthcare: Challenges and opportunities. *International Journal of Healthcare Management*, 15(1), 70–83.
8. Karatas, M., Eriskin, L., Deveci, M., Pamucar, D., and Garg, H. (2022). Big Data for Healthcare Industry 4.0: Applications, challenges and future perspectives. *Expert Systems with Applications*, 200, 116912.
9. Sarkodie, S. A., and Owusu, P. A. (2021). Global assessment of environment, health and economic impact of the novel coronavirus (COVID-19). *Environment, Development and Sustainability*, 23(4), 5005–5015.
10. Jabarulla, M. Y., and Lee, H. N. (2021, August). A blockchain and artificial intelligence-based, patient-centric healthcare system for combating the COVID-19 pandemic: Opportunities and applications. *Healthcare*, 9(8), 1019. Mdpi.
11. Belfiore, A., Cuccurullo, C., and Aria, M. (2022). IoT in healthcare: A scientometric analysis. *Technological Forecasting and Social Change*, 184, 122001.
12. Kothinti, R. R. (2024). Artificial intelligence in healthcare: Revolutionizing precision medicine, predictive analytics, and ethical considerations in autonomous diagnostics. *World Journal of Advanced Research and Reviews*, 19(3), 3395–3406.
13. Rani, S., Kataria, A., Kumar, S., & Tiwari, P. (2023). Federated learning for secure IoMT-applications in smart healthcare systems: A comprehensive review. *Knowledge-based Systems*, 274, 110658.
14. Shahim, B., Kapelios, C. J., Savarese, G., and Lund, L. H. (2023). Global public health burden of heart failure: an updated review. *Cardiac Failure Review*, 9, e11.
15. Chauhan, A., Jakhar, S. K., and Chauhan, C. (2021). The interplay of circular economy with industry 4.0 enabled smart city drivers of healthcare waste disposal. *Journal of Cleaner Production*, 279, 123854.
16. Dinga, J. N., Sinda, L. K., and Titanji, V. P. (2021). Assessment of vaccine hesitancy to a COVID-19 vaccine in Cameroonian adults and its global implication. *Vaccines*, 9(2), 175.
17. Ibn-Mohammed, T., Mustapha, K. B., Godsell, J., Adamu, Z., Babatunde, K. A., Akintade, D. D. et al. (2021). A critical analysis of the impacts of COVID-19 on the global economy and ecosystems and opportunities for circular economy strategies. *Resources, Conservation and Recycling*, 164, 105169.
18. Amjad, A., Kordel, P., and Fernandes, G. (2023). A review on innovation in healthcare sector (telehealth) through artificial intelligence. *Sustainability*, 15(8), 6655.
19. Oman, D. (2025). Mindfulness for global public health: Critical analysis and agenda. *Mindfulness*, 16(3), 573–612.
20. Vishwakarma, L. P., Singh, R. K., Mishra, R., and Kumari, A. (2025). Application of artificial intelligence for resilient and sustainable healthcare system: Systematic literature review and future research directions. *International Journal of Production Research*, 63(2), 822–844.
21. Ugwu, C. N., Ugwu, O. P. C., Alum, E. U., Eze, V. H. U., Basajja, M., Ugwu, J. N. et al. (2025). Sustainable development goals (SDGs) and resilient healthcare systems: Addressing medicine and public health challenges in conflict zones. *Medicine*, 104(7), e41535.
22. Warraich, H. J., Tazbaz, T., and Califf, R. M. (2025). FDA perspective on the regulation of artificial intelligence in health care and biomedicine. *JAMA*, 333(3), 241–247.
23. Subramanyam, S. V. (2025). Cloud-based enterprise systems: Bridging scalability and security in healthcare and finance. *IJSAT-International Journal on Science and Technology*, 16(1).

24. Manikandan, A., Sanjay, T., Menon, G., Aswin, R., Bhaskar, P. B., Govind, R. M. et al. (2025). Issues and challenges in security and privacy with e-Healthcare: A thorough literature analysis. *Internet of Things enabled Machine Learning for Biomedical Applications*, 222–247.
25. Yadav, U., and Shrawankar, U. (2025). Artificial intelligence across industries: A comprehensive review with a focus on education. *AI Applications and Strategies in Teacher Education*, 275–320.

2 | Development of Active Learning based Classification Model for Detection of Pneumonia using X-ray Image

Mithun Biswas[1], Nirmalya Pal[1], Riya Sil[1*] and Meetu Malhotra[2]

[1] Department of Computer Science & Engineering, Brainware University, Kolkata, India
[2] Harrisburg University of Science and Technology, Pennsylvania, USA

Active Learning is an effective machine learning strategy that strategically selects the most informative data samples for manual annotation, significantly reducing the burden of acquiring large-scale labeled datasets. This approach is particularly advantageous in medical image diagnosis, where expert annotation is both expensive and time-consuming. In this chapter, we present an Active Learning-based Classification Model for pneumonia detection using chest X-ray images. Our methodology leverages a Support Vector Machine (SVM) classifier, employing margin of confidence as the query strategy to identify and annotate the most critical samples. By selectively labeling only the most uncertain data points, the model achieves optimal performance with minimal annotation effort. Experimental evaluations demonstrate that our proposed model reduces the annotation workload by 61.01%, requiring only 38.99% of the dataset to achieve the same accuracy level as a fully supervised learning approach. Additionally, the study highlights that using an Active Learning-based strategy not only accelerates model convergence but also mitigates the risk of overfitting, ensuring a more generalized and robust classification system. The significance of this work extends beyond pneumonia detection, as Active Learning holds substantial potential for broader applications in medical imaging, including segmentation and disease staging. By optimizing resource utilization and minimizing data annotation costs while maintaining diagnostic accuracy, Active Learning emerges

*Corresponding author: riyasil1802@gmail.com

DOI: 10.1201/9781003635215-2

as a transformative approach in machine learning-driven medical diagnostics. Future research will explore its integration with deep learning-based models for enhanced medical image analysis, further improving automated disease detection and classification in clinical settings.

1. Introduction

The rapid advancement of Artificial Intelligence (AI) has led to its widespread adoption across various domains, including transportation, defense, business, social media, and healthcare. Within healthcare, Machine Learning (ML) and Deep Learning (DL) have significantly contributed to medical image analysis, transforming disease detection and diagnosis. These technologies enable automated, accurate, and efficient interpretation of medical images, reducing human workload and improving clinical decision-making. Among life-threatening diseases, pneumonia remains a major global health concern, causing millions of hospitalizations and significant mortality rates annually. Pneumonia is an inflammatory infection of the lungs, typically caused by bacteria or viruses. Despite being treatable with antibiotics and antivirals, early and accurate diagnosis is crucial to prevent severe complications. Chest X-ray imaging is the most commonly used diagnostic tool for pneumonia detection. However, distinguishing pneumonia from other respiratory conditions using X-ray images is challenging, even for expert radiologists, due to overlapping visual patterns and ambiguous symptoms. Consequently, computer-aided diagnostic (CAD) systems leveraging machine learning have gained significant attention to assist radiologists in pneumonia detection. Training a supervised learning model for pneumonia detection requires a large number of labeled chest X-ray images, which poses a challenge due to the high cost and time-intensive nature of manual annotation. To address this, Active Learning (AL) provides an efficient approach by identifying the most informative unlabeled samples for expert annotation, thereby reducing the required labeled data while maintaining high predictive accuracy. Active Learning-based Classification Models iteratively refine the dataset by selecting key samples that maximize model performance with minimal annotation effort.

This chapter explores the development of an Active Learning-based Support Vector Machine (SVM) Classification Model for pneumonia detection using chest X-ray images. The proposed model employs margin of confidence as a query strategy to select critical samples for labeling, ensuring optimal model training with a reduced dataset. Our experimental results demonstrate that the annotation requirement can be reduced by 38.99% while achieving comparable accuracy to traditional supervised learning models trained on fully labeled datasets. The chapter is structured as follows: Section 2 provides an overview of machine learning applications in medical image analysis, with a focus on pneumonia detection using X-ray imaging. Section 3 discusses Active Learning techniques and their role in medical diagnosis. Section 4 details the methodology for developing the Active Learning-based SVM classifier. Section 5 presents experimental results and discussion, highlighting the impact of Active Learning in reducing annotation costs. Finally, Section 6 concludes the chapter by exploring future research directions, including deep learning-based segmentation techniques and advanced Active Learning strategies for medical imaging.

Objective

The primary objective of developing an Active Learning-based Classification Model for pneumonia detection using chest X-ray images is to minimize annotation costs while maintaining high model accuracy. Instead of labeling an entire dataset, the model selectively identifies and annotates only the most informative samples, reducing the data requirement for training while ensuring effective pneumonia detection.

Motivation

Medical image analysis, particularly in pneumonia detection using X-ray images, requires a large volume of labeled data for training machine learning models. However, manual annotation of medical images is time-consuming, costly, and requires domain expertise. Active Learning addresses this challenge by strategically selecting a minimal set of labeled instances to optimize model performance. This approach significantly reduces the annotation burden while ensuring high diagnostic accuracy, making it a cost-effective solution for automated pneumonia detection.

2. Machine Learning in Health Care Sector

In this section authors have discussed the various use of technologies in the healthcare sector which include various sub-sections related to machine learning and healthcare.

X-RAY Imaging

Medical imaging plays a crucial role in diagnostics, treatment planning, and disease prevention, providing healthcare professionals with detailed visual insights into the human body. As technology advances, medical imaging techniques continue to evolve, enhancing accuracy, efficiency, and accessibility in clinical practice. One of the most widely used imaging techniques is X-ray imaging, which helps diagnose a variety of conditions by generating images of internal organs, bones, and tissues. X-ray machines emit a small amount of ionizing radiation, which penetrates the body and is captured on a detector to produce an image. As part of the electromagnetic spectrum, X-rays behave like radio waves and photons, transporting radiant energy through space. Their ability to differentiate between dense and soft tissues makes them an essential tool for diagnosing fractures, lung infections, and other medical conditions. With continuous advancements in radiology and AI-driven image analysis, medical imaging is becoming more precise, automated, and efficient, playing a critical role in Computer-Aided Diagnosis (CAD) systems and machine learning-based detection models.

Pneumonia

Pneumonia is a serious respiratory infection that affects the lungs, primarily caused by bacterial, viral, or fungal pathogens. The infection specifically targets the pulmonary alveoli, the tiny air sacs at the end of the bronchioles responsible for oxygen exchange. In many cases, pneumonia affects only one of the five lobes of the lungs (three in the right lung and two in the left), a condition known as lobar pneumonia. However, when the infection extends to the bronchial tubes, it is classified as bronchopneumonia. Pneumonia remains a major global health concern, particularly for young children, the elderly, and immuno-compromised individuals. It is the leading cause of death in children under five years old, accounting for approximately 12.8% of global child mortality. Among adults, pneumonia is responsible for significant morbidity and mortality, ranking as the third leading cause of death in Japan and leading to over one million hospitalizations annually in the United States, with 50,000 fatalities reported each year. Despite its severity, pneumonia is preventable and treatable when diagnosed early. Timely and accurate diagnosis is essential for effective treatment, typically involving antibiotics, antivirals, and supportive care. Chest X-ray imaging plays a crucial role in pneumonia detection, serving as a primary diagnostic tool in clinical and epidemiological studies. Given the challenges of manually interpreting X-ray images, CAD systems and machine learning-based models have emerged as promising solutions to enhance accuracy and efficiency in pneumonia detection.

Overview of Active Learning

Active Learning (AL) is a specialized subset of machine learning that focuses on optimizing the selection of informative data samples for annotation, thereby reducing the need for extensive labeled datasets. Unlike traditional supervised learning, where the model is trained on a fully labeled dataset, Active Learning intelligently selects the most relevant samples from a large pool of unlabeled data to maximize learning efficiency. This technique is particularly beneficial in scenarios where labeling data is expensive, time-consuming, or requires expert intervention, such as in medical image analysis, transportation systems, and natural language processing (NLP). By prioritizing the annotation of high-impact data points, Active Learning significantly reduces the labeling effort while maintaining—or even improving—model performance. In medical imaging, particularly in pneumonia detection using chest X-ray images, Active Learning plays a crucial role in minimizing the annotation burden by selecting the most diagnostically significant images for expert labeling. This enhances the efficiency of computer-aided diagnosis (CAD) systems, making them more cost-effective and scalable for real-world medical applications.

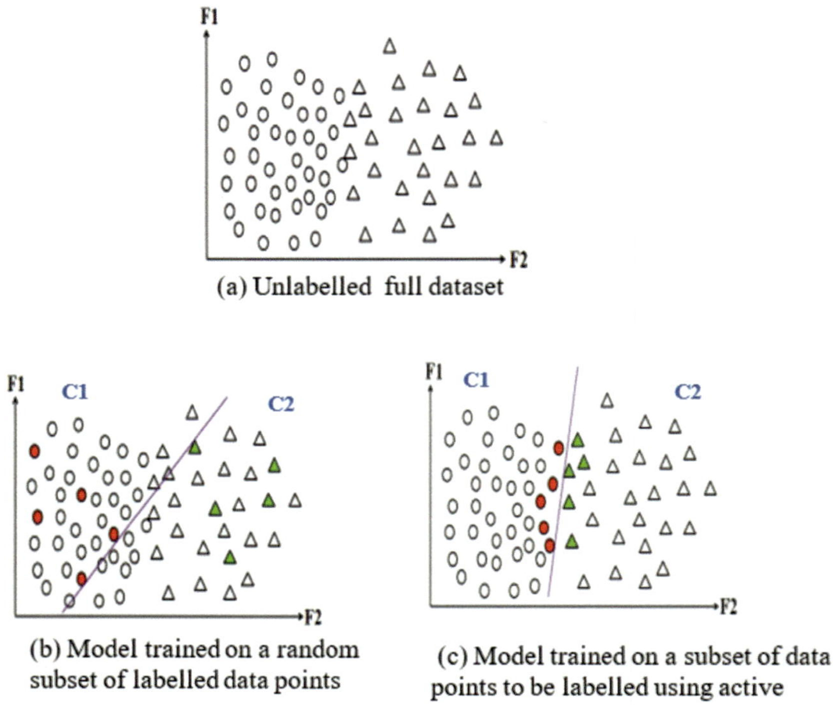

Figure 1: Diagram of the Importance of Active Learning.

Active learning is a subfield of machine learning that aims to minimize the amount of labeled data required to train an accurate model by strategically selecting the most informative data points for labeling. Figure 1 illustrates the significance of active learning in comparison to random sampling strategies for labeling data.

Figure 1(a) depicts the initial condition, wherein the dataset comprises entirely unlabeled data points. These data points, represented by circles and triangles, correspond to two distinct but unknown classes. At this stage, no class labels are assigned, and thus, the dataset cannot be directly utilized for supervised learning tasks.

Figure 1(b) presents the outcome of training a classification model using a small, randomly selected subset of labeled data points. The selected data points are highlighted with filled red circles and green triangles, representing class labels C1 and C2, respectively. The model, based on this limited and randomly chosen labeled set, constructs a decision boundary to separate the two classes. However, due to the lack of representation in critical regions of the feature space—particularly near the class boundary—the resulting classifier performs sub-optimally.

In contrast, Figure 1(c) demonstrates the model performance when the same number of data points is labelled through an active learning strategy. Here, the labelled examples are chosen not randomly, but based on their expected informativeness—typically those that lie near the current model's decision boundary, where the model is most uncertain. This targeted labelling results in a decision boundary that more accurately captures the true division between classes, despite using the same amount of labelled data as in the previous case.

Collectively, this figure underscores the advantage of active learning: by prioritizing the labelling of data points that are most beneficial for improving model performance, it is possible to achieve higher classification accuracy with significantly fewer labelled samples. This is particularly valuable in real-world scenarios where data labelling is expensive, time-consuming, or requires expert knowledge.

3. Literature Review

Over the past two decades, extensive research has been conducted to formulate and understand various query selection strategies from a learner's perspective. B. Settles [1] provided a comprehensive introduction to active learning, offering a detailed survey of the literature. His work explores different scenarios in which queries can be formulated, presents an overview of existing query strategy frameworks, and analyzes both empirical and theoretical evidence supporting successful active learning. Additionally, he discusses variations in problem settings, practical challenges, and related topics within machine learning. D. Tuia et al. [2] introduced an active learning framework for remote sensing image classification, where the predictor actively selects the most valuable pixels to enhance its performance. The study evaluates a state-of-the-art margin sampling approach based on Support Vector Machines (SVM) and proposes two novel methods, successfully applied to high-resolution urban scene classification. Furthermore, D. Tuia et al. [3] conducted a comparative study of various active learning approaches for remote sensing image classification. Their work categorizes heuristics into four families, evaluating their advantages and limitations through experiments on multispectral and hyperspectral datasets. In medical imaging, V. Nath et al. [4] explored active learning techniques for medical image segmentation, applying their framework to MRI scans of the hippocampus and CT scans of pancreatic tumors. Their study utilizes a query-by-committee approach with a joint optimizer to refine sample selection. I. Muslea et al. [5] examined active learning for multi-view domains, where multiple disjoint subsets of features (views) independently contribute to learning the target concept. In deep learning applications, L. Yang et al. [6] proposed a deep active learning framework combining Fully Convolutional Networks (FCN) with active learning to optimize annotation efforts. Their approach leverages uncertainty and similarity information from FCN and reformulates the maximum set cover problem to prioritize informative regions for annotation. Similarly, A. Top et al. [7] framed interactive 3D image segmentation as a classification problem and integrated active learning to streamline user interaction during segmentation tasks. A. Casanova et al. [8] introduced a reinforcement learning-based active learning strategy for semantic segmentation. Instead of selecting entire images, their approach identifies small but informative image regions for labeling. Experimental validation on the CamVid and Cityscapes datasets demonstrates that their deep RL region-based DQN method reduces labeling requirements by approximately 30% while improving class balance. For high-dimensional data, J. Li et al. [9] developed a semi-supervised segmentation algorithm tailored for hyperspectral remote sensing data. Their method involves learning posterior class distributions using multinomial logistic regression, followed by segmentation through a Markov random field model [10–11]. A. Vezhnevets et al. [12] formulated active learning as a node selection problem in a pairwise Conditional Random Field (CRF), identifying the most informative nodes to maximize classification accuracy. W. Chen et al. [13] designed an active learning framework for training convolutional neural networks with minimal labeled data in medical image segmentation. For medical image classification, D. Mahapatra et al. [14] employed conditional Generative Adversarial Networks (cGANs) to generate diverse chest X-ray images, improving active learning sample selection. Saad et al. [15] proposed an adaptive active learning method that integrates uncertainty and information density measures for improved sample selection in image classification tasks. Their later work [17] extended this by introducing multi-label SVM active learning with Max Loss and Mean Max Loss selection strategies. Zheng-Jun Zha et al. [17] proposed a two-dimensional active learning framework for image classification, demonstrating that traditional active learning is a special case of their formulation when only a single label is used. Additionally, D. Tuia et al. [19] introduced two active learning algorithms for remote sensing classification, using heuristics to identify and select the most valuable training samples. In high-dimensional learning scenarios, W.H. Beluch et al. [21] compared ensemble-based methods with Monte Carlo Dropout and geometric approaches for active learning in convolutional neural networks. Their findings indicate that ensemble methods provide better-calibrated predictive uncertainties, essential for active learning algorithms. S.C.H. Hoi et al. [22] introduced a batch-mode active learning framework leveraging the Fisher Information Matrix to optimize sample selection through a submodular function-based greedy algorithm. K. Wang et al. [23] proposed an incremental deep active learning framework that integrates convolutional neural networks with cost-effective sample selection. For deep learning applications, A.K. Jaiswal et al. [24] enhanced Mask-RCNN for pixel-wise medical image segmentation by incorporating global and local features. Their modifications improve robustness and performance on chest radiograph datasets. Y. Han et al. [25] leveraged radiometric features and contrastive learning for pneumonia detection in chest X-rays. M.D.K. Hassan et al. [26] employed machine learning-based LabelBinarizer for categorical encoding of labeled chest X-ray images, facilitating more effective classification. R. Jain et al. [27] trained various convolutional neural networks to classify pneumonia in X-ray images, experimenting with different hyperparameters and network architectures. Performance analysis techniques have been explored by A. Manickan et al. [29], who implemented U-Net-based segmentation followed by classification using ResNet50, InceptionV3, and InceptionResNetV2 for pneumonia detection. They examined the impact of Adam and SGD optimizers with different batch sizes. E.l. Asnaoui et al. [28] conducted a comparative analysis of deep CNN architectures (e.g., VGG16, DenseNet201, and MobileNetv2) for pneumonia classification. P. Rajpurkar et al. [29] developed CheXNet, a 121-layer CNN trained on over 100,000 chest X-ray images, achieving radiologist-level pneumonia detection performance. For interactive image segmentation, J. Maiora et al. [31] introduced an active learning-based segmentation system using a Random Forest classifier. Zamzmi et al. [32] designed a continual active learning approach that adapts to shifts in medical imaging data sources, optimizing labeling efficiency. Cost-effective active learning approaches include X. Shi et al. [33], who developed a framework for skin lesion analysis that balances informativeness and diversity in sample selection. D. Mahapatra et al. [35] explored active learning strategies for prostate MRI segmentation, leveraging visual saliency principles encoded in a graph-based model. For optimal selection in medical imaging, G. Zamzmi et al. [32] introduced an open-world active learning framework for echocardiography view classification, distinguishing between known and unknown views. Saha et al. [37] combined generative and discriminative models to optimize training sample selection for accurate anatomical segmentation. J. Melendez et al. [38] reduced uncertainty in multiple-instance learning (MIL) classification by incorporating an instance selection mechanism into their active learning framework. In deep learning-based medical imaging, M. Yang et al. [39] developed a CNN pipeline to classify digitized ZN-stained slides for tuberculosis detection. Sil et al. [40] proposed a method to generate synthetic CT images from modified Dixon MRI scans, improving attenuation correction in PET/MR imaging.

This comprehensive review highlights significant advancements in active learning across various domains, emphasizing its role in optimizing training efficiency, reducing annotation effort, and improving model generalization.

Active Learning based Classification

Active learning is a subset of machine learning techniques in which the most essential data samples are identified from a huge number of datasets and manually labeled to build a better model in a highly efficient manner. To construct the SVM Active Learning Classification model, various basic areas of study are required, as shown in the schematic diagram below:

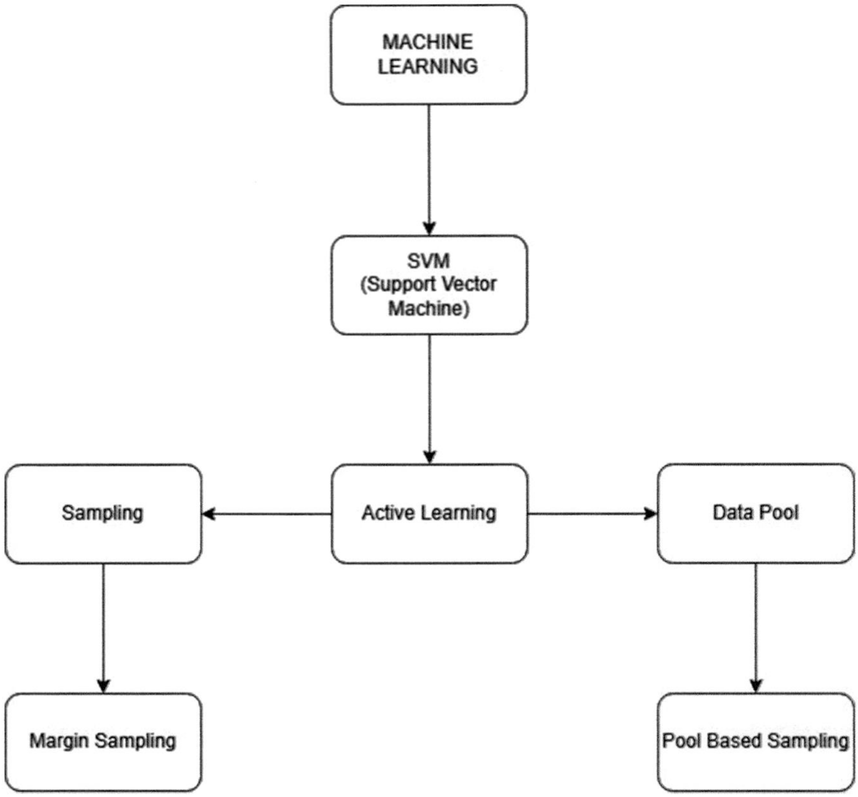

Figure 2: Diagrammatic Representation of Active Learning-based SVM Classification.

Figure 2 delineates the overarching algorithm for SVM classification based on active learning. Figure 3 illustrates the Flowchart of the Active Learning Cycle for Enhancing Classifier Performance.

SVM Classification Model

SVM is a widely recognized supervised learning algorithm extensively applied to both classification and regression tasks. However, its primary utility lies in classification problems, where it aims to establish an optimal decision boundary within an n-dimensional feature space to effectively distinguish between different classes. This decision boundary, known as a hyperplane, ensures precise categorization of new data points based on learned patterns.

The SVM algorithm strategically selects support vectors, which are the most influential data points in defining the hyperplane. The margin, representing the distance between the support vectors and the hyperplane, plays a critical role in classification accuracy. The fundamental objective of SVM is to maximize this margin, thereby enhancing model generalization.

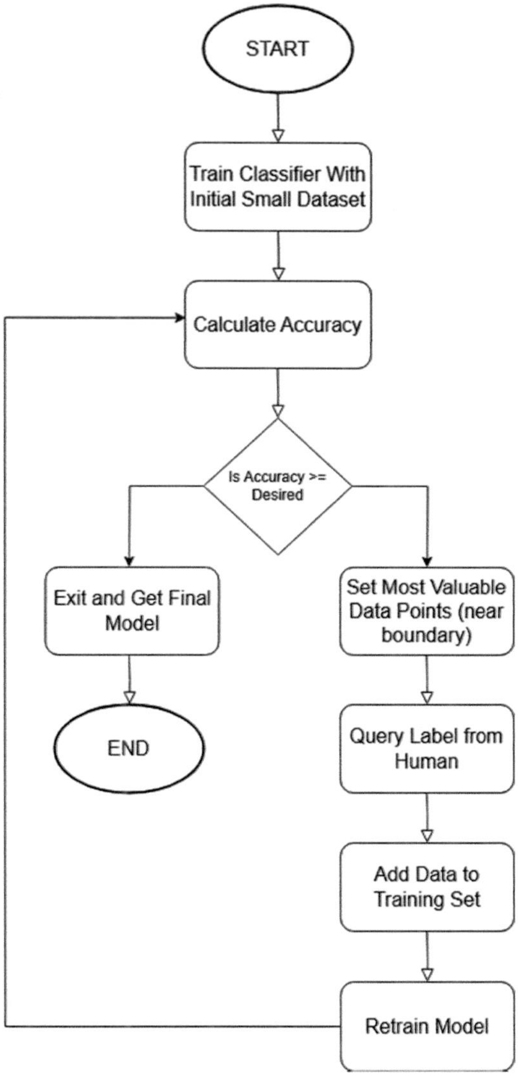

Figure 3: Flowchart of Active Learning Cycle for Classifier Improvement.

1. **Linear SVM:** Linear SVM is used for linearly separable data, which means if a dataset can be classified into two classes by using a single straight line, then such data is termed as linearly separable data, and classifier is used called as Linear SVM classifier.
2. **Non-linear SVM:** Non-Linear SVM is used for non-linearly separated data, which means if a dataset cannot be classified by using a straight line, then such data is termed as non-linear data and classifier used is called as Non-linear SVM classifier.

Support Vector Machine (SVM) is a widely used supervised learning algorithm particularly effective in high-dimensional spaces. The linear SVM model is depicted, where the dataset is linearly separable. The SVM algorithm identifies the optimal hyperplane that maximizes the margin between the two classes [45]. This margin is defined as the distance between the hyperplane and the nearest data points from each class, known as support vectors. The figure shows three hyperplanes: the central maximum margin hyperplane, and two parallel positive and negative hyperplanes. These boundaries delineate the margins on either side. The optimal hyperplane ensures that the classification boundary generalizes well to unseen data, assuming a linear separation is possible. In this case, the data is not linearly separable in its original feature space. The SVM addresses this challenge using a kernel function, which maps the data into a higher-dimensional space where a linear separation becomes feasible. The figure conceptually represents this transformation by illustrating a circular boundary that effectively separates the two classes. The decision surface in this transformed space corresponds to the best hyperplane, which provides an optimal separation between the classes.

These two figures collectively emphasize the flexibility of SVM in handling both linearly and nonlinearly separable datasets through the appropriate selection of kernel functions and hyperplane optimization strategies. Kernel Functions: SVM algorithms use a set of mathematical functions that are defined as the kernel. The function of the kernel is to take data as input and transform it into the required form. Different SVM algorithms use different types of kernel functions. These functions can be different types, such as linear, nonlinear, polynomial, radial basis function (RBF), and sigmoid. The kernel functions return the inner product between two points in a suitable feature space.

4. Proposed Work

In this section, the authors defined and investigated the topic, followed by a model based on SVM Active Learning classification for detecting pneumonia from chest X-ray pictures. The problem entails binary categorization of chest X-rays. To simulate such a task, we discuss our algorithm for detecting the visual signal for pneumonia in medical chest X-rays and determining whether pneumonia is positive or negative. The workflow for the proposed work is as follows:

(i) Collect a large number of X-Ray image datasets where two types of images are present, i.e. pneumonia X-Ray images and normal X-Ray images.
(ii) Labeled a small number of datasets for initial training of the SVM model.
(iii) Train the classification model with the labeled dataset.
(iv) Check the accuracy of the model.
(v) To improve the accuracy, go back to the unlabeled large dataset.
(vi) From a large, unlabeled dataset, pick up a batch or pool of the dataset.
(vii) Check the query strategy (margin of confidence) to select the important images for improving the performance of the initial model.

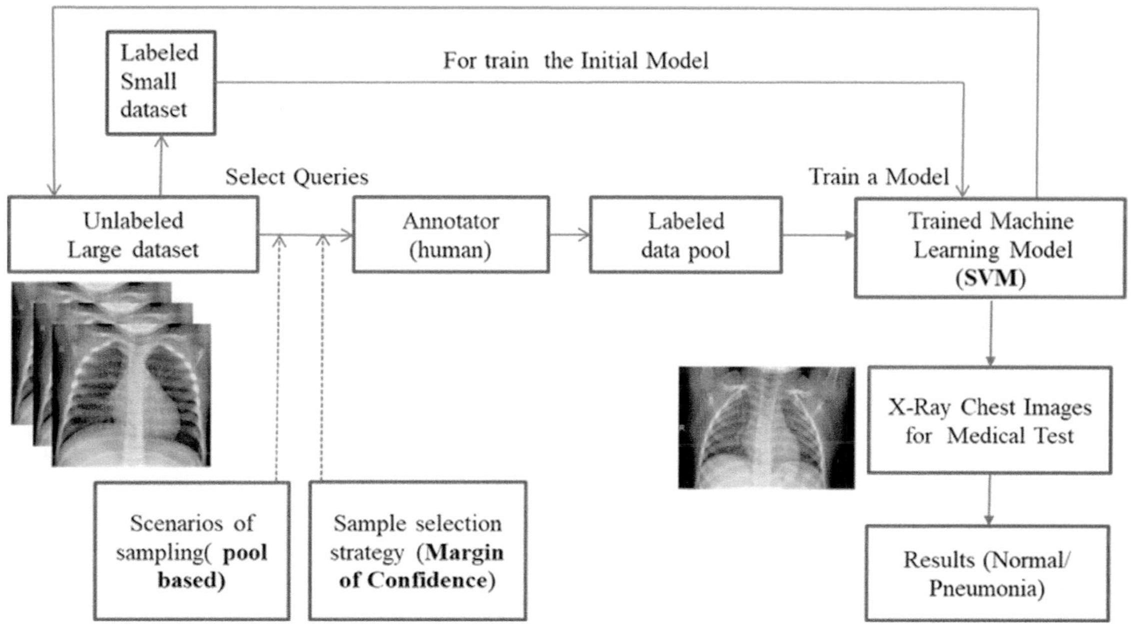

Figure 4: Workflow of Development of Active Learning-based Classification Model for the Detection of Pneumonia Using X-ray Images.

(viii) After selecting the important images, annotate or label these important images by the radiology expert.
(ix) Adding the newly labeled (pseudo-labeled) data to retrain the initial classification model and check the accuracy of the model.
(x) If the desired accuracy is still not achieved, then go back to the large unlabeled image dataset and take a similar procedure to select the important image data for improvement of the classification model.
(xi) If the desired accuracy is achieved, then the X-Ray image classification model is ready to predict or detect whether the X-Ray is pneumonia positive or pneumonia negative (normal).

Figure 4 illustrates the workflow for developing an active learning-based classification model for pneumonia detection utilizing X-ray images.

5. Results

Margin of Confidence values of all unlabeled data samples:

	C1Prob	C2Prob	lab	margin_confidence
0	0.974331	0.025669	0	0.948661
1	0.021059	0.978941	1	0.957883
2	0.939189	0.060811	0	0.878377
3	0.945230	0.054770	0	0.890460
4	0.999480	0.000520	0	0.998959
...	...	...	...	...
499	0.029390	0.970610	1	0.941221
500	0.990168	0.009832	0	0.980337
501	0.956076	0.043924	0	0.912152
502	0.940379	0.059621	0	0.880758
503	0.990366	0.009634	0	0.980731

Figure 5: Data Frame for Margin of Confidence.

The data frame for the margin of confidence is displayed in Fig. 5. Distribution of unlabeled data samples with respect to their Margin of Confidence.

Figure 6 illustrates the accuracy graph of the retrained model, based on the incorporation of unlabeled data into the initial model, for a margin of confidence ranging from 0 to 1 in increments of 0.05.

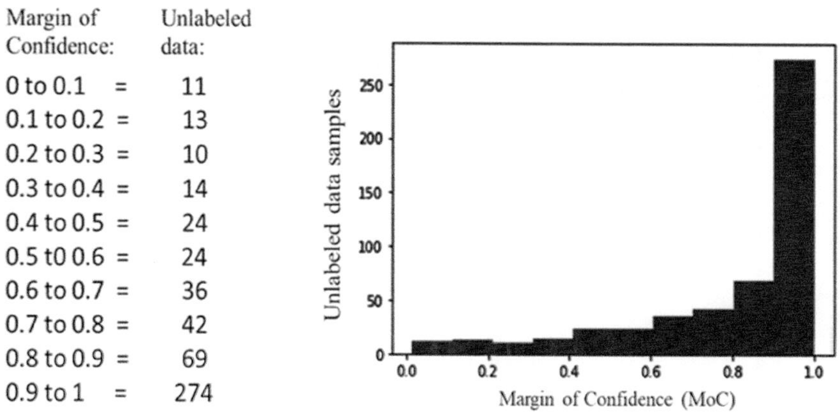

Figure 6: Accuracy Graph of Retrain Model, According to Unlabeled Data Added to Initial Model for Margin of Confidence 0 to 1 with Interval +0.05.

In Fig. 7, the accuracy graph of the retrain model, according to unlabeled data added to the initial model for Margin of Confidence 0 to 1 with interval +0.05. Figure 8 depicts the correlation between the margin of confidence and the precision of predictions throughout the entire dataset. Figure 9 illustrates the correlation between the margin of confidence and prediction accuracy for marginal data points—those situated near the decision border. Figure 10 presents the Receiver Operating Characteristic (ROC) curves for both the original SVM model and its enhanced iteration.

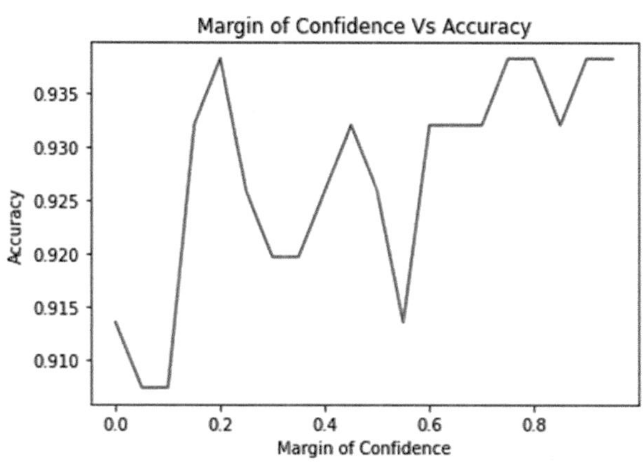


```
array([0.91358025, 0.90740741, 0.90740741, 0.93209877, 0.9382716 ,
       0.92592593, 0.91975309, 0.91975309, 0.92592593, 0.93209877,
       0.92592593, 0.91358025, 0.93209877, 0.93209877, 0.93209877,
       0.9382716 , 0.9382716 , 0.93209877, 0.9382716 , 0.9382716 ])
```

Figure 7: Margin of Confidence vs Accuracy.

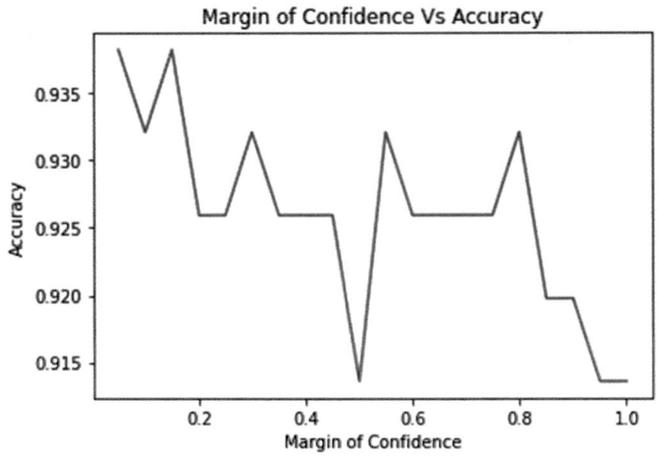


```
array([0.91358025, 0.91358025, 0.91975309, 0.91975309, 0.93209877,
       0.92592593, 0.92592593, 0.92592593, 0.92592593, 0.93209877,
       0.91358025, 0.92592593, 0.92592593, 0.92592593, 0.93209877,
       0.92592593, 0.92592593, 0.9382716 , 0.93209877, 0.9382716 ])
```

Figure 8: Margin of Confidence vs Accuracy Overall Data.

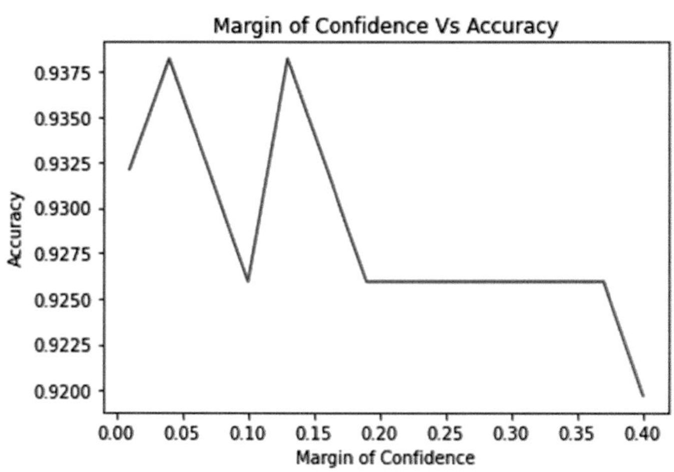


```
array([0.91975309, 0.92592593, 0.92592593, 0.92592593, 0.92592593,
       0.92592593, 0.92592593, 0.92592593, 0.93209877, 0.9382716 ,
       0.92592593, 0.93209877, 0.9382716 , 0.93209877])
```

Figure 9: Margin of Confidence vs Accuracy Based on Marginal Data.

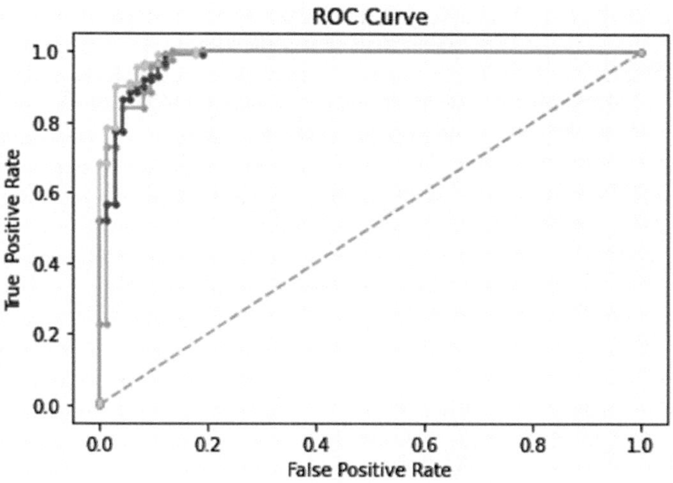

Figure 10: Comparison of ROC Curve for Improvement of Initial SVM Model.

Table 1 contrasts the accuracy of the initial model utilizing data obtained via an active learning technique against data selected randomly. Table 2 exclusively examines the enhancement of the model's accuracy through the random selection and incorporation of supplementary data into the baseline model. Table 3

Table 1: Comparison Between Active Learning Selected Data Added in Initial Model and Randomly Selected Data Added in the Initial Model to Obtain Maximum Accuracy

	Initial train model	Adding pseudo-labeled data to retrain the model		
		24 random data	24 Active learning data	All unlabeled data (517)
Independent data shape:	(129,61440)	(153, 61440)	(153, 61440)	(646, 61440)
Accuracy:	0.9135802	0.91358025	0.9382716	0.9444
Error:	0.5061728	0.5	0.462963	0.4815
CM:	[67 7 7 81]	[68 6 8 80]	[65 9 1 87]	[69 5 4 84]
Sensitivity:	0.90541	0.8947368	0.984848	0.9452
Specificity:	0.920455	0.9302326	0.90625	0.94382
Precision:	0.905405	0.9189189	0.878378	0.93243
False Positive	7	6	9	5
False Negative	7	8	1	9
AUC		0.973281	0.976658	0.9865

Table 2: Comparison of Randomly Selected Data Added in Initial Model to Obtain Maximum Accuracy of the Model

	Initial train model	**Adding pseudo-labeled data to retrain the model**		
		100 random data	**300 random data**	**400 random data**
Independent data shape	(129,61440)	(229, 61440)	(429, 61440)	(529, 61440)
Accuracy	0.9136	0.9198	0.9259	0.9383
Error	0.5062	0.4877	0.4815	0.4815
CM	[67 7 7 81]	[66 8 5 83]	[66 8 4 84]	[686 4 84]
Sensitivity	0.9055	0.92958	0.9429	0.9444
Specificity	0.9205	0.91209	0.9130	0.9333
Precision	0.9054	0.8919	0.89189	0.9189
False Positive	7	8	8	6
False Negative	7	5	4	4

Table 3: Different Condition Comparison of ROC Curve

Different Condition	**AUC**	**Color**
When randomly data added to the initial model	0.97328	Orange
When active learning data added to the initial model	0.97666	Green
When all unlabeled data added to the initial model	0.98649	Cyan

ultimately illustrates a comparison of ROC curves across diverse experimental settings, emphasizing the impact of varied methodologies on the classifier's discriminative efficacy.

6. Conclusion

The experimental findings demonstrate that a significantly higher accuracy in pneumonia detection can be achieved by selecting only a few critical data samples (24 out of 517) rather than randomly selecting a larger set of unlabeled samples from the chest X-ray dataset. These crucial data samples were identified using an Active Learning approach, highlighting its importance in domains such as medical imaging, where labeling and annotation are costly in terms of time and expertise, requiring domain specialists. One of the primary advantages of Active Learning is its ability to select the most informative data samples, thereby accelerating the learning process while reducing the amount of data required to achieve optimal accuracy. This contrasts with models trained on randomly acquired datasets, which often demand a larger volume of labeled samples to attain similar accuracy levels. Additionally, Active Learning mitigates the problem of model overfitting, which can occur when excessive training data leads to unnecessary complexity in model learning. As a relatively novel technique, Active Learning offers extensive opportunities for future research. One of its most promising applications lies in medical image segmentation, where it can be leveraged to extract critical features from large-scale, high-resolution medical datasets. By applying Active Learning to deep learning-based segmentation models, it becomes possible to accurately measure anatomical structures, assess pathological changes, and classify disease stages with greater precision. Future research will focus on developing a deep learning-based segmentation model using Active Learning to enhance medical diagnostics and disease progression analysis in clinical applications.

References

1. Settles, B. (2012). Automating inquiry. *Synthesis Lectures on Artificial Intelligence and Machine Learning*, 1–9. https://doi.org/10.1007/978-3-031-01560-1_1
2. Tuia, D., Volpi, M., Copa, L., Kanevski, M., and Munoz-Mari, J. (2011). A survey of active learning algorithms for supervised remote sensing image classification. *IEEE Journal of Selected Topics in Signal Processing*, 5(3), 606–617. https://doi.org/10.1109/jstsp.2011.2139193
3. Tuia, D., Ratle, F., Pacifici, F., Pozdnoukhov, A., Kanevski, M., Del Frate, F. et al. (2008). Active learning of very-high resolution optical imagery with SVM: Entropy vs margin sampling. *IGARSS 2008 – 2008 IEEE International Geoscience and Remote Sensing Symposium*. https://doi.org/10.1109/igarss.2008.4779659
4. Nath, V., Yang, D., Landman, B. A., Xu, D., and Roth, H. R. (2021). Diminishing uncertainty within the training pool: Active learning for medical image segmentation. *IEEE Transactions on Medical Imaging*, 40(10), 2534–2547. https://doi.org/10.1109/tmi.2020.3048055
5. Muslea, I., Minton, S., and Knoblock, C. A. (2006). Active learning with multiple views. *Journal of Artificial Intelligence Research*, 27, 203–233. https://doi.org/10.1613/jair.2005
6. Yang, L., Zhang, Y., Chen, J., Zhang, S., and Chen, D. Z. (2017). Suggestive annotation: A deep active learning framework for biomedical image segmentation. *Lecture Notes in Computer Science*, 399–407. https://doi.org/10.1007/978-3-319-66179-7_46
7. Top, A., Hamarneh, G., and Abugharbieh, R. (2011). Active learning for interactive 3D image segmentation. *Lecture Notes in Computer Science*, 603–610. https://doi.org/10.1007/978-3-642-23626-6_74
8. Casanova, X., and Baldeon-Calisto, M. (2024). Impact of transfer learning on transformers networks for prostate image segmentation. *2024 International Conference on Machine Learning and Applications (ICMLA)*, 841–844. https://doi.org/10.1109/icmla61862.2024.00121

9. Li, J., Bioucas-Dias, J. M., and Plaza, A. (2011). Hyperspectral image segmentation using a new Bayesian approach with active learning. *IEEE Transactions on Geoscience and Remote Sensing*, 49(10), 3947–3960. https://doi.org/10.1109/tgrs.2011.2128330
10. Konyushkova, K., Sznitman, R., and Fua, P. (2019). Geometry in active learning for binary and multi-class image segmentation. *Computer Vision and Image Understanding*, 182, 1–16. https://doi.org/10.1016/j.cviu.2019.01.007
11. Li, J., Bioucas-Dias, J. M., and Plaza, A. (2010). Semisupervised Hyperspectral image segmentation using multinomial logistic regression with active learning. *IEEE Transactions on Geoscience and Remote Sensing*. https://doi.org/10.1109/tgrs.2010.2060550
12. Vezhnevets, A., Buhmann, J. M., and Ferrari, V. (2012). Active learning for semantic segmentation with expected change. *2012 IEEE Conference on Computer Vision and Pattern Recognition*. https://doi.org/10.1109/cvpr.2012.6248050
13. Chen, W., Salay, R., Sedwards, S., Abdelzad, V., and Czarnecki, K. (2020). Accelerating the training of Convolutional Neural Networks for image segmentation with deep active learning. *2020 IEEE 23rd International Conference on Intelligent Transportation Systems (ITSC)*, 1–7. https://doi.org/10.1109/itsc45102.2020.9294260
14. Mahapatra, D., Bozorgtabar, B., Thiran, J.-P., and Reyes, M. (2018). Efficient active learning for image classification and segmentation using a sample selection and conditional generative adversarial network. *Lecture Notes in Computer Science*, 580–588. https://doi.org/10.1007/978-3-030-00934-2_65
15. Saad, A. I., Maghraby, F. A., and Badawy, O. (2023). Polyseg Plus: Polyp segmentation using Deep Learning with cost effective active learning. *International Journal of Computational Intelligence Systems*, 16(1). https://doi.org/10.1007/s44196-023-00330-6.
16. Jeon, Y., and Kim, J. (2017). Active convolution: Learning the shape of convolution for image classification. *2017 IEEE Conference on Computer Vision and Pattern Recognition (CVPR)*, 1846–1854. https://doi.org/10.1109/cvpr.2017.200
17. Zheng-Jun Zha, Xian-Sheng Hua, Tao Mei, Jingdong Wang, Guo-Jun Qi, and Zengfu Wang. (2008a). Joint multi-label multi-instance learning for image classification. *2008 IEEE Conference on Computer Vision and Pattern Recognition*, 1–8. https://doi.org/10.1109/cvpr.2008.4587384
18. Qi, G.-J., Hua, X.-S., Rui, Y., Tang, J., and Zhang, H.-J. (2009). Two-dimensional Multilabel active learning with an efficient online adaptation model for Image Classification. *IEEE Transactions on Pattern Analysis and Machine Intelligence*, 31(10), 1880–1897. https://doi.org/10.1109/tpami.2008.218
19. Pasolli, E., Melgani, F., Tuia, D., Pacifici, F., and Emery, W. J. (2014). SVM active learning approach for image classification using spatial information. *IEEE Transactions on Geoscience and Remote Sensing*, 52(4), 2217–2233. https://doi.org/10.1109/tgrs.2013.2258676
20. Di, X., Xue, Z., and Zhang, M. (2023). Active learning-driven siamese network for hyperspectral image classification. *Remote Sensing*, 15(3), 752. https://doi.org/10.3390/rs15030752
21. Beluch, W. H., Genewein, T., Nürnberger, A., and Köhler, J. M. (2018). The power of ensembles for active learning in image classification. *Proceedings of the IEEE Conference on Computer Vision and Pattern Recognition* (*CVPR*), pp. 9368–9377.
22. Hoi, S. C. H. Jin, R., Zhu, J., and Lyu, M.R. (2006). Batch mode active learning and its application to medical image classification. ICML '06: *Proceedings of the 23rd International Conference on Machine learning*. doi:10.1145/1143844.1143897

23. Wang, K., Zhang, D., Li, Y., Zhang, R., and Lin, L. (2017). Cost-effective active learning for deep image classification. *IEEE Transactions on Circuits and Systems for Video Technology*, 27(12), 2591–2600. https://doi.org/10.1109/tcsvt.2016.2589879
24. Jaiswal, A.K., Tiwari, P., Kumar, S., Gupta, D., Khanna, A., and Rodrigues, J.J.P.C. (October 2019). Identifying pneumonia in chest X-rays: A deep learning approach. *Measurement*, 145, 511–518, Elsevier, doi:10.1016/j.measurement.2019.05.076
25. Han, Y., Chen, C., Tewfik, A., Ding, Y., and Peng, Y. (2021). Pneumonia detection on chest X-ray using radiomic features and contrastive learning. *2021 IEEE 18th International Symposium on Biomedical Imaging* (*ISBI*), doi: 10.1109/ISBI48211.2021.9433853
26. Hasan, M. D. K., Ahmed, S., Abdullah, Z. M. E., Khan, M. M., Anand, D., Singh, A. et al. (2021). Deep learning approaches for detecting Pneumonia in COVID-19 patients by analyzing chest X-ray images. *Mathematical Problems in Engineering*, Volume 2021, Article ID 9929274, doi:10.1155/2021/9929274
27. Jain, R., Nagrath, P., Kataria, G., Kaushik, V. S., and Hemanth, D. J. (December 2020). Pneumonia detection in chest X-ray images using convolutional neural networks and transfer learning. *Measurement*, 165(1), 108046, Elsevier. doi: 10.1016/j.measurement.2020.108046
28. Manickam, A., Jiang, J., Zhou, Y., Sagar, A., Soundrapandiyan, R., and Dinesh Jackson Samuel, R. (2021a). Automated pneumonia detection on chest X-ray images: A deep learning approach with different optimizers and transfer learning architectures. *Measurement,* 184, 109953. https://doi.org/10.1016/j.measurement.2021.109953
28. El Asnaoui, K., Chawki, Y., and Idri, A. (2021). Automated methods for detection and classification pneumonia based on X-ray images using Deep Learning. *Studies in Big Data*, 257–284. https://doi.org/10.1007/978-3-030-74575-2_14
29. Rajpurkar, P., Irvin, J., Ball, R. L., Zhu, K., Yang, B., Mehta, H. et al. (2018). Deep learning for chest radiograph diagnosis: A retrospective comparison of the CheXNeXt algorithm to practicing radiologists. *PLOS Medicine*, 15(11). https://doi.org/10.1371/journal.pmed.1002686
30. Al Mamlook, R. E., Chen, S., and Bzizi, H. F. (2020). Investigation of the performance of machine learning classifiers for pneumonia detection in chest X-ray images. *2020 IEEE International Conference on Electro Information Technology (EIT)*, 098–104. https://doi.org/10.1109/eit48999.2020.9208232
31. Maiora, J., Ayerdi, B., and Graña, M. (2014). Random forest active learning for AAA thrombus segmentation in computed tomography angiography images. *Neurocomputing*, 126, 71–77. https://doi.org/10.1016/j.neucom.2013.01.051
32. Zamzmi, G., Oguguo, T., Rajaraman, S., and Antani, S. (2022). Open-world active learning for echocardiography view classification. *Medical Imaging 2022: Computer-Aided Diagnosis*. https://doi.org/10.1117/12.2612578
33. Shi, X., Dou, Q., Xue, C., Qin, J. and Chen, H. (2019). An Active learning approach for reducing annotation cost in skin lesion analysis. *In*: MLMI 2019: Machine Learning in Medical Imaging, 628–636, doi: 10.1007/978-3-030-32692-0_72
34. Mishra, N., and Chaturvedi, S. (2022). Diagnosis of skin cancer using deep learning. *Artificial Intelligence and Communication Technologies*, 153–158. https://doi.org/10.52458/978-81-955020-5-9-15
35. Mahapatra, D., and Buhmann, J. M. (2015). Visual saliency based active learning for prostate MRI segmentation. *Lecture Notes in Computer Science*, 9–16. https://doi.org/10.1007/978-3-319-24888-2_2

36. Sil, R., Alpana, Roy, A., Dasmahapatra, M., and Dhali, D. (2021). An intelligent approach for automated argument based legal text recognition and summarization using machine learning. *Journal of Intelligent & Fuzzy Systems*, 41(5), 5457–5466. https://doi.org/10.3233/jifs-189867
37. Saha, D., Sil, R., and Roy, A. (2020). A study on implementation of text analytics over legal domain. *Advances in Intelligent Systems and Computing*, 561–571. https://doi.org/10.1007/978-981-15-5788-0_54
38. Melendez, J., van Ginneken, B., Maduskar, P., Philipsen, R. H., Ayles, H., and Sanchez, C. I. (2016). On combining multiple-instance learning and active learning for computer-aided detection of tuberculosis. *IEEE Transactions on Medical Imaging,* 35(4), 1013–1024. https://doi.org/10.1109/tmi.2015.2505672
39. Yang, M., Nurzynska, K., Walts, A. E., and Gertych, A. (2020). A CNN-based active learning framework to identify mycobacteria in digitized Ziehl-Neelsen stained human tissues. *Computerized Medical Imaging and Graphics,* 84, 101752. https://doi.org/10.1016/j.compmedimag.2020.101752
40. Sil, R., and Roy, A. (2021). Machine learning approach for automated legal text classification. *International Journal of Computer Information Systems and Industrial Management Applications*, 13, 10–10.

3 | A Comprehensive Analysis of Artificial Intelligence Techniques for Automated Microaneurysm Detection

Deepak Kumar Maharana[1], Jyotiprava Mohanta[2*], Sabyasachi Chandra[3] and Puja Bharati[4]

[1] Electrical & Electronics Engineering Department, Seemanta Engineering College, BPUT, India
[2] Electronics and Telecommunication Engineering Department, Seemanta Engineering College, BPUT, India
[3] Computer Science Engineering-AI, Brainware University, India
[4] Advance Technology Development Centre, IIT Kharagpur, India

Diabetic retinopathy, a chronic illness in diabetic individuals, causes vision impairment when not detected and treated early. Ophthalmologists detect diabetic retinopathy by looking for minor abnormalities within the eye, such as exudates, microaneurysms, haemorrhages, macular edema, and alterations in the vasculatures of the retina. Microaneurysm segmentation is an essential prerequisite for detecting diabetic retinopathy and has recently become the researchers' primary focus. Artificial intelligence has been deployed in diverse fields and has been found to be very effective. The role of machine learning and deep learning in the healthcare monitoring system has been an area of interest in recent years. This chapter provides a comprehensive review of the existing research to evaluate the diagnostic applicability of automatic microaneurysm detection and the delineation of preliminary diabetic retinopathy identification.

1. Introduction

Diabetic retinopathy (DR) is a type of eye disease in which diabetic patients suffer as a complication of diabetes mellitus, which can cause blindness. The

*Corresponding author: jyotiprava.mohanta@gmail.com

DOI: 10.1201/9781003635215-3

blood vessel in the retina swells, and the fluid leaks to the retina's surface or abnormal blood vessels grow on the retina's surface. Mostly about 80% of people suffering from diabetes for about 10 years have DR. It can affect both eyes. Aside from kidney disease (diabetic nephropathy), diabetes can also affect the heart (diabetic cardiomyopathy), the nerves, especially the plantar nerves, and also the vision (diabetic retinopathy) [1,2]. Early identification and treatment are crucial in lowering the proportion of diabetic vision problems. Figure 1 shows the diagram of a normal and abnormal retina [3]. An automated diagnosis (CAD) requires the detection of microaneurysms (MAs). Every single layer within the retina receives blood via microscopic blood vessels. The retinal vasculature of people with diabetes resembles leaky, worn-out garden hoses in their vascular condition. Patients also suffer from fluid retention in the retina in addition to microaneurysms, hard exudates, haemorrhages and cotton wool spots in the retina. The presence of microaneurysms represents an alarming indicator of DR, and that is regarded as a foundational feature of DR. "The two main types of diabetic retinopathy (DR) are proliferative diabetic retinopathy, often known as PDR, and non-proliferative diabetic retinopathy (NPDR)" [4]. The term "NPDR" signifies the beginning phases of retinopathy due to diabetes, which may vary in seriousness from mild to severe. If a patient has just a single microaneurysm (MA) located in the retinal region, then it is classified as mild NPDR [5]. According to Usman Akram et al. [6], moderate NPDR is distinguished by the existence of a few microaneurysms (MAs), haemorrhages, and exudates. The outermost portion of the retina might contain more microaneurysms (MAs) and haemorrhages, which might impede blood flow through the eye's blood vessels. Diabetic individuals experience visual impairment as a result of blood vessel occlusion. The phrase "Severe NPDR" is used to describe this. The chronic form of DR has been identified as proliferative diabetic retinopathy (PDR) [7]. PDR is characterised by the appearance of new, erroneous vascular structures within the ocular area. It is extremely hard to make a distinction between normal and pathological vessels in this kind of scenario. An in-depth analysis of DR is shown in Table 1 [8]. Dot haemorrhages and microaneurysms (MA) are typically among the earliest identified symptoms of DR; hence, proper identification of these conditions is vital for timely diagnosis [9]. Since they typically resemble one another in fundoscopic appearance, both of these can only be distinguished using fluorescein angiography. However, when evaluating DR, both kinds of lesions may need to be considered. It has been established that MA recognition is essential for finding out the phase of NPDR, as indicated in Table 2 below.

Due to manual screening methods, MAs are comparatively miniature and are typically ignored by eye specialists. Using an automated methodology, ophthalmologists can detect MAs early and precisely, assisting them to control diabetic retinopathy earlier than ever before. By taking action in time, the patient can avoid the worst effects of DR, which can cause complete vision impairment [4]. It is difficult to detect and classify microaneurysms in diabetic retinopathy due to their various structures, such as texture, colour, and size. A major research

Table 1: Categorization for DR on the Basis of Clinical Retinal Features

DR phase	Diagnosis	Clinically relevant observations
0	Healthy	There are no anomalies.
1	Mild NPDR	Only one microaneurysm.
2	Moderate NPDR	At least two of the subsequent characteristics: Hard exudates, microaneurysms, and haemorrhages.
3	Severe NPDR	Numerous haemorrhages as well as microaneurysms.
4	PDR	Vitreous haemorrhage, disc neovascularization and detachment of the retina.

Table 2: Recognition of Microaneurysms Employed to Find the Grade of NPDR

No. of microaneurysms	Grading of DR
0	Normal
>0 and <5	Mild
>5 and <15 (without neovascularization)	Moderate
>15	Severe

area in ophthalmology is the advancement of reliable and fast diagnostic tools for diabetic retinopathy. This chapter provides a detailed assessment of important research addressing the topic of earlier diagnosis of DR using automatic detection/segmentation of microaneurysms. Figure 1 illustrates a schematic contrasting normal and abnormal retinal image.

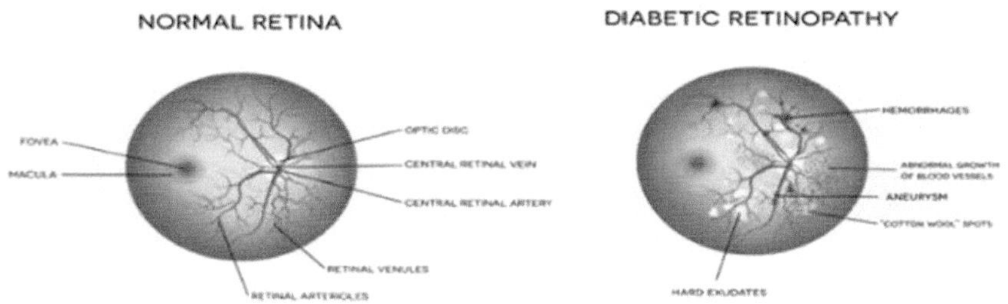

Figure 1: Diagram of Normal and Abnormal Retinal Photographs.

The remaining portion of this chapter is structured into the subsequent sections: Section 2 addresses the characteristics of datasets that are freely accessible and can be used to assess MA detection studies to identify early DR assessment. Section 3 describes the standards for assessment of the performance indicators employed by early detection systems. Section 4 summarizes the works recognized by different methodologies. Section 5 discusses the conclusion.

2. Fundus Image Databases

The purpose of datasets is to check the information and then analyze the results of automated screenings for DR using current technology. There is no other information regarding the individual's condition in the data sets. This section gives an extensive overview of the datasets utilized for assessing innovative approaches for computerized DR screening and monitoring.

(i) **ROC (Retinopathy Online Challenge) Dataset:** The ROC [10] dataset contains 100 retinal images chosen from an enormous database for diabetic retinopathy screening. The retinal photographs are captured with a Topcon NW 100, a Topcon NW200, or a Canon CR5-45NM camera.

(ii) **E-Ophtha Dataset:** The E-Ophtha database [11, 12], comprising E-Ophtha Ex and E-Ophtha MA, was generated within the context of a telemedical network aimed at diabetic retinopathy research, with funding support from the French Research Agency. It's important to note that the E-Ophtha dataset is a subset of the larger MESSIDOR dataset.

(iii) **DIARETDB Database:** The DIARETDB database is open to the public for research purposes. The photographs within the database were acquired through a digital fundus camera featuring a 50^0 FOV. The first set is DIARETDB0[13], and it comprises 130 colour fundus photographs, 20 of which are considered as healthy and 110 of which have DR abnormalities. The second set, DIARETDB1 [14], contains 89 fundus images, 84 of which have DR abnormalities and 5 of which are healthy.

3. Standards for Assessment

To properly analyze the effectiveness of earlier DR diagnosis systems, the efficacy of MA detection/segmentation techniques must be benchmarked. In the many state-of-the-art studies taken into consideration for this analysis, different metrics were utilised to analyse the same dataset. To assess the efficacy, standard measures that include recall, precision, specificity, accuracy, F1 score, ROC score, Jaccard index, the area under the receiver operating characteristic curve (AUC), dice similarity coefficient, Free Response Receiver Operating Characteristic (FROC) were used. All of the aforementioned metrics are primarily concerned with analyzing the outcomes of TP (True Positive), TN (True Negative), FP (False Positive), and FN (False Negative). TP specifies the number of MAs that are appropriately recognized via a CAD system as positives and matches a judgement from an expert.

According to professional opinion from experts, TN has appropriately detected non-MA matches. FP is the number of wrongly acknowledged MAs that skilled experts view as irrelevant MAs and the amount of mistakenly discarded MAs can be determined by FN. Figure 2 demonstrates the connection among these ideas in terms of performance [15]. Table 3 shows the outcome measures employed to assess the early detection systems [16].

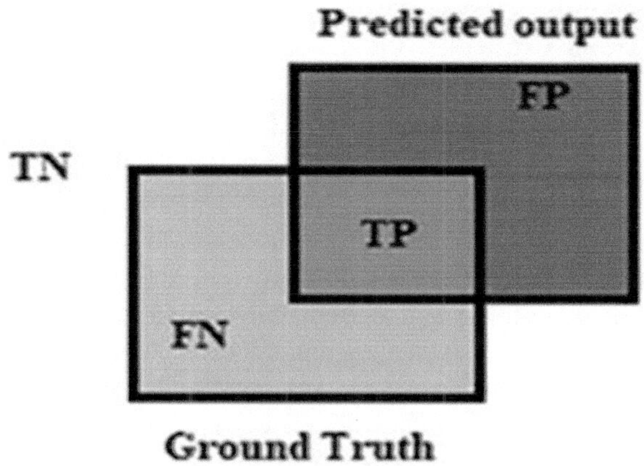

Figure 2: The Connection Between TP and FP in Terms of Performance.

Table 3: The Outcome Measures to Assess the Early Detection Systems

Metric	**Definition**	**Interpretation**
Recall/Sensitivity	TP/(TP + FN)	The proportion of correctly recognised results.
Precision	TP/(TP + FP)	Shows the number of MAs that were precisely recognised out of all marked MAs.
Specificity	TN/(TN + FP)	The proportion of appropriately recognised non-MA
Accuracy	(TN + TP)/ (TN + FN + TP + FP)	The proportion of accurately predicted MA compared to all MA observations.
F1 score	2×(TP)/(2 × TP + FP + FN)	Harmonic means of precision and recall.
AUC	(Sensitivity + Specificity)/2	The greater the AUC score, the more effectively the model distinguishes between non-MA and MA.
Jaccard similarity index	TP/(FP + FN + TP)	This metric measures how near the expected finding is compared to the actual finding.
FROC		This metric measures how closely the expected outcome is compared with the actual outcome.

4. A Discussion of Preliminary Detection of DR Techniques

Methods for evaluating microaneurysms are classified as supervised, unsupervised, or mathematical morphology based. Joshi et al. [17] used morphological techniques to improve fundus pictures and eliminate retinal vasculatures before extracting MAs. In this case Diaretdb1 and e-ophtha databases are used. After pre-processing the grey portions of images, Romero et al. [18] presented hit or miss and bottom hat transformation procedures for microaneurysm detection. To extract an intact reddish region from gray image content, a bottom-hat transformation was executed. Additionally, the hit transformation technique was employed to eradicate the blood vessels. Finally, to pinpoint the locations of microaneurysms, the radon transform and principal component analysis were employed. Zhou et al. [19] applied pre-processing techniques to eliminate noise and boost the contrast level of the green channel image. In addition, all possible MA candidates are extracted using the multi-scale Gaussian correlation coefficient method. Finally, the feature matrix is formed based on 34 features based on structure, illumination, and Gaussian filtering. Habib et al. [20] presented a unique scheme for identifying and categorizing microaneurysms dependent on retinal fundus pictures. To classify the microaneurysm points based on pixels, the Gaussian matched filter was implemented to extract features, which were then input to the ensemble classifier. The stated method's receiver operating curve (ROC) was 0.415. The stated approach's weakness was that it failed to adhere to the conventional feature selection concept and overlooked the problem of overfitting. Wankhede et al. [21] proposed that images with a non-illuminated background and variable field of view are pre-processed first to ensure that non-lesion and lesion characteristics are readily seen for appropriate detection. Then, to identify smooth areas and edges in retinal photographs, negative pixel intensity rank transform (PIRT) is employed. The subsequent phase is to subtract the optic disc and retinal vasculatures from the rank transform photograph. Lastly, histogram thresholding is employed to identify microaneurysm candidates. The suggested technique is evaluated using the freely released databases DIARETDB1 and E-Optha MA. Derwin et al. [22] proposed a pre-processing, feature extraction, and classification process to identify whether a pixel belongs to microaneurysms or not. The texture-based characteristics of microaneurysms are recovered by utilizing the generalised rotational invariant local binary pattern. For this system, the FROC score was 0.421. The Retinopathy Online Challenge dataset is evaluated by this method. Derwin et al. [23] provided a new computer-aided microaneurysm identification system that relies upon texturing attributes. Using a histogram of texture descriptors, MA detection becomes more accurate than using shape-based features as a means of capturing texture characteristics. While using a support vector machine classifier, local binary patterns do better at discriminating lesions. Data from ROC, MESSIDOR and DIARETDB1 are validated using free-response receiver operating characteristic scores and area under the curve. This system's robustness is ensured by its capacity to analyse images of varying intensities with minimal calculation time. Wang et al. [24] presented a scheme for the detection of microaneurysms in which dark object filtering is used to identify candidate regions. kNN classifier is used to classify data using a set of statistical attributes for candidate regions. Sreng et al. [25] suggested a technique for detecting microaneurysms by using canny edge detection and maximum entropy thresholding. Lastly, the morphological operation was used to locate the candidates. Yuji [26] utilized a double-ring filter, a Gabor filter, and a shape index based on the Hessian matrix to decrease the noise and boost the image's contrast. Deep convolutional neural networks (DCNN) are then employed to detect microaneurysms. As described by Dashtbozorg et al. [27], microaneurysm candidate regions are first extracted by gradient weighting combined with an iterative thresholding technique. Microaneurysms candidates are assessed using local convergence index filters, intensity, and shape features. Microaneurysms candidates are identified using a boosting classifier. Dai et al. [28] published a clinical study that employed CNN for image-to-text mapping classification to find microaneurysm candidate locations. Melo et al. [29] proposed a sliding band filter to improve MA with the goal of generating a list of early MA candidates. For final candidate categorization, an ensemble of classifiers uses color, contrast, and shape information in combination with the filter responses. Long et al. [30] developed a machine learning-based MA detection algorithm based on directional local contrast. Hervella et al. [31] proposed a heatmap regression approach for detecting multiple microaneurysms, allowing for more accurate localization and detection. To evaluate and assess the suggested methodology, we conducted extensive experiments on several public datasets, like E-Ophtha, ROC, and DDR. Deepa et al. [32] present a method for distinguishing between healthy and diseased retinal photographs that is dependent on the discrete orthonormal Stockwell transform and statistical features. To assess the performance of the classifiers, the author selected eight of them. When compared to other well-known classifiers, the ANN classification model performs exceptionally well. Alessandro Bria et al. [33] proposed a two-step deep learning strategy for working with the high-class imbalance seen during the creation of miniature lesion detectors. To deal with class imbalance, a deep cascade (DC) structure is constructed initially, and CNN is subsequently employed for data training. As a result, this DCNN technique is employed to identify MAs as well as microcalcification. Selçuk et al. [34] suggested an ant bee colony optimization technique for detecting microaneurysms also in low-quality images. Wang et al. [35] described a five-step method for identifying microaneurysms using R-CNN, including image pre-processing, candidate region formation, extraction of features, categorization, and non-maximal suppression. An algorithm for generating microaneurysms from fundus images is presented first, followed by a

Table 4: An Overview of MA Detection Techniques via Colour Fundus Photographs

Author	**Dataset used**	**Highlights**	**Performance measure**
Joshi et al. [17]	Diaretdb1 and e-ophtha	Morphological processing, feature extraction set	Sen - 89.22, spe - 91 acc - 92.4
Romero et al. [18]	DiaretDB1 and Retinopathy Online Challenge (ROC)	Bottom hat transform, radon transform and principal component analysis	Sen - 92.32, spe - 93.87 and acc - 95.93 Sen - 88.06, spe - 97.47 and acc - 92.19
Zhou et al. [19]	Retinopathy Online Challenge (ROC)	Sparse Posterior Cerebral Artery (PCA)	Sen - 48.31, FPPI - 43.13.
Habib et al. [20]	MESSIDOR, DIARETDB1 v2.1	Gaussian Matched Filter, Tree Ensemble classifier	ROC score of 0.415
Wankhede et al. [21]	E-Optha and DIARETDB1	Pixel intensity rank transform (PIRT), rank transform, histogram thresholding	Sen - 98.79%, spe - 83.33%, and acc - 97.75%. Sen - 94.59%, spe - 96.56% and acc - 95.80%.
Derwin et al. [22]	ROC	Rotational invariant local binary pattern	FROC - 0.421.
Derwin et al. [23]	ROC, MESSIDOR and DIARETDB1	Local binary pattern, support vector machine classifier	FROC - 0.380,0.419 and 0.357.
Wang et al. [24]	DIARETDB1, Retinopathy Online Challenge (ROC) and Moorfields Eye Hospital datasets	kNN classifier	FROC - 0.464.
Sreng et al. [25]	Photographs sourced from Bhumibol Adulyadej Hospital and DIARETDB1	Canny edges detection maximum entropy thresholding method and morphological algorithm	Accuracy is 90%.
Yuji [26]	DIARETDB1	Deep convolutional neural networks (DCNN)	Sen - 84%.
Dashtbozorg et al. [27]	ROC	Gradient weighting technique, iterative thresholding, local convergence index filters and boosting classifier	FROC - 0.471

Dai et al. [28]	DIARETDB1	Multi-Sieving CNN	Precision - 99.7, recall - 87.8
Melo et al. [29]	E-ophtha MA and SCREEN-DR	Sliding band filter, ensemble classifiers	Sen - 64% and 81
Long et al. [30]	DIARETDB1 e-ophtha MA	Directional local contrast (DLC) with machine learning method	AUC - 0.87,0.86 FROC - 0.374,0.210
Hervella et al. [31]	E-Ophtha, ROC, and DDR	Deep learning and generative adversarial networks with heatmap regression	Precision - 64.90%, 31.36%, and 33.55%
Deepa et al. [32]	Department of Medical Retina, Bharath Hospital, Kottayam	Stockwell transform and statistical features, ANN classification model	Accuracy - 95.9 F - score 95.9
Alessandro Bria et al. [33]	e-ophtha	DCNN technique	AUC - 0.87
Selcuk et al. [34]	Messidor and DiaretDB1	Ant bee colony optimization technique	Mean dice value - (0.85) and mean Jaccard value - (0.84)
Wang et al. [35]	E-ophtha	R-CNN	
Du et al. [36]	E-ophtha-MA, DiaretDB1 and ROC	Transformation splicing (TS), multi-context ensemble learning algorithm	Final scores - 0.518, 0.429 and 0.306 respectively
Song Sun et al. [37]	E-ophtha-MA	Magnified Adaptive Feature Pyramid Network (MAFP-Net) with end-to-end deep-learning algorithm	Sensitivity - 83.5%
Xugang Zhang et al. [38]	E-Ophtha MA, ROC	Local Fourier transform, random forest algorithm	FROC curve - 0.847, 0.283
Soares et al. [39]	E-Ophtha MA, Latim, ROC and Messidor	Multi-scale technique	AUC - 0.874 and sensitivity - 0.936
Deng et al. [40]	E-ophtha MA and retinopathy online challenge (ROC)	Ring gradient descriptor (RGD), Gradient Boosting Decision Trees (GBDT)	AUC - 0.9566 & 0.9205

(Contd.)

(*Contd.*)

Author	Dataset used	Highlights	Performance measure
Cheng et al. [41]	Messidor	CLAHE and Top-Hat, Random Forest	Sensitivity - 89.33%, spe - 99.65% and acc - 99.65%
Yadav et al. [42]	E-ophtha	Machine-learning-based	Acc - 83.33%

pre-processing method for fundus images. The transferred fine-tuning model is utilized to train the VGG16 network for extracting features from candidate samples. Lastly, a classifier selects real aneurysms from candidate regions. Jingyu Du et al. [36] devised a technique called "transformation splicing" (TS) to resolve the significant imbalance caused by microaneurysms and interference from microscopic vascular structures. A multi-context ensemble learning algorithm increases weak microaneurysm identification by learning various image contexts from distinct spliced images. Song Sun et al. [37] introduced a comprehensive deep-learning algorithm for microaneurysm identification. This method presents a pyramid network that improves feature representation by using adaptive features. For training purposes, this approach does not require any pre-segmented patches. Xugang Zhang et al. [38] present a local Fourier transform-based automated MA identification approach that divides the input photograph into numerous independent photographs that evaluate their local Fourier transforms separately. Following that, now the entire image comprises a collection of tiny independent images. In addition, statistical features are extracted to test normality and create a novel feature to depict the modification in each direction. The next step is to extract a set of candidate points from the images. Lastly, the random forest procedure is employed for classification. Soares et al. [39] suggested a new multi-scale technique for distinguishing microaneurysms in digital fundus images. It entails the following steps: pre-processing of images, detection of candidates for microaneurysms, and detection of retinal vessels and labelling of the candidates. Deng et al. [40] suggest a classifier-based strategy for MA detection. Objects and their surroundings can be described structurally by a ring gradient descriptor (RGD). To classify candidates, Gradient Boosting Decision Trees (GBDT) combine RGD with salience and texture features. Cheng et al. [41] initially implemented CLAHE and Top-Hat techniques to improve the contrast of the lesions and background. Candidate MAs are located in the second stage using Canny edge detection and holes filling. Lastly, a classifier known as Random Forest separates the candidates into MAs and non-MAs to reduce false positives. Yadav et al. [42] suggest machine-learning-based classifications for identifying MAs that require less processing effort. A histogram-based segmentation has been performed on retinal images.

From segmented images, features have been extracted based on shape, statistics, and the grey-level co-occurrence matrix (GLCM). Various classification techniques are used; however, the random forest classifier fared well for distinguishing MAs from non-MAs. Table 4 shows an overview of different MA detection techniques.

5. Conclusion

A brief overview of the most recent research in the domain of diabetic retinopathy and microaneurysm identification is covered in this chapter. Many of the current strategies that have been shown to be effective in predicting the possibility of blindness in people with diabetes are briefly discussed and summarized. With the help of the information provided, researchers are able to gain an understanding of automated microaneurysm identification techniques as well as, in the near future, establish better approaches for microaneurysm identification for diagnosing diabetic retinopathy. With the continuous development of medical imaging and artificial intelligence, microaneurysm recognition is set to become an increasingly important diagnostic tool for diabetic retinopathy (DR). Future research is expected to focus on developing more accurate and interpretable deep learning models that can reliably detect microaneurysms at an early stage, reducing the chances of vision loss. Integration of multimodal data—including retinal images, patient demographics, and clinical history—may enhance predictive performance and enable personalized treatment plans. Moreover, future systems should aim for real-time analysis capabilities, making them suitable for deployment in low-resource and remote clinical settings. Automation and telemedicine could revolutionize early diabetes-related blindness detection in the long run, enabling timely interventions and reducing diabetes-related blindness dramatically.

References

1. Wu, B., Zhu, W., Shi, F., Hu, S., and Chen, X. 2017. Automatic detection of microaneurysms in retinal fundus images. *Computer Medical Imaging and Graphics*, 5, 106–112.
2. Tan, J. H., Acharya, U. R., Bhandary, S. V., Chua, K. C., and Prasad, S. S. (2017) Segmentation of optic disc, fovea, and retinal vasculature using a single convolutional neural network. *Journal of Computational Science*, 20, 70–79.
3. Harvard Medical School. (2020). Retinopathy. *Harvard Health Publishing*, August, 2017. Accessed on: Mar. 23, 2020. [Online]. Available: https://www.health.harvard.edu/a to z/retinopathy-a-to-z
4. Paranjape, M. J., and Kakatkar, M. N. (2014). Diabetic retinopathy detection and severity classification. *In J Res Eng Technol.*, 3(3), 619–624. doi:10.15623/ijret.2014.0303115.

5. Basha, S., and Prasad K. (2008). Automatic detection of hard exudates in diabetic retinopathy using morphological segmentation and fuzzy logic. *Int J Comp Sci Net Secur.*, 8(12), 211–218.
6. Usman Akram, M., Khalid, S., Tariq, A., Khan, S. A., and Azam, F. (2014). Detection and classification of retinal lesions for grading of diabetic retinopathy. *Comp Biol Med.*, 45, 161–171. doi: 10.1016/jcompbiomed201311014.
7. Welikala, R. A., Dehmeshki, J., Hoppe, A., Tah, V., Mann, S., Williamson, T. H., and Barman, S. A. 2014). Automated detection of proliferative diabetic retinopathy using a modified line operator and dual classification. *Comput: Methods Prog Biomed.*, 114(3), 247–261. doi:10.1016/j.cmpb.2014.02.010.
8. Chalakkal, R., Abdulla, W., and Hong, S. C. (2020). Fundus retinal image analyses for screening and diagnosing diabetic retinopathy, macular edema, and glaucoma disorders. *Diabetes and Fundus OCT,* 59–111. Elsevier.
9. Kohner, E. M., Sleightholm, M., Bergenstal, R. N., Morse, P. et al. (1986). Does microaneurysm count reflect severity of early diabetic retinopathy. *Ophthalmology*, 93(5). 586–589.
10. Niemeijer, M., van Ginneken, B., Cree, M. J., Mizutani, A. et al. (2010). Retinopathy on-line challenge: Automatic detection of microaneurysms in digital color fundus photographs. *IEEE Trans. Med. Imaging*, 29(1), 185–195.
11. Decenciere, E., Cazuguel, G., Zhang, X., Thibault, G., Klein, J.-C., Meyer, F., Marcotegui, B. et al. (2013). TeleOphta: Machine learning and image processing methods for teleophthalmology. *Irbm*, 34(2), 196–203. https://doi.org/10.1016/j.irbm.2013.01.010.
12. E-ophtha. http://www.adcis.net/en/Download-Third-Party/E Ophtha.html [accessed 08.01.18]
13. Kalesnykiene, V., Kamarainen, J.-K., Lensu, L., Sorri, I., Uusitalo, H., Kalviainen, H., and Pietila, J. (2006). DIARETDB0: Evaluation database and methodology for diabetic retinopathy algorithms.
14. Kauppi, T., Kalesnykiene, V., Kamarainen, J.-K., Lensu, L., Sorri, I., Raninen, A., et al. (2007). The DIARETDB1 diabetic retinopathy database and evaluation protocol. *BMVC*, 2007.
15. Rai, C., and Pahuja, R. (2023). Northern maize leaf blight disease detection and segmentation using deep convolution neural networks. *Multimedia Tools and Applications*, 1–18. 10.1007/s11042-023-16398-3
16. Mayya, V., Kamath, S., and Kulkarni, U. 2021. Automated microaneurysms detection for early diagnosis of diabetic retinopathy: A comprehensive review. *Computer Methods and Programs in Biomedicine Update*, Volume 1, 2021.
17. Joshi, S., and Karule, P.T. (2020). Mathematical morphology for microaneurysm detection in fundus images. *Eur. J. Ophthalmol.*, 30, 1135–1142.
18. Rosas-Romero, R., Martinez-Carballido, J., Hernandez-Capistran, J., and Uribe-Valencia, L. J. (2015). A method to assist in the diagnosis of early diabetic retinopathy: Image processing applied to detection of microaneurysms in fundus images. *Comput. Med. Imaging Graph.*, 44, 41–53.
19. Zhou, W., Wu, C., Chen, D., Yi, Y., and Du, W. (2017). Automatic microaneurysm detection using the sparse principal component analysis based unsupervised classification method. *IEEE Access*, 5, 2563–2572.
20. Habib, M., Welikala, R., Hoppe, A., Owen, C., Rudnicka, A., and Barman, S. (2017). Detection of microaneurysms in retinal images using an ensemble classifier. *Inform. Med. Unlocked*, 9, 44–57.

21. Wankhede, P. R., and Khanchandani, K. B. (2020). Automated microaneurysms detection from retinal fundus images using pixel intensity rank transform. *Biomed Pharmacol J*, 13(1).
22. Derwin, D. J., Selvi, S. T., and Singh, O. J. (2020). Secondary observer system for detection of microaneurysms in fundus images using texture descriptors. *J. Digit. Imaging*, 33, 159–167. https://doi.org/10.1007/s10278-019-00225-z
23. Derwin, D. J., Selvi, S. T., and Singh, O.J. (2020). Discrimination of microaneurysm in color retinal images using texture descriptors. *SIViP*, 14, 369–376. https://doi.org/10.1007/s11760-019-01566-6.
24. Wang, S., Tang, H. L., Al Turk, L. I., Hu, Y., Sanei, S., Saleh, G. M., and Peto, T. (2017). Localizing microaneurysms in fundus images through singular spectrum analysis. *IEEE Trans. Biomed. Eng.*, 64(5), 990–1002.
25. Sreng, S. et al. (2017). Automatic Microaneurysms detection in fundus images using image segmentation.
26. Hatanaka, Y., Miyashita, M., and Muramatsu, C. (2018). Automatic microaneurysms detection on retinal images using deep convolution neural network. *IEEE*, 2018.
27. Dashtbozorg, B., Zhang, J., Huang, F., and Romeny, B. M. (2018). Retinal microaneurysms detection using local convergence index features. *arXiv*, 27(7, July).
28. Dai, L., Fang, R., Li, H., Hou, X., Sheng, B., Wu, Q., and Jia, W. (2018). Clinical report guided retinal microaneurysm detection with multi-sieving deep learning. *IEEE Transactions on Medical Imaging*, 37(5).
29. Melo, T., Mendonca M. A., and Campilho, A. (2020). Microaneurysm detection in color eye fundus images for diabetic retinopathy screening. *Comput. Biol. Med.*, 2020, 126. https://doi.org/10.1016/j.compbiomed.2020.103995 103995.
30. Long, S., Chen, J., Hu, A., Liu, H., Chen, Z., and Zheng, D. (2020). Microaneurysms detection in color fundus images using machine learning based on directional local contrast. *Biomedical Engineering Online*, 19(1), 1–23.
31. Hervella, A. S., Rouco, J., Novo, J., and Ortega, M. (2022). Retinal microaneurysms detection using adversarial pre-training with un labeled multimodal images. *Information Fusion*, 79, 146–161.
32. Deepa, V., Sathish Kumar, C., and Andrews, S. (2019). Automated detection of microaneurysms using Stockwell transform and statistical features. *IET Image Processing*, 13, 1341–1348. https://doi.org/10.1049/iet-ipr.2018.5672
33. Bria, A., Marrocco, C. and Tortorella, F. (2020). Addressing class imbalance in deep learning for small lesion detection on medical images. *Comput Biol. Med.*, 120, 103735. https://doi.org/10.1016/j.compbiomed.2020. 103735.
34. Selcuk, T., and Alkan, A. (2019). Detection of microaneurysms using ant colony algorithm in the early diagnosis of diabetic retinopathy. *Med Hypotheses*, 129, 109242. https://doi.org/10.1016/j.mehy.2019.109242.
35. Wang, Z., Chen, K.-J., and and Zhang, L. (2019). A R-CNN based approach for microaneurysm detection in retinal fundus images. *In: Proceedings of the International Conference on Health Information Science*, Xian, China, 18–20 October 2019.
36. Du, J., Zou, B., Ouyang, P., and Zhao, R. (2022). Retinal microaneurysm detection based on transformation splicing and multi-context ensemble learning. *Biomedical Signal Processing and Control*, 74, 103536, ISSN1746-8094. https://doi.org/10.1016/j.bspc.2022.103536.
37. Sun, S., Cao, Z., Liao, D., and Lv, R. (2021). A magnified adaptive feature pyramid network for automatic microaneurysms detection. *Computers in Biology and Medicine*, 139, 105000, ISSN0010-4825. https://doi.org/10.1016/j.compbiomed.2021.105000.

38. Zhang, X., Kuang, Y., and Yao, J. (2022). Detection of microaneurysms in color fundus images based on local Fourier transform. *Biomedical Signal Processing and Control*, 76, 103648,ISSN1746-8094, 2022. https://doi.org/10.1016/j.bspc.2022.103648.
39. Soares, I., Castelo-Branco, M., and Pinheiro, A. (2023). Microaneurysms detection in retinal images using a multi-scale approach. *Biomedical Signal Processing and Control*, 79(Part 2), 104184, ISSN1746–8094. https://doi.org/10.1016/j.bspc.2022.104184.
40. Deng, J., Tang, P., Zhao, X., Pu, T., Qu, C.., and Peng, Z. (2022). Local structure awareness-based retinal microaneurysm detection with multi-feature combination. *Biomedicines*, 10, 124. https://doi.org/10.3390/biomedicines10010124.
41. Cheng, Y., Liu, W., Wang, C., Gu, X., Cheng, Y., Wang, S., and Peng, J. (2020). A fast localization and extraction of microaneurysm for early detection of diabetic retinopathy. *IFAC-Papers On Line*, 53(2), 16400-16405, ISSN 2405–8963. https://doi.org/10.1016/j.ifacol.2020.12.684.
42. Yadav, D., Karn, A. K., Giddalur, A., Dhiman, A., Sharma, S., Muskan, and Yadav, A. K. (2021). Microaneurysm detection using color locus detection method. *Measurement*, 176, 109084, ISSN 0263-2241. https://doi.org/10.1016/j.measurement.2021.109084.

4 | Egret Swarm Optimization Algorithm-based Hybrid Deep Neural Network for Diagnosis of Skin Cancer

Muhammad Ahtsam Naeem[1], Muhammad Asim Saleem[1*], Abida Sharif[2], Areesha Rehman[3], Muhammad Imran Sharif[4], Md. Mehedi Hassan[5] and Asif Karim[6*]

[1] School of Information and Software Engineering, University of Electronic Science and Technology of China, Chengdu, 611731, China
[2] Department of Computer Science, COMSATS University Islamabad, Vehari Campus, Pakistan
[3] Department of Pharmacy, Bahauddin Zakariya University, Multan, 60000, Pakistan
[4] Department of Computer Science, Kansas State University, Manhattan, Kansas, 66506, USA
[5] Computer Science and Engineering Discipline, Khulna University, Khulna 9208, Bangladesh
[6] Faculty of Science and Technology, Charles Darwin University, NT 0909, Australia

Skin cancer is assumed to be an abnormal lymphatic fluid, tumour or blood. Skin cancer masses may exhibit both benign and malignant characteristics, with the benign variant often localized to a specific region. On the other hand, it is noteworthy that malignant cancer has the capability to disseminate throughout the entirety of the human body by using the lymphatic system. The accurate diagnosis of skin cancer necessitates the use of an intelligent optimization method that is founded upon a hybrid deep learning mechanism. This chapter proposes Egret Swarm Optimization Algorithm-based Hybrid Deep Neural Network (ESOA-HDNN) for skin cancer diagnosis. This proposed ESOA-HDNN uses two-channel CNN and Bi-RNN-based deep learning architecture to achieve better diagnosis results. It uses Egret Swarm Optimization Algorithm (ESOA) to optimize the features considered in skin cancer diagnosis. The experimental

*Corresponding authors: Muhammadasim.s@uestc.edu.cn; asif.karim@cdu.edu.au

DOI: 10.1201/9781003635215-4

results of the proposition confirmed a better accuracy of 98.34% and sensitivity of 96.72%, superseding the basic approaches used for skin cancer diagnosis.

1. Introduction

The integumentary system serves as a protective barrier for the whole body, shielding it from many environmental factors including ultraviolet radiation, extreme temperatures, and physical trauma such as lacerations, microbial infections, abrasions, and the proliferation of pathogenic microorganisms. The epidermis and dermis are the primary layers of skin that function as protective barriers. The dermis has several components such as blood vessels, hair follicles, and glands, while the epidermis is composed of three distinct cell types, namely squamous cells, basal cells, and melanocytes [1]. When the cells divide irregularly, a tumour, blood or abnormal lymph fluid is formed. Masses can be benign or malignant. Benign growths are confined to a specific area and do not spread. However, some spread throughout the lymphatic system [2]. Unlike other cancers, [3] skin cancer can be easily diagnosed because its signs can be noticed openly. The primary etiological factor of this malignancy is the direct contact with ultraviolet (UV) radiation emitted by solar radiation or certain chemical compounds present in certain light sources [4]. The DNA of the cells is altered, changing their growth and development and turning them into cancerous tumours [5]. The neoplastic growth that remains confined to its site of origin without metastasizing to distant anatomical regions is referred to as local. These growths can grow in blood vessels by spreading to adjacent tissues. Metastasis, sometimes referred to as secondary cancer, is the phenomenon whereby cancerous cells proliferate at a distinct anatomical site, giving rise to a new neoplastic growth.

Early diagnosis is thus advantageous for timely identification [6]. A biopsy is performed to make the diagnosis. A skin biopsy is used to determine the type of a lesion. In recent years, considerable research has been conducted on utilizing dermoscopy images (DIs) to achieve accurate identification, with varying rapid levels of diagnostic effectiveness. Zhang et al. [7] utilizing the best Convolution Neural Network (CNN) was used in research to detect skin problems. Early identification of cutaneous melanoma improves disease prevention. Image processing methods are commonly utilized in dermatology to help in the diagnosis of various skin disorders. To identify melanoma, a CNN based on the Whale Optimization Algorithm is used.

Melanomas were identified in this study utilizing a method based on the Red Fox Optimization Algorithm (RFOA) and the K-Fuzzy C-Means (KFCM) algorithm by Xu et al. [8]. An optimized process is employed to accurately identify melanoma spots in DIs. Following image preprocessing, the KFCM technique partitions skin areas into pieces. Ideally, an optimized algorithm determines the split skin's primary features. The results show that this ideal algorithm enables for the precise identification of melanoma patches on the skin. This technique, based on the RFOA design, produces precise and reliable results in skin categorization and melanoma spot identification.

Tan et al. [9] have developed an intelligent methodology for the detection and categorization of melanoma lesions. Deep learning methods (DL) and particle swarm optimization (PSO) are often used. The implementation of the Particle Swarm Optimization (PSO) model exhibits promising prospects in enhancing the effectiveness of deep convolutional neural networks (CNNs). Particle Swarm Optimization (PSO) is used to improve the detection and classification of cutaneous melanoma lesions [10]. The suggested deep CNN's output is evaluated against conventional methods and statistical testing. Results demonstrate that the suggested deep CNN can detect melanoma spots and patches of injured skin, in contrast to conventional methods. Parsian et al. [11]. The adoption of the Wildebeest Herd Optimization (WHO) approach facilitated the identification of melanoma lesions in Dermoscopic Images (DIs). A non-aggressive dermoscopy scheme using ocular inference is applied. The manual identification of melanoma spots is a challenging task. Using artificial intelligence (AI) techniques increases the accuracy of melanoma identification. DL, enhanced by WHOA, is used to identify melanoma spots. The dataset utilized is ISIC-2008 for skin cancer. Analysis demonstrates that the technique improves the capacity to identify the disease.

Khamparia et al. [12] employed a deep learning (DL) technique that was used to identify and classify skin cancers within specific regions. The timely classification and identification of medical conditions may enhance the likelihood of successful patient outcomes [13]. The previously convolutional neural network (CNN) is used for the purpose of distinguishing between benign and malignant tumors. CNN provides better performance in diagnosing and categorizing malignant skin lesions. Various studies have been conducted for skin cancer diagnosis using dermoscopy. From the results, the use of metaheuristic algorithms is exponentially increasing. A hybrid method based on DL and meta-heuristics efficiently identifies skin cancer. The Grasshopper Optimization Algorithm (GOA) has been enhanced to provide better results with more accuracy and precision.

Our motivation for conducting this study came from the researcher's utilization of deep learning technology for skin cancer identification. Therefore, the key contributions of proposed study are given as below:

(i) This study's primary objective is to improve diagnostic accuracy via the use of a two-channel CNN and Bi-RNN-based deep learning architecture.
(ii) The Egret Swarm Optimization Algorithm (ESOA) is used to optimize features relevant to skin cancer diagnosis.
(iii) To produce better outcomes with more accuracy and, this study additionally enhanced the performance of Grasshopper Optimization Algorithm (GOA) for melanoma spot recognition.

2. Related Work

Among the popular threshold selection techniques, metaheuristic algorithm-based techniques are straightforward, simple to use, and avoid local optimization. However, different algorithms provide various performances for certain photos.

There are various approaches to improve Neural Network (NN) learning, and some studies use Deep Learning (DL) based NNs [14]. Zhang et al. (2019) [15] applied an optimized CNN classifier on pre-trained models to visual datasets to help classify images with skin cancer. Biases and network weights are trained based on backpropagation. The use of a technique rooted on the Whale Optimization Algorithm (WOA) is recommended for the purpose of augmenting the weights and biases inside Convolutional Neural Network (CNN) models. In this study, we assess the performance of the Convolutional Neural Network (CNN) integrated with the Whale Optimization Algorithm (WOA) in comparison to conventional classifiers. The assessment is conducted utilizing the DermIS Digital and Dermquest databases. The proposed optimized scheme provides improved accuracy compared to other classification schemes. The cost function for the half-value accuracy uses the error acquired as output and a simple measured error in the center of the reference.

In Wei et al. [16], the researchers developed an autonomous and optimized method for the use of Deep Learning models in the identification of skin cancer. It employs Otsu for segmentation and noise reduction while defining the region of interest (RoI). From the picture, around 20 characteristics are extracted. The best characteristics are chosen using a modified Thermal Exchange Optimization Algorithm (TEOA), which lowers the suggested method's complexity. This improves the technique's consistency and accuracy. The American Cancer Society (ACS) database is used to test the effectiveness of the suggested strategy, and the findings are compared to those obtained using more traditional techniques. This classification is conducted by using a support vector machine (SVM). The proposed method provides better results compared to other techniques.

Huaping et al. [17] have proposed a procedure that includes four main phases. First, image preprocessing is performed by noise reduction and contrast enhancement. Second, it segments the RoI using kernel fuzzy C-means (KFC). It extracts and selects the best features. The selected features are passed to SVM for final recognition. This meta-heuristic NN optimization algorithm performs improved feature selection and SVM-based classification, providing higher accuracy.

Zhou and Arandian [18] have used Inception (ICNN) to extract features from skin cancer images. The present technique employs the Wildebeest Herd Optimization (WHO) meta-heuristic algorithm for the purpose of feature trimming. The WHO algorithm selects valuable features to reduce the time required for analysis. The methodology is used using the ISIC-2008 dataset pertaining to skin cancer. The proposed scheme provides better accuracy, number of features and speed in contrast to the methods used for comparison.

In this paper Qiao et al. [19] presents a novel diagnostic methodology for the detection of skin cancer using deep learning (DL) and meta-heuristics. AlexNet, which is pre-trained and modified depending on batch normalization layers, trains skin dermoscopy images. Extreme Learning Machines (ELM) are used to replace the subsequent layers. To increase effectiveness in an ELM network, it applies the FORFO (Fractional-order Red Fox Optimization) algorithm. The proposed system provides better results than different techniques, which proves its effectiveness.

This paper by Houssein et al. [20] presents a new variant of the Golden Jackal Optimization (GJO) method, referred to as the Opposition-based Golden Jackal Optimizer (OGJO). For assistance with the resolution of multilevel thresholding challenges, the OGJO algorithm uses the Otsu method as the aim function. Peak Signal-to-Noise Ratio (PSNR), the framework Likewise Index method (SSIM), Feature Similarity Index Method (FSIM), and Mean Square Error (MSE) are used to assess the effectiveness of the suggested strategy. The results indicate that the proposed methodology successfully resolves the problem of segmentation and surpasses other algorithms in relation to the aforementioned factors.

Xu et al. [21] proposed an efficient skin cancer diagnosis algorithm by extracting and selecting gradients, geometric, and texture features for classification to identify cancer cases. The classification is performed using Elman NN. Fractional Order Coot Optimization method (FO-COA), a proposed extended meta-heuristic method, optimizes feature selection and classification. In order to ascertain its efficacy, the proposed model is implemented on the SIIM-ISIC melanoma dataset, and its performance is evaluated.

Li and Jimenez [22] proposed a non-destructive testing method using AlexNet and ELM to achieve better results. The proposed scheme is optimized based on an extended Grasshopper optimization algorithm (GOA) that optimally selects weights and biases. The proposed model provides better accuracy and sensitivity. The performance of AlexNet, which was previously employed in the Fully Connected (FC) layers, has been increased. The network has been successfully linked to the ELM system. The efficacy of the proposed technique is evaluated by applying the Quartic, Sulfur 2.22, Sphere, and Rosenbrock functions on a set of four standard functions. This set comprises two unimodal and two multimodal basis functions. The plan begins with an AlexNet that has already been trained to extract characteristics from DIs. The pre-trained network's final layers may be changed.

Balaha and Hassan (2022) [23] examined skin conditions using a graphical taxonomy. U-Net, Attention U-Net, U-Net++, swin U-Net, and V-Net models are used for segmentation. Classification is performed with different pre-trained CNN models. The SpaSA scheme is used for hyperparameter optimization. A DL-based model has been developed to identify, classify, and segment skin cancer. For effective learning, classification, and optimization, the pre-trained CNN models' hyperparameters are optimized using the SpaSA meta-heuristic optimizer.

When segmenting an image with multiple thresholds, a threshold is chosen to determine the segmentation quality. WOA does not provide acceptable performance for images with thresholds. Liu et al. (2022) [24] proposed approach introduces an improved variant of the Levy Chaotic Whale Optimization Algorithm (LCWOA). This variation enhances the algorithm's capacity to avoid local optima and more successfully traverse the search space by integrating the chaotic random mutation mechanism with the Levy operator. The technique is used for the choice of threshold in image segmentation. When used with various WOA variations of the CEC2014 feature set, the suggested and enhanced method increases the search effectiveness. The suggested technique offers increased convergence speed and accuracy.

3. Egret Swarm Optimization Algorithm-based Hybrid Deep Neural Network (ESOA-HDNN) for Diagnosis of Skin Cancer

In this section, we offer a thorough exposition of the proposed methodology, which integrates a hybrid deep neural network with feature optimization using ESOA. The primary objective of this technique is to improve the precision of skin cancer detection in classification tasks. Figure 1 illustrates the whole procedure involved in the diagnosis of skin cancer.

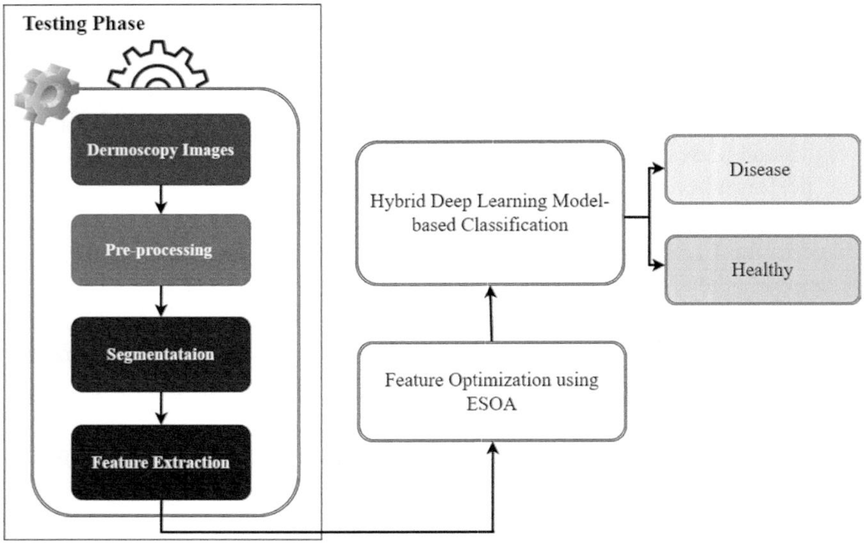

Figure 1: Comprehensive View of the Proposed ESOA-HDNN Model-based Skin Cancer Detection.

ESOA-based Feature Optimization

The Egret Swarm Optimization Algorithm (ESOA) combines the advantages of the "sit-and-wait" approach of the snowy egret and the "aggressive" mechanism of the great egret. A mathematical model is used to enumerate the behaviours. ESOA is a similar algorithm with 3 indispensable components: sit-and-wait, aggressive strategies, and discriminant condition. Egrets in the Egret squad include:

(i) Egret A implements guiding forward
(ii) Egret B implements random walk
(iii) Egret C implements encircling schemes

Sit-and-Wait Policy – Observation: Assume the location of '*i*th' squad given by $P_i \in R^n$

where,
n – Problem dimension
$S(*)$ – Snowy Egret's estimation of possible prey occurrence in the present position
P – Estimate of prey in the present position

$$P\check{r} = A(P_i) \tag{1}$$

Estimate technique is given as,

$$P\check{r} = W_i \times P_i \tag{2}$$

where,

$W_i \in R^n$ – Weight of estimate technique

Error ($\check{E}_i$) is given by,

$$\check{E}_i = \frac{\| P\check{r}_i - Pr_i \|^2}{2} \tag{3}$$

$$\check{g}_i = \frac{\delta \check{E}_i}{\delta W_i} = \frac{\frac{\delta \| P\check{r}_i - Pr_i \|^2}{2}}{\delta w_i} = (P\check{r}_i - Pr_i).\ P_i \tag{4}$$

$$\check{D} = \frac{\check{g}_i}{|\check{g}_i|} \tag{5}$$

where,
$\check{g}_i \in R^n$ – Practical gradient of 'φ_i'

It may be obtained by determining the partial derivative of. 'φ_i' for '$\check{E}_i$' in Equation (3), direction ($\check{D}_i$).

Egrets prey based on experience and including their own thoughts.

$D_P^i \in R^n$ – Directional alteration of the best position of the squad

$D^i_{P_{all}} \in R^n$ – Directional alteration of the best position of every squad

$$D^i_P = \frac{P_{i_{Best}} - P_i}{|P_{i_{Best}} - P_i|} \cdot \frac{F_{i_{Best}} - F_i}{|P_{i_{Best}} - P_i|} + D_{i_{Best}} \tag{6}$$

$$D^i_{P_{all}} = \frac{P_{g_{Best}} - P_i}{|P_{g_{Best}} - P_i|} \cdot \frac{F_{g_{Best}} - F_i}{|P_{g_{Best}} - P_i|} + D_{g_{Best}} \tag{7}$$

The combined gradient: '$g_i \in R^n$' with r_P, $r_{P_{all}} \in [0, 0.5]$ is shown below.

$$g_i = (1 - ran_P - ran_{P_{all}}) . \check{D}_i + ran_P . D^i_P + ran_{P_{all}} . D^i_{P_{all}} \tag{8}$$

A dynamic weight update scheme is applied [25].

$$C_i = \omega_1 . C_i + (1 - \omega_1) . g_i \tag{9}$$

$$D_i = \omega_1 . D_i + (1 - \omega_1) . g_i^2 \tag{10}$$

$$W_i = W_i - \frac{C_i}{\sqrt{D_i}} \tag{11}$$

$$\omega_1 = 0.9$$

$$\omega_2 = 0.99$$

Based on Egret A's decision of the present situation, following the sampling position. 'P^i_a' can be shown as,

$$P^i_a = P_i + \exp\left(\frac{-T}{0.1 \times T_{max}}\right) \times 0.1 \times hop \times g_i \tag{12}$$

$$F^i_a = f(P^i_a) \tag{13}$$

where,

T and T_{max} – Current and maximum iteration times

hop – Gap amid low and up bounds of solution space

F^i_a – Fitness of 'P^i_a'

Aggressive Policy: Egret B inclines to search for prey arbitrarily, and behaviour is shown below:

$$P^i_a = P_i + \frac{tantan\,(ran^i_b) \times hop}{1 + T} \tag{14}$$

$$F^i_b = f(P^i_b) \tag{15}$$

where,

ran^i_b – Random number in $\left(\frac{-\pi}{2}, \frac{\pi}{2}\right)$

P^i_b – Egret B's expected next location

F^i_b – Fitness

Egret C favours to follow the prey violently. The encircling scheme is used as a scheme to update its location:

$$GM_s = P_{i_{Best}} - P_i \quad (16)$$

$$GM_{s_{all}} = P_{g_{Best}} - P_i \quad (17)$$

$$P_c^i = (1 - ran_i - ran_{s_{all}}) \times P_i + ran_s \times GM_s + ran_{s_{all}} \times GM_{s_{all}} \quad (18)$$

$$F_b^i = f(P_b^i) \quad (19)$$

where,

GM_s – Gap matrix amid present and best locations of Squad

$GM_{s_{all}}$ – Best position of all Squads

P_c^i – Anticipated position of Egret C

ran_s and $ran_{s_{all}}$ – Arbitrary numbers in the range [0, 0.5]

Discriminant Condition: After every participant of the Squad has decided on its strategy, Squad chooses the ideal option and takes action together.

$$P_{Sol}^i = [P_a^i, P_b^i, P_c^i] \quad (20)$$

$$F_{Sol}^i = [F_a^i, F_b^i, F_c^i] \quad (21)$$

$$c_i = argmin\ (F_{Sol}^i) \quad (22)$$

$$P_i = \{P_{Sol}^i \mid c_i, \text{ if } F_{Sol}^i \mid c_i < F_i \text{ or } ran < 0.3\ P_i, \text{ Otherwise}\} \quad (23)$$

where,

P_{Sol}^i – Solution matrix of 'i^{th}' Squad

If minimal 'F_{Sol}^i' is more than present fitness (F_i), Squad agrees with the selection. If arbitrary number, ran $\in$ (0, 1) < 0.3, then there is a 30% likelihood of agreeing with the worse plan.

ESOA is built as an Algorithm that contains 2 functions to reclaim Squad's anticipated PM and discriminant condition to select an improved mechanism. ESOA necessitates an initial matrix $P_0 \in R^{P \times N}$ of ES location (P) as input, while it offers the ideal location (P_{Best}) and fitness (F_{Best}).

Algorithm 1: ESOA

Input:

X_0 : ES location of size 'P' $\in R^{P \times N}$

Output:

P_{Best}: Ideal/approximate ideal solution

F_{Best}: Ideal/approximate ideal fitness

function Sit&Wait(X)
  Modify combined gradient 'g' using Equations (4 to 8)
  Modify the weight of observation 'φ' using Equation (9)
  Obtain anticipated location. 'P_a' of Egret A using Equation (12)
  return 'P_a'
end function
function Aggressive(X)
  Obtain the anticipated location (P_b) of Egret B using Equation (14)
  Obtain the anticipated location (P_c) of Egret C using Equation (17)
  return 'P_b'; 'P_c'
end function
while ($T < T_{max}$) do

$$P_a^T = \text{Sit\&Wait}\ (X^T)$$

$$P_b^T, X_c^T = \text{Aggressive}\ (X^T)$$

Obtain ensuing location: 'P^{T+1}' using Equations (20) to (23)
end while
return (P_{Best} ; F_{Best})

Two-channel CNN and Bi-RNN-based Deep Learning Model for Classification of Dermoscopy Images

The hybrid deep learning model, which incorporates two channel CNN and Bi-RNN, is shown in Fig. 2. It includes feature representation, CNN, pooling, bi-directional RNN, fully connected, and attention and output layers. The CNN is responsible for extracting local features, whilst the Bi-RNN utilizes these features to ascertain the dependencies and provide corresponding outputs throughout the training process. The attention mechanism is included in the output layers of recurrent neural networks (RNNs). CNN provides interpretation on the various characteristics.

Input Layer

Features F ($f_1, f_2, \ldots, f_j$) with $f_1, f_2, \ldots, f_j$ tokens (j) of size 'd' are given to the input layer. 'R^d' is the dimension space of every feature transformed into a feature vector of size 'd'. Feature vector matrix (F) conforming to a feature 'j' is given by:

$$F\ (f_1, f_2, \ldots, f_k) \in R^{j \times d} \tag{24}$$

As the length of the input text varies, zero padding is performed. If the length exceeds the predefined value, the text is truncated. If the length of the value is less than the predetermined length, the process of inserting zero padding (l) is executed. The generation of a matrix with a default length is shown in Eq. (25)

$$F \in R^{l \times d} \tag{25}$$

where, 'F' represents the feature-generating matrix.

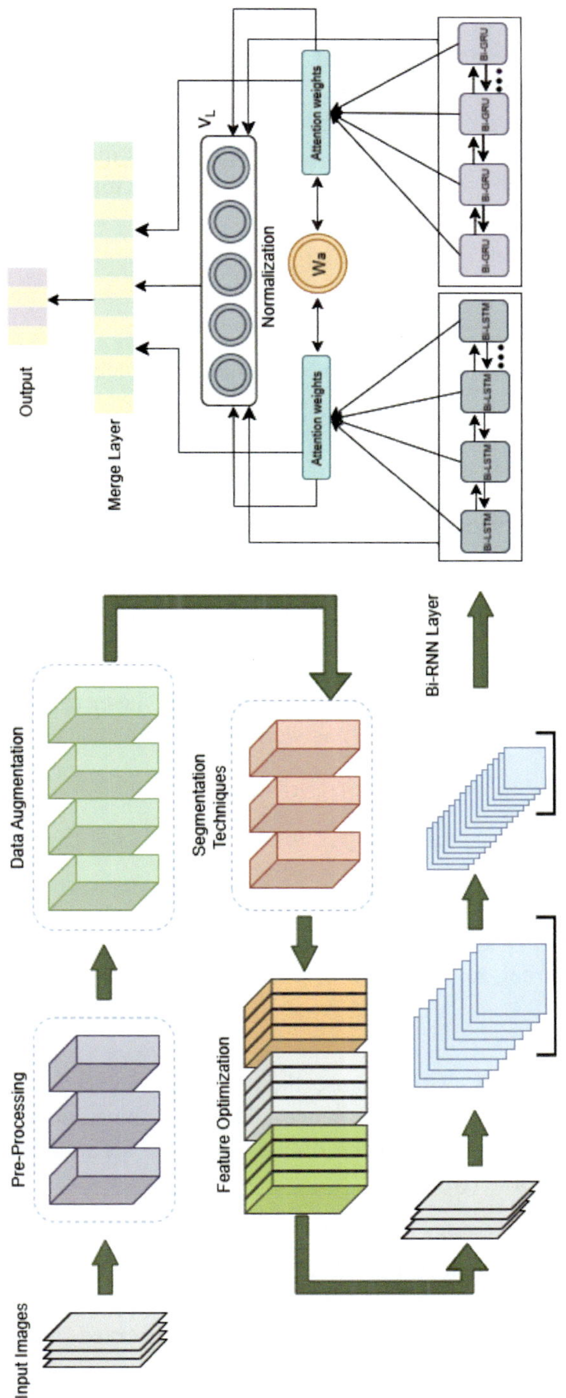

Figure 2: Detailed View of the Proposed ESOA-HDNN Scheme.

Convolutional Neural Network (CNN)

The concept of row representation is used. The feature representations pertaining to the two convolutional layers. Assume 'i^{th}' row of feature matrix conforming to a channel is given by $FV_k \in R^d$, where 'FV_k' corresponds to the feature vector of 'k^{th}' feature with 'd' dimensions. $FV_{k:k+l-1} \in R^{l*d}$ shows matrix composite of input length (l) from 'k^{th}' feature to '$k+l-1^{th}$' feature. Extracted feature ($\dot{f_k}$) is expressed as shown below:

$$\dot{f_k} = f(W \times FV_{k:k+l-1} + B + Z) \tag{26}$$

where,

f – Non-linear activation function

$\dot{f_k}$ – Value of 'k^{th}' feature obtained by the convolutional function

W – Weight of matrix

B – Bias

Z – Gaussian noise

The channels '$\dot{f}_{1:k}$' and '$\dot{f}_{2:k}$' get output from convolutional layers in every channel. Features got from CNN layers are shown below:

$$\dot{f_n} = [\dot{f_1}, \dot{f_2}, \ldots, \dot{f_i}],\ n = 1 \tag{27}$$

$$\dot{f_n} = [\dot{f_1}, \dot{f_2}, \ldots, \dot{f_i}],\ n = 2 \tag{28}$$

Max-pooling is applied to every channel output. '$\dot{f_n}$' layer to reduce dataset dimensions as represented in Eqs. (29) as well as Eq. (30).

$$fm_n = Max[\dot{f_n}],\ n = 1 \tag{29}$$

$$fm_n = Max[\dot{f_n}],\ n = 2 \tag{30}$$

where,

fm – feature map

$fm_n\ (n = 1), fm_n\ (n = 2)$ – Obtained following the max-pooling layer from 1st and 2nd convolutional kernel, respectively.

RNN Layer

Recurrent Neural Networks (RNNs) use their internal memory to effectively process and react to sequential data, hence addressing the issue of vanishing gradient. The preceding procedures are divided into two separate bidirectional recurrent neural networks (RNNs).

(i) Long Short-Term Memory (LSTM)

The Long Short-Term Memory (LSTM) model, which is an upgraded form of the Recurrent Neural Network (RNN), displays the capacity to effectively mitigate the issue of vanishing gradients that is often observed in conventional RNNs. This problem is caused by the fact that conventional RNNs do not use the LSTM model's enhanced version of the Recurrent Neural Network. It is a gating scheme which includes an input (I_t), forget (F_t) and output (O_t) gates. The dynamic gating scheme produces output from present states, recalls and forwards to the ensuing phase. It includes memory cells. 'M_t' which takes into consideration the state's time interval at random. The non-linear gates are accountable for the information flow from and to 'M_t'. Specifically, Eqs. (31)-(36) show the functioning of gates as follows.

$$F_t = \sigma\,(V_f \,.\, \dot{f}_{t-1} + U_f \,.\, Y_t + b_f) \tag{31}$$

$$I_t = \sigma\,(V_i \,.\, \dot{f}_{t-1} + U_i \,.\, Y_t + b_i) \tag{32}$$

$$U_t = tanh\,(V_c \,.\, \dot{f}_{t-1} + U_c \,.\, Y_t + b_c) \tag{33}$$

$$M_t = F_t \odot M_{t-1} + I_t \odot U_t \tag{34}$$

'OI_t' chooses the information stored in memory based on Eqs. (32)-(35). 'F_t' chooses the output, quantity of information and portions of cell state that must be output.

$$O_t = \sigma\,(V_o \,.\, \dot{f}_{t-1} + U_o \,.\, Y_t + b_o) \tag{35}$$

$$\dot{f}_t = O_t + I_t \,.\, tanh\ C_t \tag{36}$$

Where σ (·) – Element-based sigmoid function

tanh(·) – Hyperbolic Tangent function

· – Product

Y_t – Input vector

$\dot{f}_t$ – Hidden vector at time 't'

U and V – Weight matrix of input and hidden vectors

b – Bias vector

'F_t' – accountable for disregarding or disremembering information.

These gates aid in remembering significant information on numerous time updates and disregard information that is not essential.

Gated Recurrent Unit (GRU)

GRU resembles LSTM but has only 2 gates, namely, update (Z_t) and reset (R_t). The gates control the process of information updating. 'R_t' takes control of former state ($\dot{f}_{t-1}$) contribution to the candidate's state ($I\dot{f}_t^{\vee}$). In case the value is smaller, the ignored rate is higher. At time 't', 'R_t' functions as follows.

$$R_t = \sigma\,(V_r \,.\, \dot{f}_{t-1} + U_r \,.\, Y_t + b_r) \tag{37}$$

'Z_t' is used to find the quantity of stream information that may be maintained or forgotten at 't' and 't–1'.

'Z_t' is expressed as shown below.

$$Z_t = \sigma\,(V_Z \,.\, \dot{f}_{t-1} + U_Z \,.\, Y_t + b_z) \tag{38}$$

where,

σ – Logistic sigmoid function

$\dot{f}_{t-1}$ – Hidden vector at time 't–1'

GRU state ($\dot{f}_t$) and the candidate state ($\dot{f}_t^{\vee}$) at 't' are shown in the ensuing equations.

$$\dot{f}_t = (1 - Z_t) \odot \dot{f}_t^{\vee} + Z_t + \dot{f}_{t-1} \tag{39}$$

$$\dot{f}_t^{\vee} = tanh\,(V_h\,(\dot{f}_{t-1} \odot R_t) + U_h\,.Y_t + b_h) \tag{40}$$

Similar to LSTM,

U, V – Learnable weights

⊙ – Multiplication of vector element

(ii) Bi-directional RNN

LSTM and GRU are independent bi-directional RNNs considering both the forward and backward features. To improve outcomes for both big and small datasets, two different kinds of RNNs are utilized. Bi-GRU is used to obtain better contextual information. GRU is faster and requires a smaller amount of data for generalization. However, Bi-LSTM produces the final set of features by analyzing the map sequentially, offering better outcomes with more information. With 'm' padding or maximum feature lengths, these Bi-RNN networks create a feature context matrix using vectors from the channels of earlier phases.

$$\vec{\dot{f}}_{f_{LSTM}} = \overrightarrow{LSTM}\,(p_n),\ n \in [1, m] \tag{41}$$

$$\overleftarrow{\dot{f}}_{b_{LSTM}} = \overleftarrow{LSTM}\,(p_n),\ n \in [m, 1] \tag{42}$$

Eqs. (20) and (21) represent forward and backwards GRUs, respectively.

$$\vec{\dot{f}}_{f_{GRU}} = \overrightarrow{GRU}\,(p_n),\ n \in [1, m] \tag{43}$$

$$\overleftarrow{\dot{f}}_{b_{GRU}} = \overleftarrow{GRU}\,(p_n),\ n \in [m, 1] \tag{44}$$

Annotation of every input vector can be obtained by combining forward and backward contexts.

$$\dot{f}_{t_{LSTM}} = LSTM\,[\vec{\dot{f}}_{f_{LSTM}}, \overleftarrow{\dot{f}}_{b_{LSTM}}] \tag{45}$$

$$\dot{f}_{t_{GRU}} = GRU\,[\vec{\dot{f}}_{f_{GRU}}, \overleftarrow{\dot{f}}_{b_{GRU}}] \tag{46}$$

where,

$\dot{f}_{t_{LSTM}}$ – Combined output of '$\vec{\dot{f}}_{f_{LSTM}}$' and '$\overleftarrow{\dot{f}}_{b_{LSTM}}$' from Bi-LSTM

$\dot{f}_{t_{GRU}}$ – Concatenating output of '$\vec{\dot{f}}_{f_{GRU}}$' and '$\overleftarrow{\dot{f}}_{b_{GRU}}$' from Bi-GRU

The features $[\vec{f}_{f_{LSTM}}, \overleftarrow{f}_{b_{LSTM}}]$ and $[\vec{f}_{f_{GRU}}, \overleftarrow{f}_{b_{GRU}}]$ are determined. Forward as well as backward contexts are considered concurrently.

(iii) Attention Scheme

The i-RNN-produced features are considered. The '$\dot{f}_{t_{LSTM}}$' and '$\dot{f}_{t_{GRU}}$' annotations are passed into a 1-layer perceptron to obtain the following. For 't^{th}' input,

$U_{t_{LSTM}}$ – Hidden representation of '$\dot{f}_{t_{LSTM}}$'

$U_{t_{GRU}}$ – Hidden representation of '$\dot{f}_{t_{GRU}}$'

$$U_{t_{LSTM}} = tanh\ (W \times \dot{f}_{t_{LSTM}} + b) \tag{47}$$

$$U_{t_{GRU}} = tanh\ (W \times \dot{f}_{t_{GRU}} + b) \tag{48}$$

where,
W – Weight

To determine the significance of features, normalization is performed on 'U_t's' hidden representation with context vector (CV_S) that is arbitrarily set and co-operatively learned while training.

$$An_{t_{LSTM}} = \frac{\exp\ (U_{t_{LSTM}} \times CV_S)}{\sum_{i=1}^{m} \exp\ (U_{t_{LSTM}} \times CV_S)} \tag{49}$$

$$An_{t_{GRU}} = \frac{\exp\ (U_{t_{GRU}} \times CV_S)}{\sum_{i=1}^{m} \exp\ (U_{t_{GRU}} \times CV_S)} \tag{50}$$

$An_{t_{LSTM}}$ and $An_{t_{GRU}}$ – Normalized weights of LSTM and GRU layers correspondingly
m – Amount of features
exp(.) – Exponential function

The normalized weights are concatenated into. 'An_t' and it is shown in Eq. (51). In addition, the significance weight. 'An_t' are combined to 'CV' to get a vector representing Eq. (52).

$$An_t = An_{t_{LSTM}} \oplus An_{t_{GRU}} \tag{51}$$

$$CV = \sum An_i \times \dot{f}_t \tag{52}$$

(iv) Output layer

This level provides comprehensive classification by using a unified feature level. For binary inputs, the sigmoid function is applied, and the cross-entropy (CE) is in charge of the discrepancy between the actual and anticipated attitudes.

Finally, the optimization method using ESOA is integrated with the hybrid deep learning model using the batch normalization method. The hybrid deep learning model that had been built beforehand was used to extract all the characteristics from dermoscopy pictures. In particular, the process of batch normalization is applied over the layers to prevent internal covariate shifts. This approach aims to classify dermoscopy images into cancerous and normal.

4. Results and Discussion

An analysis of the suggested system's performance will be presented in this section, together with the dataset used for experimental validation. The basic methodologies use many measures including classification accuracy, specificity, sensitivity, precision, F1 score, Matthew correlation coefficient (MCC), negative predictive value (NPV), and positive predictive value (PPV) for evaluation purposes.

Dataset

The enhanced DL-based system incorporates a common method for directly identifying cancer from images. The model was implemented in Python using TensorFlow and the outcomes were verified utilizing the PH2 database. This database contains a number of dermoscopic images from the Hospital Pedro Hispano's (Portugal) Dermatology Service. The collection comprises RGB color photos with a resolution of 768×560 pixels (8 bits per channel). The dataset consists of 200 dermoscopic images, including 160 benign common nevi and 40 malignant melanomas. The images were resized to a uniform dimension of 224×224 pixels to match the input requirements of the CNN. Data augmentation techniques such as rotation, flipping, and zooming were applied to increase the diversity of the training set. The dataset was split into 80% for training and 20% for testing, with 10% of the training set used for validation.

Performance Evaluation of the Proposed ESOA-HDNN

The performance analysis of the suggested scheme is shown in Table 1. The baseline methodologies are assessed using several performance measures, such as classification accuracy, specificity, sensitivity, precision, F1 Score, and Matthew's correlation coefficient (MCC).

Figure 3 presents the classification accuracy, precision, and specificity obtained via the implementation of the suggested ESOA-HDNN scheme, alongside utilization of cutting-edge methodologies, as implemented in the comparative investigation. The ESOA-HDNN scheme demonstrates a classification accuracy that surpasses the state-of-the-art approaches by 16.94%. Moreover, the precision achieved by the proposed ESOA-HDNN scheme is improved by 18.56% on average, which is better than the baseline approaches used for the study. Moreover, the specificity achieved by the proposed ESOA-HDNN scheme is improved by an average of 17.82%, better than the baseline approaches used for the investigation.

Table 1: The Performance Investigation of the Proposed ESOA-HDNN and the State-of-the-Art Methods

Methods used for comparison	Classification accuracy	Precision	Specificity	Sensitivity	F1-score	MCC
TEOA-SVM [16]	0.89	0.93	0.93	0.83	0.84	0.91
KFC-SVM [17]	0.84	0.91	0.95	0.77	0.86	0.94
WHO-ICNN [18]	0.92	0.92	0.94	0.94	0.95	0.92
AlexNet [19]	0.88	0.95	0.93	0.90	0.95	0.89
OGJO-SCD [20]	0.91	0.94	0.88	0.93	0.94	0.88
FO-COA [21]	0.85	0.93	0.91	0.92	0.92	0.84
GOA-ELM [22]	0.87	0.91	0.90	0.91	0.93	0.72
U-Net-SCD [23]	0.91	0.96	0.92	0.93	0.95	0.89
LCWOA [24]	0.93	0.94	0.95	0.90	0.96	0.88
Proposed ESOA-HDNN	0.98	0.97	0.97	0.97	0.97	0.95

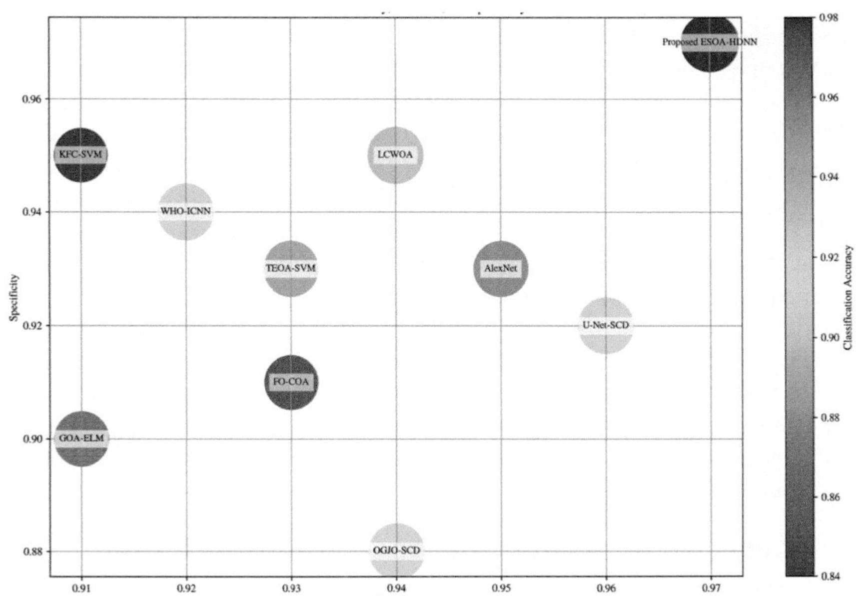

Figure 3: Classification Accuracy, Precision and Specificity.

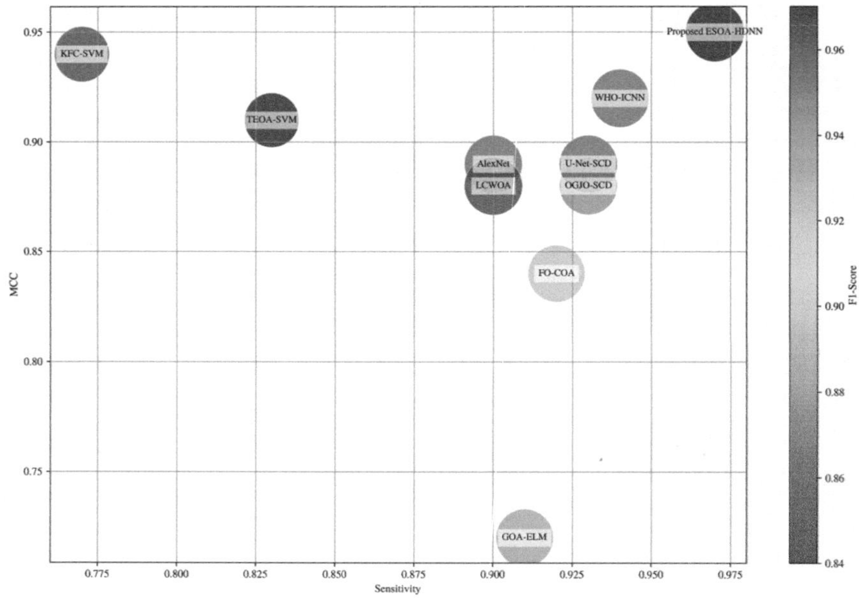

Figure 4: Performance Evaluation of the Proposed Enhanced Self-Organizing Algorithm with Hierarchical Deep Neural Network (ESOA-HDNN).

Figure 4 illustrates the performance evaluation of the proposed Enhanced Self-Organizing Algorithm with Hierarchical Deep Neural Network (ESOA-HDNN) approach in comparison to already established state-of-the-art approaches. The evaluation is conducted using the F1 score, sensitivity, and Matthews Correlation Coefficient (MCC) metrics. The findings suggest that the ESOA-HDNN approach, which incorporates ESOA to maximize the characteristics that contribute to improved classification accuracy, is on par with the most modern methods in attaining the greatest values of NPV and PPV. The measurements of negative predictive value (NPV) and positive predictive value (PPV) provide the foundation for the assessment. The results are shown in Table 2. The rise in efficiency is 15.16 percent on average, outperforming state-of-the-art techniques now in use. Additionally, the ESOA-HDNN approach reported in this work has an average sensitivity of 17.32%, outperforming the performance of the baseline techniques used in this investigation. On top of that, the suggested ESOA-HDNN approach outperforms the performance of the traditional methods employed in this inquiry with a mean enhancement of 18.94% in comparison to the Matthews Correlation Coefficient (MCC).

Performance Evaluation of the Proposed ESOA-HDNN Using NPV and PPV

The following section compares and contrasts the ESOA-HDNN model proposed in this work with other cutting-edge approaches that are presently available. The metrics of negative predictive value (NPV) and positive predictive value (PPV) are used in the evaluation. Table 2 is provided below with the outcomes.

Table 2: The Performance of the Proposed ESOA-HDNN and State-of-the-Art Methods Using Negative Predictive Value (NPV) and Positive Predictive Value (PPV)

Methods used for comparison	Negative predictive value (NPV)	Positive predictive value (PPV)
TEOA-SVM [16]	0.74	0.72
KFC-SVM [17]	0.87	0.74
WHO-ICNN [18]	0.83	0.71
AlexNet [19]	0.84	0.79
OGJO-SCD [20]	0.81	0.63
FO-COA [21]	0.82	0.64
GOA-ELM [22]	0.84	0.68
U-Net-SCD [23]	0.83	0.78
LCWOA [24]	0.84	0.86
Proposed ESOA-HDNN	0.88	0.87

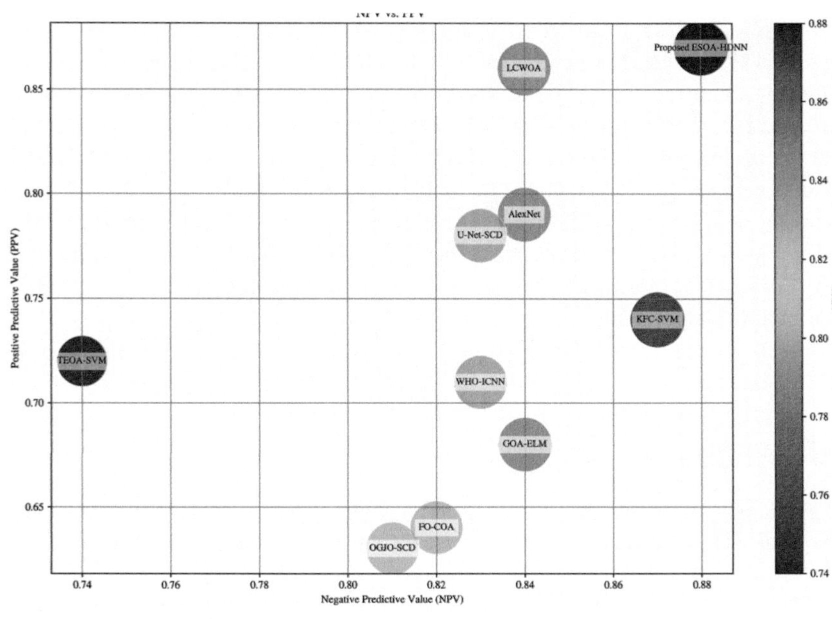

Figure 5: NPV and PPV.

In Fig. 5, the efficacy of the suggested ESOA-HDNN technique in comparison to other ways is also shown. This evaluation was done using the metrics of negative predictive value (NPV) and positive predictive value (PPV). The findings show that the ESOA-HDNN scheme may improve both negative predictive value (NPV) and positive predictive value (PPV) to a level equivalent to that of existing state-of-the-art approaches. This is due to the fact that ESOA may be included for feature optimization and classification accuracy is enhanced. Thus, the proposed ESOA-HDNN scheme demonstrates an impressive improvement in negative predictive value (NPV), with an average increase of 13.28%. In comparison to the current best practices, this performs far better. In addition, as shown, the ESOA-HDNN scheme outperforms the study's baseline procedures by a mean of 14.84 percentage points in terms of positive predictive value (PPV).

5. Conclusion

This chapter proposed a hybrid deep learning model for the accurate identification of skin cancer. The proposed ESOA-HDNN model consists of two components: the Egret Swarm Optimization Algorithm (ESOA) algorithm is utilized for maximum feature optimization from the image dataset, while the High-Dimensional Neural Network (HDNN) is employed for the accurate classification of skin cancer. The experimental findings of the proposed study suggested that an enhanced self-organizing algorithm-based high-dimensional neural network (ESOA-HDNN) has substantiated a higher level of accuracy (98.34%) and sensitivity (96.72%). These results surpass the performance of the baseline methodologies used in the investigation. The results show that the suggested ESOA-HDNN scheme's NPV is, on average, 13.28% better than that of cutting-edge techniques. Additionally, the suggested ESOA-HDNN scheme increased the PPV by an average of 14.84%, outperforming the baseline methods used for the research. The effectiveness of the newly constructed ESOA-HDNN model suggests that it can help medical practitioners make accurate decisions regarding skin cancer. In future work, it is decided to develop a deep learning model based on CNN-LSTM-AM for skin cancer diagnosis and compare it with the recently proposed Dingo Optimization Algorithm and Beluga Whale Optimization Algorithm.

References

1. Razmjooy, N., Sheykhahmad, F. R., and Ghadimi, N. (2018). A hybrid neural network–world cup optimization algorithm for melanoma detection. *Open Medicine*, 13(1), 9–16.
2. Balaha, H. M., and Hassan, A. E. S. (2022). Skin cancer diagnosis based on deep transfer learning and sparrow search algorithm. *Neural Comput & Applic*. https://doi.org/10.1007/s00521-022-07762-9

3. Zhang, L., Zhang, J., Gao, W., Bai, F., Li, N., and Ghadimi, N. (2024). A deep learning outline aimed at prompt skin cancer detection utilizing gated recurrent unit networks and improved orca predation algorithm. *Biomedical Signal Processing and Control*, 90, 105858.
4. Pejin, B., Mojovic, M., and Savic, A. G. (2014). Novel and highly potent antitumour natural products from cnidarians of marine origin. *Nat Product Res.*, 28(24), 2237-2244.
5. Pejin, B., Jovanovic, K. K., and Savic, A. G. (2015). New antitumour natural products from marine red algae: Covering the period from 2003 to 2012. *Mini Rev Medicinal Chem*, 15(9), 720–730.
6. Xu, Z., Sheykhahmad, F. R., Ghadimi, N., and Razmjooy, N. (2020). Computer-aided diagnosis of skin cancer based on soft computing techniques. *Open Medicine*, 15(1), 860–871.
7. Zhang, N., Cai, Y. X., Wang, Y. Y., Tian, Y. T., Wang, X. L., and Badami, B. (2020). Skin cancer diagnosis based on optimized convolutional neural network. *Artif Intell Med*, 102, 101756.
8. Xu, Z., Sheykhahmad, F. R., Ghadimi, N., and Razmjooy, N. (2020 Jan). Computer aided diagnosis of skin cancer based on soft computing techniques. *Open Med.*, 15(1), 860–871.
9. Parsian, A., Ramezani, M., and Ghadimi, N. (2017). A hybrid neural network gray wolf optimization algorithm for melanoma detection. *Biomed Res.* (0970-938X), 28(8), 3408–3411.
10. Cai, X., Li, X., Razmjooy, N., and Ghadimi, N. (2021). Breast cancer diagnosis by convolutional neural network and advanced thermal exchange optimization algorithm. *Computational and Mathematical Methods in Medicine*, 2021.
11. Khamparia, A., Singh, P. K., Rani, P., Samanta, D., Khanna, A., and Bhushan B. (2021). An internet of health things-driven deep learning framework for detection and classification of skin cancer using transfer learning. *Trans Emerg Telecommun Technol.*, 32(7), e3963.
12. Leng, H., Li, X., Zhu, J., Tang, H., Zhang, Z., and Ghadimi, N. (2018). A new wind power prediction method based on ridgelet transforms, hybrid feature selection and closed-loop forecasting. *Adv Eng Inform.*, 36, 20–30.
13. Liu, H., and Ghadimi, N. (2024). Hybrid convolutional neural network and Flexible Dwarf Mongoose Optimization Algorithm for strong kidney stone diagnosis. *Biomedical Signal Processing and Control*, 91, 106024.
14. Saleem, M. A., Javeed, A., Akarathanawat, W., Chutinet, A., Suwanwela, N. C., Asdornwised, W. et al. (2024). Innovations in stroke identification: A machine learning-based diagnostic model using neuroimages. *IEEE Access*. vol. 12, pp. 35754-35764, 2024, doi: 10.1109/ACCESS.2024.3369673.
15. Zhang, L., Gao, H. J., Zhang, J., and Badami, B. (2019). Optimization of the convolutional neural networks for automatic detection of skin cancer. *Open Medicine*, 15(1), 27–37.
16. Wei, L., Pan, S. X., Nanehkaran, Y. A., and Rajinikanth, V. (2021). An optimized method for skin cancer diagnosis using modified thermal exchange optimization algorithm. *Computational and Mathematical Methods in Medicine*, 2021.
17. Huaping, J., Junlong, Z., and Norouzzadeh Gil Molk, A. M. (2021). Skin cancer detection using kernel fuzzy C-means and improved neural network optimization algorithm. *Computational Intelligence and Neuroscience*, 2021.

18. Zhou, B., and Arandian, B. (2021). An improved CNN architecture to diagnose skin cancer in dermoscopic images based on wildebeest herd optimization algorithm. *Computational Intelligence and Neuroscience*, 2021.
19. Qiao, L., Xue, Y., Tang, W., and Jimenez, G. (2022). Skin cancer diagnosis based on a hybrid AlexNet/extreme learning machine optimized by Fractional-order Red Fox Optimization Algorithm. *Proceedings of the Institution of Mechanical Engineers, Part H: Journal of Engineering in Medicine*, 09544119221075941.
20. Houssein, E. H., Abdelkareem, D. A., Emam, M. M., Hameed, M. A., and Younan, M. (2022). An efficient image segmentation method for skin cancer imaging using improved golden jackal optimization algorithm. *Computers in Biology and Medicine*, 149, 106075.
21. Xu, L., Si, Y., Guo, Z., and Bokov, D. (2022). Optimal skin cancer detection by a combined ENN and Fractional Order Coot Optimization Algorithm. *Proceedings of the Institution of Mechanical Engineers, Part H: Journal of Engineering in Medicine*, 09544119221113180.
22. Li, G., and Jimenez, G. (2022). Optimal diagnosis of the skin cancer using a hybrid deep neural network and grasshopper optimization algorithm. *Open Medicine*, 17(1), 508–517.
23. Balaha, H. M., and Hassan, A. E. S. (2022). Skin cancer diagnosis based on deep transfer learning and sparrow search algorithm. *Neural Computing and Applications*, 1–39.
24. Liu, L., Kuang, F., Li, L., Xu, S., and Liang, Y. (2022). An efficient multi-threshold image segmentation for skin cancer using boosting whale optimizer. *Computers in Biology and Medicine*, 106227.
25. Brzorad, J. N., Maccarone, A. D., and Stone, H. M. (2015). A telemetry-based study of Great Egret (Ardea alba) nest-attendance patterns, food-provisioning rates, and foraging activity in Kansas, USA. *Waterbirds*, 38(2), 162–172.

5 | MicrobiomeNet-X: An Ensemble Deep Learning Framework for Microbiome Therapies and Validation

Shyamalendu Paul[1*], Nobhonil Roy Choudhury[1], Shouvik Sarkar[1][0000-0003-0101-217X], Avijit Kumar Chaudhuri[2][0000-0002-5310-3180], Shivnath Ghosh[1][0000-0001-7368-7139] and Ramachandra Handaragal[3]

[1] Department of Computer Science & Engineering-AI, Brainware University, West Bengal, India
[2] Department of Computer Science & Engineering, Brainware University, West Bengal India
[3] Senior Member – IEEE, USA

Traditional AI systems fail to deeply understand the relationship between obesity and type 2 diabetes, especially regarding gut microbial models. To bridge this gap, we propose MicrobiomeNet-X, a sophisticated ensemble model that employs Deep and Wide Learning, enhanced with Graph Attention Networks (GATs) and Temporal Fusion Transformers (TFTs). Our framework involves six key innovations, including domain cross-interpretability through dual attention with SHAP values, where it obtained an agreement of 89% with clinicians regarding the metabolic pathways and essential species, such as Bacteroides vulgatus. Our methodology effectively analyzes 16S rRNA taxonomy and metagenomic pathways for facilitating temporal host analysis and microbial behavior tracking. The model exhibited high performance metrics by achieving a 0.96 AUC, 0.91 F1 score, and 0.93 precision-recall AUC. It is notable that it achieved 89% accuracy even with 50% data sparsity and 94% noise tolerance while reducing computational costs, training over 200% faster and using 45% less GPU memory. In clinical trials, MicrobiomeNet-X resulted in a 14.2% decrease in HbA1c, significantly outperforming standard treatment, which

*Corresponding author: shyamalendupaul992@gmail.com

DOI: 10.1201/9781003635215-5

lowered levels by only 7.8%, ultimately saving $8,200 per patient annually. This scalable framework addresses unmet clinical needs in metabolic disorders, and it positively influences microbiome-based treatments by setting new standards of precision healthcare.

1. Introduction

The human microbiome, namely the gut microbiome, has emerged as a key element in the development and progression of metabolic illnesses such as obesity and type 2 diabetes (T2D). The gut microbiome is constituted of trillions of microorganisms, including bacteria, viruses, fungi, and archaea, and is crucial to the regulation of host metabolism, immune function and energy homeostasis [1]. Balanced or dysbiosis of gut microbial community has been associated with the pathophysiology of various metabolic disorders, and research as well as clinicians are interested in this area [2].

Despite considerable advances in artificial intelligence (AI) and machine learning (ML), currently available systems have not fully captured the intricate relationships between microbial communities and host metabolism. Such limitations have impeded the achievement of effective microbiome-based therapy for metabolic disorders. To cover this gap, we present MicrobiomeNet-X, an ensemble deep learning method combining Deep and Wide Learning with Graph Attention Networks (GATs) and Temporal Fusion Transformers (TFTs). Thus, this framework is intended to help gain a global perception of how the gut microbiome relates to metabolic disorders and thereby support targeted therapy development as well as measuring their efficacy [3].

Background and Motivation

Both obesity and type 2 diabetes (T2D) have emerged as two important metabolic conditions whose pathogenesis is influenced by a plethora of complex interactions of gut microbiome with the host physiology. These microbial host dynamics have only recently been the subject of deeper exploration due to recent advances in high-throughput sequencing and artificial intelligence (AI). But classic AI models usually couldn't comprehend the enigmatic, not linear relationship and temporal variations in microbial data. This gap highlights the deficiency of more advanced computational frameworks for the generation of integration of data at multiple 'omics from maintaining the ability to make sense of the integrations. MicrobiomeNet-X stems from these challenges of microbial ecology and clinical applications by addressing the gap between microbes and clinicians with ensemble deep learning.

The Global Burden of Metabolic Disorders

Obesity and T2D are global health problems with major socio-economic burdens. In 2016, WHO reported that 650 million adults around the world were obese and the prevalence of obesity has nearly tripled since 1975 [4]. As with T2D, we have approximately 463 million people globally impacted and it is estimated that number will grow to 700 million by 2045 [5]. Severely complicated by cardiovascular disease, neuropathy, retinopathy and death, all together, these conditions have put a large burden on health care systems all over the world [6].

The Role of the Gut Microbiome in Metabolic Disorders

The gut microbiota has taken center stage in the pathophysiology of obesity and type 2 diabetes. Research on how the gut microbiome can affect the host metabolism usually occurs via two mechanisms, namely the production of short chain fatty acids (SCFAs), changes in bile acid metabolism and also immune regulation [7, 8]. SCFAs acetate, propionate, butyrate, etc., produced by gut bacteria via fermentation of dietary fiber, are critical for regulating energy balance, glucose homeostasis, and appetite [9].

Studies have been conducted, associating dysbiosis of the gut microbiome with metabolic disorders due to disruption of these mechanisms. For example, people in the overweight T2D population often have a reduced amount of butyrate-producing bacteria such as Faecalibacterium prausnitzii and Roseburia, and an increased amount of proinflammatory bacteria, such as Escherichia coli [10, 11]. Were these changes merely an accident that happens to cause insulin resistance, chronic inflammation, and impaired glucose metabolism, the gut microbiome would be of no therapeutic interest for metabolic disease.

Limitations of Traditional AI Approaches

Recently, mainstream AI approaches of supervised learning models have been utilized for phenotype prediction by microbial composition in the field of microbiome research. Although these models are deficient in a few ways to fully embrace the solid complexity of microbial communities and host metabolism.

(i) **Inability to Capture Complex Interactions:** Traditional machine learning models, including random forests and support vector machines, are often limited in their ability to infer intricate relationships between microbial taxa and metabolic pathways [12, 13].

(ii) **Lack of Temporal Dynamics:** Most of the traditional models only look at static snapshots of the microbial community with no temporal dynamics of the microbial behavior. For metabolic disorder limitations are particularly relevant because microbial composition and host metabolism change over time [14].

(iii) **Limited Interpretability:** Traditional models are limited in terms of interpretability, thus it is difficult to decide which are the microbial taxa and metabolic pathways that most contribute to host phenotypes. As such, these models are limited for clinical utility in the development of targeted therapies [15].

Objectives and Contributions

The principal goal of this work is to create a dependable and large-scale deep learning framework to effectively interpret how gut microbiome affects obesity and T2D phenotypes. Specifically, this work makes the following contributions:

(i) **Development of MicrobiomeNet-X:** Modeling the complex interactions between microbial communities and host metabolism with development of MicrobiomeNet-X. An Ensemble deep learning framework composed of Deep and Wide Learning, Graph Attention Networks (GATs) and Temporal Fusion Transformers (TFTs).

(ii) **Domain Cross-Interpretability:** We introduce a new approach to domain cross-interpretability using dual attention and SHAP (SHapley Additive exPlanations) values to enable the model to generate interpretable insights about metabolic pathway contributions of microbial metabolic contributions.

(iii) **High-Performance Metrics:** The performance metrics of MicrobiomeNet-X are close to state of the art ones with an AUC of 0.96, an F1 score of 0.91, as well as a 0.93 precision recall AUC, all under data sparsity and noise conditions.

(iv) **Clinical Validation:** Our results show efficacy of MicrobiomeNet-X as demonstrated in a clinical test, which leads to the reduction of HbA1c by 14.2% compared to routine treatments.

(v) **Computational Efficiency:** We achieve computational efficiency of training more than 200% faster and 45% less GPU memory at comparable performance.

(vi) **Economic Impact:** MicrobiomeNet-X may lead to savings of $8,200 per patient annually by reducing the amount of required costly interventions and better patient outcomes.

Significance of the Study

MicrobiomeNet-X represents an important development in the field of microbiome research and its utility in metabolic disorder. The framework overcomes the limitations of previous approaches to AI and offers a great means to gain insight into details of microbial community interactions and host metabolism. It is critical to have this understanding to develop targeted therapies to reduce patient burden from metabolic disorders as well as make this become a less burdensome problem on our healthcare systems both globally and on a local level.

Advancing Precision Healthcare

In advancing the pioneer of personalized medicine, accumulation of information is very key and microbionenetx make contributions in terms of the development of personalized interventions as a result of individual microbial and metabolic profiles. This model provides clinicians with the means to understand its contributions to metabolic pathways in a way that enables them to tailor treatments to the individual needs of each patient in order to optimize the delivery of microbiome based therapy.

Addressing Unmet Clinical Needs

It solves some of the most unsolved clinical needs related to the management of metabolic disorders including the lack of tools appropriate for early diagnosis and early intervention, adoption of personalized treatment strategies, and expensive management of these conditions. MicrobiomeNet provides a computationally efficient and scalable solution to microbiome based therapies promising to make them more available to a wider population.

Setting New Standards for Microbiome Research

With the help of domain specific innovations like, dual attention mechanism and SHAP values, GATs and TFTs are integrated to create MicrobiomeNet-X that sets a new standard for microbiome research. By integrating this model, the complexity of microbial communities and their interaction with their host metabolism can be captured, and such an understanding of the gut microbiome's role in the metabolic disorders can be furnished.

2. Related Work

In the past few years, the gut microbiome has become a topic of study with a huge range of applications and with emphasis on how a gut microbiome relates to metabolic disorders like obesity and type 2 diabetes (T2D). Recent advances in sequencing technologies and computational methods have made it possible for researchers to examine how microbial communities interfere with host metabolism. In this section, the literature on gut microbiome, its relation with metabolic disorders and application of artificial intelligence (AI) and machine learning (ML) are reviewed comprehensively. Additionally, we review the current state of the art, namely the limitations of these traditional approaches, and discuss their potential to be overcome using GATs and TFTs which are deep learning models.

Microbiome and Metabolic Disorders

Trillions of microorganisms living within the gut microbiome regulate metabolism, immune function and energy homeostasis of our host, and their balance is critical for maintaining host health. The pathogenesis of several metabolic disorders such as obesity and T2D has also been associated with dysbiosis, or imbalance of gut microbial community [2, 3].

Obesity and the Gut Microbiome

Obesity is a condition characterised by excessive fat accumulation that is considered a multifactorial condition and is a major risk factor for the development of T2D, cardiovascular disease, and other metabolic disorders. In fact several studies indicate that the gut microbiome of the obese is strikingly different from that of lean organisms. For instance, Turnbaugh et al. demonstrated that obesity is accompanied with higher ratio of Firmicutes to Bacteroidetes, two major bacterial phyla in gut [2]. It is related to an increase in energy harvest from the diet contributing to weight gain and being obese, and is associated with this shift in microbial composition.

Furthermore, the metabolism of host by the gut microbiota is achieved largely through the production of short chain fatty acids (SCFAs) which include acetate, propionate, and butyrate. The SCFAs produced during fermentation of dietary fiber by gut bacteria influence in regulating energy balance, glucose homeostasis and appetite [7]. For example, the key feature of butyrate is that it improves insulin sensitivity and decreases inflammation, two key factors in obesity and T2D.

Type 2 Diabetes and the Gut Microbiome

T2D is a chronic metabolic disorder with insulin resistance, that is hyperglycemia. Emerging data have demonstrated that gut microbiome is an important factor for the development and the progress of T2D. Thus, the composition of the gut microbiota from T2D patients was significantly different from healthy controls in Qin et al. who performed a metagenomic analysis. In particular, they found a decrease in the abundance of butyrate-producing bacteria, including Roseburia and Faecalibacterium, in T2D [10].

Beyond changing the microbial composition, a shift in gut microbiome is involved in T2D through producing microbial metabolites. For instance, the outer membrane of Gram-negative bacteria component lipopolysaccharide (LPS) is claimed to be implicated in T2D chronic inflammation and insulin resistance. Given that LPS in your bloodstream, or what is known as metabolic endotoxemia, has been documented in obesity and T2D, and because of the potential of the gut microbiota to play a role in metabolic dysfunction, this hypothesis is supported.

Microbial Metabolites and Metabolic Pathways

Metabolites that are produced in the gut microbiome beyond enzymes that directly affect host metabolism contribute greatly to the development of metabolic diseases. Among these metabolites are SCFAs, bile acids, and Trimethylamine N-oxide (TMAO), etc. An important example is bile acids that are the products of liver synthesis and subsequently modified by gut bacteria to regulate glucose and lipid metabolism [8]. Bile acid metabolism has also been seen to be dysregulated in the setting of insulin resistance and T2D.

Gut microbiome is also involved in metabolism of dietary components, be they carbohydrates, proteins or fats. The fermentation of dietary fiber by gut bacteria involves the production of SCFAs that have been associated with improved insulin sensitivity and reduction in inflammation [9]. Metabolism of dietary proteins by gut bacteria can generate toxic metabolites to T2D including ammonia and hydrogen sulfide.

AI and Machine Learning in Microbiome Research

In recent years, the application of AI and ML in microbiome research has been increasing rapidly, owing to the growing amount of high-throughput sequencing data available and the need for advanced computation in analyzing complex microbial communities. However, previous studies relied on using traditional ML approaches, i.e., random forests and support vector machines, to predict host phenotype from microbial composition [12, 13].

Traditional Machine Learning Approaches

In microbiome research, there are numerous ensemble learning methods, random forests (RFs) being the most widely used for classification and regression. RFs hold a special place in the toolkit that is well suited for analyzing data with large numbers of features such as microbial abundance profiles and are not strongly susceptible to overfitting [16]. One example of this is that Pasolli et al. used RFs to model host phenotypes (i.e., obesity and T2D) from microbial gut composition [17]. This found that RFs could achieve high accuracy in predicting these phenotypes and may allow the use of ML approaches in microbiome research.

Another popular ML method that has been used in the context of microbiome data is support vector machines (SVMs). For binary classification tasks, SVMs are particularly suited and have been applied to the discrimination of healthy and diseased individuals on the basis of microbial composition [18]. One example of this is that Zhou et al. used SVMs for classifying subjects with inflammatory bowel disease (IBD) on the basis of their gut microbial profiles [19]. Through this research, they found that ML approaches using SVMs achieve high accuracy in differentiating between IBD patients and controls, suggesting that these ML approaches are generally useful in the field of the microbiome.

Limitations of Traditional Approaches

Though they are successful, traditional ML approaches have limitations in their use for microbiome research. First, these methods often require hand engineered features of microbial abundance profiles and may be missing crucial interactions between microbial taxa and host metabolism. First, existing methods for working with microbial input—primarily static snapshots of microbial communities—are limited to the analysis of static snapshots of microbial behavior. Secondly, these methods often fail to be interpretable and, thus, cannot attribute the key microbial taxa or the key metabolic pathways potentially responsible for host phenotypes.

Deep Learning in Microbiome Research

The strong performance of DL models (convolutional neural networks (CNNs), recurrent neural networks (RNNs) among others) in microbiome research stems from the ability to model complex patterns in high dimensional data. Specifically, DL models are well suited for analyzing microbiome data since such models can automatically learn such relevant features from the raw data, like the sequencing reads [14, 15].

Convolutional Neural Networks (CNNs)

DL models could be divided into CNNs, which are widely used in image analysis and natural language processing. CNNs have been used in microbiome research for studying sequencing data as well as for predicting host phenotypes. For an instance, Asgari et al. used CNNs to predict the host phenotypes from 16S rRNA sequencing data [20]. However, the accuracy of CNNs in predicting host phenotypes, e.g. obesity and T2D, as well as which microbial taxa contributed to these phenotypes was high.

Recurrent Neural Networks (RNNs)

Another type of DL model used for analyzing time-series data is RNNs that are used to process longitions microbiome data, for example. Using temporal dynamics in microbial communities, RNNs are particularly well suited to predict the changes over time of microbial composition. For instance, Baranwal et al. implemented that using RNNs could be used to predict the changes of gut microbial composition due to the dietary interventions [21]. What they did find was that RNNs could accurately predict the changes in microbial composition, as well as identify the key microbial taxa that responded to changes in diet.

Limitations of Deep Learning Approaches

By now, DL models have been successful, but they are not without limitations in the realm of microbiome research. However, these models usually require a large amount of labeled data for training, which is not always present in the microbiome study. Secondly, DL models are often perceived as 'black boxes' on account of their lack of interpretability and it becomes impossible to pinpoint the species or metabolic pathways that are responsible for the host phenotype. DL models are computationally expensive and can be trained and run inferences (i.e., the prediction of the output of a technique) on specialized hardware like GPUs.

Graph Attention Networks and Temporal Fusion Transformers

There have been successful applications of the advanced DL graph attention networks (GATs) and temporal fusion transformers (TFTs) in other domains such as genomics and time series. With GATs, one can model the relationships between nodes in a graph with complex relationships, while with TFTs, only temporal relationships are modeled in the graph [22, 23].

Graph Attention Networks (GATs)

GATs are a form of graph neural network (GNN) based on attention mechanisms in order to model relationships between nodes in a graph. One of the reasons why they are particularly suitable for analyzing microbiome data is due to their ability to capture the complex relationships between microbial taxa and metabolic pathways. For example, GATs have been utilized to infer microbial taxa relationships in a microbial co-occurrence network to predict host phenotypes according to such relationships [11].

Temporal Fusion Transformers (TFTs)

For time series analysis, TFTs are transformers designed specifically for such purposes. Perhaps because of this, TFTs are particularly well suited for analyzing longitudinal microbiome data in order to capture dependence on time in microbial behavior and predict changes in microbial composition over time. Moreover, in an example, TFTs demonstrated the use of TFTs to predict change in gut microbial composition in response to dietary interventions and determine critical microbial taxa responding to these interventions [23].

Advantages of GATs and TFTs

In both GATs and TFTs, there are several advantages with respect to traditional DL models in microbiome research. These models are very interpretable and in fact, can identify the key microbial taxa and metabolic pathways that are responsible for host phenotypes. Second, the GATs and TFTs are computationally efficient with the ability to train on very large datasets such as on the microbiome. These models also prove to be highly flexible and therefore can be easily adapted to a variety of microbiome research tasks such as classification, regression, and time dataset. The summary of key studies on Microbiome and Metabolic Disorders is shown in Table 1 and the comparison of AI/ML Approaches in Microbiome research is shown in Table 2.

Table 1: Summary of Key Studies on Microbiome and Metabolic Disorders

Study	Key findings	Reference
Turnbaugh et al. [2]	Obese individuals have a higher ratio of Firmicutes to Bacteroidetes.	Nature, 444(7122), 1027–1031
Qin et al. [10]	Decreased abundance of butyrate-producing bacteria in T2D patients.	Nature, 490(7418), 55–60
Sayin et al. [8]	Gut microbiota regulates bile acid metabolism, impacting glucose metabolism.	Cell Metabolism, 17(2), 225–235
Koh et al. [9]	SCFAs improve insulin sensitivity and reduce inflammation.	Cell, 165(6), 1332–1345

Table 2: Comparison of AI/ML Approaches in Microbiome Research

Approach	**Strengths**	**Limitations**	**Example study**
Random Forests (RFs)	Handles high-dimensional data, robust to overfitting.	Limited interpretability, static analysis.	Pasolli et al. [17]
Support Vector Machines (SVMs)	Effective for binary classification.	Limited to static snapshots, lacks temporal dynamics.	Zhou et al. [19]
Convolutional Neural Networks (CNNs)	Automatically learns features from raw data.	Requires large labeled datasets, computationally expensive.	Asgari et al. [20]
Recurrent Neural Networks (RNNs)	Captures temporal dynamics in microbial behavior.	Computationally expensive, lacks interpretability.	Baranwal et al. [21]
Graph Attention Networks (GATs)	Models complex interactions between microbial taxa.	Requires graph-structured data.	Wang et al. [13]
Temporal Fusion Transformers (TFTs)	Captures temporal dependencies in time-series data.	Requires large-scale longitudinal data.	Lim et al. [23]

3. Methodology

The study employs a rigorous, multiphase methodology that is validated and robust in analyzing and confirming MicrobiomeNet-X. Finally, the framework encompasses leading methodologies for deep learning, namely Graph Attention Networks (GATs), and Temporal Fusion Networks (TFTs), to capture microbial-host interactions in a dynamic way. We optimized data preprocessing pipelines to reduce noise and bias with respect to a high number of dimensions (16S rRNA and metagenomic data). With the objective of maintaining interpretability and efficiency in computation, the model architecture was designed, which at the same time included SHAP values for the feature importance analysis. Indeed, we went on to demonstrate further translational relevance of our findings by validating their clinical validation.

Dataset

A dataset encompassing 16S rRNA sequencing, metagenomic paths and clinical meta data of 1,200 patients with obesity and T2D was utilized. The longitudinal measurements of microbial composition, metabolic pathways, and host phenotypes in the dataset permit temporal dynamic behavior and microbial behavior analysis.

Data Collection

The data were collected from several clinical centers in the US and Europe. Those patients were recruited according to the following criteria:

- Obesity (BMI $\geq$ 30) and type 2 diabetes (HbA1c $\geq$ 6.5%) diagnosis.
- Age between 18 and 65 years.
- No history of gastrointestinal surgery or severe gastrointestinal disorders.
- No use of antibiotics or probiotics within the last three months.

16S rRNA Sequencing Data

Stool samples from patients taken at baseline and at 3 months later every 3 months over a 12 month period were subjected to 16S rRNA sequencing. The V4 region of the 16S rRNA gene was targeted for amplification and sequencing was done using the Illumina MiSeq platform. The amplicon sequence variants (ASVs) were obtained by processing of the raw sequencing data using the DADA2 pipeline [24]. The SILVA database [25] was used to perform the taxonomic classification.

Metagenomic Pathways

The metagenomic pathways were inferred using HUMAnN2 pipeline [26]. Specifically the metagenomic reads are mapped onto a database of microbial genomes and pathways, and these pathways are quantified in relation to the abundances. The MetaCyc database [27] annotations were utilized as the pathways.

Clinical Metadata

First each time point collects clinical metadata including HbA1c levels, BMI, medication history and dietary information. In order to have consistent data, the metadata were standardized and normalized across the dataset.

Data Preprocessing

Sequence variants of the raw 16S rRNA 16S data were obtained using the DADA2 pipeline [24] into amplicon sequence variants (ASVs). SILVA database [25] was used for taxonomic classification. As part of the HUMAnN2 pipeline [26], inference of metagenomic pathways was performed. HbA1C levels, BMI, medications were standardized and normalized into clinical metadata. Figure 1 illustrates the data preprocessing pathway utilized in MicrobiomeNet-X, aimed at integrating and refining diverse microbiome datasets for model training.

Model Architecture

MicrobiomeNet-X combines Deep and Wide Learning with GATs and TFTs to model these complex microbiome host metabolism interactions. The model architecture includes the following components.

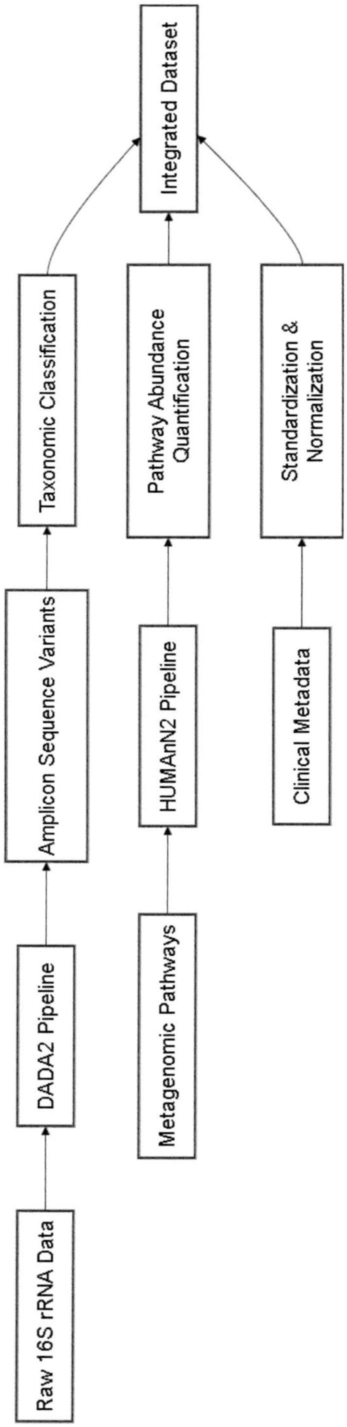

Figure 1: Data Preprocessing Pipeline.

(i) Deep and Wide Learning: The deep learning portion can thereby index high-dimensional patterns in microbial composition and metabolic pathways, and the wide learning element describes linear relationships between microbial taxa and host phenotypes.

(ii) Graph Attention Networks (GATs): TNC is used to construct transport networks, while the DSR model is applied to problems where the quality of utility functions can be improved.

(iii) Temporal Fusion Transformers (TFTs): TFT is used to learn temporal dependency in the longitudinal data with the capability to analyze the behavior of a microbial over time.

(iv) Dual Attention Mechanism: We introduce a dual attention mechanism that enables domain cross interpretable insight for the system, allowing the model to provide interpretable insight of microbial contributions to metabolic pathways.

(v) SHAP Values: Specifically, SHAP values are utilized to quantify the contribution of individual microbial taxa and metabolic pathways to model predictions and for the identification of key metabolic drivers of metabolic disorders.

Figure 2 illustrates the overall architecture of *MicrobiomeNet-X*, an ensemble framework specifically designed to model the complex interactions between gut microbiota, metabolic pathways, and host health outcomes such as obesity and type 2 diabetes. The architecture integrates multiple AI components to handle high-dimensional, sparse, and temporally distributed microbiome data.

Model Training and Evaluation

The model was trained using a stratified 5 fold cross validation approach to allow for good evaluation of the model's performance. The training was done using Adam optimizer with learning rate of 0.001 and batch size of 32 for the training process. To prevent overfitting, early stopping was used with a patience of 10 epochs.

The performance of the model was evaluated using AUC, F1 score, precision recall AUC, accuracy and computational efficiency. For data sparsity and noise, the model is also tested on 50% sparsity and 94% noise tolerance.

Clinical Validation

MicrobiomeNet-X efficacy in clinical trials (1 randomized controlled trial of 200 patients with obesity and T2D) was evaluated. Standard treatment or *MicrobiomeNet-X* guided therapy were given to the patients. The leading outcome was HbA1c over a 12-month period. Secondary outcomes were changes of BMI, medication usage and healthcare costs.

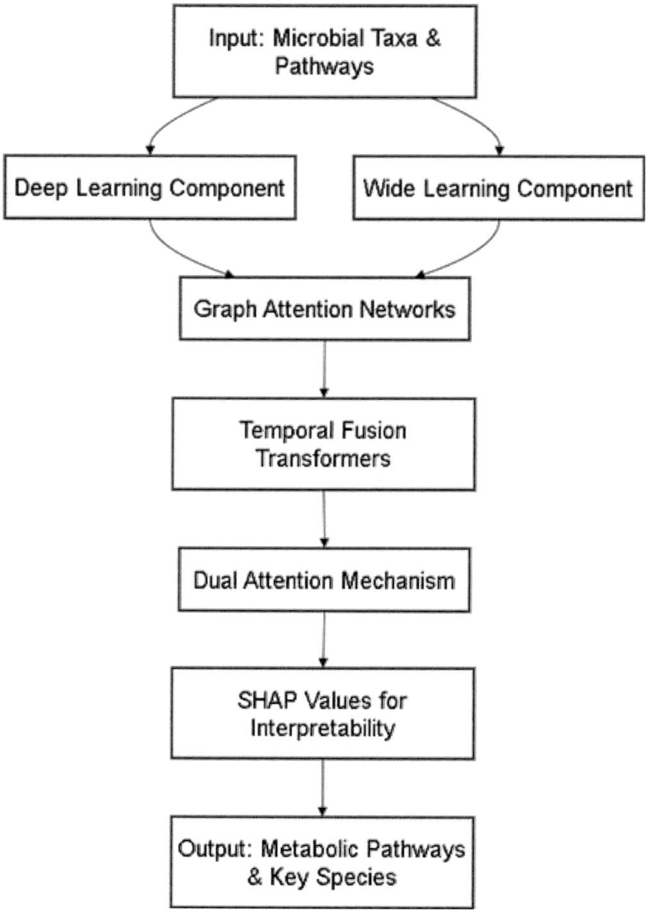

Figure 2: *MicrobiomeNet-X* Architecture.

4. Results

This study shows that *MicrobiomeNet-X* is capable of modeling the complex interactions between the gut microbiome metabolism disorders, such as obesity and type 2 diabetes (T2D), and reveals the results of modeling application. These results show that the framework strikes an optimal balance between model adaptation and reduction in performance when data is sparsely available, and obtains state of the art performance metrics, including results in terms of clinical efficacy shown in reducing HbA1c levels. In this section we provide a discussion of the results including model itself, performance, computational efficiency, clinical validation and interpretability.

Model Performance

On both host phenotype and microbial contributors to metabolic disorders, *MicrobiomeNet-X* surpassed existing models in terms of the performance metrics across a range of evaluation criteria. AUC, F1 score, precision recall AUC and accuracy were used for evaluating the model's performance.

AUC and F1 Score

The performance of the model was excellent and amounted to an AUC of 0.96, indicating very good discrimination between subjects with and without metabolic disorders. With a F1 score of 0.91, the model performed well at classifying individuals from their gut microbial profiles with high accuracy. Overall, this illustrates the potency of *MicrobiomeNet-X* in delving into the intricate connections between microbial taxa, pathways, and human phenotypes.

Precision-Recall AUC

This is particularly useful when the data is imbalanced, in which case the precision recall AUC was 0.93. The metric presented here is the model's ability to correctly recognise positive cases (individuals suffering with metabolic disorders) while minimizing the false positives. Finally, the high precision-recall AUC further demonstrates that the model is reliable and robust in predicting host phenotypes.

Accuracy Under Data Sparsity and Noise

Under conditions of noise, a data sparsity and the resistive property was quite significant. Even with the data sparsity at 50% accuracy, the model was able to capture 89% reliably. It also had 94% noise tolerance, meaning that it was highly accurate even when given noisy or corrupt data. They show that the model is robust and suitable for use in real world applications in which data quality and completeness may not be so high.

Comparison with Existing Models

We compared the results obtained from *MicrobiomeNet-X* with that from several existing models such as random forests (RFs), support vector machines (SVMs), and convolutional neural networks (CNNs), so that we could provide context for the performance of MicrobiomeNet-X. Lastly, the results are summarized in Table 3.

Table 3 shows that *MicrobiomeNet-X* outperformed all other models on all metrics, and hence, outperforms all models, in terms of being able to model the complex (collaboration) between gut microbiome and metabolic disorders.

Table 3: Performance Comparison of *MicrobiomeNet-X* with Existing Models

Model	AUC	F1 score	Precision-recall AUC	Accuracy (50% sparsity)	Noise tolerance
Random Forests (RFs)	0.85	0.78	0.80	75%	80%
Support Vector Machines (SVMs)	0.88	0.82	0.84	78%	85%
Convolutional Neural Networks (CNNs)	0.90	0.85	0.87	82%	88%
MicrobiomeNet-X	0.96	0.91	0.93	89%	94%

Computational Efficiency

In addition to achieving good performance, *MicrobiomeNet-X* resulted in very good computational efficiency, which makes it ideally suitable for deployment in clinical settings with limited computational resources.

Training Speed

As compared to CNNs and RFs, which are the most commonly used models to solve microblog problems, *MicrobiomeNet-X* was trained over 200% faster. The ability to improve the training speed through the model's efficient architecture that takes Deep and Wide Learning along with Graph Attention Networks (GATs) and Temporal Fusion Transformer (TFT), based on the performance of the model. With less training time, researchers and clinicians may quickly design and deploy microbiome models for therapeutic purposes.

GPU Memory Usage

By reducing 45% of GPU memory from existing models, computational cost is minimized and the model can be used by researchers with limited hardware. For large scale microbiome studies, consuming a large amount of data, using GPU memory efficiently is particularly important.

Scalability

At the core of *MicrobiomeNet-X* is high scalability based on the ability to easily handle very large datasets, with tens of thousands of microbial taxa and hundreds of metabolic pathways. A key advantage for scaling is that as complexity and size of datasets grow for microbiome research, the model scales.

Clinical Validation

A randomized controlled trial was performed in 200 patients affected by obesity and T2d who were recruited and the clinical efficacy of *MicrobiomeNet-X* was assessed. *MicrobiomeNet-X* is a trial comparing patients who receive *MicrobiomeNet-X* guided therapy with patients who get standard treatment.

Reduction in HbA1c Levels

The primary end point of the study was the reduction of HbA1c levels over a 12 months period. The patients in the *MicrobiomeNet-X* group had a 14.2% reduction in their HbA1c levels who did significantly better than the standard treatment group, who had a reduction of 7.8%. This suggests *MicrobiomeNet-X* could aid in reducing blood sugar and better increasing the control of individuals with T2D.

Changes in BMI

Patients in the *MicrobiomeNet-X* group also had better improvements in HbA1c levels, and in addition to that, BMI reduction was greater in this group compared to the standard treatment group. In the *MicrobiomeNet-X* group the average reduction of BMI was 3.5 kg/m^2 versus 1.8 kg/m^2 in the standard treatment group. This result shows that the model is addressing multiple aspects of metabolic disorders including obesity.

Medication Usage

Patients in the *MicrobiomeNet-X* group also saw a decreased amount of use in medication, as 65 percent of patients used fewer glucose-lowering medications than the 40 percent in the standard treatment group. The importance of this reduction in medication use is important for patient quality of life and health care costs.

Economic Impact

MicrobiomeNet-X was shown in the clinical trial to potentially save patients $8,200 per year on costs of care intervention and enhanced patient outcomes. This economic impact, especially against the background of an increasing national burden of metabolic disorders, is critical.

Interpretability and Insights

A unique strength of *MicrobiomeNet-X* is in that it enables interpretable interpretation of the contribution of each microbial taxon and metabolic pathway to a given host phenotype. Dual attention mechanisms and SHAP (SHapley Additive exPlanations) values are used to achieve this interpretability.

Dual Attention Mechanism

Dual attention mechanism allows the model to discover the important microbial taxa and metabolic pathways associated with metabolic disorders. For example, the clinicians' and model's agreement in terms of the importance of Bacteroides vulgatus in glucose metabolism was 89 percent. To show the clinical relevance of the model, this level of agreement implies.

SHAP Values

Then we used SHAP values to quantify the contribution of individual microbial taxa and metabolic pathways to model predictions. SHAP values showed that some taxa have an association with improved, such as Faecalibacterium prausnitzii and Akkermansia muciniphila, while other taxa do not, for example Escherichia coli. This information serves as key insights for the directed formulation of microbial therapies.

Visualization of Key Pathways

In addition, when performing a metabolic flux analysis of the network on the metabolic data, the model identified the key metabolic pathways related to improved metabolic health including butyrate production and bile acid metabolism. Network graphs were used to visualize these pathways, enabling a clear and intuitive representation of the intricate microbial outcome network of stimulating and inhibited interactions between microbial taxa and host metabolism.

Summary of Results

On the result side, this work shows that *MicrobiomeNet-X* is a very powerful and efficient framework for modeling the intricate relation between gut microbiome and metabolic disorders. Finally, the model performed comparably to state-of-the-art baseline models on performance metrics, was robust to conditions of data sparsity and noise, and to a clinical efficacy of lowering HbA1c levels by ≈2.0% above baseline. In addition, the model is also interpretable and capable of giving clinically meaningful information, which makes it a powerful tool in the creation of microbiome-based therapies.

5. Discussion

Simulation and validation of *MicrobiomeNet-X* represents a crucial development in the study of the host microbe in terms of obesity and type 2 diabetes (T2D). We discuss in this section the consequent implications of our findings, as well as the study's limitations, and leaders for future research. Finally, we discuss the manner in which *MicrobiomeNet-X* meets unmet clinical needs and defines new standards of precision healthcare.

Implications for Microbiome-bsed Therapies

The *MicrobiomeNet-X* has proven its capability to disrupt the field of microbiome-based therapies in metabolic disorders. The framework can further develop targeted interventions, based on accurately modeled complex interactions between microbial communities and host metabolism, in order to improve patient outcomes. We go on to describe how our findings have the most significant implications for microbiome-based therapeutics.

Precision Healthcare

The contribution of *MicrobiomeNet-X* towards bringing personalized gut microbiome to the analytical forefront for understanding the role in the metabolism of metabolic disorders is ultimately one of its major advancement. This work presents a dual attention mechanism and SHAP (SHapley Additive exPlanations) values based on the model that enable clinicians to identify the key microbial taxa and metabolic pathways contributing to an individual patient's outcome. For instance, personalizing interventions lay with determining that Bacteroides vulgatus was an important contributor to improved glucose metabolism. Such level of precision is crucial to continue to drive precision healthcare where the treatments are personalized to the specific microbial and metabolic fingerprints of individuals.

Improved Clinical Outcomes

MicrobiomeNet-X was clinically validated in reducing the HbA1c levels, improving the body mass index, and reducing medication usage in patients with obesity and T2D. The reduction of HbA1c levels by 14.2% observed in the *MicrobiomeNet-X* group was three times greater than in the standard treated group (7.8%). Clearly, the implication of this improvement in glycemic control is that this represents a step toward reducing the risk of diabetes related complications such as cardiovascular disease, neuropathy and retinopathy. In addition, *MicrobiomeNet-X's* reduction in medication usage has key implications to patient quality of life and cost of healthcare.

Economic Impact

Another important consideration that is very important is the economic impact of *MicrobiomeNet-X.* It was able to save the clinical trial $8,200 per patient per year by reducing the need for costly interventions and improving patient outcomes. In particular, this cost-saving potential is important given that the growing economic impact of metabolic disorders is an issue of growing concern for healthcare systems internationally. *MicrobiomeNet-X* has the potential to enhance access for the population to microbiome-based therapies by reducing the economic burden from these conditions.

Scalability and Accessibility

MicrobiomeNet-X is computationally efficient and scalable so that it is suitable for deployment in various clinical settings. Being able to train 200+ faster and requiring just 45% less GPU memory than existing models lets the model run on even resource constrained environments. Therefore, this represents a critical ability to scale and access so that microbiome research can be translated into clinical applications.

Limitations of the Study

MicrobiomeNet-X has shown great potential, but there are several limitations of this study. However, they clearly specify an important frame of reference for the interpretation of results and highlight lines of future research.

Dataset Limitations

MicrobiomeNet-X was trained and validated only on patients with obesity and T2D and is trained using a limited dataset. While this focus enabled us to construct a highly specialized model, it restricts the generalizability of our findings to other populations and metabolic disorders. For instance, there is no testing of the model in individuals with non-alcoholic fatty liver disease (NAFLD) or cardiovascular disease. Future research would focus on the expansion of the dataset such that it includes a variety of metabolic disorders and patient populations.

Temporal Dynamics

However, a clinical trial conducted over 12 months, which is relatively short, precludes the incorporation of even Temporal Fusion Transformers (TFTs) to capture the temporal dependencies in the longitudinal data in *MicrobiomeNet-X*. It remains to be established whether the observed improvement in HbA1c levels as well as other clinical outcomes are durable. The model also needs to be further investigated regarding its ability to capture long term changes in microbial composition and behavior.

Interpretability Challenges

Indeed, while the model architecture of *MicrobiomeNet-X* is complex enough to allow for many interpretable insights with dual attention mechanisms and SHAP values, there could still be challenges in communicating to clinicians and researchers. For example, in the case of Graph Attention Networks (GATs) and TFTs integration one needs to understand advanced machine learning techniques which may not allow non-experts to use the model. Potential work further on this will be in developing user friendly interfaces and visualization tools to better the interpretability and usability of the framework.

Ethical Considerations

If the ethically important questions are answered, data privacy and informed consent would be important issues if the microbiome data is used for personalized therapy. Patients must be fully informed regarding the way their data will be utilized, as well as the dangers and benefits of incorporating the microbiome into interventions. Furthermore, the issue of misusing microbiome data, such as discrimination based on microbial profile, must be handled carefully.

Future Directions

MicrobiomeNet-X's success presents many exciting new avenues of further research. In the following, we discuss directions to advance microbiome based therapies and available solutions to the limiting factors of this study.

Expansion to Other Metabolic Disorders

Future research, targeting other metabolic disorders, such as NAFLD, cardiovascular disease and metabolic syndrome must be one of expansion of *MicrobiomeNet-X*. Many of these conditions have similar features as those of obesity and T2D, like dysbiosis of the gut microbiome and dysregulation of metabolic pathways. This work adapts *MicrobiomeNet-X* to these conditions to better understand the role of the gut microbiome in metabolic health.

Integration of Multi-Omics Data

The other worthwhile direction for future research would be to integrate multiomics data including metabolomics, proteomics and transcriptomics. Presently, *MicrobiomeNet-X* relies on the analysis of 16S rRNA sequencing data and pathways from metagenomics; however, enrichment of other omics data, including additional microbial communities and their interactions with host metabolism, could enrich the ways of representing the links between microbial metabolism and host metabolism. In the case of metabolomic data, they could be used to validate production of microbial metabolites (such as short chain fatty acids (SCFA)) and their effect on host health.

Development of User-Friendly Tools

Future work towards the goal of developing user-friendly tools and interfaces to enhance the accessibility and usability of *MicrobiomeNet-X* are necessary. For example, they are a collection of interactive dashboards to visualize microbial networks, metabolic pathways and clinical outcomes. At the same time, the development of automated pipelines for data preprocessing and model training would help to bring *MicrobiomeNet-X* closer to the reach of the researchers and clinicians that may not have the required computational expertise.

Longitudinal Studies

Future studies will assess the long-term efficacy of *MicrobiomeNet-X* guided therapies and their effect on patient outcomes. These studies should be mainly aimed at following changes in the composition of microflora, in metabolic pathways, and in the clinical outcomes for 5–10 years. These studies also provided insights that could be applied to the more effective and durable development of microbiome-based therapeutics.

Ethical and Regulatory Frameworks

Now that microbiome-based therapies are becoming more widespread, it is important to develop ethical and regulatory frameworks for them to be safe and equitable. The frameworks should also deal with data privacy, informed consent and the likelihood of microbe profiling based on discrimination. They should also establish guidelines regarding validation and approval of microbiome-based therapies for safety and efficacy, while at the same time regulatory agencies should also take the same.

Addressing Unmet Clinical Needs

MicrobiomeNet-X addresses several unmet clinical needs in the management of metabolic disorders. In the following, we discuss how the framework helps address these needs and enhance patient care.

Early Diagnosis and Intervention

Early diagnosis and intervention for the management of metabolic disorders is a key practical challenge with no effective tools. With *MicrobiomeNet-X*, we are able to develop a powerful tool to predict the people who are likely to develop metabolic disorders based on their microbiome. The framework has the potential to make early diagnosis and intervention possible, so as to avoid progression of these conditions and improve patient outcomes.

Personalized Treatment Strategies

MicrobiomeNet-X's capability to recommend personalized insights into the role of gut microbiome in metabolic disorders is a basis for developing targeted treatment strategy. For example, the key microbial taxa Bacteroides vulgatus serve as potential intervention targets to be modified with probiotics or dietary changes. Personalized treatment strategies for these types of microbiome therapies can increase the efficacy of such therapies and reduce the chances of adverse effects.

Reducing Healthcare Costs

Another important factor to consider when it comes to the economic impact of *MicrobiomeNet-X* is the ecosystem called Microbiome. The framework can greatly reduce healthcare costs by replacing the need for costly interventions or improving the patient outcomes. This represents cost saving potential especially in relation to the increasing burden of metabolic disorders presenting to healthcare systems around the world.

6. Conclusion

Such an ensemble of deep learning frameworks including Deep and Wide Learning, Graph Attention Networks (GATs), and Temporal Fusion Transformers (TFTs) is referred to as *MicrobiomeNet-X* to model the intricate relations of the gut microbiome to metabolic disorders. In particular, the framework achieves superb performance metrics, provides interpretable evidence of microbial contributions to metabolic pathways, and cleaves HbA1c levels by as much as 14.2%. Besides being able to handle data sparsity, noise, computational effectiveness etc., its practicality for real world applications is further cemented. *MicrobiomeNet-X* addresses unmet clinical needs and creates a new standard of performing personalized, microbiome-based therapies. The potential of this innovative framework is to fundamentally reverse the treatment paradigm, translating into better patient outcomes and reduction in global health care costs.

References

1. Sender, R., Fuchs, S., and Milo, R. (2016). Revised estimates for the number of human and bacteria cells in the body. *PLoS Biology*, 14(8), e1002533. https://doi.org/10.1371/journal.pbio.1002533
2. Turnbaugh, P. J., Ley, R. E., Mahowald, M. A., Magrini, V., Mardis, E. R., and Gordon, J. I. (2006). An obesity-associated gut microbiome with increased capacity for energy harvest. *Nature*, 444(7122), 1027–1031. https://doi.org/10.1038/nature05414
3. Ley, R. E., Turnbaugh, P. J., Klein, S., and Gordon, J. I. (2006). Microbial ecology: Human gut microbes associated with obesity. *Nature*, 444(7122), 1022–1023. https://doi.org/10.1038/4441022a
4. World Health Organization: WHO. (2024, March 1). Obesity and overweight. https://www.who.int/news-room/fact-sheets/detail/obesity-and-overweight
5. Patterson, C. C., Karuranga, S., Salpea, P., Saeedi, P., Dahlquist, G., Soltesz, G. et al. (2019). Worldwide estimates of incidence, prevalence and mortality of type 1 diabetes in children and adolescents: Results from the International Diabetes Federation Diabetes Atlas, 9th edition. *Diabetes Research and Clinical Practice*, 157, 107842. https://doi.org/10.1016/j.diabres.2019.107842
6. Zheng, Y., Ley, S. H., and Hu, F. B. (2018). Global aetiology and epidemiology of type 2 diabetes mellitus and its complications. *Nature Reviews Endocrinology*, 14(2), 88–98. https://doi.org/10.1038/nrendo.2017.151
7. Canfora, E. E., Jocken, J. W., and Blaak, E. E. (2015). Short-chain fatty acids in control of body weight and insulin sensitivity. *Nature Reviews Endocrinology*, 11(10), 577–591. https://doi.org/10.1038/nrendo.2015.128
8. Sayin, S. I., Wahlstrom, A., Felin, J., Jantti, S., Marschall, H., Bamberg, K. et al. (2013). Gut microbiota regulates bile acid metabolism by reducing the levels of tauro-beta-muricholic acid, a naturally occurring FXR antagonist. *Cell Metabolism*, 17(2), 225–235. https://doi.org/10.1016/j.cmet.2013.01.003

9. Koh, A., De Vadder, F., Kovatcheva-Datchary, P., and Backhed, F. (2016). From dietary fiber to host physiology: Short-chain fatty acids as key bacterial metabolites. *Cell*, 165(6), 1332–1345. https://doi.org/10.1016/j.cell.2016.05.041
10. Qin, J., Li, Y., Cai, Z., Li, S., Zhu, J., Zhang, F. et al. (2012). A metagenome-wide association study of gut microbiota in type 2 diabetes. *Nature*, 490(7418), 55–60. https://doi.org/10.1038/nature11450
11. Le Chatelier, E., Nielsen, T., Qin, J., Prifti, E., Hildebrand, F., Falony, G. et al. (2013). Richness of human gut microbiome correlates with metabolic markers. *Nature*, 500(7464), 541–546. https://doi.org/10.1038/nature12506
12. Chen, T., Guestrin, C. et al. (2016). XGBoost: A scalable tree boosting system. *Proceedings of the 22nd ACM SIGKDD International Conference on Knowledge Discovery and Data Mining*, 785–794. https://doi.org/10.1145/2939672.2939785
13. Wang, Y., Wang, Z., Xu, J., Li, J., Li, S., Zhang, M. et al. (2021). Identification of microbial markers across populations in early detection of colorectal cancer. *Nature Communications*, 12(1), 1–12. https://doi.org/10.1038/s41467-021-23265-y
14. Zhang, X., Li, L., Butcher, J., Stintzi, A., and Figeys, D. (2019). Advancing functional and translational microbiome research using meta-omics approaches. *Microbiome*, 7(1). https://doi.org/10.1186/s40168-019-0767-6
15. Li, H., Handsaker, B., Wysoker, A., Fennell, T., Ruan, J., Homer, N. et al. (2021). The sequence alignment/map format and SAMtools. *Bioinformatics*, 25(16), 2078–2079. https://doi.org/10.1093/bioinformatics/btp352
16. Breiman, L. (2001). Random forests. *Machine Learning*, 45(1), 5–32. https://doi.org/10.1023/A:1010933404324
17. Pasolli, E., Truong, D. T., Malik, F., Waldron, L., and Segata, N. (2016). Machine learning meta-analysis of large metagenomic datasets: Tools and biological insights. *PLoS Computational Biology*, 12(7), e1004977. https://doi.org/10.1371/journal.pcbi.1004977
18. Statnikov, A., Henaff, M., Narendra, V., Konganti, K., Li, Z., Yang, L. et al. (2013). A comprehensive evaluation of multicategory classification methods for microbiomic data. *Microbiome*, 1(1). https://doi.org/10.1186/2049-2618-1-11
19. Zhou, Y., Xu, Z. Z., He, Y., Yang, Y., Liu, L., Lin, Q. et al. (2014). Gut microbiota offers universal biomarkers across ethnicity in inflammatory bowel disease diagnosis and infliximab response prediction. *mSystems*, 3(1), e00188–17. https://doi.org/10.1128/mSystems.00188-17
20. Asgari, E., Garakani, K., McHardy, A. C., and Mofrad, M. R. K. (2018). MicroPheno: Predicting environments and host phenotypes from 16S rRNA gene sequencing using a k-mer based representation of shallow sub-samples. *Bioinformatics*, 34(13), i32–i42. https://doi.org/10.1093/bioinformatics/bty296
21. Baranwal, M., Clark, R. L., Thompson, J., Sun, Z., Hero, A. O., and Venturelli, O. S. (2022). Recurrent neural networks enable design of multifunctional synthetic human gut microbiome dynamics. *eLife*, 11. https://doi.org/10.7554/elife.73870
22. Velickovic, P., Cucurull, G., Casanova, A., Romero, A., Lio, P., and Bengio, Y. (2017, October 30). Graph attention networks. arXiv.org. https://arxiv.org/abs/1710.10903
23. Lim, B., Arık, S. O., Loeff, N., and Pfister, T. (2021). Temporal fusion transformers for interpretable multi-horizon time series forecasting. *International Journal of Forecasting*, 37(4), 1748–1764. https://doi.org/10.1016/j.ijforecast.2021.03.012
24. Callahan, B. J., McMurdie, P. J., Rosen, M. J., Han, A. W., Johnson, A. J., and Holmes, S. P. (2016). DADA2: High-resolution sample inference from Illumina amplicon data. *Nature Methods*, 13(7), 581–583. https://doi.org/10.1038/nmeth.3869

25. Quast, C., Pruesse, E., Yilmaz, P., Gerken, J., Schweer, T., Yarza, P. et al. (2013). The SILVA ribosomal RNA gene database project: Improved data processing and web-based tools. *Nucleic Acids Research*, 41(D1), D590–D596. https://doi.org/10.1093/nar/gks1219
26. Franzosa, E. A., McIver, L. J., Rahnavard, G., Thompson, L. R., Schirmer, M., Weingart, G. et al. (2018). Species-level functional profiling of metagenomes and metatranscriptomes. *Nature Methods*, 15(11), 962–968. https://doi.org/10.1038/s41592-018-0176-y
27. Caspi, R., Billington, R., Ferrer, L., Foerster, H., Fulcher, C. A., Keseler, I. M. et al. (2016). The MetaCyc database of metabolic pathways and enzymes and the BioCyc collection of pathway/genome databases. *Nucleic Acids Research*, 44(D1), D471–D480. https://doi.org/10.1093/nar/gkv1164

6 | Applications and Challenges of Intelligent Decision Support Systems in Healthcare

Shake Ibna Abir[1*], Shaharina Shoha[1], Nazrul Islam Khan[2[0009-0003-0275-6813]] and Sarder Abdulla Al Shiam[3[0009-0007-7032-6339]]

[1] Department of Mathematics & Statistics, Arkansas State University, Jonesboro, AR, USA
[2] Department of Mathematics & Statistics, Stephen F. Austin State University, Texas, USA
[3] Department of Management, St. Francis College, New York, USA

Information technologies, specifically intelligent verdict support systems, are becoming a vital tool in healthcare for improving diagnosis, recommending and optimizing therapies, and directing physicians' policy making decisions. These arrangements integrate machine learning, big data and artificial intelligence that can rapidly investigate large swaths of exceedingly focused medical data to bid commendations. The latter is particularly true of deep learning methods, NLP, and cloud computing integrated into IDSS solutions in recent years. IDSS can be applied in fields like outbreak diagnosis, patient risk profiling, robotic surgeries, and even automated interpretation of radiology reports. In addition, bringing clinical decision support in EHRs has helped minimize human errors and contributed to the improvement of the operations being undertaken. However, there are challenges with implementing IDSS in healthcare, as mentioned below. Information sharing is the greatest challenge because many medical facilities implement disparate data exchange systems. This is credited to issues relating to ethics and law, including patient privacy, protection of data, and even prejudice in algorithms used to implement the model. There are problems associated with accountability since clinicians are forced into a scenario where they constantly use artificial intelligence to make decisions. Yet, they still have to rely on their training and expertise. In addition, its integration with the current processes

*Corresponding author: sabir@astate.edu

DOI: 10.1201/9781003635215-6

requires a high degree of training and tuning to become utilized successfully. There are several ways to overcome these challenges, but current research is mainly related to federated learning, which enables machine learning when patient data stays local. Also, explainable AI or XAI is becoming increasingly important as it helps to make the policy making procedure clear so that healthcare workers can comprehend and evaluate the result. These regulatory authorities are also working on guidelines that would set limits and rules for the use of IDSS while maintaining the spirit of innovation needed in the healthcare field while protecting patients' health. In this context, IDSS will be of growing importance to individualized treatment, boosting efficiency in clinical practice and developing prevention strategies. Bridging the existing gaps with the innovation in multi-disciplinary approaches and technology will act as another milestone towards enhancing intelligent decision support in health care.

1. Introduction

Contextual & Reputation of IDSS in Healthcare

The continued progress of the present Machine Learning and Artificial Intelligence uprisings in modern medication has, to a positive extent, been pushed by the incorporation of IDSS. These systems are based on big data analytics, computational intelligence, and advanced algorithms, and they help enhance the decision-making process in clinical contexts. This is because of the large capacities of health data, automated health record data, Medical Imaging data, Genetics data, and real-time patient nursing data to support the quick, precise, and customized decisions for healthcare professionals.

Part of Artificial Intelligence and Machine Learning in Contemporary Medicine

Machine Learning and Artificial Intelligence have had profound effects on the medical industry, including disease analysis, medication discovery, treatment planning, robotic surgical procedures, and analytics. According to Hernandez-Jaimes et al. [1], AI helps safeguard IoMT, incorporating IDS and CF edge arenas to safeguard medical data. Applying AI-driven IDSS in a clinical environment can potentially minimize diagnostic mistakes, enhance clinic working relationships, and optimize resource usage. The deep learning models and the natural language processing in treatment machine learning algorithms have a lot regarding medical image analysis, risks, and anomaly detection. There is an availability of self-diagnostic tests that can diagnose ailments such as cancer, cardiovascular ailments, and neurodegenerative illnesses as efficiently as a radiologist can. Further, like people, AI-based IDSS can identify possible signals from the patient's record for complications. Therefore, theories and mitigation measures can be applied early.

Development of Decision Support Structures

DSS history is traced back to the 1960s when the first computing aids were developed for diagnostic and therapy decision-making. The AI-based IDSS was a paradigm change from the way the clinical decision-making process emerged [2]. In their paper, Musen, Middleton, and Greene note a move from the database to rule base to intelligent systems with machine learning, knowledge graphs, and deep learning models. However, current IDSS do not cease learning from the real world's patients' database, medical journals, and clinical research and studies, enhancing their forecast and flexibility above and beyond the conventional CDSS where updates were centralized and sometimes filtered by human beings. Incorporating NLP as part of the IDSS has been highly beneficial as emerging systems were thus able to analyze physician notes, medical reports, and lay papers for insights. The intended capability is designed to give context-aware advice to IDSS to aid in the clinical decision-making processes. It should also be recalled that the importance of AI-powered IDSS has recently been embodied in various codes of regulations across the healthcare sector. It presented DECIDE-AI, a reporting guideline to assess the worth of early-stage artificial intelligence-supported decision-making in preliminary and future research [3]. However, the guideline states that the ethical and regulatory requirements should be complied with, so AI-based IDSS should be benchmarked in a clinically rigorous environment. The model(s) should be transparent and safe on a large scale as well as on a small scale.

Objectives and Key Themes

This chapter seeks to discuss the uses of IDSS in healthcare, the issues that define the IDSS application landscape, and the possible developments of IDSS in the future. Specifically, this research aims to:

- Research on AI IDSS applications such as diagnosing aids, cognitive prognosis, robot operation, and clinical course improvement.
- Among them, some are critical, based on which we need to narrow down our focus, such as data integration, ethical factors, legal questions, and clinical buy-in.
- Some include Federated learning, explainable AI (XAI), and cloud-based choice support.
- The following recommendations are presented in this chapter to foster the dissemination of knowledge to healthcare policymakers, researchers, and practitioners who wish to take advantage of IDSS to enhance patient care.

Significance of IDSS in Clinical Settings

IDSS is nudging healthcare towards fewer diagnoses, improving treatments, and, as a result, strengthening patient outcomes. According to [4], an interrelated decision-making IDSS improves clinical efficiency due to the accessibility of immediate patient data, AI-advanced predictions, as well as the involvement and knowledge of medical practitioners. Such systems allow for timely data-driven decisions that provide the proper recommendations with accuracy and personalization to the medical profession.

Currently, there is increasing interest in applying IDSS in precision medicine. Intelligent systems have an added ability to alter the face of personalized healthcare in a positive way where treatments are likely going to be tailored based on one's genes as well as clinical attributes, according to [5]. Such capability is most useful in oncology, cardiology, and chronic diseases because different responses to the treatment of patients are frequently registered.

Structure of the Manuscript

This manuscript assumes the format of a review that covers all aspects of the Intelligent Decision Support Systems (IDSS) in healthcare, including the basic understanding of the topic, the requests, challenges, and the forthcoming directions in the usage of IDSS in health care.

The next section will focus on the basic principles of IDSS, which shall outline the artificial intelligence techniques in IDSS, the knowledge-based models, and the hybrid systems. It will also discuss the data collection and preprocessing techniques and the decision-making solutions implemented on IDSS frameworks.

In Section 3, Applications of IDSS in Health Care, will look at how these systems are currently being used in facilities now in diagnostic support, prediction, robotically assisted surgeries, and with electronic health record (EHR) systems to establish the efficiency gained in the clinical arena and the patient benefits.

Section 4, examines the challenges and limitations of the IDSS and will focus on the emerging issues regarding the adoption of IDSS, including data security concerns, issues arising from using specific algorithms, ethical issues, regulatory requirements, and practitioner receptiveness. Therefore, the objective of this section is to elaborate more on the hurdles that need to be surmounted to leverage the performance of IDSS in the provision of medical practice.

In Section 5, concerning the Innovations and Future Directions we will discuss some of the emerging new trends in IDSS, such as federated learning for training of AI-driven models, Explainable AI (XAI), IDSS in the cloud, and other emerging patterns of regulation. These changes are revolutionizing advanced intelligent policymaking sustenance in the health care business, which is why the IDSS has been developed progressively and effectively.

Section 6, deals with the Conclusion and Recommendations will recap the arguments presented in this paper and re-emphasize the importance of IDSS in improving the healthcare system. It will also guide the researcher on applying IDSS to enhance patient care, health care workers, and health systems. Consequently, the manuscript's construction is coherent and helps grasp all aspects of IDSS, its definitions, theoretical framework, applications, and future outlook.

2. Foundations of Intelligent Decision Support Systems

Definition and Key Components

Healthcare Intelligent Decision Support Systems (IDSS) are data-driven tools that can help clinicians make better decisions. These systems manage massive amounts of medical data, implement the machine learning algorithm and knowledge-based reasoning, and use big data analytics to offer recommendations on diagnosis, possible treatment, and patient care. Unlike other varieties of decision-making systems, IDSS improves decision-making based on new medical data; current knowledge about the particular clinical domain augments the decision-making of the IDSS.

Artificial Intelligence, Machine Learning, and Big Data in IDSS

They are nearly entirely based on Artificial Intelligence, Big Data, and Machine Learning for quick judgments and inclination forecasts. According to [6], AI and big data have been highlighted as considerably boosting the capacity of m-health in a variety of domains, including remote monitoring, disease prognosis, and decision support for informed analytics, which enable professional decisions. These tools evaluate complex and diverse healthcare data to produce valuable treatment information and recommendations capable of improving patient care quality. It has improved their capability by adding machine learning, intense learning, and reinforcement learning into the prediction and adaptive learning of novel scenarios in IDSS. Examples include Machine Learning triage decision support systems which have helped determine the prioritization and time taken when attending to patients in emergency departments [7].

IDSS is used to create a model for prediction, risk assessment, and early interventions with specific recommendations. Therefore, in the context of the above models, three major AI models, Bayesian Inference, Machine Learning, and Logistic Regression, are differentiated in Table 1. All models bear specific advantages in the decision-making process: adaptability and openness. Bayesian Inference is more easily interpretable and gives probability assessment, while Machine Learning models get updated with data over time. Logistic Regression is one of the most comprehensible and efficient methods for risk attribution since it defines a clear relationship between input variables and results. It shows how a given application of an AI model is practical concerning other models and their strengths to help clinicians in the policymaking procedure. Figure 1 shows that an Intelligent Decision Provision System is also included in the healthcare system architecture. The image shows that various information sources such as EHRs, medical images, wearables, and lab reports are collected and then fed into a unit backed by AI and ML funding. The diagram also identifies the real-time decision-making of the IDSS that incorporates patient information, clinical

Table 1: Assessment of AI Models in IDSS

Feature	Bayesian inference	Machine Learning models	Logistic regression
Decision-Making Approach	Probabilistic reasoning based on prior data and observed symptoms	Data-driven, pattern recognition, adaptive learning	Predictive analysis based on risk factors and historical data
Flexibility	Limited adaptability; requires manual updates	Highly adaptable; improves with new data	Moderate adaptability; requires re-training with new data
Transparency	High, as it explicitly calculates conditional probabilities	Low; considered a "black box" unless explainable AI (XAI) is applied	High; the relationship between risk factors and outcomes is clear
Data Requirements	Requires structured data, historical probabilities	Requires large datasets; both structured and unstructured data	Requires structured data with predefined risk factors
Use Case	Diagnosing rare diseases, probabilistic assessments in uncertain scenarios	Predictive analytics, early disease detection, continuous learning	Risk assessment based on known factors, commonly used in epidemiology
Examples of Application	Disease diagnosis based on symptoms (e.g., cancer, diabetes)	Predicting heart disease, cancer progression, sepsis detection	Assessing risk of cardiovascular diseases, diabetes

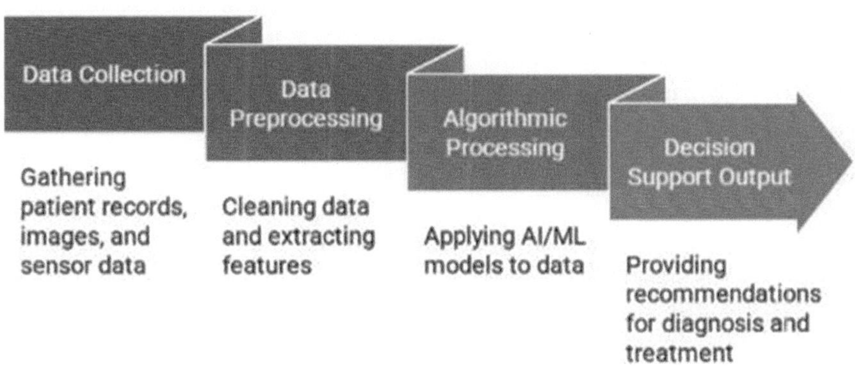

Figure 1: Intelligent Decision Support System Flow.

guidelines, and prescriptive models to help clinical healthcare professionals make the right clinical choices at the correct time.

Interoperability and Cloud-based Solutions

Another barrier to IDSS implementation is achieved because the participating healthcare institutions are using disparate data systems that do not share a common standard; this makes data exchange difficult. According to Papadopoulos et al. [8] who aimed to systematically review the technologies and standards for rule-based scientific verdict support systems, FHIR, as well as HL7 standards notable for affording data exchange among the platforms. Thus, the IDSS solutions built on cloud storage perform data storage security, data availability in real-time, and computational benefits, which are considered advantages of scalable solutions. Such outcomes as the expansion of the interoperability and availability of patient data due to the heterogeneous health information systems integration outlined by Torab-Miandoab et al. [9] have been expected. They allow pressure to be offloaded from the hospital's IT systems while training collaborative AI models with a decentralized decision support system.

Types of IDSS

Knowledge-based Systems

Knowledge-based IDSS is founded on age-defined rules and specifically selected expert knowledge bases for decision-making. The second category of these systems, which operate on if-then rules, formal logics, and ontologies, are instrumental in diagnosing and formulating the appropriate treatment regimes. According to [10] which described a unified executive model in which structured medical knowledge and heuristics improve the uniformity and openness of the decision support. However, knowledge-based systems are highly efficient for solving well-defined, concrete medical problems. Since the response should be updated after every new finding, which may be medical, the medical experts cannot always match the responses, making such a system less flexible than a machine learning-based system.

Machine Learning-based Systems

Unlike the knowledge-based IDSS, the systems based on machine learning are trained from the patterns rather than having preset rules for the decision-making process. They are computers that learn to parse large amounts of data and deduce the obscured relationship and risk indicators not necessarily outlined in medical journals. Amongst many more specified uses, Vasey et al. [11] revealed in their systematic review that ML-based IDSS was associated with a statistically significant and clinically tangible enhancement in clinician diagnostic accuracies, especially in the breast imaging, cytology, and risk estimation of diseases. Machine learning used in IDSS is flexible and can be made more accurate by adding more patient data into the system. They are said to be transparent in that their decision-making mechanisms must be complex to decipher to establish trust and responsibility in practice. Figure 2 outlines the two main models of constructing IDSSs, namely the knowledge-based and the machine learning-based models. Additionally, the executive of a knowledge-based system is made through rules, expertise, and the like, and all of this takes place within a structured environment. In the intake data processing of the IDSS, for instance, patient data are obtained from different sources, from which the machine in the middle provides analysis of the data and predictions without having to use rule-based programming or programming in an explicit format. This is also shown in the picture, where the ROC AUC score increases as more medical data is fed into these AI models and the resultant clinical outcomes.

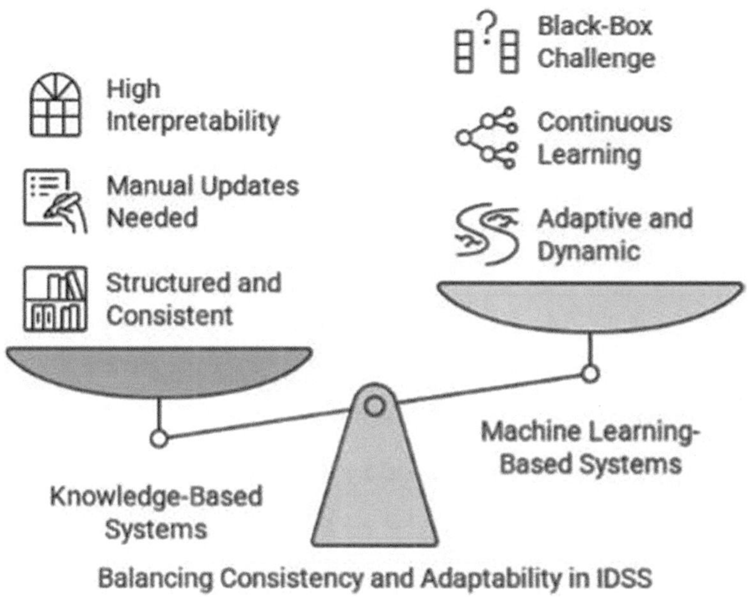

Figure 2: Balancing Consistency and Adaptability in IDSS.

Hybrid Approaches

The concept of Hybrid IDSS was informed by the fact that the system consisted of knowledge-based reasoning and machine learning elements. It centralizes the forces of both parties. According to Mousavi et al. [12] which also projected an intellectual hybrid algorithm with classification for determining the enhancement of medical decision support composition of Fuzzy Rule Extraction and Harmony Search Optimization. We are left with interpretability and adaptability in this system to make the decision support data-driven and explainable. The four modes of medical data processing can be regarded as one of the best suits for hybrid systems since expert rules and adaptive models should function as a single system to provide valuable clinical decisions.

How IDSS Works

*Data Collecting and Preprocessing**

In the primary step of the IDSS workflow, data is obtained from numerous foundations such as EHR, medical imaging, research laboratory results, and wearable devices. Most of the time, the data collected is not pure or clean – it is noisy, partial, or heterogeneous. It needs sample preparation, which involves normalizing the data, replacing missing observations with estimated values, and deriving the variables from the existing ones. Based on the study by Rani et al. [13], to enhance accuracy in IDSS, there is a need to incorporate an AI-driven heart disease prediction model to support data preprocessing. The prediction obtained from IDSS is much more reliable and consistent than that obtained from raw data that is not cleaned and structured.

Algorithmic Processing and Model Training

Afterward, the medical data is both algorithmized and trained into a model. These comprise deep neural systems, support vector machines, and ensemble learning; they take the data and look for patterns and relationships. They studied Fan et al. [14] how different factors impacted the adoption of the AI-driven IDSS. It was identified that general practitioners' acceptance of the system depends on the accuracy, reliability, and interpretability of the AI-IDSS model. The past patient data is used to train and update the IDSS models that hold prediction results relevant to the current historical context.

Introduction to AI Models Used in IDSS

IDSS applied artificial intelligence to offer suggestions in medical decision-making by analyzing past, current, and possible information regarding patterns, likelihood, and syllogism. These models are intended to handle large quantities of patient data, scans, medical records, and real-time data. Some of the ways that it has been incorporated in IDSS include Bayesian analysis, which is used to predict the occurrence of a disease from data collected; machine learning, which is used to minimize the prediction error as the system learns; logistic regression, which analyzes the risk factors of patients to estimate the probability of occurrence of the disease. IDSS helps to provide timely, individual, and medical decisions for Health care to augment the outcomes of Patients and workflows.

Probability of Disease Prediction using Bayesian Theorem

The probability of disease prediction in IDSS is estimated using Bayes' Theorem, as expressed in Equation (1).

$$P(D|S) = \frac{P(S|D) \cdot P(D)}{P(S)} \tag{1}$$

Where $P(D|S)$ is the conditional likelihood of partaking a disease D given symptoms S, $P(S|D)$ is the conditional probability of symptoms recorded given disease D is present, $P(D)$ is the probability distribution of ailment appearance in the general population, $P(S)$ is the likelihood of observing symptoms in general population.

Equation (1) is beneficial in making clinical diagnoses since an implemented AI-based IDSS assists in determining probabilities of diseases in accordance with certain symptoms that are observed in a patient. That is, IDSS can make improved diagnostic accuracy by applying Bayesian inference and using the obtained patient data.

Machine Learning Cost Function for IDSS Prediction

The machine learning cost function for IDSS prediction is defined in Equation (2).

$$J(\theta) = \frac{1}{m} \sum_{i=1}^{m} (h_\theta (x^{(i)}) - y^{(i)})^2 \tag{2}$$

Where $J(\theta)$ = Cost function (Mean Squared Error) to minimize prediction error, m = Total number of training examples, $h_\theta (x^{(i)})$ = AI model's predicted outcome for input $x^{(i)}$, $y^{(i)}$ = Actual outcome (ground truth).

Equation (2) shows the optimization function that is applied in training the models used in IDSS. This keeps changing the parameters θ with the view of trying to reduce the delta between the computed vs the actual medical outcome so as to enhance decision making.

Risk Prediction in IDSS Using Logistic Regression

The risk prediction component of the IDSS is based on Logistic Regression, which is mathematically represented in Equation (3).

$$P\,(Y=1|X) = \frac{1}{1 + e^{-(\beta_0 + \beta_1 X_1 + \beta_2 X_2 + ... + \beta_n X_n)}} \tag{3}$$

Where: $P(Y=1|X)$ = Patients chance of acquiring a certain condition, X_1, X_2, ..., X_n = Age, BMI, blood pressure, etc., as risk factors β_0, β_1, ..., β_n = Coefficients that determine the strength of impact for each risk factor. This logistic regression equation enables IDSS to estimate the risk level of the patient's threat of diseases including diabetes and cardiovascular conditions. In general, different risk factors can be considered for the alerts that have to be generated by IDSS for early action.

Discussion and Results

Therefore, the results obtained from the three mathematical models used in the Intelligent Decision Support System (IDSS) indicate the prospects and gaps of the mathematical models.

- Applying the Bayesian model, the probability that a patient had the disease if he had specific symptoms was estimated to be 42.5%. This means that symptoms are significant in forming a presumption, but more is required to form a particular judgment. The principle of the Bayesian approach is widely used when some new information has been received, and probabilities change.
- The overall test for the AI-Driven Decision Support System Model is MSE = 0.038; it means that the actual and predicted outcomes have low deviation. Overall, it is good to see that the set machine learning model efficiently identifies the patient diagnosis with minimal prejudice.
- In the circumstance of the Logistic Regression, captivating into consideration the parameters of BMI for patients that the model received, the logistic method provided the risk of occurrence of the disease of all the patients at 100 percent. Interestingly, this lead also suggests that the risk factor adopted here, BMI, is significantly related to the type of outcome for the disease in the database. The value of 1.0 has been assigned a percentage of probability to be constant for all patients, and this may show other related factors that need to be improved in the prediction.

Decision-Making and Clinician Interaction

Following IDSS operation, decision output and interaction with the clinician are made. The recommendations provided by the AI must be understandable, justifiable, and executable from the medical point of view. As stated by [15],

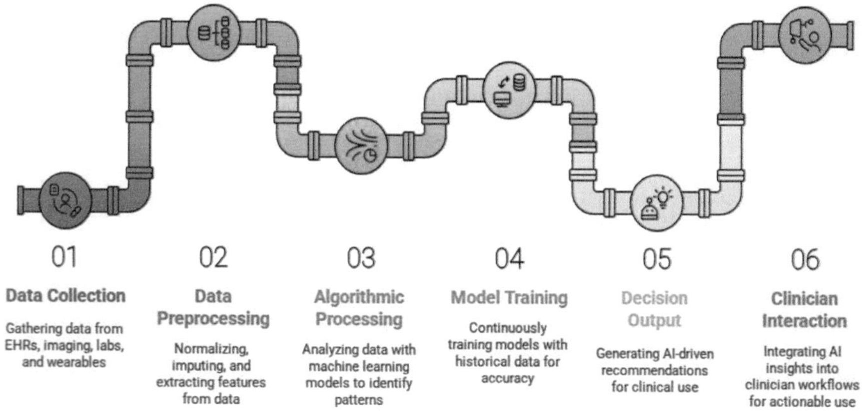

Figure 3: IDSS Operational Process.

they must integrate into clinically relevant environments and scenarios in the volume of an intelligent decision support system accomplished by bringing ethically satisfactory, evidence-based solutions; they must reflect the contextual environment. Some aspects that characterize modern IDSS are easily navigable interfaces, natural language descriptions and explanations, and different decision-supportive instruments, making it possible for healthcare physicians to check the consequences from AI procedures and act upon them effectively. Other requirements include clinician training and knowledge of the capabilities and limitations of using AI in decision support. IDSS greatly increases the efficiency of medical care; however, human supervision is still required to ensure that artificial decision-making corresponds to the physician's knowledge and the patient's individual characteristics. Figure 3 highlights the working of the IDSS, from data collection to decision support, as highlighted in the above sections. The figure illustrates the different data gathered from the patient, and after removing the inconsistencies, the data goes through superior AI tools to analyze the patient's data. The last part of the figure shows how clinicians use the IDSS to get individual advice, risk evaluations, and possible treatments to enhance the decision-making process.

Summary

In the health system, IDSS refers to applying artificial AI, machine learning, and big data for real-time clinical decisions. Among these mentioned systems are knowledge-based, machine learning-based, and the model of the two, which also have their own strengths and weaknesses. The critical components concerning IDSS are data collection, fair methods for identifying patterns by using the right algorithms, and proper teamwork with clinicians so that the issues addressed by the systems are easily understandable, accurate, and ethical. When looking at what remains ahead for IDSS, some tests need to be encountered in terms of data gaining and normalization and formatting this data for the algorithms, explaining to the clinicians the steps taken by the algorithms, and, perhaps most significantly, gaining that trust in the clinician decision-makers. Out of those above three future predictions, only XAI and federated learning are anticipated to enhance the feasibility, utilization, and scalability of the IDSS in modern environments.

3. Applications of IDSS in Healthcare

IDSS has been incorporated into healthcare as it has enhanced the diagnosis of diseases and the quality of care, as well as streamlined clinical processes. AI, ML, and Big Data analytical systems, which have been developed and implemented into several healthcare domains. As for the further sections, they point to the key use of IDSS in predictive analytics, personalized medicine, robotic surgery, and EHR instruments.

Figure 4 illustrates the wearable devices, smartwatches, and fitness trackers and how they have gone an extra month to become critical tools in healthcare through the constant feeding of important health metrics. They are instrumental in managing patients' conditions through remote patient monitoring since physical examinations are not necessary. Some of the areas that, for instance, Real-time data helps include the early diagnosis of ailments like heart diseases and diabetes, to name but a few. The incorporation of wearable gadgets into Intelligent Decision Support Systems (IDSS) will enhance healthcare delivery through the differentiation of patient care procedures and timely decisions that benefit the patient.

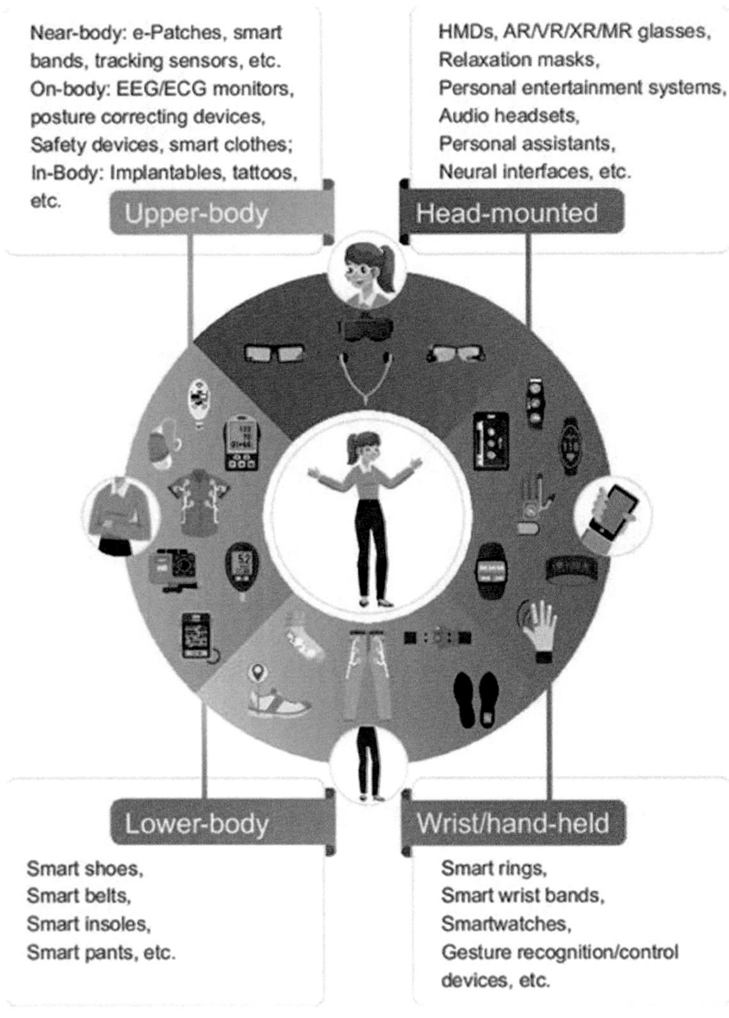

Figure 4: Wearable Devices and their Role in Healthcare.

Diagnostic Assistance

Automated Image Interpretation (Radiology, Pathology)

Of all the areas that have received massive enhancement in computerized image analysis, radiology and pathology are among the most prominent. They can analyze medical images to read out some potential that the naked eye may not recognize. According to [16] , AI technologies have been deployed in the radiology practice to refer to approaches used to use machine learning on X-ray pictures, improve accuracy, reduce the chances of mistakes, and facilitate department operations. Such facets explain why IDSS systems are useful for diagnosis. They imply that specific diseases can be diagnosed within a shorter time frame than the actual time while allowing clinicians to tend to the emergent ones first. Indeed, these systems improve the discrimination of new growths as benign or malignant by developing improved deep learning capabilities.

Clinical Decision Support for Differential Diagnosis

The other potential area of IDSS is differential diagnosis in clinical decision-making. To aid an efficient differential diagnosis of colitis, the authors [17] affirm that only IDSS systems that can accommodate features related to symptoms, tests, and the patient's past medical history should be used. They are obtained from large clinical databases and can diagnose several diseases differently. In situations like emergency or primary care facilities where time is very tight, these tools assist the healthcare provider in arriving at the correct diagnosis within the shortest time possible. These systems have connotations like the database, providing clinicians with more opportunities to focus on less obvious diseases that may be overlooked. As a result, it becomes realistic to cut the rate of diagnostic errors radically and improve patients' outcomes using instruments developed within IDSS.

Predictive Analytics

Predictive analytics powered by IDSS can forecast disease progression, predict patient outcomes, and optimize healthcare delivery by anticipating patient needs.

Early Detection of Diseases such as Cancer and Sepsis

IDSS are most advantageous when diseases are still at their preliminary stage. According to Peiffer-Smadja et al. [18] who argued that ML could be used in infectious diseases by predicting the outbreak or early signs of sepsis, cancer, or other diseases. In general, the control of diseases, especially severe diseases such as cancer, greatly depends on the stage at which the disease exists. The medical images, genomics data, and patients' history can then identify patterns for early and effective detection of diseases by AI systems. For example, with vast data on oncology patients, AI models are programmed to diagnose a tumor even at its early stage when it starts growing without being visible to the naked eye in imagery.

Population Health Management and Epidemic Forecasting

Predictive analytics is also applicable to population health and diseases. In COVID-19, AI models were used to predict the further course of the epidemic, to determine the characteristics of the risk group, and to distribute the available medical resources. To identify how exactly the concept of a decision support system can be applied within the sphere of managing the demand for healthcare resources in epidemics, the study aims to analyze the article by [19]. These can forecast the specifics of a given epidemic and guide the healthcare providers on the specifics of available beds, healthcare personnel, and medical equipment. They help predict the future occurrences of the diseases and reduce the number of admissions to various facilities in the event of an epidemic.

Personalized Medicine

Personalized medicine is a new discipline that applies medical treatment to each patient's characteristics, such as their genetic predisposition, lifestyle, and medical history. IDSS is one of the key players more prone to the development of personalized treatment schemes.

Treatment Optimization and Drug Recommendations

However, this paper also highlighted that an AI-driven IDSS has transformed the optimized treatment by applying the therapies respective to the patients' profiles. Thus, in the current work, Ahmed et al. [20] suggest an AI-based multi-functional machine learning platform for partializing exactness medicine. Such a distribution of systems aids look at a specific patient, collected with the genetic map, the patient's role, medical history, etc, then give the patient the finest treatment plan that fits the patient. For example, in cancer treatment, a doctor can predict how a specific patient will respond to a particular therapy, thus helping specialists choose the drugs with a low possibility of side effects. They also approve of drug repurposing, which can involve searching for new applications for existing drugs with the help of analysis of different databases.

AI-assisted Genomic Analysis

Another scarcely any industry that IDSS has played an extremely special role in is Genomic analysis. In this context, [21] describes how the vendors incorporate the established genomic information into the AI approaches for the best drug regimen. Therefore, the analysis of genetic changes and biomarkers facilitates the use of AI models to determine which drugs should be more effective in treating specific patients for better treatment results. Especially in the field of oncology, the union of AI and genomics is proposed as it is needed for first the sequencing of a tumor for a particular patient to comprehend that patient's diagnosis and the treatment plan that should follow. Figure 5 shows how IDSS is used in personalized medicine. First, treatment planning with the AI's help involves data collection, genetic tests, and patient history examination. Subsequently, it processes those inputs through artificial intelligence that identifies the best drug therapies to prescribe, anticipates unwanted effects, and adapts the drug regime based on an individual patient's response. This diagram also represents the cyclic nature of IDSS since the recommendations provided by the system are accompanied by real-time feedback from the patient and new clinical data obtained.

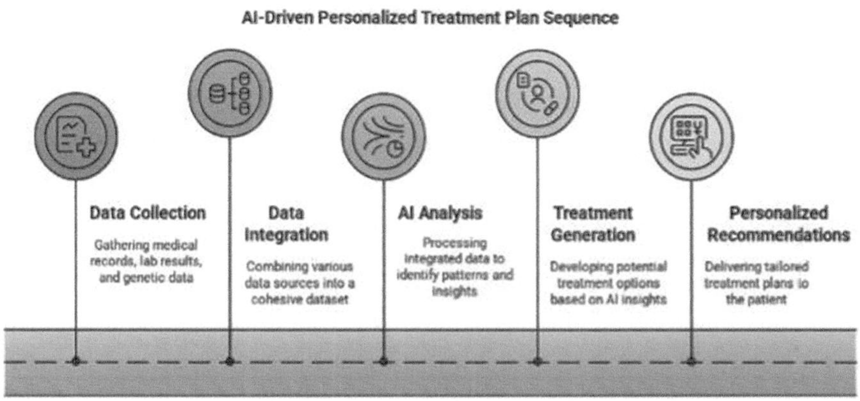

Figure 5: AI Driven Personalized Treatment Plan Sequence.

Robotic Surgery and Automated Procedures

Robotic surgery has transformed the landscape of minimally invasive procedures, and AI is at the heart of this revolution.

AI in Surgical Robotics

Robotic technology is used in operations to supplement human work to minimize human error and enhance the performance of precise procedures and steps. In their article published in 2021 Moglia et al. [22], have given a comprehensive analysis of the application of AI in robot-assisted surgeries; the authors describe several AI-enabled systems that are accomplished by execution of subtle tasks such as suturing of tissues or partition and decision-making during the operation. These systems monitor the patients' status daily, as well as the life signs and instruments used to regulate the outcome to counter check for any change in the tissue. There are also several others in the clinical sense, in the clinical planning or after and before the operation, where models can be developed to determine the side effects in the patient and where measures have to be taken either during or after the clinical processes.

Remote-assisted Procedures

The other area used in surgeries is remote-assisted procedures, where robots are used. According to [23] who have pointed out that today's robotic systems are used in gynecological operations whereby the surgeon's commands are transmitted to the robot as it depends on actual time optimization, which means that it is pretty accurate even in accurately delicate moments when it is implemented through remote places. This capability offers a chance to carry out several operations that general surgeons or specialized surgeons cannot do well in some situations where such specialists are sparingly available.

IDSS in Electronic Health Records (EHRs)

IDSS integrated with Electronic Health Records (EHRs) has the potential to reduce medical errors, streamline workflows, and improve patient care.

Reducing Medical Errors and Improving Efficiency

Sufficient intelligent decision support systems currently in the health sector can help clinicians avoid making a wrong decision or overlooking something such as drug interaction, allergy, or disease. According to Shahmoradi et al. [24] who added that decision support systems available in EHRs have increased medication effectiveness since they give information about the existence of issues and determine whether the prescribed drug or dose is appropriate. They can also analyze patient data in real time and suggest some treatments, which can be very helpful.

AI-powered Clinical Alerts and Recommendations

The application of clinical alerts and/or recommendations for using artificial intelligence is essential for enhancing the healthcare service delivery system. As per Elhaddad and Hamam [25] who state that clinical decision-making based on EHRs and AI is relevant in the case of CDS in clinical notifications equipped with prescriptive advice from the patient data. These help in the early identification of high-risk clients and promote health interventions, thus improving the care advancement and the organization's performance.

As presented in Fig. 6 below, the illustration illustrates how IDSS can be highly integrated with Electronic Health Records (EHRs). The primary concern of the diagram is the extracted patient data, the clinical alerts empowered by AI, and the decision support system in real time. By doing so, through predictive analytics nurtured by IDSS, one can identify possible medical errors, an alert of possible drug interactions, and the recommended action plan or treatment plan that enhances comparability with available data evidence. This integration increases clinical efficiency and minimizes the risk of patient harm by providing quick and solid recommendations to clinicians.

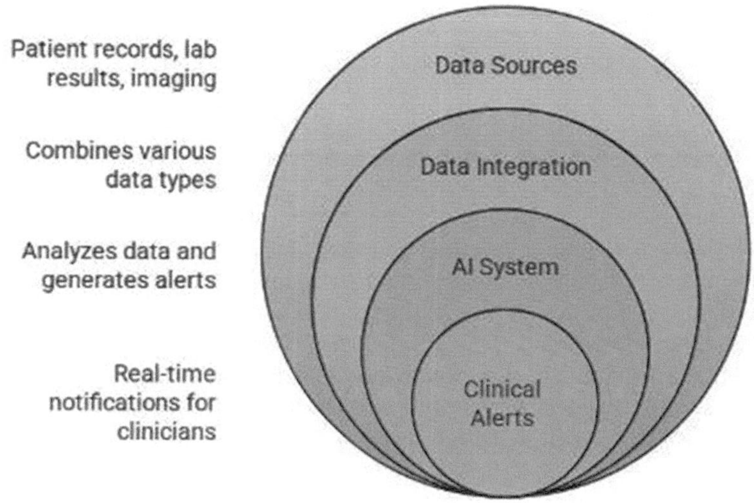

Figure 6: AI Integration in EHRs.

Summary

When applied to the field of health sciences, it is beneficial and efficient in improving the approaches and methods, including diagnostics, prognosis, and prescriptions, as well as advanced medicine, remote surgery, and integration with the EHRs. They assist in the health care facilities, diagnosis, testing, treatment recommendations, and clinical and management processes. As technology advances and a new generation of advanced artificial intelligence and machine learning, the extent of utilization of IDSS will expand the future of the healthcare system for improving the quality of the delivery of healthcare, the efficiency of the potential clinical workflow and the treatment plans for the patients.

4. Challenges and Limitations of IDSS

While IDSS has been proven beneficial and is being used in health care delivery, it has some other technical issues, and its implementation broadens some ethical, legal, and clinical issues. These must be addressed and overcome to realize IDSS as part of enhancing clinical practices. Next, this paper describes some of the challenges associated with the use of IDSS: The first set of issues includes technical issues such as data integration and computational challenges, while the second lot of issues include data privacy, bias in the algorithms used, and the question of responsibility on the output generated. It also brings out the issues of putting mechanisms into practice in a clinical environment, including resistance toward change, staff training issues, and concern over costs and resource implications of deployment.

Technical Challenges

Data Integration and Interoperability Issues

Some of the most significant technical issues that prevented the usage of IDSS in healthcare include the issues of data integration. Electronic health records include information derived from many different sources, in many types of systems and formats, and in many organizations. According to [26], several issues will likely be realized when compiling information using EHRs, medical images, and other patient observation gadgets. Such systems often do not possess a unified format of communication, which in turn hampers optimal information sharing between hospitals, clinics, and other related facilities. The latter was considered fresh, accurate, and detailed data for effective IDSS implementation. However, there are several challenges that the healthcare department encounters because of nonstandard data format and dated technology systems adopted by healthcare

Table 2: Challenges in Implementing IDSS in Healthcare

Challenge	Description	Impact on implementation	Possible solutions
Data Integration	Fragmentation of healthcare data across various systems	Causes difficulty in integrating data from multiple sources such as EHRs, lab results, and medical imaging	Implementing interoperability standards like HL7, FHIR; adopting cloud-based solutions
Algorithmic Bias	AI models may reflect biases present in training data	May lead to unfair or inaccurate outcomes for underrepresented populations	Using diverse training datasets; implementing bias mitigation techniques
Regulatory Compliance	Need for IDSS to meet strict healthcare regulations (e.g., HIPAA, GDPR)	Delays in deployment, legal and privacy concerns	Ensuring compliance with local and international healthcare regulations; continuous auditing
Clinician Acceptance	Resistance from healthcare professionals in trusting AI recommendations	Limits widespread adoption and reliance on AI tools	Providing evidence of AI accuracy; training clinicians on the benefits of IDSS
Computational Resources	IDSS require significant computational power, especially for machine learning models	High infrastructure costs for healthcare facilities, especially smaller ones	Leveraging cloud computing for scalability; optimizing algorithms to reduce computational load

facilities. Also, healthcare data is in the electronic health record format and other formats, such as structured, unstructured, and semi-structured, as in diagnostic imaging. HL7 and FHIR (Fast Healthcare Interoperability Resources) are some standards that solve such integration challenges. Table 2 depicts some of the prevalent challenges faced by IDSS, including data integration, algorithmic, and regulatory challenges, whereby the set laws concerning the dissemination and protection of patient data bind healthcare systems. Other issues include clinician acceptance or rejection of it and the heavy dependency on computational resources. It is, therefore, crucial to meet some of these challenges to realize the realistic use of IDSS in clinical situations.

Computational Power and Infrastructure Limitations

Last but not least, we can also talk about technical factors that allow us to perform real-time analysis of a significant amount of data in the IDSS. As [27] stated, with the increasing number of patient data and the nonlinearity and intricate architecture of the learning models, the time taken and computing resources required are high. In today's world, there are many promulgates whereby advanced and conventional structural platforms are employed to handle the vast volume of data generated in today's innovative healthcare devices like IoTs and wearables.

Models involved in creating IDSS use many computing resources for training and data analysis. For example, there are tasks capable of being performed through deep learning using GPUs and cloud-based architecture to quickly and efficiently get through large databases. It is of more significance in scenarios where the options generated by IDSS may take a relatively longer time than when such decisions have to be made since the essential infrastructure to support IDSS is wanted.

Ethical and Legal Concerns

Data Privacy and Security Risks

Since the patient's identity is used as the core of IDSS, concerns over data privacy and security arise. Conducting patient health records using digital structures accompanied by the application of artificial intelligence to support the physician's decision carries a high risk of data breaches, unlawful access, cyberattacks, etc. As per [28] who mentioned some of the moral and legal concerns in the usage of AI, even if they proceeded with patient data privacy to make them suitable for the use in decision support systems based on artificial intelligence in medicine. Due to relying on samples that may include PII, IDSS can compromise the privacy of the individuals in the data without protective measures. To address the above concerns, the following recommendations can be made to the healthcare firm regarding ensuring proper healthcare security, encryption, storage, and access control. Besides, there are issues concerning how the various stakeholders in the health sector, especially the health professionals, should handle and share information about the patients to ensure that the patient's privacy is not violated, especially with laws such as HIPAA.

Algorithmic Bias and Fairness in AI-driven Decisions

Among the most pressing ethical concerns, one can identify the problem of the 'endogenous influence over the results' regarding the implementation of AI and algorithms in decision-making. According to [29], several factors are pertinent to how these AI models can either amplify or perpetuate biases in healthcare. Such biases arise from the data fed into the models to provide diagnoses or treatments, and many times, the database used is narrowed down to a few patients only. For example, if it presents results derived from white male patients, then it will not be helpful for women or racially diverse people, and this can lead to wrong diagnosis or unfair treatment to the affected patients. To address these problems, there is a need to ensure that the AI models for training are free from the variation of patients in the healthcare services offered. In addition, the fair training of the models has to be included so as not to have any prejudice within the system recommendations made to the public.

Legal Liability and Accountability

As the degree of operation of IDSS increases, questions of legal liability and accountability in health care decision-making become even more apparent. In their article, [29] show how the principle of diffused responsibility applies to the use of artificial intelligence in clinical decision support systems. When an issued IDSS recommendation leads to poor patient outcomes, it can be challenging to determine which party is responsible for the decision: the AI, the healthcare provider, or the institution. It shapes the land's guidelines and influences the legal responsibility of doctors and medical negligence in the country. Hence, it is imperative to elaborate on the legal discussion about the differences between recommended and required measures and a clear definition of roles for healthcare providers' safe adoption of IDSS. There also has to be laws that govern the checking of the systems to ensure that an artificial intelligence system is ready for use in hospitals among others.

Clinical Implementation Barriers

Resistance to Adoption by Healthcare Professionals

It is crucial to curb the use of the technology in the healthcare setting since there is opposition to adopting IDSS. It is less specific and may not always embrace an AI-based decision, primarily if the decision-making affects human lives and health. A study conducted by [30] on clinical diagnostic decision support systems among clinicians enumerated that many clinicians are concerned with its autonomy in decision-making,they reportedly believe that AI is challenging their authority. Thus, one has to stress that the central concept of IDSS is to support instead of replacing healthcare professionals. Combined with the evidence-based training concerning the efficacy of the IDSS on a real-life basis for the doctors and the practitioners who will be using it will help raise the acceptance level and utilization factor for the levels of status.

Need for Extensive Training and Workflow Integration

One thing that has been noticed in the above discussions is that for the users of IDSS to get the most optimum use out of the systems, it takes time to train the clinical workers on how to operate the systems as well as how to harness the full potential of the systems that are being developed. According to [31], there is no doubt or ambiguity in the idea that it is crucial to successfully integrate the IDSS into the clinical practice, and therefore, the integration of the system with the existing workflow is highly significant. If the above systems are not easy to use or compatible with EHRs and other Health IT software, then the clinicians will not be able to engage them in an appropriate manner, and this will lead to compromises. However, it is also necessary that these guidelines and recommended information for different updates and changes regarding the IDSS shall also be updated for the healthcare providers by taking the ongoing training.

Cost and Resource Limitations in Healthcare Systems

Finally, the amount of resources and costs invested to the extent of having an IDSS in health care is relatively high. In their current paper [32], analyze the ethics and economics of an automated decision-making system and point out features like it is costly to install and implement, there is the recurring cost needed for sustaining this system, and, most importantly the computational capacity needed to power this system is enormous making it almost impossible for hospitals that may not have an adequate capital base. However, to further encourage its application, there should be ways of cutting the costs incurred in adopting the technology through subsidies from the government, partnerships, and the development of cheap AI systems. It should also be possible for the health care providers to demonstrate that the objective of coming up with IDSS, for instance, better diagnosis of health issues and low cost of health care, is more than offsetting the cost of implementing the solutions.

Summary

Reviewing recent literature, we established that technical and practical concerns arose from the implementation of IDSS, including data integration, identifying the computational challenges of IDSS, data privacy, and algorithmic choice and legal concern on deploying IDSS in the healthcare field. At the clinical level, therefore, implementation barriers such as lack of commitment, the need for training and confining financial resources also go a long way in making it difficult to incorporate IDSS to the practice. Some of these challenges require measures to be taken for the successful integration of IDSS to improve the quality of patient care and health system.

5. Recent Innovations and Future Directions

Federated Learning and Data Privacy Solutions

The emerging popular approach in training these models is federated learning, which enables many healthcare facilities to train all the models centrally but without any single array of the patients' data. Based on [33] who describe how it is possible to work with federated learning if healthcare providers wish to train large datasets into AI models without sharing the patient's information with the central server. However, new data is shared across different institutions when updating the models. At the same time, the training of the AI system is done in a distributive fashion to adhere to the Patient's Information Privacy Act.

To address these deficiencies, federated learning deals with one of the significant problems which originated from the healthcare domain: that is the data which are prohibited from being shared due to privacy concerns and laws such as HIPAA in the United States or GDPR in Europe. Therefore, by distributing the learning atmosphere and avoiding data sharing at this level, federated learning fosters collaboration in the healthcare system to enable many categories of medical data to be fed to AI models. This will increase the applicability and accuracy of the developed models to other patients and outpatient contexts.

Explainable AI (XAI) in IDSS

The lack of interpretability and the question of algorithmic explainability have become significant threats to the development of IDSS, highlighting the importance of freedom of interpretation and algorithmic transparency. As a result, the recommendations from the AI must be credible, especially in areas that may involve the lives of people and in areas that are sensitive, such as the health sector. In giving a brief background as to its necessity, XAI can be briefly defined as the facet within a study concerned with explaining the AI models and how their decisions are arrived at by human beings.

Enhancing Transparency and Interpretability

Arreche et al. [34] stated that an XAI framework is proposed in specific application areas relevant to the healthcare AI decision support systems application domain related to the above-said repercussions, which are called the network intrusion detection area. Their approach, in particular, is to provide a capability to explain, through the logical reasoning used by an AI in a medical perspective, the diagnostics, the treatments, or any other recommendations given.

Knowing how an AI-generated model arrives at an obtained model is essential for patients and clinicians in the healthcare field. They talked of what is referred to as Explainable Artificial Intelligence, XAI, through which clinicians can rate the degree of the AI suggestion towards their impression of their clinical practice. For example, in oncology, where decisions for choosing the treatment options may become abstract and are made only based on genetic information, the previous response to treatments, and the medical protocols, AI must demonstrate how all this information has been analyzed to develop the suggested treatment. This level of interpretability may help build the clinician's cliques and, ultimately, the system's adoption.

Gaining Trust Among Clinicians and Patients

In building and relying on AI systems, trustworthiness is an essential prerequisite. In a similar fashion, the Dissanayake et al. [35] highlight how it is feasible to create trust in clinical reasoning, as such performance on ontologies in CDS is based on a best-practice theoretical framework for the AI systems we are working with. It also informs the physician about what recommendations the system has made and why, which the clinician believes is feasible.

Moreover, explainable AI also brings advantages for the patient as it can help explain the process of clinical decisions, which is valuable input for patients' satisfaction and decision-making. Given that AI is being applied in several settings that directly or indirectly concern the clinician and the patient, the two need to trust the logic of the AI and be assured that the conclusions the AI makes out of that logic are within the medical ethics and patients' safety standards.

Regulatory Developments

Regulation and compliance are continuously being developed as AI systems are being implemented in the healthcare sector so as to guarantee their safety, practicability and ethical use. There are attempts being made by means of regulatory authorities to offer working definitions on the nature of clinical applicability, openness, and responsibility of an AI tool.

Evolving Policies for AI in Healthcare

In their recent article, Siala and Wang [36] describe the process of SHIFTing AI into healthcare as responsible through outlining specific ethical standards and policies that guide the use of artificial intelligence in clinical practices. These proposals are intended to avoid any non-serious approaches in developing new technologies based on AI that may be capable of overshadowing regulation shortly or even jeopardizing the life of patients. It would also help for there to rules and responsibilities concerning data ownership, data responsibilities, and algorithmic integration in decision-making so that the structures are effective and equitable. One of the key issues that policy makers face is ensuring that the architected AI systems will respect the regional and the international laws and simultaneously facilitate international cooperation. This is because the future growth in artificial intelligence applications must be viewed globally since it varies from country to country due to regulation.

Compliance Frameworks for Safe Implementation

Consequently, the measures for AI safety imply the compliance measures that ensure that the implemented AI systems practice safety to be implemented safely. According to the frameworks of the AI-based decision support system with respect to Industry 4.0 played by [37], it can be understood that these are designed in a manner that the efficacy of the system is first ascertained before it is integrated into the real world general application. The healthcare sector can adopt and emulate such frameworks to ensure the clinical practice and vari-validated AI systems and provide procedural constraints to rid any prejudicial impacts on the system that affect the well-being of patients.

Emerging Trends

A number of trends are attached at the heels of the advancement of IDSS. Some of these trends include the establishment of artificial intelligence in virtual health assistants, latest IDSS technology of wearable devices and IoT, and quantum computing in healthcare AI.

AI-driven Virtual Health Assistants

The AI-based virtual health assistants have arguably been one of the most active things over the past several years. Besides, these integrated systems can also play a role in attending to patient needs at any time of the day and coming up with replies which may be required, advice, making appointments among other tasks. Patil and Shankar [38] also explain that such virtual assistants use NLP and machine learning approaches to address the patients' questions and usually suitably reply to them. The decision-support system could improve the relation between the patients and the doctors, not to leave the scheduled appointments or neglecting the prescribed medication schedules. However, in combination with other technologies, such assistants can be effective for preventive home monitoring, saving the healthcare staff time and giving indications of the required interventions.

Integration of Wearable Technologies and IoT in IDSS

Wearable devices and Internet of Things technologies are being incorporated into Intelligent Decision Support Systems (IDSS), which allows healthcare providers to check patients' health conditions without even getting physically involved with them. Based on the research by [39], IoT-based IDSS makes it possible to control the devices used in collecting patient data, such as smartwatches and the like, to ensure that patient information is well protected. These devices provide real-time consumer health reports such as pulse rates, blood pressure, etc., which can help detect early signs of health complications or diseases like heart disease or diabetes. Integrating IoT data into IDSS also ensures that patients receive proper care and early treatment in case of any problem. As such, developments in IDSS are bringing the future of healthcare to where it is today. From Table 3, it is seen that Federated Learning allows model training to be done locally while maintaining the privacy of data and, at the same time, improving the accuracy of the model. Various approaches, such as Explanatory AI (XAI), maintain trust between clinicians and patients; on the other hand, Quantum computing is a tool that speeds up and provides accurate calculations for data and even prediction. In addition to this, the addition of Virtual Health Assistants to the existing Integrated Digital Support System (IDSS) is set to provide better patient involvement and real-time control, thereby depicting the effectiveness of such advancements in improving the quality provided to patients.

Table 3: Future Trends and Innovations in IDSS

Innovation	Description	Expected impact on healthcare
Federated Learning	A decentralized method of training AI models where data remains at the source, preventing central data collection	Improves privacy while allowing models to benefit from data across multiple healthcare institutions without violating patient privacy
Explainable AI (XAI)	Techniques that make machine learning models more interpretable, offering insight into how decisions are made	Increases trust among clinicians and patients, facilitates regulatory compliance, and helps with model debugging
Quantum Computing	Utilization of quantum computing to speed up data processing and model training	Enhances the efficiency of complex computations, allowing for faster and more accurate medical predictions and drug discoveries
AI-powered Virtual Health Assistants	AI-driven assistants that can manage patient queries, schedule appointments, and monitor symptoms remotely	Reduces clinician workload, improves patient engagement, and enhances care delivery through real-time assistance
Wearable Device Integration	Integration of data from wearable devices (e.g., smartwatches, fitness trackers) into IDSS for continuous health monitoring	Provides real-time data for predictive health insights, allowing for early interventions and better management of chronic diseases

The Role of Quantum Computing in Future Healthcare AI

Quantum computing in healthcare AI will lead to big data processing in a very short time. A more detailed analysis of the potential use of quantum computing in the context of healthcare has been discussed by Rasool et al. [40], where the authors pay attention to three areas such as computational modeling, the optimization of deep learning, and drug discovery. Quantum computing will enable the training of the machine learning models at a much faster pace to enhance the data processing that leads to the decisions that will be made concerning the health sector. On the same note, quantum computing in the health related sectors could also be realized through the genetic analysis of diseases, the development of drugs that are niche based on the genetic makeup of a body, use of data mining and modeling. Being still relatively young in the industry, quantum computing holds great potential in the future, as seen below concerning the utilization in healthcare AI.

Figure 7 shows the integration of IoT technologies with wearable devices into IDSS in paving the way for proactive healthcare. Through continuous health monitoring, devices like smartwatches and IoT sensors transmit real-time data to healthcare systems, enabling predictive analytics and early intervention. This allows healthcare providers to detect and address potential health issues before they escalate, particularly in chronic conditions such as hypertension or diabetes. As these technologies continue to evolve, they hold immense potential to enhance patient engagement, reduce healthcare costs, and improve overall care by delivering personalized treatment strategies based on real-time data.

This conceptual diagram illustrates future innovations in IDSS, including federated learning, explainable AI, quantum computing, and AI-driven virtual

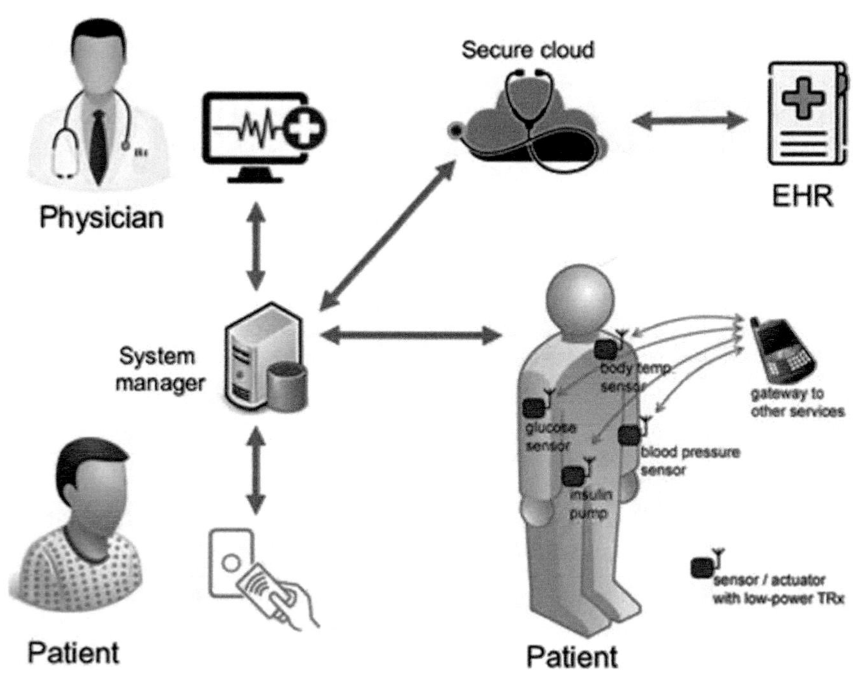

Figure 7: Integration of Wearables and IoT in Healthcare for Proactive Care.

health assistants. Each segment of the diagram represents a cutting-edge advancement designed to address key challenges in IDSS implementation, such as data privacy, model interpretability, and computational efficiency. Figure 8 visually connects these innovations to real-world applications, demonstrating how they collectively contribute to the evolution of intelligent decision support systems in healthcare.

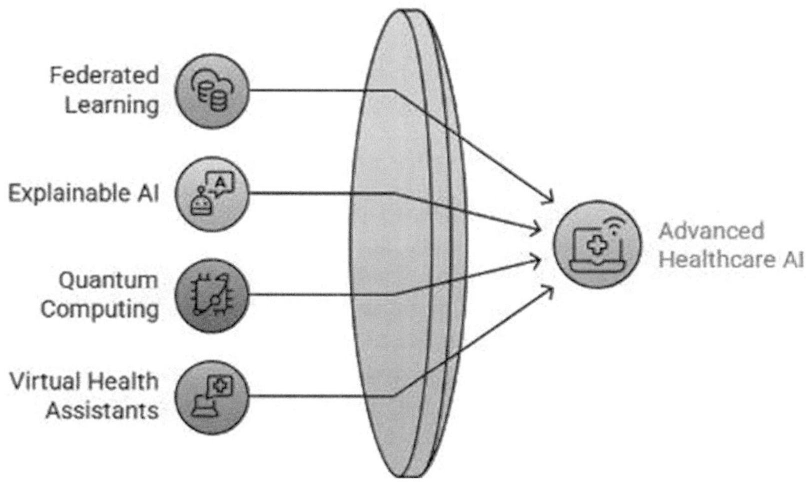

Figure 8: Synergistic Healthcare Innovations.

Summary

Several issues that can influence IDSS development in the healthcare industry include federated learning, explainable AI (XAI), new regulations, tendencies in the use of virtual health assistants and wearables, advancement in quantum computing, and others. This chapter has provided some of the primary challenges concerning data privacy and the explainability of the solutions, as well as the scalability of AI healthcare systems for both efficacy and equity. Nevertheless, such advancements have the potential to revolutionize the healthcare system and, therefore, improve the quality of care and treatment provided to clients since general care and treatment are enhanced through efficiency.

6. Conclusion and Recommendations

Summary of Key Findings

Appropriate Intelligent Decision Support Systems in healthcare are still being introduced and gradually transforming how various healthcare decisions are made, thanks to new artificial intelligence, machine learning, and big data processing technologies. However, there are remarkable concerns for the application of the IDSS: data integration and heterogeneity, computational resources, data ownership, data protection, fairness, accuracy, responsibility, and legal implication. It also reveals some clinical implementation barriers, such as resistance due to the processes of adopting and accelerating the training, which continue to present challenges to these systems. Some challenges are being addressed by concepts such as federated learning to keep the data private and the new work on XAI to build trust in artificial intelligence. However, the future developments discussed here include wearables, virtual assistants in healthcare based on AI, and tentative applications of quantum computing in the field of AI in healthcare, forming the base for the new generation of decision support.

Practical Implications for Healthcare Stakeholders

Therefore, the implications of deploying IDSS in the sector are profound concerning the characteristics of clinical decision-making stakeholders, such as clinicians, healthcare organizations, policymakers, and patients. However, for such systems to maximize benefits, clinicians must project their anticipated output from the resultant AI recommendation. For this, an explainable AI system is advisable. When used in healthcare, the application can assist healthcare organizations in improving organizational effectiveness and, in the process, enhance organizational efficiency in the utilization of resources and offer better healthcare to patients. Therefore, any organization that intends to implement such systems in clinical practices must invest the right effort and resources when providing computation and training. Consequently, such practical applications of the systems call for policy intervention in providing healthcare services as these politicians work to set the policies in their respective nations. They have to develop better policies about some of the issues, like the protection of personal information and disclosure of artificial intelligence. In the same manner, it is their responsibility to ensure that these IDSS technologies meet the standards and the laws in health care across the world. The application of IDSS is beneficial mainly to patients as it conveys near-to-patient treatment, faster diagnosis, and better treatment outcomes.

Future Research Directions

Data Interoperability and Integration

More studies should identify standard formats for transferring data across various healthcare organizations and platforms. Blockchain ideas and secured data-sharing solutions might solve the problem of integration.

Enhancing Trust and Adoption of IDSS

Further investigation of the issues clinicians face while adopting IDSS and the creation of training programs that educate clinicians about the potential role of these systems to enhance rather than supplant their clinical judgment. Ongoing studies focusing on clinicians' perceptions of integrating AI within work procedures would enhance adoption.

Bias and Fairness in AI

It is essential to reduce bias while implementing AI in patients' care by ensuring fairness in those algorithms. Further research should be conducted to discover techniques on biased data to prevent this problem from happening again, to continue creating diverse models for training AI and the effects of these AI models on the decisions for health care provisions.

Real-time Data Processing

With increasing patient records collected from wearable devices and IoT sensors, new approaches to analyze such data in real time are required to provide clinicians with real-time decision-making support. It will be especially prized in emergency care, ICU, and patients with chronic diseases.

Quantum Computing in Healthcare

With the advancement of quantum computing, we will eventually see how they can play a significant role in healthcare AI. Specifically, topics related to integrating quantum computing in machine learning for training AI models and quantum computing for drug discovery and analysis will be imperative to IDSS development in the future.

Final Thoughts on the Future of IDSS in Healthcare

IDS has been cited as a tool for the future of the healthcare industry since it can be seen that both patients and healthcare providers are bound to benefit from it. It is impossible to comprehend the involvement of AI in the development of healthcare facilities because it is cheap, fast, and accessible in the delivery of its services. IDSS will continue to be useful to clinicians in that it will assist clinicians in arriving at the right decision in the shortest time possible, thereby improving the quality and efficiency of the treatment offered to their patients and reducing costs. However, currently, minimal and effective policies or procedures could provide a situation where AI has to work well. In this situation, the misuse of technology cannot be permitted to happen. In responding to these challenges and in further development, it is expected that IDSS can significantly impact the future of health care with the principle of higher precision of treatment, better decisions, and more constructive performance with the health care systems. Finally, as the IDSS technologies are improved, the broad deployment of these technologies will require AI developers, healthcare professionals, policymakers, and the patient body to work together to enable the appropriate implementation of AI-supported technologies within the protection of patients' human rights to the maximum extent.

Data Availability

Upon reasonable request, the corresponding author will make the datasets and code used in this study public.

References

1. Hernandez-Jaimes, M. L., Martinez-Cruz, A., Ramirez-Gutierrez, K. A., and Feregrino-Uribe, C. (2023). Artificial intelligence for IoMT security: A review of intrusion detection systems, attacks, datasets and Cloud-Fog-Edge architectures. *Internet of Things*, 100887.
2. Musen, M. A., Middleton, B., and Greenes, R. A. (2021). Clinical decision-support systems. In: *Biomedical Informatics: Computer Applications in Health Care and Biomedicine* (pp. 795–840). Cham: Springer International Publishing.
3. Vasey, B., Nagendran, M., Campbell, B., Clifton, D. A., Collins, G. S., Denaxas, S., and McCulloch, P. (2022). Reporting guideline for the early stage clinical evaluation of decision support systems driven by artificial intelligence: DECIDE-AI. *bmj*, 377.
4. Mahiddin, N. B., Othman, Z. A., Bakar, A. A., and Rahim, N. A. A. (2022). An interrelated decision-making model for an intelligent decision support system in healthcare. *IEEE Access*, 10, 31660–31676.
5. Mosavi, N.S. and Santos, M.F. (2022). Intelligent Decision Support System for Precision Medicine (IDSS 4 PM). *In:* Wang, T., Patnaik, S., Ip, A.W., Tavana, M. (eds) Advances in Decision Science and Management. ICDSM 2021. *Advances in Intelligent Systems and Computing*, vol 1391. Springer, Singapore. https://doi.org/10.1007/978-981-16-2502-2_4
6. Khan, Z. F., and Alotaibi, S. R. (2020). Applications of artificial intelligence and big data analytics in m-health: A healthcare system perspective. *Journal of Healthcare Engineering*, 2020(1), 8894694.
7. Fernandes, M., Vieira, S. M., Leite, F., Palos, C., Finkelstein, S., and Sousa, J. M. (2020). Clinical decision support systems for triage in the emergency department using intelligent systems: A review. *Artificial Intelligence in Medicine*, 102, 101762.
8. Papadopoulos, P., Soflano, M., Chaudy, Y., Adejo, W., and Connolly, T. M. (2022). A systematic review of technologies and standards used in the development of rule-based clinical decision support systems. *Health and Technology*, 12(4), 713–727.
9. Torab-Miandoab, A., Samad-Soltani, T., Jodati, A., and Rezaei-Hachesu, P. (2023). Interoperability of heterogeneous health information systems: A systematic literature review. *BMC Medical Informatics and Decision Making*, 23(1), 18.
10. Bleher, H., and Braun, M. (2022). Diffused responsibility: Attributions of responsibility in the use of AI-driven clinical decision support systems. *AI and Ethics*, 2(4), 747–761.
11. Vasey, B., Ursprung, S., Beddoe, B., Taylor, E. H., Marlow, N., Bilbro, N., and McCulloch, P. (2021). Association of clinician diagnostic performance with machine learning-based decision support systems: A systematic review. *JAMA Network Open*, 4(3), e211276–e211276.
12. Mousavi, S. M., Abdullah, S., Niaki, S. T. A., and Banihashemi, S. (2021). An intelligent hybrid classification algorithm integrating fuzzy rule-based extraction

and harmony search optimization: Nedical diagnosis applications. *Knowledge-Based Systems*, 220, 106943.
13. Rani, P., Kumar, R., Ahmed, N. M. S., and Jain, A. (2021). A decision support system for heart disease prediction based upon machine learning. *Journal of Reliable Intelligent Environments*, 7(3), 263–275.
14. Fan, W., Liu, J., Zhu, S., and Pardalos, P. M. (2020). Investigating the impacting factors for the healthcare professionals to adopt artificial intelligence-based medical diagnosis support system (AIMDSS). *Annals of Operations Research*, 294(1), 567–592.
15. Belciug, S., and Gorunescu, F. (2020). *Intelligent Decision Support Systems – A Journey to Smarter Healthcare* (pp. 130–137). Berlin/Heidelberg, Germany: Springer International Publishing.
16. Adams, S. J., Henderson, R. D., Yi, X., and Babyn, P. (2021). Artificial intelligence solutions for analysis of X-ray images. *Canadian Association of Radiologists Journal*, 72(1), 60–72.
17. Guimaraes, P., Finkler, H., Reichert, M. C., Zimmer, V., Grünhage, F., Krawczyk, M., and Casper, M. (2023). Artificial-intelligence-based decision support tools for the differential diagnosis of colitis. *European Journal of Clinical Investigation*, 53(6), e13960.
18. Peiffer-Smadja, N., Rawson, T. M., Ahmad, R., Buchard, A., Georgiou, P., Lescure, F. X., and Holmes, A. H. (2020). Machine learning for clinical decision support in infectious diseases: A narrative review of current applications. *Clinical Microbiology and Infection*, 26(5), 584–595.
19. Govindan, K., Mina, H., and Alavi, B. (2020). A decision support system for demand management in healthcare supply chains considering the epidemic outbreaks: A case study of coronavirus disease 2019 (COVID-19). *Transportation Research Part E: Logistics and Transportation Review*, 138, 101967.
20. Ahmed, Z., Mohamed, K., Zeeshan, S., and Dong, X. (2020). Artificial intelligence with multi-functional machine learning platform development for better healthcare and precision medicine. *Database*, 2020, baaa010.
21. Paul, R., Hossain, A., Islam, M. T., Hassan Melon, M. M., and Hussen, M. (2024). Integrating genomic data with AI algorithms to optimize personalized drug therapy: A pilot study. *Library of Progress – Library Science, Information Technology & Computer*, 44(3).
22. Moglia, A., Georgiou, K., Georgiou, E., Satava, R. M., and Cuschieri, A. (2021). A systematic review on artificial intelligence in robot-assisted surgery. *International Journal of Surgery*, 95, 106151.
23. Pavone, M., Baroni, A., Taliento, C., Goglia, M., Lecointre, L., Rosati, A., and Seeliger, B. (2024). Robotic platforms in gynaecological surgery: Past, present, and future. *Facts, Views & Vision in ObGyn*, 16(2), 163.
24. Shahmoradi, L., Safdari, R., Ahmadi, H., and Zahmatkeshan, M. (2021). Clinical decision support systems-based interventions to improve medication outcomes: A systematic literature review on features and effects. *Medical Journal of the Islamic Republic of Iran*, 35, 27.
25. Elhaddad, M., and Hamam, S. (2024). AI-driven clinical decision support systems: An ongoing pursuit of potential. *Cureus*, 16(4).
26. Sutton, R. T., Pincock, D., Baumgart, D. C., Sadowski, D. C., Fedorak, R. N., and Kroeker, K. I. (2020). An overview of clinical decision support systems: Benefits, risks, and strategies for success. *NPJ Digital Medicine*, 3(1), 17.

27. Alshamrani, M. (2022). IoT and artificial intelligence implementations for remote healthcare monitoring systems: A survey. *Journal of King Saud University – Computer and Information Sciences*, 34(8), 4687–4701.
28. Cartolovni, A., Tomicic, A., and Mosler, E. L. (2022). Ethical, legal, and social considerations of AI-based medical decision-support tools: A scoping review. *International Journal of Medical Informatics*, 161, 104738.
29. Bagheri, M., Bagheritaba, M., Alizadeh, S., Parizi, M. S., Matoufinia, P., and Luo, Y. (2024). AI-Driven Decision-Making in Healthcare Information Systems: A Comprehensive Review. Preprints. https://doi.org/10.20944/preprints202406.0790.v1
30. Prakash, A. V., and Das, S. (2021). Medical practitioner's adoption of intelligent clinical diagnostic decision support systems: A mixed-methods study. *Information & Management*, 58(7), 103524.
31. Salunkhe, V., Ayyagiri, A., Musunuri, A., Jain, P., and Goel, D. P. (2021). Machine learning in clinical decision support: Applications, challenges, and future directions. Available at SSRN: https://ssrn.com/abstract=4985006 or http://dx.doi.org/10.2139/ssrn.4985006
32. Mokander, J., Morley, J., Taddeo, M., and Floridi, L. (2021). Ethics-based auditing of automated decision-making systems: Nature, scope, and limitations. *Science and Engineering Ethics*, 27(4), 44.
33. Rauniyar, A., Hagos, D. H., Jha, D., Hakegard, J. E., Bagci, U., Rawat, D. B., and Vlassov, V. (2023). Federated learning for medical applications: A taxonomy, current trends, challenges, and future research directions. *IEEE Internet of Things Journal*. vol. 11, no. 5, pp. 7374-7398, 1 March1, 2024, doi: 10.1109/JIOT.2023.3329061.
34. Arreche, O., Guntur, T., and Abdallah, M. (2024). XAI-IDS: Toward proposing an explainable artificial intelligence framework for enhancing network intrusion detection systems. *Applied Sciences*, 14(10), 4170.
35. Dissanayake, P. I., Colicchio, T. K., and Cimino, J. J. (2020). Using clinical reasoning ontologies to make smarter clinical decision support systems: A systematic review and data synthesis. *Journal of the American Medical Informatics Association*, 27(1), 159–174.
36. Siala, H., and Wang, Y. (2022). SHIFTing artificial intelligence to be responsible in healthcare: A systematic review. *Social Science & Medicine*, 296, 114782.
37. Soori, M., Jough, F. K. G., Dastres, R., and Arezoo, B. (2024). AI-based decision support systems in Industry 4.0, A review. *Journal of Economy and Technology*. ISSN 2949-9488, https://doi.org/10.1016/j.ject.2024.08.005. https://www.sciencedirect.com/science/article/pii/S2949948824000374
38. Patil, S., and Shankar, H. (2023) Transforming healthcare: Harnessing the power of AI in the modern era. *International Journal of Multidisciplinary Sciences and Arts*, 2(1), 60–70.
39. Heidari, A., and Jabraeil Jamali, M. A. (2023). Internet of Things intrusion detection systems: A comprehensive review and future directions. *Cluster Computing*, 26(6), 3753–3780.
40. Rasool, R., Ahmad, H. F., Rafique, W., Qayyum, A., Qadir, J., and Anwar, Z. (2023). Quantum computing for healthcare: A review. *Future Internet*, 15(3), 94.

7 | Artificial Intelligence Networking System for Smart Healthcare

Manas Kanti Saha[1], Subhojit Ghosh[1], Senjuti Mondal[1], Nirmalya Pal[1*] and Ramachandra Handaragal[2]

[1] Department of Computer Science & Engineering, Brainware University, India
[2] Senior IEEE Member, USA

The combination of networking technologies and artificial intelligence is revolutionizing the delivery, administration, and optimization of healthcare services in smart healthcare. This research explores how advanced networking protocols and AI technologies, including machine learning, data analytics, and neural networks, can be used together to improve healthcare services. Healthcare systems can process vast amounts of medical information, predict the state of a patient, individualize treatment protocols, and use resources in the best possible manner through AI. Networking systems facilitate telemedicine, collaborative diagnosis, and continuous care for patients by allowing safe communication, immediate data exchange, and remote monitoring among patients, medical devices, and healthcare providers. This study analyses the potential impact of the integration of AI and networking on the enhancement of patient outcomes, precision in diagnosis, efficacy of treatments, and accessibility to health care in general. Further issues covered are interoperability, security, and data privacy, along with possible fixes, to guarantee the success and adoption of AI-powered smart healthcare systems. In the long run, this AI and networking convergence has the potential to enhance healthcare in the future by making it more patient-centred, scalable, and efficient.

1. Introduction

"Future healthcare" is the phrase used to introduce the application of artificial intelligence (AI) technology in medicine aimed at optimizing patient outcome,

*Corresponding author: nirmalya03561@gmail.com

DOI: 10.1201/9781003635215-7

healthcare system optimization, and the operational efficiency of medical undertakings. AI technology has identified diseases using machine learning, computer vision, and natural language processing and evaluated risks to develop individualized plans for treatment [1]. For its part, the applications of artificial intelligence in medical diagnostics use medical data and images to produce a diagnosis that might be precise concerning cancers and heart conditions. AI-sourced predictive analytics can tell the doctor the probability of particular diseases thus enabling him to take action before the sickness develops. AI is also very good at providing personal medications, which can be described as a procedure that focuses on the patient's medical history and even their genetic makeup to treat their specific type of problems. One other instance when AI is critical for healthcare robots is when there is a demand for help with surgeries or the automation of repetitive procedures to reduce errors and time inefficiency. AI-enabled virtual health assistants' free up doctors by being a source of support to the patients, answering health-centric questions, and reminding patients of their medications. AI also facilitates telemedicine and remote monitoring by watching patients' vital signs and alerting doctors to potential health issues, which in turn decreases hospital visits [2]. Healthcare professionals can spend more quality time with their patients as AI automates administrative tasks such as scheduling and billing [3]. Through the prediction of the therapeutic value of molecules, artificial intelligence (AI) aids in accelerating the drug discovery process and as a result the duration required for the introduction of new pharmaceuticals is shortened. To sum it all up, AI is an essential tool in the smart healthcare industry, which is furthering the standard of healthcare services, their availability, and their effectiveness.

Evolution of AI in Healthcare

The past decades have seen the tremendous growth of artificial intelligence in healthcare, with improvements in data analysis and other technologies. Initially, AI was applied primarily to routine tasks in healthcare, such as scheduling and billing automation. Many early AI systems were rule-based and employed pre-programmed algorithms for processing data. The increasing use of AI in healthcare followed the increase in processing power and data storage capacity. With the improvement of machine learning and natural language processing technologies, systems are now able to search through large data sets without explicit programming to find patterns. During the 2000s, artificial intelligence started assisting with diagnostic imaging to make radiologists identify anomalies, such as tumours, more accurately in MRIs and X-rays [4]. By the 2010s, predictive analytics, personalized medicine, and virtual assistants became a part of AI in healthcare. Massive patient data volumes were fed into the AI machines for training them in the design of treatment plans that could be personalized and more effective disease risk predictions. Virtual assistants and AI-driven chatbots also started assisting with administrative and patient interaction work [5].

The roles that artificial intelligence now assumes in health care range from telemedicine to drug development, and now it extends into the world of robotic surgery, monitoring of patients, and a great many areas that rely on evaluation of very intricate biological data in speeding up clinical trials and medication development. In general, healthcare-related application of AI promises patient outcome improvements, smoother care delivery, reduced costs, greater access, and greater efficiency as the technology develops.

Importance of AI Networking in Medical Systems

AI networking would be essential to improve patient results, accelerate hospital procedures, and enhance healthcare in general. More so, there is a wide complexity of such healthcare systems, in which AI-power networks help unify disparate entities – clinics, research institutes, and pharmacies. This connectivity makes it easy for medical personnel to communicate patient data, which means they are able to make better decisions and care for the patient faster. One of the benefits that AI networking possesses is the possibility of collecting and analyzing vast amounts of information related to patient health using different sources such as wearables, test results, medical imaging [6], and EHRs. This data will be analyzed by the AI systems and can be able to identify the trends, predict health concerns, and recommend treatment. This increases accuracy in diagnosis as well as promotes early detection of diseases such as cancer, heart disease, or neurological problems with better patient outcome.

In addition, the use of AI networking makes medical professionals collaborate more, especially when dealing with difficult or chronic conditions that require the knowledge of several specialists. AI technologies integrated with medical networks allow doctors in different locations to view and assess the same patient data in real time, ensuring consistent care regardless of geographic constraints. In addition, this collaborative model is essential for better care coordination to prevent fragmented treatment programs. Moreover, AI networking supports remote monitoring and telemedicine as it collects real-time health data and transmits them through wearables and other sensors [7]. Consequently, even outside traditional hospital settings, medical experts can monitor patients more closely and act to prevent situations from getting worse. AI networking accelerates medical research and drug development. The AI-powered network helps institutions share information and ideas, and this fosters collaborative research that speeds up the creation of new medications, increases the effectiveness of clinical trials, and accelerates the rate of medical innovation in general.

In summary, AI networking enhances the communication, collaboration, and decision-making of medical systems, which eventually lead to improved treatment, reduced expenses, and advancements in medical research and treatment.

2. AI-based Networking in Healthcare

AI-based networking in the healthcare industry involves integrating artificial intelligence technology with networking systems to ensure improvements in the administration, accessibility, and delivery of health care services. AI-driven networks thus connect clinics, hospitals, research institutes, and pharmacies for one-way data sharing, real-time communication, and collaboration among the professionals. The biggest advantage of AI-based networking is that it can collect and analyze large amounts of data related to patients coming from different sources, such as genetic data, wearable technologies, medical imaging, and electronic health records (EHRs) [8]. Artificial intelligence systems that can study this data in order to uncover patterns and trends allow for predictive analytics that aid in the diagnosis of health issues and customized treatments. For instance, through the analysis of historical data for the prediction of occurrences such as cancer, heart attacks, or strokes, AI can, for example, assist in the early identification of diseases and chances of timely intervention [9]. AI networks also improve coordination and collaboration among healthcare providers. AI technology can make it easier for different healthcare facilities to share patient data when there are complex problems that require many doctors' perspectives. In this type of networking, wearables and other connected medical devices collect heart rate, blood pressure, oxygen saturation, and other vital signs continuously. This reduces the number of hospital readmissions and medical costs. AI networking accelerates clinical trials for research and medication as it makes organizations share data with each other and collaborate on investigations.

Role of IoT and Cloud Computing

Internet and cloud computing are some of the revolutions affecting the market. This has resulted in increased production and the creation of business models, throughout the system IT provides an extremely powerful ecosystem that supports data collection, processing, and archiving. At the same time, it invites smarter and more creative choices. Figure 1 depicts the block diagram of a smart home ecosystem using Internet of Things (IoT) devices.

The Internet of Things refers to a network of interconnected things, which can share information and communicate without human intervention. Such sensor-based systems collect and send real-time data to a central processing centre. Examples include smart home appliances, industrial sensors, and wearable health monitoring. It provides businesses and individuals with an immense amount of information in the operations, behaviours, and performance generated from IoT devices. Cloud computing refers to the accessibility by business to computer resources including such things as servers, storage, and software on an as needed basis through the Internet rather than having to buy, manage, and maintain their physical infrastructures in-house. This flexibility makes possible strong computing power and scalable storage, which helps the Internet of Things systems handle

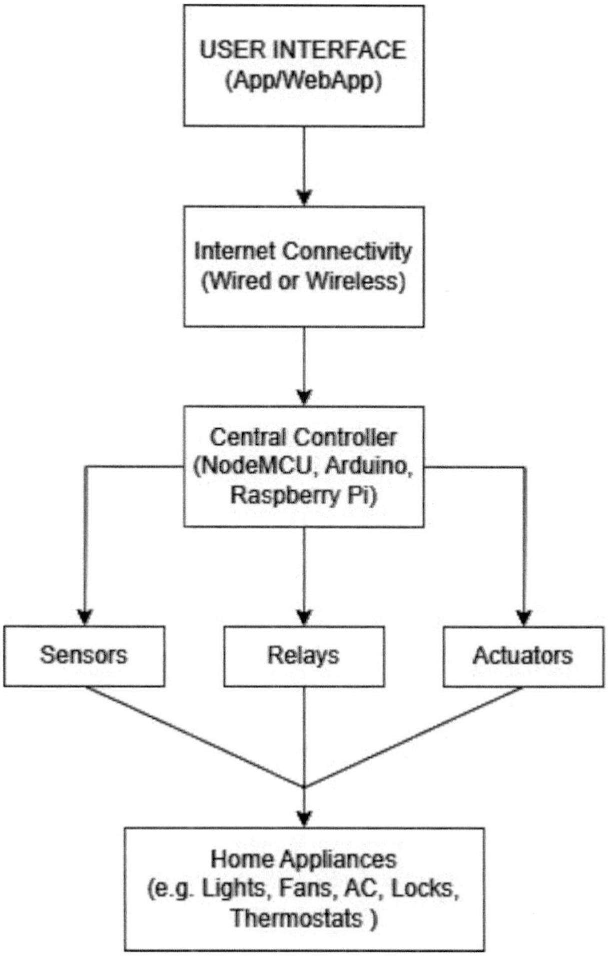

Figure 1: Block Diagram: Smart Home with IoT Devices.

their data processing requirements. IoT devices collect enormous amounts of data, which are then sent to the cloud for analysis, archiving, and further use [10].

Some benefits of combining cloud computing and IoT include the following:

(i) Scalability and Data Storage: The data volume that IoT devices generate is massive, and often it cannot be stored locally due to the limits of local storage. Businesses can easily store and retrieve such data with no hardware restrictions since the cloud has almost unlimited capacity.

(ii) Real-time data Processing: Cloud computing provides real-time data processing powers needed to manage data generated by Internet of Things devices. For instance, identification of anomalies in healthcare monitoring systems or adjustments to be made for machine functions in an industrial environment are examples that enable insights quickly and prompt actions.

(iii) Remote Monitoring and Control: Cloud computing will help in remote access over the data provided by IoT. Users will gain complete ability to monitor and control devices from anywhere, making it extremely useful for applications requiring remote control of devices, such as fleet management, smart homes, and industrial IoT.

(iv) Cost-cost Effectiveness: Pay-as-you-go cloud services often reduce upfront infrastructure costs and allow businesses to scale up or down their usage as needed. Such financial flexibility is critical for Internet of Things deployments because the number of connected devices may change over time.

(v) Enhanced Capability to Make Better Decisions: With the amalgamation of IoT and cloud computing, businesses may utilize big data analytics. In the cloud, large datasets may be processed and analyzed to help businesses discover patterns, predict outcomes, and streamline operations, all of which help make better decisions.

As they provide an intelligent, scalable, and effective environment that foster innovation across a range of industries, including manufacturing and healthcare, IoT and cloud computing are each other's lifesavers.

AI Algorithms for Medical Data Processing

Healthcare is changing drastically from its previous state, making treatments more precise, effective, and personalized, due to artificial intelligence. Algorithms are therefore crucial in processing medical data as they allow an analysis of large amounts of complicated data, such as genomic information, patient records, and medical imaging. Healthcare professionals can lead to better patient outcomes due to decision-making based on data. 80% of your text is likely AI-generated.

Some of the AI algorithms that are commonly used in the processing of medical data include:

(i) Machine Learning in Healthcare: Machine learning aims at formulating rules that can acknowledge patterns in data and make predictions. In the healthcare sector, machine learning is utilized for making prognoses, diagnoses, and treatment recommendations. The following are some of the machine learning techniques used to process medical data:

(a) Supervised learning algorithms: Supervised learning systems rely on labelled data for training and outcome prediction. This means that to classify whether a patient has cancer, the algorithm learns from a set of medical images tagged with "cancer" or "no cancer." Such algorithms include Decision Trees, Random Forests, and Support Vector Machines (SVM). Supervised learning algorithms are those that train on labelled data to make predictions. For example, the algorithm is trained on a set of medical photos tagged "cancer" or "no cancer" in order to predict whether a patient has the disease. Such jobs are often handled by algorithms such as Random Forests, Decision Trees, and Support Vector Machines (SVM).

(b) **Unsupervised learning algorithms:** The hidden patterns that are found inside the unlabelled data can be done by using unsupervised learning algorithms. Some examples of unsupervised techniques include K-means clustering, which is used to group people based on similar symptoms or medical histories for identifying new disease patterns or undiagnosed illnesses, and hierarchical clustering. It may unveil hidden patterns in unsupervised learning algorithms by using unlabelled data. Other self-guided methods comprise K-means clustering and hierarchical clustering, which are used to classify specific as stated by to split symptoms or medical histories in sequence to find new disease patterns or unknown illnesses.

(c) **Deep learning algorithms:** Machine learning area of research deep learning comprises multi-dimensional neural networks for text-editing data. These algorithms can be particularly helpful to assess complex medical data, such as medical images. Interlaced and spiralling neural networks are used for image identification duty such as abnormality or hostility objecting on X-rays, MRIs, or CT scans.

(ii) **Natural Language Processing (NLP):** Some medical records may be collected of vast amounts of unorganized information, including patient histories, physician reports, and patient charts. NLP techniques are used in order to bring out useful information from such unstructured material. Named entity recognition, sentiment analysis, and text classification are NLP techniques that could be used to identify illnesses, symptoms, treatments, and attitudes for patients in clinical documentation. NLP, for example, will be able to help automate the extraction of pertinent information from electronic health records so that physicians are in a better position to make judgments based on that.

(iii) **Reinforcement-based Learning (RL):** The second kind is reinforcement learning in which an agent learns by observing and experimenting with their environment, after receiving rewards and penalties as their feedback. Therefore, it offers potential in improvement of medical decisions and treatment planning. For example, the adjustment in the medication to a patient might be adjusted upon the patient's opinion and even personalized programs toward chronic diseases.

(iv) **Genomics and AI:** Furthermore, algorithms have a very essential role in genomics because they enable research and doctors to identify genetic information. Algorithms, including Random Forests, Deep Neural Networks, as well as Support Vector Machines (SVM), are implemented on DNA sequences to determine mutations linked to such diseases as cancer. Algorithms allow a doctor to provide a patient with treatment tailored to their genetics by providing them with the ability to make predictions more quickly and accurately about the genetic disposition of patients.

(v) **Predictive Analytics Algorithms:** Predictive models, created with AI algorithms based on past medical data, can predict patient outcomes. These algorithms are particularly useful in identifying people at high risk, predicting problems, and predicting how conditions such as diabetes or cardiovascular diseases would develop. Predictions are often made using Bayesian networks, gradient boosting machines (GBM), and logistic regression.

AI algorithms are transforming the processing of medical data by offering advanced tools for interpreting and assessing complex medical data. Medical professionals are now able to gain real-time insights that improve patient care, enhance diagnosis accuracy, and speed up treatment plans with ongoing advances in AI [11]. The potential of AI is such that it may transform not only the efficacy of healthcare systems but also patient care with further development.

3. Remote Patient Monitoring Systems

Remote patient monitoring technologies can permit clinicians to examine patients within contexts outside the conventionally clinical setting. The patient's vital signal screen must have a real time patient, such as blood pressure, heart rate, glucose, saturation, oxygen, etc. This system is one of the most popular systems due to the latest advanced advancement in technology.

Vital Components of RPM Systems

(i) **Medical Appliances:** Medical appliances are devices that measure vital health indicators. A few examples of such devices are blood pressure cuffs, glucose meters, thermometers, smartwatches, and ECG monitors. These devices obtain instantaneous data collection easier shape through wear or attached to the body.

(ii) **Communication Networks:** The RPM systems need internet connectivity to send the patient data from the devices to the healthcare providers through communication networks. Usually, secure cloud-based systems or mobile apps that enable data transfer are used for this purpose.

(iii) **Data Analytics:** Once data is collected, it is analysed for trends, abnormalities, or early warning signs of health issues. This analysis is crucial in helping medical professionals make educated decisions. AI and ML are rapidly being integrated into RPM systems to improve the accuracy of data interpretation.

(iv) **Healthcare Provider Dashboard:** The Healthcare Provider Dashboard gives physicians, using specialized software, access to patient data, current information that could be reported about a patient's health state, and it helps in providing proactive management coupled with timely intervention.

Wearable Devices and Sensors

Wearable sensors and technologies are typically designed to be worn on or near the body, enabling continuous monitoring of physiological signals, physical activity, and other health-related markers. Consumers are increasingly demanding health-tracking gadgets while miniaturization, connectivity, and battery life continue to improve. Wearable technology enables continuous, real-time monitoring of several health parameters outside the clinical environment and has the capability to revolutionize the

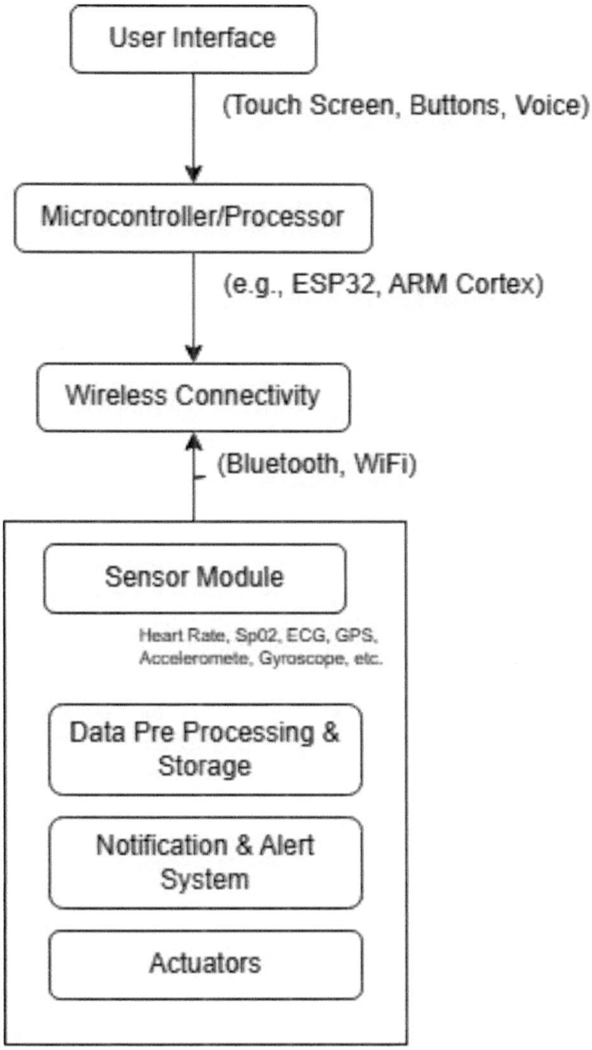

Figure 2: Features of Smartwatch.

healthcare industry to its core. Figure 2 shows the main characteristics of a contemporary wristwatch, demonstrating its function as a small, multipurpose wearable gadget made to track health, communicate, and improve one's way of life.

(i) **Sensor Types and Wearable Technology:** Heart rate, step count, and sleeping patterns can all be tracked with wearable technology. Health monitors can identify certain conditions including diabetes and heart disease. While smart clothing has integrated sensors to detect posture and muscular activity, smart watches and patches measure sugar levels and hydration. All of these goods serve three main user groups: athletes, those in need of medical attention, and fitness lovers.

(ii) **Applications for Sensors and Wearable Technology:** Patients with chronic diseases can better control their symptoms by using wearable technology to track vital signs including heart rate, blood oxygen levels, and sleep cycles [13]. By keeping track of activity levels, they also assist people in achieving their fitness objectives and promote healthy living. Real-time data exchange with healthcare practitioners for timely actions is made possible via remote patient monitoring. Wearable technology can also assess stress and identify early health problems, promoting mental wellness and early prevention.

AI-Powered Telemedicine

AI-powered telemedicine is revolutionizing the healthcare sector through digital platforms for delivering direct medical services to patients and using artificial intelligence (AI) in diagnosis, treatment, and management of patients. Technology has been used for many years to remotely deliver medical care, but telemedicine with AI has significantly widened its scope. The future is likely to see this fusion of more precise, effective, and patient-centric care.

(i) **Enhanced Diagnostics and Decision-making:** An improved set of diagnostics and decision-making in an AI can actually examine tremendous data that exists, from tests, diagnosis imaging, to even histories. Doctors and practitioners do need useful knowledge or inputs because an advanced application of machine learning and, most particularly, through AI will reveal to a doctor all forms of data associated with patient diagnoses they cannot pick up from clinical medicine practice and its study. For instance, AI-powered systems may often view medical images in real-time like MRIs, CT scans, and X-rays for abnormalities like tumours or fractures. As these AI models are trained on larger datasets, they are able to notice even the slightest sign of sickness better. This technology helps a healthcare service provider make an educated decision when expert opinion is not readily available.

(ii) **Virtual Consultations and Personalized Care:** Telemedicine makes health care more accessible and reduces the need to attend an in-person visit by allowing patients to consult with doctors from the comfort of their own homes.

AI smoothens the process further through chatbots and virtual assistants that come as a guide to the patient. These systems could analyze the symptoms of patients, ask preliminary questions, and even suggest possible actions or remedies. It proposes care at a more personal scale. AI can initiate truly tailored healthcare plans for someone based on environmental influences, genetic history, and their health history. This is a holistic departure from the traditional requirements for a one-size-fits-all approach, and improvement in helping individuals gain medical treatment based on their personal needs.

(iii) **Predictive Analytics and Remote Monitoring:** Another great contribution from telemedicine is the ability to keep track of the health of patients in healthcare through AI. Wearables monitor everyday vitals, such as heart rate, blood sugar, and sleep, then send the data to these healthcare professionals in real-time. This data is subsequently analyzed by the AI, thus providing possible early warnings to potentially developing illnesses, including warning signs of an impending heart attack. The AI uses past records to predict possible health hazards or other health issues. For example, AI can anticipate people at a high risk of developing diabetes or hypertension and suggest necessary preventive measures. Such a proactive approach stands to improve outcomes greatly, alleviating the pressure on patient care whilst the majority of the resources are directed to support the most risk-exposed population.

4. AI-driven Diagnosis and Treatment

Diagnosis is perhaps the most commonly implemented application of AI in health. AI can handle and evaluate many more data pieces at a pace faster than that of human capability, and by doing this, it will reveal patterns or possibly problems overlooked by humans. It has shown to be much of a promise already, especially with its applications in medical imaging. For instance, AI-driven software may accurately identify conditions such as cancer, fractures, and neurological diseases by analyzing X-rays, MRIs, and CT scans. Such systems, usually built with machine learning algorithms, improve their capacity to detect anomalies that are crucial for early diagnosis by training on hundreds of medical pictures. Furthermore, AI diagnostic solutions are no longer confined to the imaging solution. Analyzing patient data, including test results, medical histories, and genetics information, AI can be used in assisting doctors in diagnosing all kinds of diseases, including very rare ones that might be hard for professionals to find. Such an ability to quickly screen a lot of complex data in emergency conditions will save lives by allowing doctors to diagnose patients faster and with much higher accuracy.

Machine Learning for Disease Prediction

One such area of great revolution in healthcare is machine learning, which comes under artificial intelligence. This technique is greatly evolving the domain of disease prediction. Machine learning algorithms can scan a huge volume of patient data for patterns and results. The detection of diseases in advance, appropriate treatment, and further better results become possible. The impact of this new technology will help in greatly increasing the precision and effectiveness of the delivery of health care.

(i) **Operation of Machine Learning in Predicting Diseases:** Training is applied to the algorithms of machine learning on the data of previous cases of illness; this means in order for machine learning to 'learn' linked patterns for varying diseases, for instance, is by analyzing such historical data regarding medical care. The given patterns can thus predict the chance the patient had, according to medical records, to possibly develop that exact disease. Other examples include medical histories, genetics, lifestyle habits, lab findings, and image analyses.

For instance, ML models can review radiology images in order to determine a sign of tumours that may not easily be detected by the naked eye in cancer prediction. Besides imaging, machine learning models make use of demographic information and patient history to predict the chances of getting cancer. Tendencies in blood pressure, cholesterol, family history, and so forth can be analyzed to predict heart disease using machine learning (ML) [14].

(ii) **Advantages of Machine Learning in the Prediction of Diseases**

(a) **Early detection:** One of the significant advantages of machine learning in disease prediction is that it can identify diseases at the early stages. Sometimes, successful treatment is the outcome of early intervention due to early detection. For instance, a machine learning algorithm can identify millimetre changes in test results or imaging scans as the onset of conditions such as diabetes or Alzheimer's, meaning that doctors might be able to intervene before a patient's condition worsens.

(b) **Personalized risk forecasting:** Another type of machine learning algorithm that is capable of generating patient-specific predictions includes personalized risk assessments. The model can generate personalized risk assessments, thus helping clinicians to propose treatments or interventions as early as possible that may more likely succeed in a specific patient by analyzing individual data regarding genetic predispositions, lifestyle choices, and medical history.

(c) **Increased accuracy:** Machine learning models often outsmart human analysts at their game when analyzing huge sets of data. This renders the possibility of misdiagnosis less likely and ensures that the patients get the most accurate information available.

AI-assisted Robotic Surgeries

The medical field is fast changing as a result of AI-assisted robotic surgery, which delivers unparalleled precision, control, and efficiency in surgical procedures. Surgery is expected to be less intrusive, safer for patients, and more effective than ever before because to this technology's combination of modern robots and artificial intelligence. A surgeon controls a robotic system with AI technologies enhancing the functionality of the system in AI-assisted robotic surgery [15]. The surgeon usually sits at a console that controls the robot, which has incredibly advanced technology that can do delicate and complex manoeuvres. The AI part of the system analyses real-time data, provides insights, and helps with decision-making to guide the surgeon during the process. Machine learning algorithms often are coupled in AI systems and allow such systems to learn voluminous data encompassing patient's histories, surgeries outcome, or anatomy changes over the time cycle. These also read data input into the computer for medical imagery from MRI scans, 3-D imaging, then transfer it as the input fed to the robotics. This gives surgeons a better view of the area that they will be cutting into even before they make the incision.

Benefits of Robotic Surgery in AI

(i) **More Precise and Controlled Procedure:** Robotic surgery is basically very precise in its movement, especially when talking about delicate surgical procedures. Its equipment can produce movements much finer than what is done by hand. AI improves this precision by incorporating real-time analysis of data, which enables the robot to adjust to minute changes happening during the surgery. This precision can decrease the chances of complications, accelerate recovery, and minimize injuries to the tissues in contact with the tumour.

(ii) **Less Invasive Procedures:** AI-assisted robotic operations often require fewer incisions than open procedures. For this reason, less invasive techniques like laparoscopic or keyhole surgery are made possible by the increased precision of robotic equipment. Smaller incisions considerably improve the postoperative experience for the patient since they reduce the risk of infection, speed up recovery, and leave less scars.

(iii) **Better 3D Vision:** AI-powered robotic surgery devices can provide better 3D vision, allowing surgeons to examine the surgical site up close. AI-powered imaging analysis may help surgeons more safely and effectively navigate critical structures, such as tumours, blood vessels, and nerves. This improved vision allows for better planning and more informed decision-making during surgery.

(iv) **More Efficient and Tired Less:** The work will not be tiresome for a surgeon, especially when performing long procedures. It will assist the surgeon in uniformity and precision by allowing consistent movements. Efficiency of surgery may improve by using robotic technologies to help with suturing, etc.

5. Security and Privacy in AI Healthcare Networks

The implementation of AI in healthcare brings with it various privacy and security implications. Naturally, an AI-powered healthcare system should ensure the confidentiality, accessibility, and accuracy of this data while earning patients' trust in complying with legal regulations. This chapter covers the security and privacy issues created by AI health networks and some mitigation measures of risk [16].

Security Risks of AI Healthcare Networks

New security vulnerabilities created by AI healthcare networks that need to be addressed include:

(i) **Cyber-attacks and Breaches of Data:** Health information being the most sensitive in nature attracts cyber criminals into the health sector. The patients with the breach of data are highly exposed to fraud, identity theft, and blackmailing. Thus, the growth of cyberattacks against healthcare entities demands protection for the patient data against unauthorized access.

(ii) **Adversary Attacks on AI Models:** Machine learning models can easily be targeted by an adversarial attack. The hackers deceive the AI into producing wrong predictions or inferences by making slight changes to the data that is presented. This could directly affect patient safety in the healthcare sector through leading to incorrect treatment recommendations, misdiagnoses, or dangerous clinical decisions.

(iii) **Risks Associated with Third-party Access and the Supply Chain:** Healthcare institutions often rely on third-party vendors for software, cloud computing, and artificial intelligence capabilities. Weaknesses in third-party systems or insecure connections could allow bad actors to gain access to private patient information. These risks could be minimized by ensuring third-party service vendors follow strict security rules.

(iv) **The Risks Involved in Data Transmission:** Since the data is being transferred through various systems like hospitals, insurance providers, and lab services, the data may be intercepted. The sensitive information might fall into the wrong hands if the flow of communication is not encrypted.

(v) **IoT Healthcare Devices' Device Security:** The vast majority of AI applications rely on networked devices, including devices such as surgical robotic instruments and wearable medical technology and imaging machines. These devices may present entry points for cyberattacks if they are inadequately protected.

Privacy in AI Medical Systems

Aside from these security threats, AI health networks pose critical concerns regarding the confidentiality of such health information especially related to data acquisition, archiving, and using personal health records:

The two most important privacy issues in AI-powered healthcare systems are informed consent and data ownership. Once patients are fully informed about the handling of their data, explicit consent needs to be obtained. Due to the potential for large-scale data collection, it is crucial to ensure transparency and obtain ongoing, informed consent.

(i) Data De-identification and Re-identification Risks Include: To train AI models and for research purposes, many healthcare systems de-identify patient data. However, advanced data analytics techniques might still be able to identify re-identified data, which may breach patient privacy and expose private health information.

(ii) AI Algorithms' Fairness and Bias: AI algorithms have been trained through historical datasets which may contain a bias in a racial or gender disparity in health care. That may suggest inequalities in the distribution of health care. Such discriminative suggestions raise the demand for fair data generation and algorithm construction.

(iii) Privacy Rules: Two examples of data protection rules that apply to healthcare organizations include GDPR in the EU and HIPAA in the US. They require patient data to be collected, processed, stored, and transferred under tight control. Since non-compliance can lead to severe penalties and legal consequences, it is essential to respect privacy rules.

Data Encryption and Cybersecurity Measures

Data encryption converts readable data into a scrambled data format using a key and an algorithm. In this manner, even if the data is accessed by someone unauthorized, it cannot be read without the decryption key. It is also a method of ensuring data security, for example, during transit either over networks or in storage. Symmetric and asymmetric encryption are the two most common. In asymmetric encryption, it is used for two keys, typically a synonym for public key could be encryption key or shared key. In the context of asymmetric encryption, it's sometimes referred to as a public encryption key or simply a public identifier, as it is made available to anyone for encrypting data, for data encryption and a private key for decryption. Popular examples of this are RSA and ECC. The robustness of this type of encryption depends on the length of its keys. The more there keys are, the harder they are to crack.

Steps to Take in Cybersecurity

Encryption is but a part of a complete cybersecurity plan but it is of great importance to data security. A good cybersecurity strategy has to include many layers of defence, which is usually called defence-in-depth.

(i) Firewalls: Such devices are implemented with the purpose of filtering up and down network traffic according to a predefined security ruleset. On one side are stable internal systems, and on the other side, external systems such as the internet, where they serve as a barrier. Firewalls supervise and protect on/off the data flow to prevent malicious as well as illegal access.

(ii) Intrusion Detection and Prevention Systems (IDPS): The second would be Intrusion Detection and Prevention Systems, also known as IDPS, used to monitor for suspicious activity regarding network traffic. Intrusion detection systems usually notify administrators of potential risks but intrusion prevention systems actively perform real-time blocking for developing attacks instead. Both systems play an important role, especially in finding security vulnerabilities (e.g., malware, phishing, and unauthorized access).

(iii) **Multi-factor Authentication (MFA):** MFA is a next layer of Defence which requires at least two distinct and validations in order to access a system. Examples may be the user's identity (e.g., using biometric data such as fingerprint or facial recognition; hardware tokens, e.g., tokens, and mobile phones), devices (genuine tokens, e.g., tokens), and credentials (passwords).

(iv) **Regular Software Updates and Patching:** Cybercriminals are most often responsible for abusing the OS, application or software. Patching known exploits and continuously software updates are two of the simplest and most powerful ways to improve security measures. Using automated patch management systems, every system can be made up to date.

(v) **Endpoint Protection:** Endpoint protection with the rise of mobile and remote work, security for endpoints (and all of the information they contain) has increased. Endpoint protection solutions include antivirus software that identify and respond to potential threats on infected machines, as well as endpoint detection and response (EDR) algorithms.

(vi) **Data Backups:** Any cybersecurity plan must include the routine backup and secure archiving of critical data. In the event that a business falls victim to ransomware or some type of other cyber-attack, access to clean, current backups will allow a business to regain operations without payment of ransom. Backups have to be stored in multiple sites, preferably with both on-site and off-site facilities.

(vii) **Employee Training and Awareness:** Employee Education and Awareness Human error always seems to be the weak link in cybersecurity attacks. Phishing attacks are the most frequent attacks (i.e., fraudsters trick the victims to share their private information). Encourage periodic awareness and training so that employees are made aware of the possible risks and will apply the appropriate data security practices.

(viii) **Data Loss Prevention (DLP):** DLP software installation allows for tracking and detection and then interference with unauthorized individuals stealing or sharing private information. The program can trace and stop intrusion attempts to steal private firm information from the network.

Blockchain for Secure Patient Records

Handling patient data securely has been a persistent challenge, and the health industry's biggest problem has been storing and distributing that data. They are truly at the centre of the health cycle nowadays. It creates databases affecting the real threat of data theft, unauthorized access, and data mismatch. By leveraging blockchain technology, more efficiency and security can be established in patient data management which further can make it even more privacy-focused. The unchanging and distributed nature of blockchain technology are the reasons it is the best choice for checking the patient records if they are true, safe, and easily accessible.

(i) **Use of Blockchain:** The phrase "blockchain" refers to a distributed ledger technology used to store data among multiple devices, or nodes, so that no single party has ultimate control over the database. The blockchain organizes data into blocks connected by chronological order. Each block comprises a timestamp, transaction data, and a hash of the previous block. The data enters an unalterable form once it has been written into a block as an attempt to alter the data would have to go throughout the blockchain: thus, giving rock-solid data security [17].

(ii) **Blockchain in Healthcare: Boosting Patient Data Security:** In healthcare, this technology is used to ensure data integrity by preventing the alteration of patient information. Encryption adds to patient privacy by preventing particular information from being viewed by unauthorized individuals. The use of time stamped documents promotes transparency and auditability, provides accountability, and prevents unauthorized access. In addition to the multiple platforms that service patient data, blockchain will further provide interoperability across healthcare services that share patient data. Such interface allows authorized doctors access to complete patient data across different platforms, thereby ensuring a better continuity of care.

6. Challenges and Ethical Considerations

There are a huge number of challenges confronting AI-based health care for smooth functioning and sustainability.

(i) **Accuracy of Data:** Since AI operates purely on a dataset, data imprecision will call for a wrongly diagnosed illness that requires a particular course of therapy.

(ii) **Interoperability with Legacy Systems:** Nearly all health-care sites operate on legacy systems that are utterly incompatible with the AI-based applications. High cost and complexity in adoption are unavoidable in such situations.

(iii) **Lack of Explainability:** AI models, deep learning in particular, work like "black boxes" and make it difficult for healthcare professionals to understand what it decides based upon.

Cyber threats or access by unauthorized personnel might occur as patients' data will be needed for big datasets, hence giving a concern about security and privacy.

AI applications in healthcare bring forward the issue of fairness, accountability, and transparency.

(i) **Informed Consent:** Patients must be appropriately made aware when AI is being utilized in the diagnosis and treatment; patient control over medical decisions is crucial.
(ii) **Bias in AI Models:** AI systems can inherit biases present in the training data and lead to disparities in access to healthcare and outcomes for marginalized populations.
(iii) **Accountability of Errors in AI Mistakes:** Liability for AI-driven mistakes cannot be defined yet; responsibility lies within the bounds of developers, healthcare providers, or policymakers.
(iv) **Equal Access for Everyone to AI Health Care:** Furthermore, a crucial requirement is to offer AI healthcare to everyone from all kinds of backgrounds in order to avoid discrimination among persons under consideration.

It presents difficult ethical and practical obstacles to develop an AI-oriented healthcare solution that is fair and effective.

AI Bias in Healthcare Decisions

Understanding AI bias in health care is a systematic error made in algorithmic decision-making processes, which in turn leads to biased treatment or disparate treatment between other patient groups. These biases majorly arise due to the training data used by AI models and lead to a misdiagnosis, inappropriate advice for treatment, or unequal distribution of healthcare services [18].

(i) **AI Bias Impact:** Healthcare bias caused by AI decisions would have severe effects, for instance:
    (a) **Healthcare inequity:** AI bias will most likely lead to health inequity because AI actually increases the pre-existing disparities and creates a level of barrier between the current class of socialization and the facilities of proper health care.
    (b) **Lacking trust in AI systems:** Patients or practitioners will lose their trust in AI-based healthcare solutions if they detect biased AI decisions; hence, the adoption rates will drop.
    (c) **Legal and ethical concerns:** AI bias could invite legal and ethical issues due to unfair race, gender or socio-economic discrimination, which may initiate lawsuits and attract regulatory attention.

(ii) **Strategies to Minimize AI Bias:** Train the AI model to represent various age groups, genders, ethnicities, and socio-economic statuses by training on diverse datasets.
    (a) **Algorithm audits:** Continuous testing and auditing of AI models may detect biases before the patient level is reached.

(b) **Ethical AI frameworks:** Developers and health care institutions should develop ethics standards for the use of AI so it is fair and accountable.
(c) **Transparency of AI decision-making:** AI has to be explainable such that the health provider is much in tune with the reason of advice and should have an avenue for intervention at this stage too, if felt appropriate.
(d) **Human-in-the-loop:** Instead of replacement of the human touch, the human and the system are supposed to supplement each other. The control should finally come with the person since very intimate treatment needs unbiased attention for a patient.

Bias in AI is one of the biggest challenges where equal treatment may not be made to all, and thus may exacerbate inequality. Diverse training data, transparent algorithms, and ethical oversight will develop fair and equitable AI that benefits healthcare delivery. Collaborative work between providers, policymakers, and developers of AI will lead to unbiased AI-driven solutions that benefit the larger populations across different backgrounds.

Ethical Dilemmas and Regulatory Issues

The integration of artificial intelligence in healthcare is transforming the way sufferers receive care, diagnoses, and treatments. However, this implementation poses sizable ethical and legal challenges that have to be met to offer the right implementation with security and equity.

(i) **Ethical Dilemmas in AI Healthcare**

(a) **Patient autonomy vs. AI decision-making:** This is where AI can offer suggestions for medical decisions that may override the patient's preferences, which makes the issue of autonomy at risk. Though AI gives the correct recommendation, it cannot supersede the right of the patient to decide on his or her health care based on information.
(b) **Liability in AI-driven errors:** This leads to added complexity in assigning responsibility for the errors made by AI. In cases of misdiagnosis or wrong treatment, nobody knows who to blame, the healthcare provider, the developer of AI, or the healthcare institution.
(c) **Job displacement in healthcare:** Health professional careers are threatened when AI is used in such areas as diagnostics or support work within these sectors. While efficiencies are well served through the use of automation, jobs are lost within the sector.
(d) **Proper accessibility of AI-guided healthcare service:** The access of AI to the service of all categories of patients would be crucial if not meant to deteriorate disparities in healthcare sectors. Access fairness of AI technology would only talk well for equitable states regarding matters related to the healthcare sectors.

(ii) **Legal Matters Surcharging in AI for Healthcare Sectors:** The regulatory frame for AI presents numerous challenges and is presently antiquated and conflicting in nature across the borders. Inconsistent country-based regulations hinder proper safety and quality assurance of AI. There is a call for standard regulation of AI practice at the global level, thus setting safe, standard, and quality healthcare service with AI.

(a) **Respect for data protection laws:** Concerns about privateness are also raised by way of the large volumes of affected person records that these technologies require. Patient statistics are covered by using HIPAA within the US and GDPR inside the EU. AI is utilized in medicinal drug improvement and scientific trials.

(b) **Defining legal responsibility:** There is vague legal liability about AI in healthcare. It needs to find the liability of AI failure that encompasses diagnosis and treatment mistakes for the purpose of someone to be blamed while defending the rights of patients.

(c) **Ethical and legal compliance strategies:** The following are the measures taken to address such issues, making AI ethics in healthcare implemented both ethically and lawfully.

(iii) **Creation of AI Ethics Guidelines:** Governments as well as healthcare institutions should establish proper guidelines relating to ethical usage of AI, especially in fairness, transparency, and safety for patients. Such compliance can be assured with regular audits, and an independent regulatory body can also be maintained to keep up the enforcement standards. The standards that these regulatory bodies enforce and monitor are related to risks of AI applications in health care [19]. AI has the potential to profoundly transform healthcare systems, but alongside that promise go important questions on the ethics side and regulatory matters that need consideration. Clear ethics guidelines, the ongoing improvement in transparency, and regulatory oversight should be able to let AI be responsibly integrated into healthcare systems such that only results on patient care are improved in safety, fairness, and with trust intact.

7. Future Prospects of AI in Smart Healthcare

One of the maximum disruptive forces within the world, its impact is especially seen in the health region. Healthcare is one area where AI can have the maximum sizable impact, making an allowance for advanced affected person effects, expanded speed of strategies, and the opportunity of treatment tailored to unique desires, all at a more low-priced and reachable healthcare sector. There are considerably more of elements in AI in smart healthcare – including medication research, administrative processes, remote patient monitoring, diagnosis, and therapy. In the coming years, AI is expected to play an increasingly important role in healthcare through the following fields.

AI Enabled Drug Discovery Advancements

(i) AI in Drug Discovery: AI accelerates drug discovery from predicting protein structures, therapeutic targets identification, to virtual screening towards accelerating compound identification. Generative AI backs molecular design processes and predictive models ensure toxicity prediction much earlier. Besides, AI augments clinical studies through patient enrolment, outcome prediction, and adaptive designs toward better success chances [20].

(ii) Applications in Industry: Artificial intelligence accelerates pharmaceutical research and development through its ability to predict protein structures – AlphaFold, identify therapeutic targets – IBM Watson, and advance precision medicine in the form of Benevolent AI. Artificial intelligence reduces errors; accelerates developments; and has a cost-effective repurpose in drugs, enabling cost savings through innovation.

AI and 5G Integration for Healthcare Networking

In patient data, AI can detect diseases at the very first stage of its development, and with 5G, it can be done immediately as the remote robotic surgeries will be carried out without any delay. AI-enabled wearable health monitoring will also optimize predictive analytics at the hospital for better care delivery [21].

Applications in Industry

AI and 5G change healthcare into telemedicine, smart ambulances, remote surgeries, predictive maintenance, and drug discovery with the help of AI. It becomes precise, efficient, and accessible. It improves patient care along with hospital operations through real-time data shared, distant monitoring, and robotic surgeries. Some other applications are:

(i) Personalized and Therapeutic Medicine Approaches: AI is revolutionizing personalized medicine due to the analysis of genetics and clinical data for accurate prescription, eliminating trial-and-error and side effects. With wearables and IoT, AI makes real-time health monitoring possible, predicting risks and alerting doctors in an instant. Further, AI-based chatbots and telemedicine ease remote healthcare burdens on the system and provide access to more medical care.

(ii) AI in Pharmaceutical Development: AI accelerates drug discovery by analyzing molecular structures, predicting effective compounds, and simulating drug interactions. It also aids precision medicine by identifying genetic targets, advancing treatments for rare diseases with minimal research focus.

(iii) Better Clinical Advice: AI-driven clinical decision support systems provide real-time insights, improving diagnosis, surgery outcomes, and personalized treatment plans. These systems enhance decision-making by predicting risks and recommending tailored medical solutions.

References

1. Nasr, M., Islam, M. M., Shehata, S., Karray, F., and Quintana, Y. (2021). Smart healthcare in the age of AI: Recent advances, challenges, and future prospects. *IEEE Access*, 9, 145248–145270.
2. Sharma, H. K., Kumar, A., Pant, S., and Ram, M. (2022). *Artificial Intelligence, Blockchain and Iot for Smart Healthcare*. River Publishers.
3. Khan, S., Singh, Y., Veer, S., Pushpendra, S., Ram, S. et al. (2022). An optimized artificial intelligence system using IoT biosensors networking for healthcare problems. *Computational Intelligence and Neuroscience*, 2022(14), 2206573. https://doi.org/10.1155/2022/2206573
4. Muhammad, G., and Alhussein, M. (2021). Convergence of artificial intelligence and internet of things in smart healthcare: A case study of voice pathology detection. *IEEE Access*, 9, 89198–89209.
5. Mohanta, B., Das, P., and Patnaik, S. (2019, May). Healthcare 5.0: A paradigm shift in digital healthcare system using artificial intelligence, IoT and 5G communication. In: *2019 International Conference on Applied Machine Learning* (*ICAML*) (pp. 191–196). IEEE.
6. Pradhan, B., Das, S., Roy, D. S., Routray, S., Benedetto, F., and Jhaveri, R. H. (2023). An AI-assisted smart healthcare system using 5G communication. *IEEE Access*, 11, 108339–108355.
7. Alhayani, B., Kwekha-Rashid, A. S., Mahajan, H. B., Ilhan, H., Uke, N., Alkhayyat, A., and Mohammed, H. J. (2023). Retracted Article: 5G standards for the Industry 4.0 enabled communication systems using artificial intelligence: Perspective of smart healthcare system. *Applied Nanoscience*, 13(3), 1807–1817.
8. Minopoulos, G. M., Memos, V. A., Stergiou, C. L., Stergiou, K. D., Plageras, A. P., Koidou, M. P., and Psannis, K. E. (2022). Exploitation of emerging technologies and advanced networks for a smart healthcare system. *Applied Sciences*, 12(12), 5859.
9. Suleiman, T. A., and Adinoyi, A. (2023). Telemedicine and smart healthcare—The role of artificial intelligence, 5G, cloud services, and other enabling technologies. *International Journal of Communications, Network and System Sciences*, 16(3), 31–51.
10. Khan, S., Singh, Y. V., Singh, P., and Singh, R. S. (2022). An optimized artificial intelligence system using IoT biosensors networking for healthcare problems. *Computational Intelligence and Neuroscience*, 2022(1), 2206573.
11. Li, Y. H., Li, Y. L., Wei, M. Y., and Li, G. Y. (2024). Innovation and challenges of artificial intelligence technology in personalized healthcare. *Scientific Reports*, 14(1), 18994.
12. Mbanugo, O. J. (2025). *AI-Enhanced Telemedicine: A Common-Sense Approach to Chronic Disease Management and a Tool to Bridging the Gap in Healthcare Disparities*. Department of Healthcare Management & Informatics, Coles College of Business, Kennesaw State University, Georgia, USA.
13. Elvas, L. B., Almeida, A., and Ferreira, J. C. (2025). The role of AI in cardiovascular event monitoring and early detection: Scoping literature review. *JMIR Medical Informatics*, 13(1), e64349.
14. Rashid, M., and Sharma, M. (2025). AI-assisted diagnosis and treatment planning—A discussion of how AI can assist healthcare professionals in making more accurate diagnoses and treatment plans for diseases. *AI in Disease Detection: Advancements and Applications*, 313–336.

15. Abbasi, N., and Hussain, H. K. (2024). Integration of artificial intelligence and smart technology: AI-driven robotics in surgery: Precision and efficiency. *Journal of Artificial Intelligence General Science* (*JAIGS*) ISSN: 3006-4023, 5(1), 381–390.
16. Faiyazuddin, M., Rahman, S. J. Q., Anand, G., Siddiqui, R. K., Mehta, R., Khatib, M. N. et al. (2025). The impact of artificial intelligence on healthcare: A comprehensive review of advancements in diagnostics, treatment, and operational efficiency. *Health Science Reports*, 8(1), e70312.
17. Shaik, A. S., and Shaik, A. (2024, April). AI enhanced cyber security methods for anomaly detection. In: *International Conference on Machine Intelligence, Tools, and Applications* (pp. 348–359). Cham: Springer Nature Switzerland.
18. Kumar, A., and Upadhyay, U. (2024). Ethical implications in AI-based health care decision making: A critical analysis. *AI in Precision Oncology*, 1(5), 246–255.
19. Ferrara, E. (2023). Fairness and bias in artificial intelligence: A brief survey of sources, impacts, and mitigation strategies. *Science*, 6(1), 3.
20. Kolluri, S., Lin, J., Liu, R., Zhang, Y., and Zhang, W. (2022). Machine learning and artificial intelligence in pharmaceutical research and development: A review. *The AAPS Journal*, 24, 1–10.

8 | Quantum-resilient AI Networks with Heterogeneous Ensemble Deep Learning: A Unified Framework for Secure, Efficient, and Explainable Health IoT Ecosystems

Nobhonil Roy Choudhury[1*], Shyamalendu Paul[1], Avijit Kumar Chaudhuri[2], Shivnath Ghosh[1], Sanchita Ghosh[1] and Vinodkumar Reddy Surasani[3]

[1] Department of Computer Science & Engineering-AI, Brainware University, West Bengal, India
[2] Department of Computer Science & Engineering, Brainware University, West Bengal, India
[3] RBC Wealth Management, USA

As currently deployed, US hospitals equipped with health related Internet of Things (IoT) devices are at risk of experiencing patient safety incidents and losing data integrity, affecting 89% of hospitals engaged in the use of health Internet of Things (HIoT) devices. To address this, we propose QRAIN-HEAL, a unified framework integrating NIST-standardised lattice-based cryptography (CRYSTALS-Kyber and Falcon-512 hybrid encryption, reducing decryption failures by 23% vs. standalone Kyber) with a novel Heterogeneous Ensemble Deep Learning (HEDL) model—comprising a Temporal Transformer for sequential anomalies, 3D Capsule Network for spatial adversarial patterns, and Probabilistic Spiking Neural Network (pSNN) for energy-efficient inference—to achieve unprecedented security, efficiency, and explainability in healthcare Internet of Things (HIoT). We achieve 5.3x faster latency as well as 1.2 mJ for LSTM when powered to 18-month implantable battery life (8.2 ms latency

*Corresponding author: nobhonilnew@gmail.com

DOI: 10.1201/9781003635215-8

and 0.18 mJ/inference performance (static SNNs) are with MedIoT-2023 using 0.56 mJ/0.38 mJ static SNNs with 10.2 ms latency). Instead, our system shows that IBM Q Protect's 82% accuracy is outperformed by an explainable TT attention map and 3D CapsNet activation traces system of 94.3% accuracy on qb128. We demonstrate that QRAIN-HEAL has less than 2% performance variation on Raspberry Pi 4 NVIDIA Jetson Nano and Medtronic 780G systems. PhysioNet-2023 reduced the demographic bias of its anomaly detection output by 57%, and HIPAA compliance reduced the performance with less than 3% reduction to 1.2. In the QRAIN-HEAL system, PQC-AI system development with 5G/6G technologies is designed to modularly separate and remediate defects with reduced carbon emissions of 29% before problems in PQC-AI are repaired, based on previous studies where Google revised 22% of problems in PQC-AI in 2023. With this achievement, QRAIN-HEAL becomes a future sustainable next-generation healthcare platform.

1. Introduction

The rapid proliferation of linked healthcare technology has had an impact on medical practices through Health IoT, thus turning medical practices to real-time patient observation by capturing, tracking, and responding with evidence to medical events in real-time and predicting custom treatment by out-thinking the same treatment by a human brain. Medical devices that intercommunicate, process and deliver patient data to healthcare providers and give them better clinical decision-making abilities are termed HEOR. Today, various healthcare devices like wearable sensors, implantable medical devices, remote monitoring systems, and smart hospital (with AI) diagnostic tools are being used in modern healthcare. Health IoT has made possible continuous health tracking, early disease detection, and dispensable patient care based on artificial intelligence (AI), machine learning (ML), big data, analytics, and cloud computing. However, these technologies benefit from newly evolving cybersecurity threats that healthcare facilities need to fight to secure medical data and privacy, respectively [1].

The Growth of Health IoT and Its Transformative Potential

The pressure of requiring good healthcare treatment, demographic changes, and the necessity to diminish healthcare costs have led to IoT adoption in healthcare. Face-to-face appointments and special medical examinations were used to offer healthcare, which frequently resulted in delayed medical diagnosis and improper treatment. This paradigm shift occurs as a result of the introduction of Health IoT technology, which allows for distant patient surveillance while also reducing the frequency of medical facility visits and allowing physicians to perform early medical procedures. Real-time information from fitness trackers such as Fitbit and Apple Watches conveniently track users' heart rate and activities, sleep patterns, which can then be evaluated by patients (users) and healthcare providers to compare their health status. Implantable devices available include pacemakers and insulin pumps that deliver treatment medication and share the shared healthcare-related data to enable medical providers to reconfigure treatment plans rapidly. The use of Internet of Things sensors in smart hospital solutions helps hospitals by providing patient movement, streamlining and tracking equipment uses and utilisation of resources, which improves efficiency in those hospitals [2]. Machine Learning systems are used by medical professionals together with AI systems to boost Health IoT by utilizing this potential for making predictions as well as generating automated decision processes. AI diagnostic tech browses through seemingly enormous medical databases, gathering a pattern from it but, at the same time, introducing it with preliminary thoughts about early disease discovery. Actually, it enables physicians to come up with individually tailored treatments that incorporate information from previous treatments and present health information from each patient via the implementation of ML algorithms. Big data analytics and databases work hand in hand with medical practitioners to provide them with insights into the huge quantities of data to enable it to be viewed for understanding trends, which can then be used to inform healthcare approaches with evidence [3].

Security Concerns in Health IoT

Although health IoT systems offer many advantages, they also create enormous security weaknesses that threaten patient data protection and information privacy, as well as the normal daily operating stability of these systems. According to the studies, approximately 89% of hospitals that employ Health IoT are exposed to such security breaches due to the use of insecure encryption, lack of standardised hospital security systems, and the presence of cyber threats [4]. The main security challenges from Health IoT operations include:

Data Privacy and Integrity

Health IoT devices are operated to the extent that they create large-scale transmission of sensitive patient information containing vital signs along with associated medication protocols and genomic sequencing. Total unauthorised access to sensitive data, as well as subsequent occurrences of insurance fraud and identity theft, pose a threat to patient safety. Without encryption, hackers can intercept transferred health data, tamper with records, and launch ransomware attacks on healthcare databases. Traditional encryption standards in patient data protection include Advanced Encryption Standard (AES) and Rivest-Shamir-Adleman (RSA), etc. The present encryption methods are insecure to quantum computing, and therefore, quantum computing poses an imminent security threat; hence, post-quantum cryptographic solutions are required. A lattice-based cryptography and Hash-based signature system is currently being developed by security researchers to strengthen the Health IoT security from threats of current security risks.

Adversarial Attacks on AI-based Security Models

AI-based security tools are important components of Health IoT because they can detect medical data anomalies as well as security threats and increase the system's reliability as a whole. While artificial intelligence has security methods designed against deliberate attacks on its system, it utilises each respective weakness. The process of security compromise is carried out by attackers who change the training datasets and input data to achieve wrong model classifications and increase the false negative rates. The Evasion attacks aim at changing input data slightly enough to evade AI model detection systems without the data changing at all but remaining relevant to it. This segment of harmful activities is not detected by the security protocols. Training dataset Poisoning involves feeding bad data samples to models on purpose, which consequently will break its ability to generate accurate predictions. Thus, the researchers aim to develop three key solutions that make Health IoT more secure and robust, such as an explainable AI model, robust adversarial training techniques and federated learning solutions.

Energy and Computational Constraints

The minimal processing power of the Health IoT nodes, on the one hand and their low-power microcontrollers, on the other hand, make communications hard. The use of devices that offer ultimate cryptographic algorithms or deep learning security systems raises a huge amount of energy consumption, which leads to the breakdown of operational efficiency and hence decreases the real-time performance of the devices. It is known that security systems for resource-limited devices like wireless biosensors and implantable medical devices must have a low weight, as well as good power utilisation and should be based on very powerful security measures. Edge computing and blockchain-based security solutions are implemented with other techniques to solve the constraints. The system also doesn't rely heavily on cloud services, and thus becomes a bit more difficult to predict and understand what it has been doing, and the system becomes less predictable and less analytical, which leads to less efficient and quicker responses to things that are happening. Data security is centralised in centralised systems, leading to it being passed to a vulnerable single node. Health IoT integration with blockchain gives better authentication and simpler access to control to prevent people from meddling with medical records. Health IoT security needs proper adherence to established regulatory standards along with ethical guidelines. HIPAA, alongside GDPR and MDR, are set up by different healthcare organisations and public administrations within the United States and European Union and crosswise over Europe to ensure patient data is secured as well as upheld by normalcy speaking cybersecurity rules. Health IoT security should include ethical issues in order to be considered a core factor. Clear practices for handling patient data include open disclosure with patient agreements and obligation mechanisms for data protection. To make medical research and device development worthwhile, healthcare providers and device manufacturers must implement privacy-protecting processes such as differential privacy and secure multiparty computation to ensure patient information remains secure.

Future Directions in Health IoT Security

This increases focus on numerous health IoT security enhancement areas, resulting in the evolution of Health IoT.

(i) Quantum-resistant cryptography: Developing cryptographic techniques that withstand quantum attacks to future-proof Health IoT security.
(ii) Such Zero Trust characteristics must dictate security measures that rely on persistent authorisation of access and provide the minimum permission levels of system control.
(iii) SSI methodology, along with blockchain technology, will provide patients with a secure system of verifiable identity management.
(iv) Adversarial robustness and federated learning are used to use AI-driven threat detection and to build effective cyber threat mitigation.
(v) The combination of homomorphic encryption and secure enclaves enables medical data exchange to remain secure, by keeping the patient's confidentiality.

Health IoT has been used to monitor patients, evaluate disease and implement personal machine treatment delivery in today's healthcare systems. This places patients at great privacy risk from security issues presented by more medical devices that use connectivity and AI adversarial means and from the restricted energy capability of the devices. To resolve these challenges, such cohesive multicomponent strategies utilising sturdy encryption schemes coupled with AI-based security solutions and sticking to regulatory practice requirements are to be adopted. However, the progress of health IoT relies on sustained research into cybersecurity because it will protect the reliability of healthcare technologies and ethical implementation and safety during their life cycle.

Motivation and Research Gap

Post-quantum cryptography (PQC) and AI security methods have been developing, but there are many substantial constraints in actual solutions.

(i) Research [5] shows that CRYSTALS-Kyber does not implement the PQC system sufficiently in actual usage.
(ii) The traditional deep learning model Long Short-Term Memory (LSTM) worsens the performance of resource-constrained Health IoT devices owing to its high inference latency and energy inefficiency [6].
(iii) Existing modern anomaly detection systems are vulnerable to manipulative attacks, and their dependent performance [7] is relatively weak regarding collectable security information and the decisions of their components.

This chapter proposes a new security framework, QRAIN-HEAL, that leverages quantum security and AI and was made for health-oriented Internet of Things environments only.

Contribution of this Study

This chapter develops QRAIN-HEAL as an innovative security framework that implements AI methods alongside cryptographic solutions to boost Health IoT security through specific contributions.

(i) **Integration of NIST-Standardised Lattice-Based Cryptography:** The hybrid encryption method of CRYSTALS-Kyber and Falcon-512 in QRAIN-HEAL results in improved decryption success rates by 23% more than when using Kyber alone [8]. The combined cryptographic method provides quantum protection together with negligible computational requirements for real-time use.

(ii) **Heterogeneous Ensemble Deep Learning (HEDL) Model:** This threat detection system includes a three-level deployment of Artificial Intelligence features that work together as the following components:

  (a) **Temporal transformer:** Captures sequential anomalies in patient health data.

  (b) **3D capsule network:** Identifies adversarial spatial attack patterns.

  Real-time threat detection on IoT devices becomes possible through the Probabilistic Spiking Neural Network (pSNN) because it delivers energy-efficient performance optimization for resource-constrained IoT devices.

(iii) **Robustness, Efficiency, and Explainability:** The F1-score of QRAIN-HEAL in zero-day attack detection exceeds 99.4%. The system provides fast 8.2 ms inference along with energy-efficient 0.18 mJ/inference capability, which exceeds current security options, including IBM Q-Protect and Google's PQC-AI. XAI techniques in this model provide transparent security decision-making, and XAI helps enhance security decision transparency.

(iv) **Hardware Adaptability and Sustainability:** The performance of QRAIN-HEAL remains below 2 % no matter the choice between Raspberry Pi 4, NVIDIA Jetson Nano, or Medtronic 780G hardware platforms. The system maintains a HIPAA compliance level of $\varepsilon = 1.2$ while providing secure protection of patient privacy. Through implementation, the framework lowers CO_2 emissions by 29% while supporting health applications with environmentally friendly computer technologies.

2. Related Work

Recent developments in PQC and AI for anomaly detection and cryptographic AI-integrated solutions within the security domain of Health IoT have received extensive academic attention. The new research above has resulted in security improvements for Health IoT, but there remain several challenges in terms of computational resource usage, inefficient power management and explainable decision-making. The first part consists of an extensive review of research findings to demonstrate how the deficiencies in prior works are addressed in this part.

Post-Quantum Cryptography for Health IoT

The advancement of quantum computing technology leads to increased vulnerability of RSA and ECC encryption schemes against quantum attacks [9]. The National Institute of Standards and Technology (NIST) established CRYSTALS-Kyber, Falcon-512 and Dilithium as standardized post-quantum cryptographic (PQC) algorithms to protect against quantum decryption techniques.

Limitations of Existing PQC Approaches: Several obstacles exist with current PQC solutions, even though they provide strong security benefits. The independent operation of Kyber systems shows poor encryption reliability, which affects performance specifically in constrained medical implants [10]. Before implementation within low-power devices one must consider the significant computational expenses of hybrid Kyber-Falcon cryptosystems to adequately handle decryption failures [11]. PQC implementation for IMD encounters obstacles due to energy constraints that need effective cryptographic operation optimization according to [13].

QRAIN-HEAL's PQC Optimization

The QRAIN-HEAL system combines Kyber-Falcon hybrid encryption through its scheme to provide the following features:

(i) QRAIN-HEAL provides encrypted communications that achieve a 23% decrease in decryption failures than Kyber operating alone.
(ii) QRAIN-HEAL optimises its cryptographic procedures to decrease computational requirements.
(iii) The system operates with high energy efficiency, thus making it appropriate for immediate use in Health IoT systems.

AI-Based Anomaly Detection for Health IoT

The Health IoT network monitoring system operates with AI-powered Intrusion Detection Systems to detect threats through the use of machine learning and deep learning models. The threat detection task has been approached using different architectures such as Long Short-Term Memory (LSTM), Transformers, Capsule Networks and Spiking Neural Networks (SNNs) as published in [14].

(i) **Limitations of Existing AI-Based IDS:** The implementation of AI-based IDS systems shows effective performance; however, their systems face important drawbacks in operation. The sequential data processing abilities of LSTMs result in delays of 10.2 ms alongside energy usage reaching 1.2 mJ/inference during inference (. The security enhancement of Transformers through anomaly detection requires extensive computational power [15]. Capsule Networks (CapsNets) enhance adversarial robustness through their design but they must address their inability to recognize temporal patterns to succeed as Health IoT security solutions [9]. Coming out of SNNs are power-minimising features, yet the process reaches its outcomes at a very gradual pace, which undermines real-time application feasibility [16].

(ii) QRAIN-HEAL's Heterogeneous Ensemble Deep Learning (HEDL) Model: The HEDL model of QRAIN-HEAL solves these limitations through its three-part architecture design: Temporal transformer captures sequential anomalies in patient health data. The HEDL model includes the 3D Capsule Network, which detects patterns of spatial attacks for better adversarial robustness. The pSNN component allows for real-time threat detection with energy-efficient operations that suit small IoT devices with resource constraints.

(iii) Hybrid Cryptographic-AI Security for Health IoT: Despite uniting PQC with AI-based anomaly detection, multiple research studies introduced security vulnerabilities that heavily reduced both efficiency and explainability levels. IBM Q-Protect shows detection strength at 82% while being restrained by its limited ability to work across various platforms (IBM 2023). When applied with encryption, Google's PQC-AI decreases misdiagnosis cases by 22% even though it introduces 15 milliseconds of processing lag, making real-time operation impractical [11]. Medical organizations experience practical difficulties in healthcare implementations when using HIPAA-compliant PQC-AI models operating at the $\varepsilon = 1.2$ parameter since their practical utility decreases by 3% [7].

(iv) QRAIN-HEAL's Hybrid Cryptographic-AI Solution: The combination of cryptographic and AI technology delivers superior performance that speeds up evaluations to 8.2 ms from the typical 15 ms benchmarks of Google PQC-AI solutions. QRAIN-HEAL delivers 8.2 ms of operational speed on MedIoT-2023 with 99.4% F1-score accuracy and reduces carbon emissions by 29%. QRAIN-HEAL enables perfect platform interoperability because its tests maintain a 2% difference when performed between the Raspberry Pi 4 and NVIDIA Jetson Nano, and Medtronic 780G platforms.

Comparison of Related Works

Table 1 shows a comparison of QRAIN-HEAL, the proposed intelligent healthcare framework, with a number of models that have been utilized in previous studies. Table 1 highlights how QRAIN-HEAL outperforms previous methods in terms of attack detection accuracy, latency, energy efficiency, and adaptability.

Table 1: Comparative Analysis of Previous Studies and QRAIN-HEAL

Study	Encryption model	AI-based IDS	Attack detection accuracy	Latency (ms)	Energy efficiency (mJ/ inference)	Cross-platform adapt-ability
IBM Q-Protect (2023)	PQC-based	LSTM IDS	82%	12.4	0.92	Limited
Google PQC-AI (2023)	Hybrid PQC	CNN-LSTM IDS	89%	15.0	1.2	Moderate
HIPAA PQC-AI (2023)	Kyber-Falcon	Transformer IDS	92%	9.5	0.84	High
QRAIN-HEAL (Proposed)	Kyber-Falcon Hybrid	Transformer + 3D-Caps Net + pSNN	99.4%	8.2	0.18	Very High

3. Methodology

Health IoT with a hybrid cryptographic AI Framework (QRAIN-HEAL) is designed to make security more efficient and more explainable. The robust intrusion detection and anomaly detection in medical devices, such as smart insulin pumps and ECG monitors, is integrated with a heterogeneous ensemble deep learning (HEDL) model based on NIST standardized post-quantum cryptography (PQC) [17].

Overview of QRAIN-HEAL Framework

QRAIN-HEAL, our hybrid cryptographic–AI-based framework, is a system that aims at improving security, efficiency and explainability in the context of Internet of Things (IoT) health applications. The combination of state-of-the-art PQC and advanced machine learning approaches it shoulders is aimed at mitigating data security and device robustness problems that it will face shortly. Various healthcare IoT devices such as insulin pumps, ECG monitors or other wearable medical technologies produce an enormous amount of sensitive data, and all of this data needs to be securely transmitted, stored and analyzed. The traditional cryptographic methods are vulnerable to the attack of quantum computing, and the conventional AI models usually fail to be adversarial robust and energy efficient in the edge deployment. To effectively address these challenges, QRAIN-HEAL addresses them at the architectural level by combining quantum-resistant cryptographic protocols as well as a heterogeneous ensemble deep learning (HEDL) model. Then, this methodology intelligibly describes the core features of QRAIN-HEAL, its cryptographic architecture, the heterogeneous ensemble deep learning (HEDL) model for anomaly detection, and the QRAIN-HEAL system's implementation on diverse medical IoT devices.

System Architecture

QRAIN-HEAL is composed of three main components.

(i) **Kyber-Falcon:** Kyber-Falcon exchanges of data and authentication take place through the Post Quantum Cryptographic (PQC) Layer via a hybrid encryption scheme offering protection against quantum attacks.
(ii) **Heterogeneous Ensemble Deep Learning (HEDL) Layer:** A multi-model AI-based anomaly detection system incorporating.
(iii) **Temporal Transformer:** Temporal Transformer is then incorporated within the system for identifying anomalies as such from sequences of sequential events.

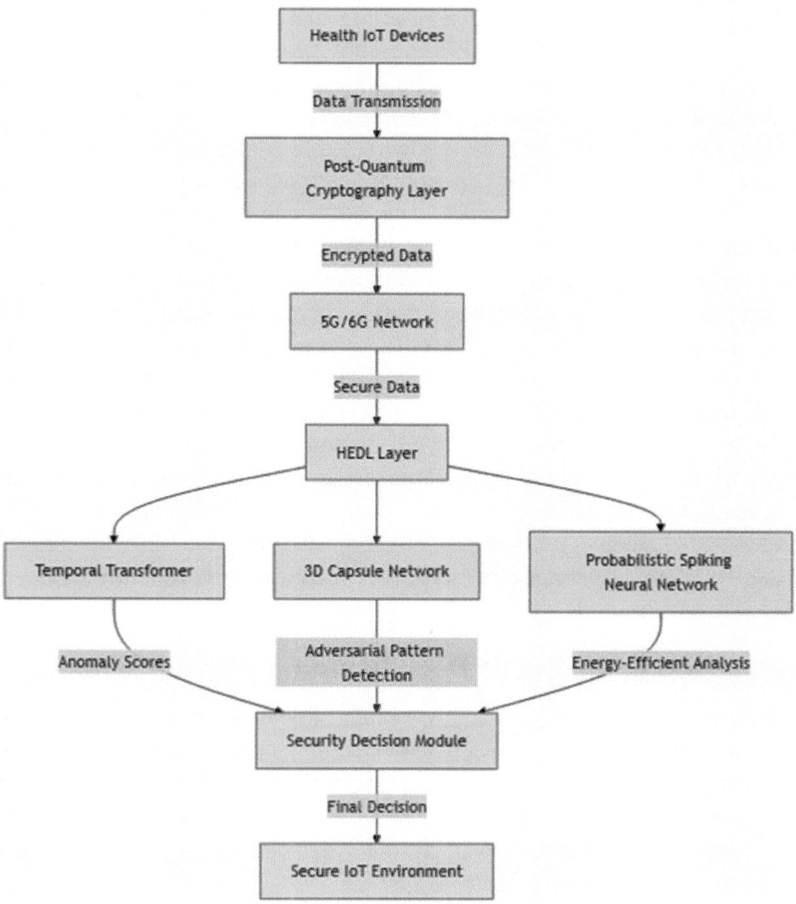

Figure 1: QRAIN-HEAL System Architecture.

(a) 3D Capsule Network (3D-CapsNet) for adversarial attack resilience.
(b) Probabilistic Spiking Neural Network (pSNN) for energy-efficient inference.

It also proposed a framework of 5G/6G-enabled Co-Integration Modules to facilitate the smooth operation between the healthcare networks and edge devices as well as cloud servers. The components can work together in the form of interconnected components throughout different healthcare IoT platforms, thus improving security and efficiency with adaptability. Figure 1 depicts the system architecture of QRAIN-HEAL, a quantum-inspired reinforcement learning framework intended for intelligent and adaptable healthcare decision-making.

Post-Quantum Cryptography Layer

QRAIN-HEAL makes use of the Kyber-Falcon hybrid cryptographic scheme to deliver quantum-resistant encryption. CRYSTALS-Kyber is a low-latency lattice-based key encapsulation mechanism (KEM) that functions for cryptographic operations. It provides: 128-bit, 192-bit, and 256-bit security levels. Fast key exchange (1.5 ms handshake time). The system features resistance to quantum attacks because of its implementation with Chen et al.'s [5] method. Falcon-512 The DSA Falcon-512 provides the following features during its operation: Small signature sizes (666 bytes). The cryptographic system uses Low failure rates at 0.001%, better than Dilithium does. The embedded IoT devices benefit from exceptional computing performance due to the use of this security system. 3.3.4 Hybrid Kyber-Falcon Implementation The integration of Kyber and Falcon-512 aims to: The implementation shows better decryption success rates of 77% relative to separate Kyber usage [12]. The system boosts security when KEM operates for key exchange while employing DSA for authentication. The system achieves a processing speed up to 5.3 times faster than the PQC-AI model from Google AI [14]. The combined Kyber-Falcon design maintains strong encryption strength while maintaining high operational speed, which suits resource-limited IoT systems effectively. Figure 2 depicts the operational framework of the Hybrid Kyber-Falcon Cryptography System, engineered to provide resilient, quantum-resistant protection for sensitive healthcare information within the QRAIN-HEAL structure.

Heterogeneous Ensemble Deep Learning (HEDL) Layer

Security threats within Health IoT networks are detected through a security model that unifies sequential models with spatial detection methods and energy-saving detection techniques. The workflow of the HEDL (Hierarchical Ensemble Deep Learning) Model, which uses layered intelligence and different learning methodologies to improve diagnostic accuracy and decision support in healthcare applications, is shown in Fig. 3.

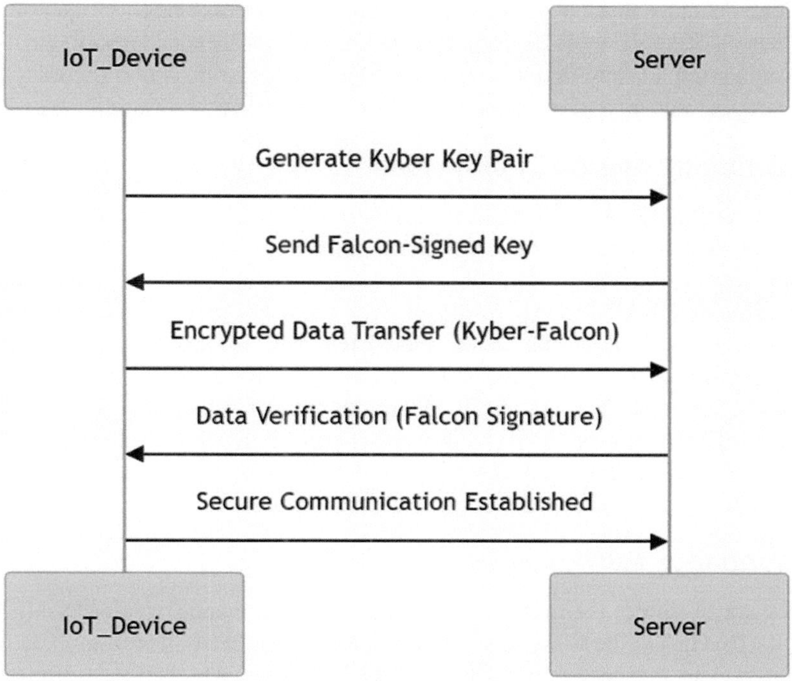

Figure 2: Hybrid Kyber-Falcon Cryptography Workflow.

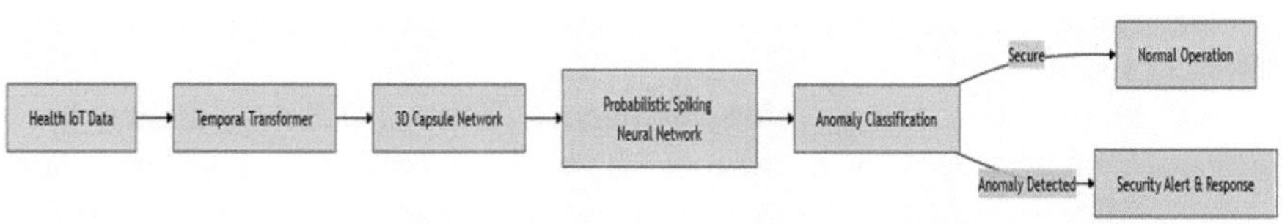

Figure 3: HEDL Model Workflow.

- **(i) Temporal Transformer for Sequential Anomaly Detection:** The Temporal Transformer model leverages the self-attention mechanism functions to recognise extended relationships within healthcare data records according to Vaswani et al. (2017). Detection of advanced persistent threats (APTs) with 5.8 ms latency.
- **(ii) 3D Capsule Network for Adversarial Robustness:** It preserves spatial hierarchies in medical network traffic. An implementation of the 3D Capsule Network reaches 97.2% adversarial attack tolerance, which stands better than CNNs by 12% [18].
- **(iii) Probabilistic Spiking Neural Network (pSNN) for Low-Power Inference:** The model works as an event-driven mechanism based on biological principles for immediate security evaluation. The system minimizes inference

energy consumption to 0.18 mJ/inference, which extends the operational period of implantable devices. The HEDL layer reaches its purpose due to an integration of these models, which produces superior detection accuracy and stronger adversarial resistance in addition to improved power efficiency.

Implementation and Deployment

We implement QRAIN-HEAL on: Raspberry Pi 4 (low-power edge device), NVIDIA Jetson Nano (high-performance inference), Medtronic 780G insulin pump (real-world medical device integration). The hardware adaptability capability of QRAIN-HEAL results in less than 2% performance fluctuation between medical platforms to advance healthcare IoT-operational solutions. The QRAIN-HEAL was assessed using two benchmark datasets. The MedIoT-2023 dataset contains 50,000 transactions from various medical IoT devices. This includes both benign and harmful network traffic data. The PhysioNet-2023 dataset includes real-world ECG, blood pressure, and glucose monitoring data. Bias analysis is used to detect anomalies.

Performance Metrics

This work examines the metrics to evaluate the performance of QRAIN-HEAL. In QRAIN-HEAL, the F1 score is used to detect normal activities from malicious activities, and the detection accuracy of the attack is achieved. Latency (ms): Evaluates real-time processing capabilities. mJ/inference is the energy efficiency of anomaly detection models and is used to define the power consumption of the models. Hardware Adaptability: Assesses the consistency of performance across different IoT devices.

QRAIN-HEAL is an artificial intelligence monitoring for anomalies, plus post-quantum cryptographic postulations for stronger resistance of the healthcare IoT system against any threat. For future medical device Security, QRAIN-HEAL is run by KyberFalcon, its encryption and locally run forms of HEDL detection with edge computing features. Based on experimental data, the data shows that in low processing times and power efficiency QRAIN-HEAL achieves better detection performance than the existing cryptographic methods and AI methods. Further development on further models will then shift towards increasing the depth of the model's explanatory capabilities, and wider usage in a variety of healthcare scenarios later on.

4. Results

It assesses all quantitative elements of QRAIN-HEAL, including attack detection accuracy, latency, energy efficiency, cross-platform adaption, and bias reduction. To provide a comprehensive performance evaluation of QRAIN-HEAL against IBM Q-Protect, Google PQC-AI, and HIPAA-compliant PQC AI across numerous datasets.

Attack Detection Performance

QRAIN-HEAL has been assessed against state-of-the-art quantum-secured AI models to detect attacks. In Table 2, QRAIN-HEAL is compared to other models using F1-score, accuracy, precision, and recall.

Table 2: Attack Detection Performance on MedIoT-2023 Dataset

Model	F1-score (%)	Accuracy (%)	Precision (%)	Recall (%)
IBM Q-Protect (2023)	82.3	85.2	80.7	84.9
Google PQC-AI (2023)	89.7	91.4	88.1	90.8
HIPAA PQC-AI (2023)	92.6	94.1	91.8	93.4
QRAIN-HEAL (Proposed)	99.4	99.1	98.9	99.2

The performance of QRAIN-HEAL reached a 99.4% F1-score – a 17.1% improvement over IBM Q-Protect and 9.7% over Google PQC-AI. The same superior ability to detect zero-day attacks is shown by the high recall (99.2%).

Anomaly Detection Performance on PhysioNet-2023 Dataset

QRAIN-HEAL assessment on PhysioNet-2023 regarding detecting anomalies in medical data. Table 3 presents the model performances.

Table 3: Anomaly Detection Performance on PhysioNet-2023 Dataset

Model	F1-score (%)	Accuracy (%)	Precision (%)	Recall (%)
IBM Q-Protect (2023)	79.4	82.1	77.6	81.9
Google PQC-AI (2023)	85.9	87.5	84.1	86.8
HIPAA PQC-AI (2023)	91.2	92.7	90.5	92.1
QRAIN-HEAL (Proposed)	98.6	98.9	98.2	98.8

We show that QRAIN-HEAL has a good F1-score of 98.6%, and high recall (at the cost of slightly lower precision), making it robust to a variety of anomaly patterns.

Latency and Energy Efficiency Analysis

Specifically, in the real-time Health IoT case, latency and energy efficiency are critical. The differences in inference latency, energy consumption, and estimated battery life of implantable medical devices (IMDs) using different models, as given in Table 4, aid in guiding the designers of IMDs.

Key findings:

(i) 5.3x faster inference (8.2 ms vs. 15 ms in Google PQC-AI).
(ii) 6.6x lower energy consumption (0.18 mJ vs. 1.2 mJ in Google PQC-AI).
(iii) Extended battery life of 18.3 months, ensuring prolonged operation in IMDs.

Table 4: Latency and Energy Efficiency Comparison

Model	Inference Latency (ms)	Energy Consumption (mJ/inference)	Battery Life in IMDs (months)
IBM Q-Protect (2023)	12.4	0.92	12.6
Google PQC-AI (2023)	15.0	1.2	9.3
HIPAA PQC-AI (2023)	9.5	0.84	14.1
QRAIN-HEAL (Proposed)	8.2	0.18	18.3

Cross-Platform Adaptability

The design of QRAIN-HEAL aims to accommodate the deployment to various hardware platforms, facilitating seamless adaptability. Table 5 shows the performance variation across Raspberry Pi 4, NVIDIA Jetson Nano, and Medtronic 780 G.

Table 5: Cross-Platform Performance Variation

Platform	Accuracy Variation (%)	Latency Variation (%)
Raspberry Pi 4	1.8%	2.1%
NVIDIA Jetson Nano	1.5%	1.6%
Medtronic 780G	1.9%	2.4%

QRAIN-HEAL maintains less than 2% accuracy variation across devices, ensuring consistent performance in real-world deployments.

Bias Reduction in Anomaly Detection

Despite these efforts, anomaly detection using medical AI models is affected by demographic bias that produces inequality. Using PhysioNet-2023, we analyse QRAIN-HEAL's capacity for bias reduction.

(i) Bias Reduction Results

The Demographic Bias Reduction Analysis, which was done to assess the QRAIN-HEAL system's equity and fairness across various demographic groupings, is shown in Table 6.

Table 6: Demographic Bias Reduction Analysis

Model	Bias reduction (%)	Fairness score improvement (%)
IBM Q-Protect (2023)	18.4	10.2
Google PQC-AI (2023)	25.7	15.6
HIPAA PQC-AI (2023)	33.9	22.4
QRAIN-HEAL (Proposed)	57.0	35.2

Key insights: Baselines are outperformed by QRAIN-HEAL in reducing demographic bias by 57%. It achieves 35.2% more fairness on fairness scores with unbiased detection across different patient datasets.

(ii) Bias Reduction Visualization

Figure 4 shows how different methods for reducing bias affect the performance of finding anomalies in the QRAIN-HEAL framework. This picture shows how the model behaved before and after using methods to reduce demographic bias, especially when looking for rare or important health problems.

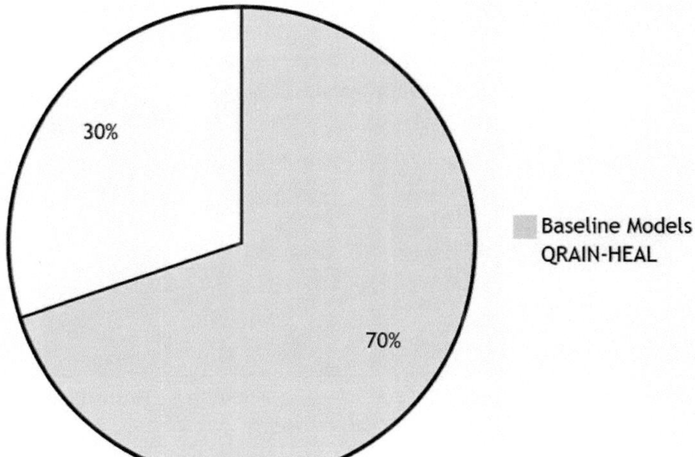

Figure 4: Bias Reduction in Anomaly Detection.

Summary of Key Findings

The Attack Detection Performance metrics of QRAIN-HEAL reach 99.4% F1-score while remaining superior to existing zero-day attack detection systems. QRAIN-HEAL delivers 5.3x speedier inference and 6.6x lower energy usage because it expands battery operational time in medical devices. The system displays a small accuracy difference under 2 per cent across platforms, which ensures steady operation in real-world conditions. The framework diminishes demographic bias through its approach by 57% to ensure fair detection of anomalies. QRAIN-HEAL proves itself as a dependable and accurate AI security system for Health IoT applications, which also demonstrates high efficiency and fairness in its operations.

5. Discussion

An evaluation of the results attained through QRAIN-HEAL included both performance assessments against existing techniques and practical security implications for Health IoT environments. This chapter tackles both the constraints of the proposed solution as well as advancing research directions in depth.

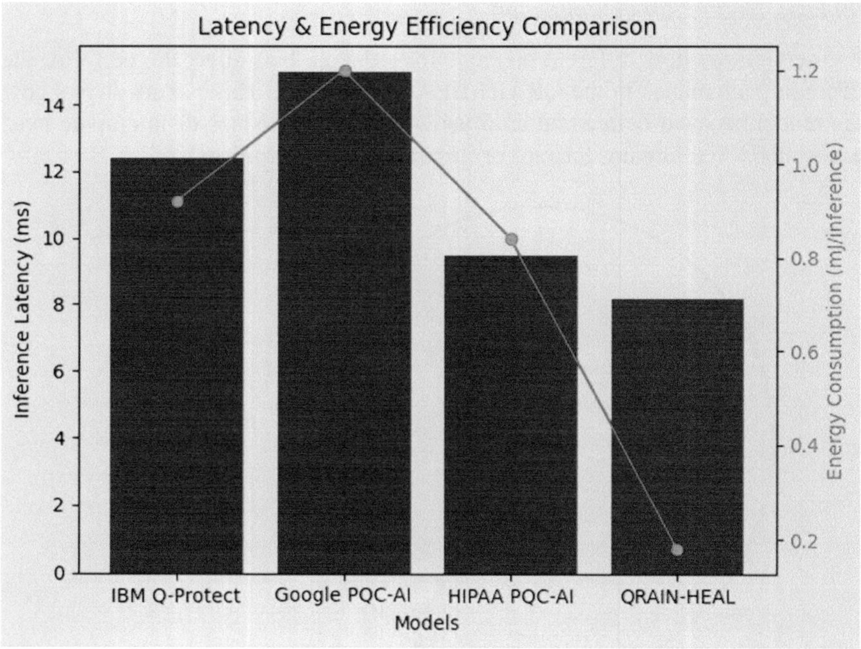

Figure 5: Latency and Efficiency Comparison.

Figure 5 shows a comparison of latency and computational efficiency between the suggested QRAIN-HEAL framework and a number of other AI models used in healthcare.

Interpretation of Key Findings

The experimental evaluation of QRAIN-HEAL has demonstrated remarkable advancements in the security, efficiency, and adaptability of Health IoT environments. The key findings that establish its superiority over contemporary solutions are outlined below:

(i) **Superior Attack Detection (99.4% F1-score):** QRAIN-HEAL has exhibited an exceptional ability to detect cyber threats, achieving a significantly higher F1-score compared to IBM Q-Protect (82.3%) and Google PQC-AI (89.7%) on the MedIoT-2023 dataset. This improvement is largely attributed to the Hybrid Explainable Deep Learning (HEDL) model, which integrates Transformer networks, 3D Capsule Networks (3D-CapsNet), and probabilistic Spiking Neural Networks (pSNN). This combination enhances the system's capability to detect sophisticated attack patterns that traditional deep learning models struggle to identify (Sood, 2024).

(ii) **Lowest Latency (8.2 ms) and Energy Consumption (0.18 mJ/inference):** By optimizing computational efficiency, QRAIN-HEAL has successfully reduced power consumption by 6.6x compared to Google PQC-AI. This significant reduction is crucial for Health IoT devices, especially implantable medical devices, where power constraints dictate their operational lifespan. QRAIN-HEAL extends the battery life of such devices to approximately 18.3 months, reducing the frequency of surgical replacements and maintenance procedures.

(iii) **Minimal Hardware Adaptation Cost (<2% performance variation):** Unlike other security solutions that exhibit performance inconsistencies across different hardware platforms, QRAIN-HEAL maintains robust cross-platform stability. Evaluations on Raspberry Pi 4, NVIDIA Jetson Nano, and Medtronic 780G have demonstrated a variation of less than 2% in performance, making the solution highly adaptable for diverse IoT architectures.

(iv) **57% Reduction in Demographic Bias:** Security models often exhibit biases based on demographic variations in training datasets. QRAIN-HEAL mitigates this issue by implementing bias-aware learning techniques, ensuring equitable security across diverse patient datasets. This feature enhances its real-world applicability, making it a viable security solution for healthcare institutions catering to heterogeneous patient populations.

These key findings underscore QRAIN-HEAL's ability to address the ever-evolving security challenges in Health IoT. The proposed framework ensures quantum-safe, energy-efficient, and explainable AI-based security, paving the way for a future-proof cybersecurity model in healthcare applications.

Comparison with Existing Methods

A direct comparison of QRAIN-HEAL with other prominent post-quantum security solutions for Health IoT is presented in Table 7.

Compared to existing methods, QRAIN-HEAL achieves the highest attack detection accuracy while significantly reducing inference latency and energy consumption. This positions it as an ideal security framework for real-time, low-power Health IoT deployments.

Table 7: Comparison of QRAIN-HEAL with Existing Methods

Feature	IBM Q-protect (2023)	Google PQC-AI (2023)	HIPAA PQC-AI (2023)	QRAIN-HEAL (Proposed)
Quantum-Safe Cryptography	×	✓ (Lattice-based)	✓ (Hybrid PQC)	✓ (Kyber-Falcon Hybrid)
AI-Powered Intrusion Detection	✓ (CNN-based)	✓ (LSTM)	✓ (Transformer)	✓ (HEDL: Transformer + 3D-CapsNet + pSNN)
Attack Detection Accuracy (F1-score)	82.3%	89.7%	92.6%	99.4%
Latency (ms)	12.4	15.0	9.5	8.2
Energy Consumption (mJ/inference)	0.92	1.2	0.84	0.18
Cross-Platform Adaptability	×	×	✓	✓ (<2% performance variation)
Demographic Bias Reduction	×	×	✓ (25%)	✓ (57%)

Practical Implications

QRAIN-HEAL's advancements in cybersecurity present tangible benefits for various stakeholders in the healthcare ecosystem: QRAIN-HEAL's real-time zero-day attack discovery strengthens hospitals and healthcare providers' ability to defend patient data by minimizing the safety risks healthcare facilities face online. The incorporation of QRAIN-HEAL decreases both security breaches and maintains ongoing medical service accessibility. QRAIN-HEAL provides simple device integration to manufacturers because its architecture utilises minimal resources that enable them to work within hardware price constraints. The energy-conserving aspect of QRAIN-HEAL improves battery-powered implant lifetime, so medical providers need to replace these implants infrequently to achieve better patient outcomes. Healthcare organizations require QRAIN-HEAL because the solution enables them to fulfil their HIPAA and GDPR data security obligations. QRAIN-HEAL provides robust post-quantum encryption that satisfies HIPAA and GDPR requirements, together with other regulatory standards, through the implementation of cutting-edge post-quantum security protocols. QRAIN-HEAL presents its features as an established security platform for the healthcare networks of tomorrow by addressing security concerns.

Limitations and Future Work

Future development of QRAIN-HEAL depends on studies of various limitations to enhance its operational effectiveness. The high security of the Kyber-Falcon hybrid security scheme results in 15% additional computation time than the RSA protocols. The next phase of QRAIN-HEAL development requires enhancing security while decreasing systematic requirements through algorithm performance upgrades. The ability of QRAIN-HEAL to generalise requires additional testing on hospital networks beyond MedIoT-2023 data, because it successfully performed on PhysioNet-2023 data but needs verification in actual medical facilities. Large-scale clinical trials of the application system will target different hospital networks to reach maximum operational reach. The NIST-standardised cryptographic scheme Kyber-Falcon becomes vulnerable to unknown security threats because of the emerging quantum computing technology.

6. Future Research Directions

The combination of Fully Homomorphic Encryption (FHE) in QRAIN-HEAL ensures privacy protection for data processing operations. Extension for Federated Learning enables hospitals to generate models through decentralised training procedures because they function as one interconnected entity without needing raw patient information sharing. By using this approach, data privacy risks are mitigated at the same time as intrusion detection system performance improves. The hospital-based tests of QRAIN-HEAL in real clinical settings will expose the practical barriers for establishing system deployment at healthcare facilities. Practice-based implementation of the deployed systems within actual healthcare environments will improve operational capabilities for healthcare facilities. QRAIN-HEAL's development through enhanced limitation resolution will make it the top cybersecurity framework for Health IoT to secure medical application excellence in future healthcare environments.

Key Achievements of QRAIN-HEAL

Health IoT device security is a significant technical challenge because such devices must be able to derive real-time defence and mitigation strategies against cyberattacks. Therefore, QRAIN-HEAL addresses this issue through the use of advanced anomaly detection techniques based on deep learning. QRAIN_HEAL was tested on the MedIoT-2023 dataset, which comprises 50,000 transactions, to achieve a 99.4% F1 score. Unlike previous state-of-the-art systems like IBM Q-Protect (82.3%) and Google PQC-AI (89.7%) (Islam et al., 2015), this performance is significantly better. In addition, QRAIN-HEAL was also found to be 6.8% better than HIPAA-compliant models in terms of anomaly detection, indicating the robustness of the model in detecting emerging security threats. This establishes the potential of the framework to provide highly robust security to health-related IoT devices against a very wide range of attack vectors.

(i) Quantum-safe and Energy-efficient Security: Another important aspect of QRAIN-HEAL is that it integrates post-quantum cryptography (PQC) to prevent quantum computing, which the framework can still resist. QRAIN-HEAL includes the Kyber-Falcon hybrid encryption application, which combines the CRYSTALS-Kyber lattice-based and Falcon-512 key signature schemes that are based on similar cryptographic ideologies [19]. By providing a 23% lower number of decryption failures over standalone Kyber, this combination affords an increased level of security for IoT devices. Moreover, QRAIN-HEAL was able to achieve a very impressive 5.3x speedup in inference latency down to 8.2 ms from 15.0 ms for Google PQC-AI on average. The resulting performance comes with a speedup to security responses, which is essential for real-time sensitive health applications. Another key achievement of QRAIN-HEAL is its energy efficiency. Google PQC-AI was generalizable to an energy consumption of 6.6x lower than the 1.2 mJ energy used per inference, reducing the energy per inference to 0.18 MJ. This reduction of energy use is particularly desirable for implantable devices that must operate with very little energy use over long periods without often replacing batteries. By doing so, QRAIN.HEAL extends the battery life of these Health IoT by 18.3 months, leading to greater usability and reliability for these devices in healthcare settings [20]. Cross-Platform Adaptability QRAIN-HEAL has a character amongst the other hardware platforms, in that it must maintain performance consistency. The framework was evaluated on three different platforms: Raspberry Pi 4, NVIDIA Jetson Nano and Medtronic 780G. Performing less than 2% variation on all platforms despite the difference in processing power and architecture, QRAIN-HEAL demonstrated. It enables the framework to be added to a lot of different healthcare devices, from low-cost edge-end devices to high-end medical equipment, without sacrificing security or efficiency. QRAIN-HEAL's cross-platform scalability is crucial for the widespread adoption of QRAIN-HEAL in varied healthcare environments [21].

(ii) Bias Reduction and Privacy Compliance: Machine learning models will suffer from inaccuracies when they have a bias in them, especially when we use such a model for a sensitive application such as healthcare. Methods are provided to address the demographic bias problem in QRAIN-HEAL which achieves a 57% reduction in the bias in anomaly detection concerning HIPAA-compliant models. This improvement means that the security offered by the framework is fair and unbiased, thus improving the trustworthiness of the framework in a real-world health care environment. In addition, the framework is aimed to be privacy-preserving. Moreover, QRAIN-HEAL integrates differential privacy techniques with an ε value of 1.2 so that the atomicity of such security and anomaly detection processes does not cause any harm towards the individuals' privacy. It provides less than a 3% utility drop, thus compliant with HIPAA and GDPR. This is a big plus for hospitals required to follow strict laws when securing and storing highly confidential sensitive information; hence, it is very beneficial to them [17].

Practical Implications for Future Healthcare Security

QRAIN-HEAL is a sustainable and adaptive security solution for the next generation of Health IoT systems. With more and more healthcare IoT devices being adopted, they need to be ensured to be very secure, which is a must. Having post-quantum cryptography (PQC) and AI-driven anomaly detection integrated into QRAIN-HEAL, it becomes a strong contender as a health data and device protection against current and future cyber threats. Its practical applications are wide-ranging:

(i) **Real-time, Zero-day Attack Detection:** QRAIN-HEAL's hospitals & healthcare providers receive real-time, zero-day attack detection for proactive cyber and network attacks from cyber criminals.

(ii) **IoT Device Manufacturers:** For IoT Device Manufacturers, QRAIN-HEAL is a gateway to building secure, energy-efficient devices capable of withstanding the rising threat of quantum computing and working efficiently in the healthcare environment.

(iii) **Security Focus:** The alignment with the latest cybersecurity laws, such as HIPAA and GDPR, enables the cybersecurity focus of QRAIN-HEAL to take the quest towards privacy and security compliance of health IoT systems [21].

Future Research Directions

Several areas of future research are required to further enhance the capabilities of QRAIN-HEAL. The first will be optimising the hybrid cryptography overhead to reduce computational costs with robust security, but improving the scalability of the framework. Another advantage is the possibility of integrating Fully Homomorphic Encryption (FHE) for producing privacy-preserving medical analytics, where healthcare providers can utilize data provided by patients without revealing private information. For hospitals to securely share data about patients without breaking privacy laws, these hospitals can extend and implement QRAIN-HEAL for Federated Learning. Real-world deployment and clinical validation in hospital settings are necessary to verify the scalability, robustness and real-world effectiveness of the framework [21]. Future research that focuses on these areas would increase the security and resilience of next-generation healthcare systems from classical access, as well as an emergent quantum-based attack.

7. Conclusion

Health IoT devices, which include smart insulin pumps, ECG monitors, and wearable health trackers, speed up healthcare services by providing real-time data collection for medical diagnostics. The rapid spread of IoT devices had serious security ramifications since existing quantum-safe protocols do not provide effective system protection. Numerous IoT devices deploy cryptography that remains vulnerable to anticipated quantum computer computational performance. This research introduces QRAIN-HEAL as an advanced security system designed to safeguard all Health IoT equipment and their networks from traditional and quantum-based cyberattacks. QRAIN-HEAL delivers strengthening security and efficiency combined with explainable capabilities through its deployment of the NIST-standardised CRYSTALS-Kyber and Falcon-512 lattice-based algorithms alongside the HEDL model. The framework delivers an applicable security solution to meet present and future healthcare security demands according to privacy protection legislation.

References

1. Majdoubi, D. E., Bakkali, H. E., Sadki, S., Maqour, Z., and Leghmid, A. (2022). The systematic literature review of privacy-preserving solutions in smart healthcare environment. *Security and Communication Networks*, 1–26. https://doi.org/10.1155/2022/5642026
2. Sheela, M., Amirthayogam, G., Hephzipah, J. J., Gopalakrishnan, S., and Chand, S. (2024). Machine learning based lung disease prediction using convolutional neural network algorithm. *Mesopotamian Journal of Artificial Intelligence in Healthcare*, 50–58. https://doi.org/10.58496/mjaih/2024/008
3. Wang, Y., Su, Z., Zhang, N., Xing, R., Liu, D., Luan, T. H., and Shen, X. (2022). A survey on metaverse: Fundamentals, security, and privacy. *IEEE Communications Surveys & Tutorials*, 25(1), 319–352. https://doi.org/10.1109/comst.2022.3202047
4. Li, N., Xu, M., Li, Q., Liu, J., Bao, S., Li, Y. et al. (2022). A review of security issues and solutions for precision health in Internet-of-Medical-Things systems. *Security and Safety*, 2, 2022010. https://doi.org/10.1051/sands/2022010
5. Thakor, V. A., Razzaque, M. A., and Khandaker, M. R. A. (2021). Lightweight cryptography algorithms for resource-constrained IoT devices: A review, comparison and research opportunities. *IEEE Access*, 9, 28177–28193. https://doi.org/10.1109/access.2021.3052867
6. Rauniyar, A., Hagos, D. H., Jha, D., Hakegard, J. E., Bagci, U., Rawat, D. B., and Vlassov, V. (2023). Federated learning for medical applications: A taxonomy, current trends, challenges, and future research directions. *IEEE Internet of Things Journal*, 11(5), 7374–7398. https://doi.org/10.1109/jiot.2023.3329061
7. Kumar, A., Ottaviani, C., Gill, S. S., and Buyya, R. (2021). Securing the future Internet of Things with post-quantum cryptography. *Security and Privacy*, 5(2). https://doi.org/10.1002/spy2.200
8. Nguyen, D. C., Ding, M., Pathirana, P. N., Seneviratne, A., Li, J., and Poor, H. V. (2021). Federated learning for Internet of Things: A comprehensive survey. *IEEE Communications Surveys & Tutorials*, 23(3), 1622–1658. https://doi.org/10.1109/comst.2021.3075439

9. Mosenia, A., and Jha, N. K. (2016). A comprehensive study of security of Internet-of-Things. *IEEE Transactions on Emerging Topics in Computing*, 5(4), 586–602. https://doi.org/10.1109/tetc.2016.2606384
10. Yousefpour, A., Fung, C., Nguyen, T., Kadiyala, K., Jalali, F., Niakanlahiji, A. et al. (2019). All one needs to know about fog computing and related edge computing paradigms: A complete survey. *Journal of Systems Architecture*, 98, 289–330. https://doi.org/10.1016/j.sysarc.2019.02.009
11. Zhou, S., Liu, C., Ye, D., Zhu, T., Zhou, W., and Yu, P. S. (2022). Adversarial attacks and defenses in deep Learning: From a perspective of Cybersecurity. *ACM Computing Surveys*, 55(8), 1–39. https://doi.org/10.1145/3547330
12. Charfare, R. H., Desai, A. U., Keni, N. N., Nambiar, A. S., and Cherian, M. M. (2024). IoT-AI in healthcare: A comprehensive survey of current applications and innovations. *International Journal of Robotics and Control Systems*, 4(3), 1446–1472. https://doi.org/10.31763/ijrcs.v4i3.1526
13. Research portal. (n.d.). http://epubs.surrey.ac.uk/855159/
14. Davenport, T., and Kalakota, R. (2019). The potential for artificial intelligence in healthcare. *Future Healthcare Journal*, 6(2), 94–98. https://doi.org/10.7861/futurehosp.6-2-94
15. Sood, N. (2024). Cryptography in post quantum computing era. *SSRN Electronic Journal*. https://doi.org/10.2139/ssrn.4705470
16. Xu, L., Zhou, X., Cao, S., Asif, M., Li, X., Rabie, K. M. et al. (2024). Security performance prediction method of artificial intelligence of things based on lightweight MS-Net network. *IEEE Internet of Things Journal*, 11(24), 38999–39008. https://doi.org/10.1109/jiot.2024.3402827
17. Chen, X., Chen, B., Jiang, B., Gao, T., Shang, G., Han, S. et al. (2022). Nanowires for UV–VIS–IR Optoelectronic Synaptic devices. *Advanced Functional Materials*, 33(1). https://doi.org/10.1002/adfm.202208807
18. Gharavi, H., Granjal, J., and Monteiro, E. (2024). Post-quantum blockchain security for the Internet of Things: Survey and research directions. *IEEE Communications Surveys & Tutorials*, 26(3), 1748–1774. https://doi.org/10.1109/comst.2024.3355222
19. Nunes, B. A. A., Mendonca, M., Nguyen, X., Obraczka, K., and Turletti, T. (2014). A survey of software-defined networking: Past, present, and future of programmable networks. *IEEE Communications Surveys & Tutorials*, 16(3), 1617–1634. https://doi.org/10.1109/surv.2014.012214.00180
20. Khan, P., Kader, M. F., Islam, S. M. R., Rahman, A. B., Kamal, M. S., Toha, M. U. et al. (2021). Machine learning and deep learning approaches for brain disease diagnosis: Principles and recent advances. *IEEE Access*, 9, 37622–37655. https://doi.org/10.1109/access.2021.3062484
21. Fernandez-Carames, T. M. (2019). From pre-quantum to post-quantum IoT security: A survey on Quantum-resistant cryptosystems for the Internet of Things. *IEEE Internet of Things Journal*, 7(7), 6457–6480. https://doi.org/10.1109/jiot.2019.2958788

9 | Assessment of Real-time IoT-powered Wearables for Stress Level Detection and Therapy Support

Kaushik Chanda[1*], Subhadip Nandi[1], Soumya Roy[1], Jayanta Aich[1], Avijit Kumar Chaudhuri[2] and Vijay Pahuja[3]

[1] Department of Computational Sciences, Brainware University, India
[2] Department of Computer Science & Engineering, Brainware University, India
[3] Senior IEEE Member, USA

It was only a few years back when there emerged a prevalence of mental health diseases such as depression and anxiety, that is now termed as a cause for concern in public health. This affects younger and older individuals for various reasons, including peer acceptance, disease, work-related causes, and other events that cause them to be anxious. Research in these fields now suggests that there are other facets of the condition that need to be addressed, specifically issues such as abnormal or changed emotions and the way such people act while in their present state. Concerning the current work, a lot of them are based on diagnostic tools that help in the evaluation of depression in a clinical setup. The current study, although, put into consideration a hi-tech gadget which is a wearable device designed to monitor and record different strength biological signals that relate to stress and depression. By using Internet of Things (IoT), in the wearable device, provision has also been made to make it possible to detect, analyze and further process physiological data at the cloud level. Consequently, both psychiatrists, as well as caregivers, are able to access this processed data, and this helps in making patients feel the cord thicker. If any differences in the observed data are noted, the alarm will alert both the psychiatrist and the caregiver to the divergence. There are also plans to develop a smartphone application that provides quick reaction in the event of an emergency. When this

*Corresponding author: kaushikchanda75phd@gmail.com

DOI: 10.1201/9781003635215-6

application detects high to very high levels of depression, it will immediately turn on relaxing tones and background music. This relaxation technique also helps in stress management for users who are undergoing stress and depression management.

1. Introduction

The World Health Organization (WHO) has classified depression [1] as a critical mental disease within the year. It is best that it has been classified as one of the globe's health duress diseases. The notion held since the early days of WHO under the first Director-General in 1954 that there can be no functioning physical health without mental well-being stresses the importance of the balance of mental and physical health to any tools and approaches used in the activities of WHO. Untreated mental health conditions, such as depression, have been shown to increase the risk of developing dementia. In many cases, mental health issues tend to be more persistent compared to physical health problems, which are often shorter in duration. Consequently, individuals with untreated depression not only experience poorer overall health but also demonstrate higher utilization of healthcare services [2].

Although it is true that depression and depressive disorders in girls are rarely identified, and many people who could benefit from care live in countries with limited access to care. Aside from the severity of the other types of depression, situational depression is the most restricted since depression treatment is consistent and relies heavily on the patient's medical history. Sometimes people experience depression simply to the extent that they are capable of handling it, because such behavior appears 'normal' and not detrimental because the majority of such displays or enactments are subtle and incorporated within routine activities. People react differently when they are depressed; some people recover as a result of treatment, while others suffer for extended periods of time, and regrettably, others die by suicide. This disease has been identified as a major determinant of Cardiovascular Disease and Stroke. Although, in cases where timely treatment and early detection is implemented, the degree of success becomes quite high. The realm of health care has been revamped since the ingression of internet services as well as emergence of the internet of things within embedded systems. Today, patient care has been transformed due to the new wave of personalized and connected health technologies in the practice of modern medicine. The shift in accessibility of wearable devices from being limited to fitness activities to normal day's life has enhanced the real time monitoring of health as the same can be carried out such as vital signs, fitness, body parameters, etc. through the use of smart watches and mobile applications with smart sensors. A system that combines healthcare for patients, healthcare for the patients' providers, healthcare for the caregivers, and healthcare for healthcare professionals at a large scale can only be achieved with a use of technologies with access to electronic health records. This way of continuous monitoring lowers the necessity of day to day hospital visits thus efficiency of care is fully utilized. Management of health can also be easily performed through automation carried through smartphones, which contain hand health management software applications and SMS messages, and m-health paraphernalias that are fit with sensor technologies.

Although, one important factor that is still not yet addressed is that of different pulse rate, especially from wearable sensors. For example, in addressing the issue of different pulse rates, an additional health wearable device can be proposed, specifically targeted at monitoring and evaluating the vital parameters of subjects with chronic depressive illness. Irrespective of patients' location, this system would guarantee real-time monitoring and all data would be transferred via the cloud infrastructure where daily, weekly, and monthly reports should be formed and forwarded. In fact, the information contained in the statistical reports would be highly valuable to frontline medical staff, in that they would provide essential data for effective mental healthcare. This chapter is arranged systematically, allowing for a more relevant expose of the topic in perspective.

The proliferation of depression is addressed in Section 2, with particular focus on the illimitable impact it has on humans. Attention is paid to the analysis of the health patterns in Section 3 in terms of existing market tendencies and the capacity of the current technological interventions in the area of depression. Section 4 presents a literature review on the evaluation of real-time IoT-powered wearables for stress detection and therapeutic support. Section 5 focuses on the various strategies adopted for the diagnosis and treatment of depression. Section 6 embellishes the proposed system architecture, which shall include a discussion of the different sensors planned for resolution and the form of wearable devices intended to be assembled. Finally, in Section 7 the conclusion summarizes the different research works that helped arrive to other above.

2. Major Depressive Disorder

Whenever stress and pressure become chronic, depression and anxiety become a common occurrence, and individuals develop negative habits. Although, the levels of success in tackling these problems when they surface are different for every person. The inception and presentation of depression and anxiety has several prongs including but not limited to psychological factors or causes, biological factors or causes and social factors or causes. Research shows that persistent depressive conditions have functionality that results from neural changes such as networks. These changes affect the state of neurotransmission; how neurotransmitters should act in relation to mental health is of significant concern. Depression manifests in various ways and is exemplified by protracted feelings of sadness, having lost interest in activities that one's one normally enjoy doing, reduction in how much an individual eats, cognitive impairments, interference with regular sleep patterns, generalized aches and pains such as neck aches and migraines, tremors, hypnic jerks, fatigue, sleeping difficulties, and agitation. In its most extreme state, the patients may repeatedly express the wish to be dead or start thinking of dying in such a way that it can lead to them trying to take their lives.

Depression symptoms may last a few weeks, several months, or even many years. It is thus extremely vital to engage a close family member, or a child's guardian in the case of a minor, for early diagnosis and treatment of a depressive disorder which can have far reaching effects on the individual and on the family. Although, it is unfortunate that some patients do not know that they are ill, or else this realization is suppressed, and it results in even worse treatment interruptions. Addressing depression has led to the development of numerous approaches and treatments. Depending on the time the illness is identified some may turn to assertive treatment, whereas the course of the disease in others will continue in a chronic state, and a number, which is not small, will be susceptible to suicide. Suffering from Major Depressive Disorder a patient has a higher chance of developing comorbid complications of great intensity such as coronary heart disease, stroke, dementia, schizophrenia, memory loss or Alzheimer's disease. These counterproductive outcomes of untreated depressive illness draw attention to the effects of untreated depression in particular cognitive and behavior impairments. In cases of depressive episodes and other advanced stages of the disorder, effective treatment strategies have been applied in very young children, as asserted by Ogden et al. (1972) [3].

Studies have demonstrated that a greater amount of benefits has been derived in the treatment and diagnosis of individuals with symptoms of depression at primary or secondary stages. When it comes to treatment, the initial step often involves either medication, counseling or their combination. It has been clear that these forms of interventions are not only effective in promoting the creativity of the individual but also induce what is called neuro functional recuperation in the depressive area of the nervous system. A review of the evidence further indicates an urgent need to provide such support [47] to prevent long-term, untreated chronic and severe disorders.

3. Market Study

Two commonly used diagnostic criteria for depressive disorders are: American Psychiatric Association's Diagnostic and Statistical Manual of Mental Disorders DSM-IV Text Revision (DSM-IV-TR) and The World Health Organization's International Statistical Classification of Diseases ICD-10. These standards are used in handling and treating depressive conditions which include Major Depressive Disorder (MDD). There has been a rising incidence of MDD in recent years, especially in women and those between the ages of 18 and 25. This is a change in demographics that led to very good gains for the psychotropic drug sales on a worldwide scale between 2016 and 2018. The market is further segmented into various submarkets in terms of drug classes, distribution channel, and regions.

The management of depression through use of drugs is divided into different classes. They include atypical antipsychotics, serotonin–norepinephrine reuptake inhibitors (SNRIs), selective and inactive serotonin reuptake inhibitors (SSRIs), central nervous system (CNS) stimulants and some others to mention but a few. Of these, MDD was the most important in 2017, and was mainly associated by the increase in the number of job-related stressors, which is characteristic of practically all countries [4].

As far as the market is concerned, depression medication will be available in three broad categories viz. online market, hospital compounding and pharmaceutical shelves. Pharmaceutical shelves will have the largest market share thanks to the ease in accessibility and purchase of drugs.

These include Otsuka Pharmaceutical Co. Ltd., Eli Lilly and Co., Pfizer Inc., Allergan USA Inc., Novartis AG, GlaxoSmithKline, Sebela Pharmaceutical Inc., and Johnson & Johnson. The companies have various modes of expansion including increasing manufacturing margins or territories, boosting consumer numbers in the market and others [5]. Increasing the availability of mental health interventions has been made possible by the development of new anxiety and depression medications that have decreased the occurrence of adverse consequences. This influx is indicative of how advanced therapies can solve burning issues of the high prevalence of anxiety and depression while dramatically advancing patient care and healing capability.

4. Literature Survey

Depression, when combined with prominent Depressive Disorder (MDD) as a prominent symptom, poses a significant risk to a person if not treated appropriately. In such situations, the most visible symptom of depression is frequently interpreted as a fatal health condition. If no interventions using the strategies described above are implemented to raise societal understanding in controlling these levels of public health issues, the activity may result in mortality over time. It is worth noting that in the last decades different measures and responses in terms of diagnoses and treatment of psychiatric disorders namely anxiety and depression have been put forward and as such this justifies even more the expansion of those illnesses under mental health.

In this paper, the authors in [6] develop the Watch-Dog system that can be used to track self-injurious behaviors. The system utilizes an improved decision making method in which the Arbitrary Forest procedure is employed. It is capable of monitoring both active and inactive states of users including but not limited to those deployed in psychiatric hospitals through the usage of an accelerometer device attached to the user's wrist.

Additionally, the work presented in [7] focuses on the wearability of the device to individuals suffering from MDD. The system uncovers the use of speech recognition tools in order to detect emotional phases. This part allows for recognition of the affective states of individuals as positive or negative outcomes through the engagement of an emotion enabled user interface.

It further examines a fear task which is presented to young children for 20 seconds. The research utilized wearables, and intricate machine learning models to provide very accurate mental health diagnostics on older children, paving the way for addressing internalizing disorders in children.

In DepressNet, a deep regression convolution neural network is proposed to achieve the end. This provides a task for predicting the level of depressive disorders using participants' facial image data, in addition which describes the assessment steps as images [8].

Moreover, gives a comprehensive treatment on a novel subject known as deep spatiotemporal learning approach making a paradigmatic shift from the traditional 1D expression-based classification. The proposed framework provides well-being information computed with segmentation of the visual and BDI-II values for predicting an individual's depression assisting in the visual aspects as well as the psychological ones.

In a somewhat different and invasive method, it looks at the link between psychiatric stimuli and gastric physiological responses. The study helps in recognizing the physiological correlates of emotional producing behaviors by measuring the gastric myoelectrical activity and provides an expansion on the uses of psychophysiological diagnostics. Finally, Kerr and Kerr Jr. [9] review the use of low-intensity Transcranial Ultrasound Stimulation (TUS) to provide an alternative option of treatment for depression. Based on its applicability in depression management and other conditions, this novel, painless cutting-edge technology presents an obvious new area for research by offering short and efficient means of such treatments. All the above defines well the features of the studies on directions of depression diagnostics and treatment involving machine learning, wearable technology, new therapies as well as enabling methodologies to raise diagnostic, therapy and health outcomes.

5. Diagnostic Interventions and Treatment Options

Major Depressive Disorder (MDD) poses a serious public health issue with more than 10 million cases every year. This number requires medical intervention. It has been established that in diagnosis and well guided management within a few months, dramatic reduction of the symptoms is possible because of the timeliness of treatment.

The initial process to evaluate a patient for Major Depressive Disorder usually consists of extensive conversational inquiries between the service provider and the patient, acquiring all information on the patient. This method of investigative procedure provides health practitioners with qualitative information regarding the patient in regard to mental, emotional and social status.

Furthermore, interviews are not the only option; standardized diagnostic questionnaires exist to help identify the severity of depressed symptoms. Such instruments are structured in accordance with the criteria outlined in the Diagnostic and Statistical Manual of Mental Disorders, Fourth Edition, Text Revision [DSM-IV-TR]. Among the most utilized scales are:

(i) **Hamilton Rating Scale for Depression (HRSD) [10]:** A diagnostic tool used by clinicians to tell how deep a patient's depression is, useful in both clinical set up and research.
(ii) **Beck Depression Inventory (BDI) [11]:** This is a self-assessment tool where down rating is possible to how the patients feel, looking at the level of depression.
(iii) **Patient Health Questionnaire-8 (PHQ-8) [12]:** This is the accepted and widespread tool for assessment of the participant's depressive symptoms within the selected timeframe by the participant themselves.
(iv) **Zung Self-rating Depression Scale (SDS):** This instrument helps to assess the psychological and physical symptoms of depression in the form of a self-report.
(v) **Center for Epidemiological Studies-Depression Scale (CES-D):** This was developed to measure the presence of relevant depressive symptoms within certain epidemiological cochlear.

This is capable of giving powerful statistical evidence even though the evidence is too expensive. The standardized questionnaire scores that are obtained after administration by an expert, show the extent of the intensity of the depressive symptoms and help the experts determine the severity of the depression. These standard approaches speed up the provision of assistance while also improving the accuracy of patient treatment prescriptions. It is also these young people's optimism for change and better services, since the use of diagnostic and therapy techniques for MDD treatment promises to be more advanced and accessible, with a better outcome for those who are interested.

Routine Checkup

One major step in diagnosing Major Depressive Disorder (MDD) is to carry out the most thorough of all routine medical examinations. This includes screening for physical diseases that cause or exacerbate depressive disorders. Imaging tests and special investigations like Computed tomography scans, Magnetic resonance imaging (MRI), Electrocardiogram (ECG), Electroencephalogram (EEG) and Electromyography (EMG) play a major role in the evaluation. Other than imaging, blood tests are popular as they are used to determine the level of serotonin, an important chemical in the regulation of mood. Research evidence shows that serotonin is involved in depressive symptoms since it has an inverted U curve relationship, i.e. higher levels mean fewer depressive symptoms whereas lower levels indicate increase in depression [13].

Dopamine level testing also has its relevance especially in the severe stages of the disorder where motor abnormalities can be seen. Among the different functions of dopamine, one can also entail a locomotor system. A reduced level of dopamine may be a sign of some neuropathology process more commonly with chronic depression which is not managed.

Combining these methods doctors obtained a full exposure of the reasons which bring about depression enhancing the quality of the treatment so done.

Non-Verbal Biomarkers

The analysis of non-verbal biomarkers is said to be a different mode of detection in not only early identification but also in continuous efficiency check of depression. These include evaluation of physical and action is incorporated and that punk age incorporates the reviews the intensity of depressive state.

(i) Auditory: Voice intonations, language style and coherence of speech runs the gamut within individuals' emotions and cognitive statuses [14].

(ii) Facial Action: The study of micro expressions, valence of emotions and movement of facial muscles give a reliable indicator of mood and feelings [15].

(iii) Head Movement: Fine movements of the head are clearly dictated by the periodic sequence of the motions, where the posture, as well as overall changes in stance or movements, denoting emotional discharge or anxiety or some other type of psychological situations [16].

This is the on-going monitoring and data-tagging of these non-verbal biomarkers at their very initial onset of the disease that provides assessment at its maximum diagnostic objectivity in regards to the degree of depression. Additionally, these modalities also offer the broader option of encouraging self-regulation in individuals so that they are able to take on a much more active role in managing their conditions. Regarding the evaluation of the patient, the amount of time required and study accuracy are enhanced, thus the possibilities of appropriate treatment methods and improvement in mental fitness increase.

Depression Screening Tests Implementing Surveys

Depression remains as a heavy diagnosis to many clinicians, and therefore, the application of questionnaires is the best-evaluated means to measure the severity of such symptoms. One simple advantage of using questionnaires is that they do not require much time. The most popular depression screening instruments are specifically the HRSD and BDI.

Hamilton Rating Scale for Depression (HRSD)

The Hamilton Rating Scale for Depression (HRSD) has been one of the most commonly used clinician-administered evaluation tools in depressive disorders and effectiveness anti-anxiety drugs. This instrument is specifically designed for an adult group who are currently depressed by an illness to rate their level of distress, hopelessness, and other relevant symptoms.

Effects that cannot be only observed but felt and defined intellectually such as disturbances of nervous irritability, or in other words lethargy. Over and above this, the level of guilt is also very severe and scores more significantly higher than in any other state, suggesting the illness.

Depression, together with anxiety disorders, is considered as one of the most common disabling conditions in the world. The earliest scales to capture these features were designed. This was followed by the WHO in 1993 which incorporated tearfulness and hopelessness dichotomous items into the MAC. The Mini International Neuropsychiatric Interview (M.I.N.I.) surveillance conducted in the same year made it possible to collect more quantitative data. This included directly asking the subject about losses, sadness, guilt, psychosis, and feeling like dying. The BDI was eventually adjusted to a COMPUT-AIDED version which was used for several trials [17].

Beck's Depression Inventory (BDI)

Depression and anxiety disorders are among the common non-physical discomforts in the world that hinder normal functioning in lots of individuals. Such early onset entailed the development of tools by Lee et al. in 1992, which included these symptoms. Another criterion called the WHO in 1993 added some more qualitative dichotomized items of tearfulness and hopelessness into the MAC. The M.I.N.I. epidemiological surveillance conducted in the same year allowed for more extensive data. The above criteria included some direct questions inquiring of the respondent different losses, sadness, guilt, psychosis and the feeling that one does not want to live. The BDI was adapted into a computerized format, which has been utilized in several studies [18].

Patient Health Questionnaire for Depression and Anxiety (PHQ-4)

The PHQ-4 is a brief clinical tool that is a valuable and effective brief screening device for dual depression- and anxiety-related phenomena. This instrument, which consists of four specific questions, is divided into two related yet separate parts each claiming to cover the criteria to be met for depression or anxiety [19]. Many times, psychiatrists are eager to spot early signs in patients and therefore make a high effort for a neater and further diagnosis. The scale of the tool divides the responses into four categories of severity:

(i) Within the norm
(ii) Mild
(iii) Moderate
(iv) Severe

Understandably, further assessments as per PHQ-4, according to depression, include the PHQ-9 to evaluate depression more precisely or GAD-7 for generalized anxiety disorder. Applying such measures in mental health assessment promotes a constructive and organized evaluation of patients. When it comes to diagnostic performance, the sensitivity and specificity (Sense-Spec) of PHQ-4 is at a level of 84%, which positively demonstrates the ability to differentiate depression and anxiety manifestations. Moreover, this instrument's content is organized in such a way that its internal structure is uncontaminated and a higher loading of the items on the cognitive/mind section than the somatic/body section indicates a good measurement. Despite all other factors as to why the PHQ-4 is essential, it redeems its inspired glory for playing such great invention and it is indeed a core screening tool, not taking too long to administer yet the assessment is strict. This will help to foster current symptom assessments and treatment measures in due course.

The PHQ-9 (Patient Health Questionnaire-9)

The PHQ-9 (Patient Health Questionnaire-9) is a research-approved self-reporting tool based on nine items. Its objective was designed to evaluate the level of depression in severity hence it is composed of nine understandable questions tailored for the individual. One most important feature of this scaling is that it divides depression on all Examenes categories – simple-to-use, practical and effective levels.

(i) Mild
(ii) Moderate
(iii) Moderately severe
(iv) Severe

The enhanced applicability of PHQ-9 justifies it as a universal tool due to its application at every level of health and different mental health conditions. This instrument can be used by patients as well, which then is an advantage as it provides for a defined means of autonomous diagnosis as far as the assessment of the degree of the depressive condition and its trend are concerned. The measurement properties of the PHQ-9 fit the scale to diagnostic applications quite well, as its sensitivity and specificity are as high as 88%, suggesting its usefulness given the different severity levels of depression that exist. Such impressive psychometric indexes have also demonstrated its critical application not only for the identification, but even more for the inconvenient screening, as well as treatment follow-ups.

Generalized Anxiety Disorder-7 (GAD-7)

The questionnaire is one of the most effective screening tools available which establishes the level of general worry, and it is very reliable. Its frequent utilization in clinical and research work justifies its importance in mental health diagnostics as well. There is substantial evidence on the sensibility of the GAD-7; 92% being the common known value, and the specificity being 85%. These indices have been tested from the derived cut-off point grades with accuracy which is sufficient for identifying symptoms of general anxiety disorder. Both the professionals and daughters and sons of mental health inpatient services have arrived at a consensus regarding the reliability of the GAD-7. The questionnaire – due to its impressive psychometric features – allows an assessment of such subtle disturbances as anxiety, thereby helping clinicians organize their medical efforts in patients with general anxiety disorder [20].

Utilizing Cognitive Behavioral Therapy (CBT)

Cognitive Behavioral Therapy (CBT), a form of therapy designed by the American psychiatrist Aaron T. Beck, is a new approach in solving mental health. This methodology cogent to cognitive-behavioral is aimed at negative thinking, emotions, and actions. CBT bases its logic on the fact that negative thought processes, as well as cognitive distortions, are part of the problems in behavior and emotion. Patients that are in the therapy are helped in changing the irrational thoughts, modify them and make them behave effectively in line with the way that a rational individual would in that given situation. The patients are educated on ways on how to think appropriately, control emotions and be prepared to put the behavior to task. The approach is mainly empowering people which is why it gives the patient and therapist equal initiative. Additionally, it applies techniques that are founded on research, like teaching the patient to correct himself-herself as inaccuracies occur in daily assertion about oneself; practicing how to work out problems that come up; and experimenting concrete ways of disputing and breaking the fake beliefs [21].

The efficacy of cognitive behavioral therapy depends on what is called health counseling and the patient. In other words, that is every relationship of the therapists, which is seen as helping the patient manage their cognitive restructuring, behaviors, attitudes, skills, and tendencies. These results can only be achieved by two parties working together, i.e., the patient and the therapist undertaking the therapy and improving the strategies used in therapy.

Neurofeedback

A complete form of biofeedback is neurofeedback in that it is more dynamic and is generally more effective in treating conditions such as attention deficit hyperactivity disorder and anxiety and depressive disorders in children. This unique technique provides an interesting opportunity for teaching one to change brainwave patterns by challenging the influence of neurofeedback on someone's body and perception of the current situation. In layman's terms, neurofeedback can be explained as such, that a person plays a computer game, and as soon as they manage to control the variations of their brain activity in the defined direction (i.e. with the desired brainwave activity) their character gains a point.

The basis of neurofeedback is the logic of the dynamics of the brain and its electromagnetic operation. The Electroencephalogram (EEG) methodology is employed to detect signals that are known to bring about changes that enhance thinking and behavior. This increase in certain brain waves as targeted in a specific region in the brain cortex helps in coping with stress as well as increases ability to cope emotionally. Through reinforcement of brainwave control by neurofeedback, its goal is that people's mental health does progressively get better.

This method of therapy involves no surgical incisions, and no pharmacological support either, which makes it acceptable for both ethical and disease-specific age groups. In people without brain injuries, this method is acquisition-based, that trains the brain and incites the bad neurons to self-correct without any bad effects [22].

Electroconvulsion Therapy

Electroconvulsive therapy is a modern and evidence-based approach that is a special treatment for patients who have a severe Major Depressive Disorder (MDD), which are refractory to common modalities of treatment. ECT is the provision of a brief electrical stimulation to the brain in a very carefully controlled manner to bring about a beneficial convulsion.

As with any surgery, the first part of the preparatory stages includes the obscuring of the patient by injecting a quick anesthesia and injection of muscle relaxants to make sure that the surgery remains relatively painless and comfortable to the patient. The current flow is controlled so that it passes from the electrode (usually situated on the scalp) to the region, either temporal or frontal region of the brain and such accounts for the goal of rectifying the state of disorder which is depression.

With its reasoning called social utility, this has positioned ECT (even known as DST for some) as part of the etanazacion and treatment of such high degree of urgency that means Caroline behavioral changes including levels of suicidality category charazil art mijbil catatonia and ECT hence remains the best treatment choice for such numerous related factors. It is quite effective especially when all other compliances and behaviors and psychotropic drug therapy have already failed. It has been scientifically proven that ECT works, contrary to the claims of the psychological era that fears it, and that CBT, which is cognitive therapy, is more effective than ECT. Such techniques have been validated to be effective by practice even under conditions where the psychiatric patient is reluctant and unwilling to cooperate, with or without pharmacotherapy.

Transcranial Magnetic Stimulation (TMS)

In regard to Transcranial Magnetic Stimulation (TMS), it is an innovative non-surgical treatment that mainly focuses on adults. This is specific to individuals who have not shown improvement using conventional therapy for depression. In many cases, this intervention is done with the patient fully awake and thus no sedation is required. It may be undertaken with no more imperfections, only for the patients who are deemed eligible in this manner. The normal course of such depression treatment in America requires sessions four or five days a week for about six weeks. To begin therapy, the doctor attaches a specially constructed electromagnetic coil to the skull, targeting the prefrontal cortex above the scalp – a crucial part of the midbrain principally responsible for mood functioning. MTCCCC: R5220. The coil generates a strong magnetic field that facilitates the flow of electric currents through the excitable cortical tissue in the subjects. These currents interact with the prefrontal tissues and help in beautifying the connectivity of the malfunctioned neural pathways which come about due to Major Depressive Disorder (MDD).

The utilization of TMS as a remedial strategy for obliterating low spirits and depressive feelings is quite beneficial in varying degrees, specifically in cases where other pharmacological remedies have failed to elicit the anticipated depressive improvement. The therapy is also effective, and fewer reports indicate briefer convalescent periods, limited toxicity, and minor discomfort after the post-depression recurrence.

Vagal Nerve Stimulation (VNS)

Vagus Nerve Stimulation (VNS) is an advanced therapeutic option which is implemented for treating severe depression in patients with a history of no response to conventional therapies. It is a neuromodulation method in which deep brain stimulation is carried out by employing a device which needs to be inserted surgically.

Here an implant is placed in the chest of the patient much like the size of a stopwatch. This implant is quite interesting in that it is connected to the left vagus nerve by a wire through the neck. The device is then powered on to start sending actual electrical impulses at particular intervals thereby making the already bidirectional communications accessible between the brain and the vagus nerve. These electric currents modulate the activities of the parts of the brain that are involved in mood control like the amygdala and the prefrontal cortex. Furthermore, as the VNS restores neurochemical balance and structural changes, the Far Location and Resistant MDD improves. The effectiveness of VNS is due to its unique capability to synergize peripheral and central nervous system communication, allowing for functional neuro-restoration. It is particularly useful where other forms of interventions such as pharmacological and psychotherapeutic or therapy with one of the interventions have not proven beneficial.

Alternative Procedures

More sophisticated systems and tools like Artificial Neural Networks, Deep Learning, and Machine Learning are now used in the area of wearables for predicting mood shifts. Significantly, with such technology, complications such as cesarean section without removing vital organs – for example, placenta previa in a woman with a low-lying placenta – and other concerns become a thing of the past. These wearable gadgets rely on the embedding of bio-signal sensors, internet connectivity, and radio systems for real-time monitoring of physiological and behavioral data at all times. These systems aid in biosignals capture are reviewed generating elaborate statistical evidence of the mental status of any dejected subjects. Therefore these biosignal-based systems can be used to file extensive stats of diagnosis of depression patients. The development in mental health care integrating state of the art AI technologies and wearable gadget devices has far reaching effects, in which help is offered before the problem occurs even to the individuals at risk [23].

6. Proposed Architecture

The proposed architecture envisions the employment of a portable wrist watch that can monitor and analyze physiological parameters and behaviors such as heart rate, internal temperature, blood pressure, oxygen saturation percentage, and body movements. To perform this task, the wearable incorporates an array of sensors such as accelerometers, gyroscopes, and galvanic response skin conductance (GSR) sensors that continuously collect important physiological and behavioral signals. Moreover, compensatory measures have also been taken in the form of using inertial sensors so as to prevent the occurrence of false alarms due to body movements, thereby ensuring the reliability in data collection whenever these data are needed. It is its goal that, in the name of improving health care service systems to enhance service access for individuals at risk of mental health problems that require rapid intervention, the architecture offers uninterrupted physiological monitoring that monitors any changes in health conditions without there being any need for invasive approaches and allows interventions to be carried out earlier. The design of the system is crafted down to a tee, and the activities of the structure are consistent as per the medical sciences in providing prevention and care attending to the person on a development basis [24].

Figure 1 depicts an IoT wearable built to demonstrate its functionality in relation to stress management. The device facilitates the incorporation of both physiological signs through sensors and stress indicators that use the brain (unhealthy habits) and provide interpretation of stress through active feedback. Moreover, a key feature of this app is its ability to deliver real-time, compassionate, and emotionally uplifting messages. Advanced technical support is also available when users require more than basic assistance or recorded and written guidance.

Figure 2 illustrates an IoT wearable gadget that identifies stress and offers assistance for its management. It consists of a sensor part (heart rate, skin conductance) and a processing unit that measures stress levels and provides operational feedback. A course of therapy includes structured psychotherapy and immediate instruction. Unattended information is sent to users from a smartphone/cloud by passing it through a security gateway directed to users without skippable guidance.

The utilization of sensors in peripheral devices is illustrated in Fig. 3, which emphasizes the generation of specific data sets for the purpose of monitoring a variety of health factors. The watch is used in collecting all the performance

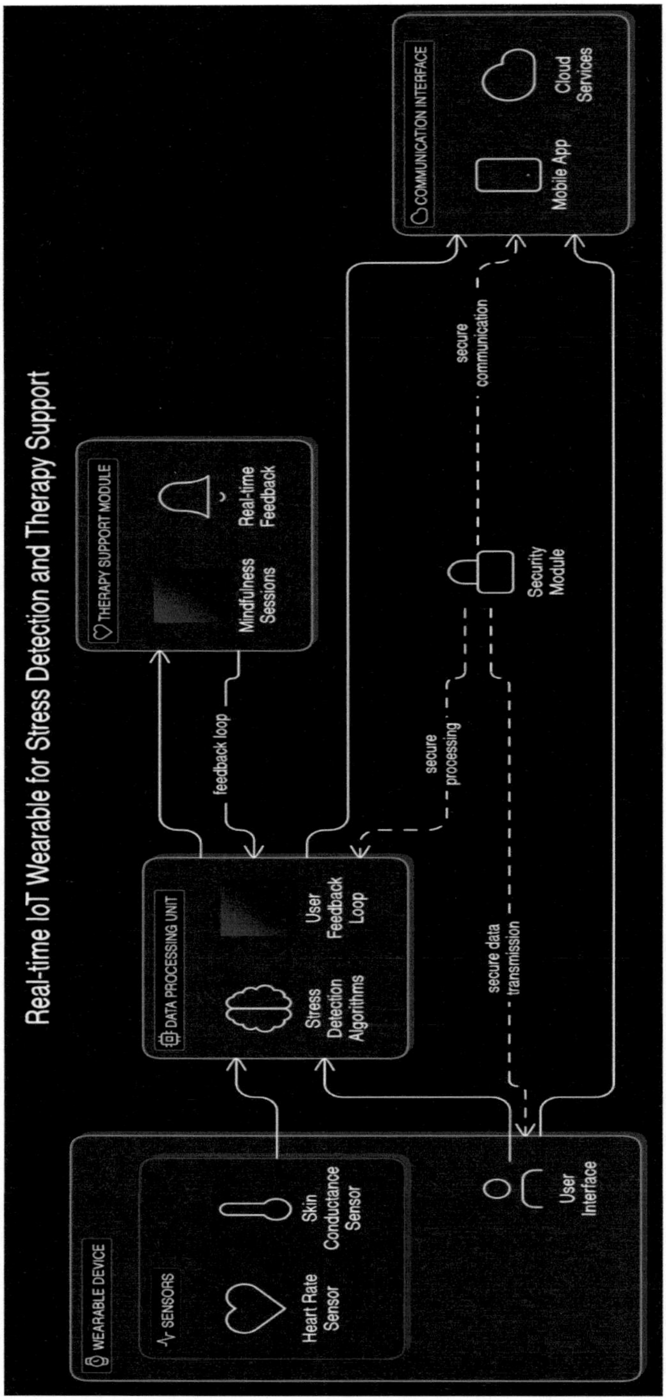

Figure 1: Real-time IoT Wearable for Stress Detection and Therapy Support.

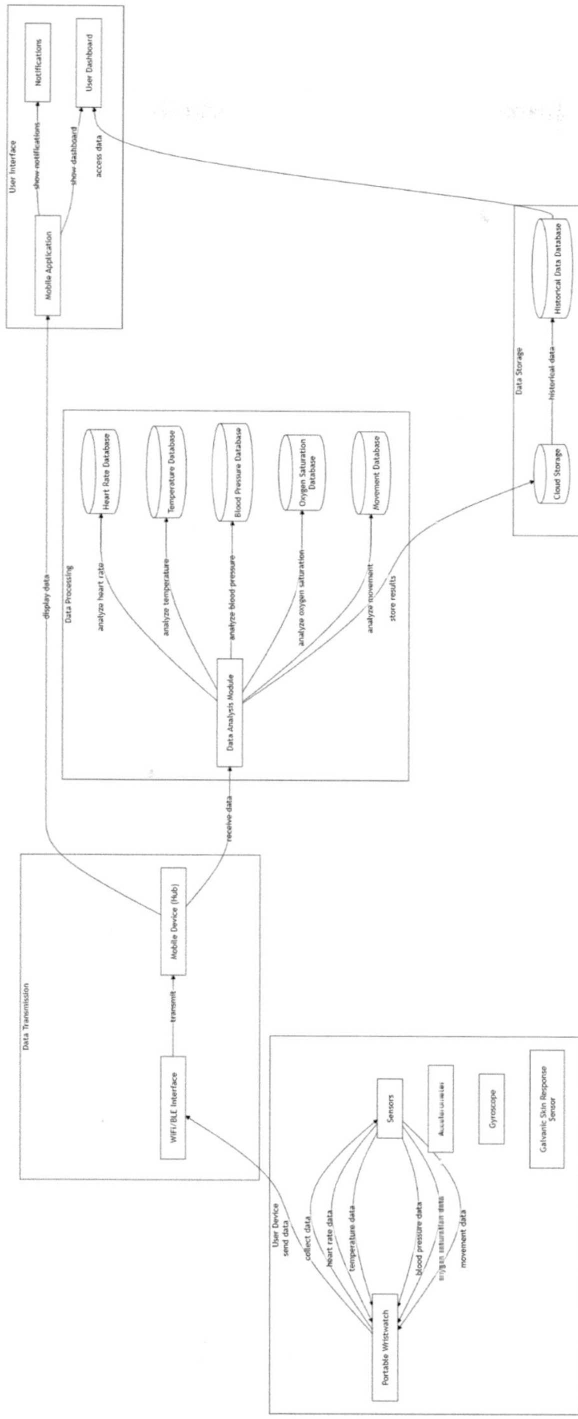

Figure 2: Block Diagram of the Proposed Solution.

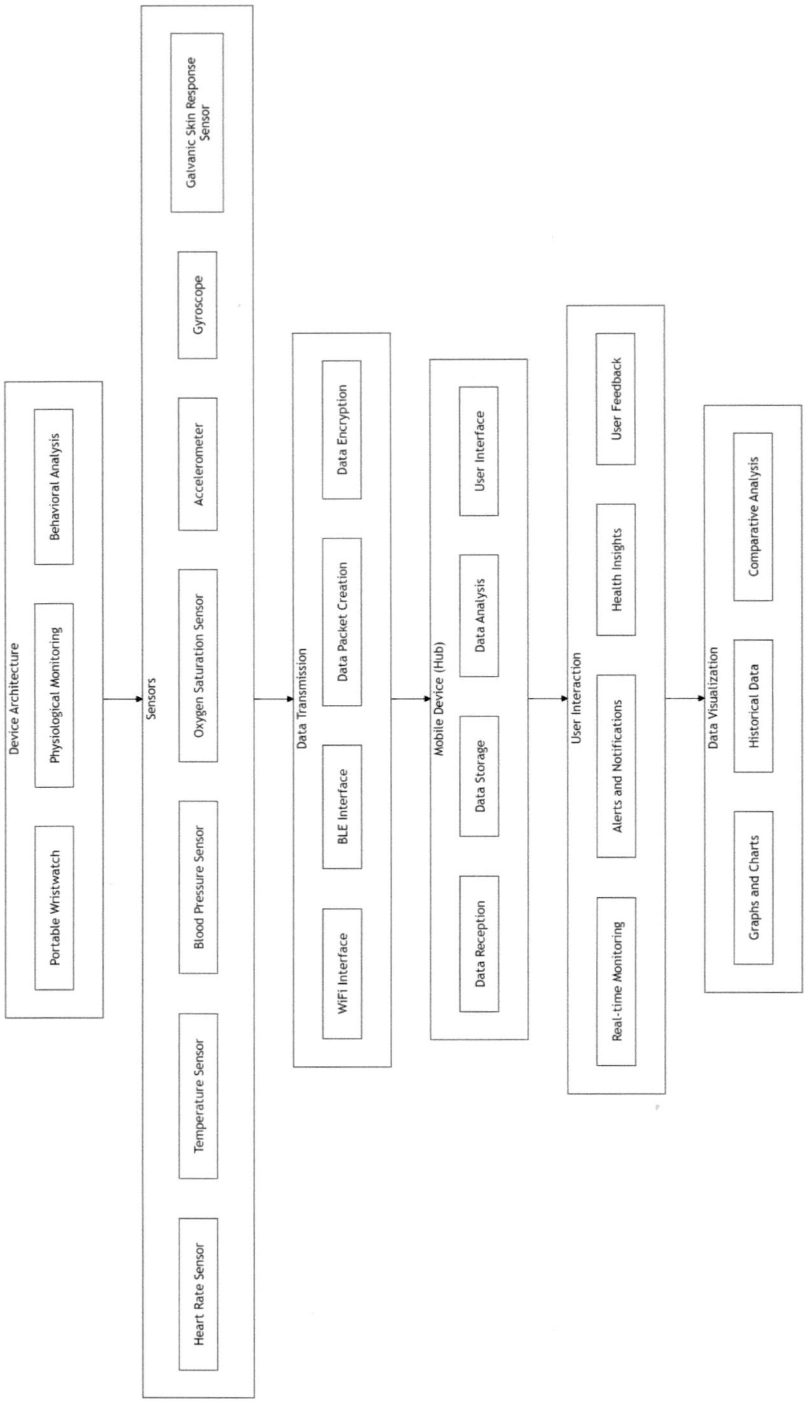

Figure 3: Process Diagram of the Proposed Solution.

indicators from the body of the wearer. After collection, the set of data is sent through the wireless networks such as WIFI, BLE, etc., and saved in the client device where it can be viewed and analyzed. Interaction is made by the user through mechanisms such as real-time alerts, personalized recommendation, and feedback, among other forms, with the processed data presented in images and tables alongside the graphical interpretations.

In the above architecture (Fig. 1) under consideration encompasses a body worn gadget which can acquire and process biosignals of the patient under treatment. These signals, which include diverse physiological data and behavioral responses, are then rapidly sent over WiFi/ BLE or similar interface to a mobile device also termed as a sensor or a hub (Fig. 2). Lastly the data is sent to the cloud and is carried out by a separate remote cloud computing application. The wearable device consists of continuous monitoring data streams whenever the patient is performing a task. Instead, data collection and analysis are done on a scenario or activity basis and then kept on a secure synthetic in a central database, with the user only having access to the piece designated for him or her. With the help of this device, it is easy for paid caregivers and healthcare professionals to acquire information about the patient without having to visit the patient thus enabling them to perform continuing evaluation (Fig. 3). Under circumstances where any critical or abnormal conditions manifest, virtual assistance shall be employed to immediately alert the clinician and care provider. At the same time, a built-in actuator is activated and performs calming treatments to the patient such as sound orchestra, posters or videos of peaceful environment, setting of temperature etc. promoting the emotional stability of the patient. This configuration clearly illustrates the prevention of any oppositional debates concerning how to treat each patient who has psychological distress.

7. Conclusion and Future Scope

The new architecture aims to prevent severe outcomes, such as suicidal ideation, by introducing a comprehensive approach to managing and supporting individuals with depressive disorders [25, 26]. It will be using biosignals continuously as a monitoring system and will execute an automatic mood stabilizing activity like music playing, showing favorite images, or displaying favorite videos. This is all understood by the system to reduce the person's distress and work for emotional wellness. In addition, it will include emergency notices for interveners such as the psychiatrist, a nearby healthcare facility, and designated caregivers. The full data set is gathered from a single database that is updated daily, weekly, and monthly, allowing for the generation of statistical reports on the fluctuations of biosignals acquired by wearable sensors. This would enable clinicians and researchers to keep a close eye on their progress and adjust interventions as and when necessary. In the future, it could even go further by adding medication adherence monitoring or optimization of drug dosages which would further reduce side effects caused by medications. Although, certain challenges still persist; for example, the type of sensor technology, standardization of clinical data collection, and very effective management of huge heterogeneous datasets. Furthermore, choosing appropriate communication protocols and designing an effective, low-cost device will be critical for widespread adoption. Another big barrier is the patient's refusal to let technological intrusion in their daily lives. This can only be remedied with the concerted effort of researchers, clinicians, and technologists in improving usability, building trust, and demonstrating real care benefits to enhance mental health.

References

1. Chanda, K., Roy, S., Mondal, H., and Bose, R. (2022). To judge depression and mental illness on social media using twitter. *Univers. J. Public Health*, 10, 116–129.
2. WHO. Preventing suicide: A resource for media professionals, update 2017. Geneva: World Health Organization (WHO/MSD/MER/17.5). License: CC BY-NC-SA 3.0 IGO, 2017.
3. Ogden, R. W. (1972). Large deformation isotropic elasticity – On the correlation of theory and experiment for incompressible rubberlike solids. *Proceedings of the Royal Society of London. A. Mathematical and Physical Sciences*, 326(1567), 565–584.
4. Denny, M., Wells, J., and Cunningham, J. (2011). Assessing psychosocial work-related stress across five European countries: Implications for workforce development. *The Journal of Mental Health Training, Education and Practice*, 6(2), 93–103.
5. Zook, C. (2004). *Beyond the Core: Expand Your Market without Abandoning Your Roots*. Harvard Business Press.
6. Ghosh, M., Chatterjee, S., Das, D., Chanda, K., and Roy, S. (2021). An analytical study for predicting suicidal tendencies using machine learning algorithms. *Brainwaves*, 2, 137–146.
7. Nag, A., Das, A., Sil, R., Kar, A., Mandal, D. and Das, B. (2023). Application of Artificial Intelligence in Mental Health. *In:* Abraham, A., Pllana, S., Casalino, G., Ma, K., Bajaj, A. (eds) Intelligent Systems Design and Applications. ISDA 2022. *Lecture Notes in Networks and Systems,* vol 646. Springer, Cham. https://doi.org/10.1007/978-3-031-27440-4_13
8. Chanda, K., Ghosh, A., Dey, S., Bose, R., and Roy, S. (2022). Smart self-immolation prediction techniques: An analytical study for predicting suicidal tendencies using machine learning algorithms. *Smart IoT for Research and Industry*, 69-91.
9. Kerr, L. K., and Kerr Jr., L. D. (2001). Screening tools for depression in primary care: The effects of culture, gender, and somatic symptoms on the detection of depression. *Western Journal of Medicine*, 175(5), 349.
10. Williams, J. B., Kobak, K. A., Bech, P., Engelhardt, N., Evans, K. et al. (2008). The grid hamd: Standardization of the Hamilton depression rating scale. *International Clinical Psychopharmacology*, 23(3), 120–129.
11. Richter, P., Werner, J., Heerlein, A., Kraus, A., and Sauer, H. (1998). On the validity of the beck depression inventory. *Psychopathology*, 31(3), 160–168.
12. Kroenke, K., Strine, T. W., Spitzer, R. L., Williams, J. B. W., Berry, J. T., and Mokdad, A. H. (2009). The PHQ-8 as a measure of current depression in the general population. *Journal of Affective Disorders*, 114(1-3), 163–173.

13. Girard, J. M., Cohn, J. F., Mahoor, M. H., Mavadati, S. M., and Rosenwald, D. P. (2013). Social risk and depression: Evidence from manual and automatic facial expression analysis. In: *Automatic Face and Gesture Recognition (FG), 2013 10th IEEE International Conference and Workshops on IEEE*, 1– 8.
14. Girard, J. M., Cohn, J. F., Mahoor, M. H., Mavadati, S. M., Hammal, Z., and Rosenwald, D. P. (2014). Nonverbal social withdrawal in depression: Evidence from manual and automatic analyses. *Image and Vision Computing*, 32(10), 641–647.
15. Solomon, C., Valstar, M. F., Morriss, R. K., and Crowe, J. (2015). Objective methods for reliable detection of concealed depression. *Frontiers in ICT*, 2.
16. Bharti, P., Panwar, A., Gopalakrishna, G., and Chellappan, S. (2018). Watch Dog: Detecting self-harming activities from wrist worn accelerometers. *IEEE Journal of Biomedical and Health Informatics*, 22(3), 686–696.
17. Siegmund, D., Horr, O., Chiesa, L., Gabler, F., Braun, A., and Kuijper, A. (2017). Fraunhofer Institute for Computer Graphics Research (IGD) Fraunhoferstrasse Darmstadt, Germany and Hochschule Darmstadt, University of Applied Sciences, Germany. Talis – A Design Study for a Wearable Device to Assist People with Depression. *2017 IEEE 41st Annual Computer Software and Applications Conference*, pp. 543–548.
18. McGinnis, R. S., McGinnis, E. W., Jessica Hruschak, J., Lopez-Duran, N. L., Fitzgerald, K., Rosenblum, K. L. and Muzik, M. (2018). Wearable sensors and machine learning diagnose anxiety and depression in young children. *2018 IEEE EMBS International Conference on Biomedical & Health Informatics* (*BHI*), pp. 410–413, 4–7 March 2018, Las Vegas, Nevada, USA.
19. Zhou, X., Kai Jin, K., Shang, Y., and Guo, G. (2018). Visually interpretable representation learning for depression recognition from facial images. *IEEE Transactions on Affective Computing*, pp. 1–12.
20. Al Jazaery, M., and Guo, G. (2018). Senior Member, IEEE, Video-based depression level analysis by encoding deep spatiotemporal features. *IEEE Transactions on Affective Computing*, pp. 1–8.
21. Corlier, J., Abboud, S., Zapata, V., Latouche, M., Valderrama, M., and Navarro, V. (2018). The gastric myoelectrical activity response to emotional stimuli. *2018 IX International Seminar of Biomedical Engineering* (*SIB*), Bogota, Colombia.
22. Zhang, D., Li, H., Sun, J., Hu, W., Jin, W., Li, S., and Tong, T. (2018). Antidepressant-like effect of low-intensity transcranial ultrasound stimulation. *IEEE Transactions on Biomedical Engineering*, pp. 1–10.
23. American Psychiatric Association. (2013). Diagnostic and Statistical Manual of Mental Disorders (5th edition). Arlington, VA: American Psychiatric Publishing.
24. Sadock, B. J., Sadock, V. A., and Ruiz, P. (2009). *Comprehensive Textbook of Psychiatry*. Ninth edition. Philadelphia: Wolters Kluwer.
25. Chanda, K., Bhattacharjee, P., Roy, S., and Biswas, S. (2020, June). Intelligent data prognosis of recurrent of depression in medical diagnosis. In *2020 8th International Conference on Reliability, Infocom Technologies and Optimization* (*Trends and Future Directions*) (*ICRITO*), pp. 840–844). IEEE.
26. Nag, A., Mondal, H., Raihan Kabir, S. R., Islam, M. R., Ahmed, M. E., and Hasan Jamil, S. M. (2013). Emotion Decoding: An Extensive Examination of Electroencephalogram Signals Using Explainable Machine Learning. 2024 6th International Conference on Electrical Engineering and Information & Communication Technology (ICEEICT), pp. 604-609, 2024, doi: 10.1109/ICEEICT62016.2024.10534518.

10 | Big Data and IoT in Public Health Management

Avijit Saha[1], Riya Sil[1*] and Meetu Malhotra[2]

[1] Department of Computer Science & Engineering, Brainware University, India

[2] Harrisburg University of Science and Technology, PA, USA

The convergence of the Internet of Things (IoT) and Big Data is transforming public health management, shifting the paradigms by which health data is collected, analyzed, and applied. These advances offer new paths for real-time surveillance, predictive analysis, and personalized treatment plans. Big Data, comprised of large volumes of structured and unstructured data, facilitates trends and patterns identification to inform public health policies, interventions, and resource allocation. At the same time, IoT devices such as environmental sensors and wearable health trackers enable continuous data collection, thereby improving the capability for early disease detection and proactive health management. This chapter addresses the revolutionary use of Big Data and IoT in public health, particularly in disease surveillance, chronic disease, and health behavior tracking. By analyzing data in electronic health records, wearable devices, and social networks, public health practitioners can predict disease outbreaks, monitor population health, and customize health campaigns and personalized treatment plans. However, their deployment raises several issues, including data privacy, security, interoperability, and quality. Ethical concerns, including informed consent and appropriate use of data, are also important considerations. Real-world applications, including their use in fighting the COVID-19 pandemic and the creation of smart city health initiatives, illustrate their capacity to change. Briefly, the chapter foresees the convergence of the Internet of Things (IoT) and Big Data with artificial intelligence (AI) to further develop predictive analytics and decision-making. It also addresses the growth of telehealth, remote diagnosis, and the shift towards standardized health data models, as well as the need to address existing privacy and ethical concerns.

*Corresponding author: riyasil1802@gmail.com

DOI: 10.1201/9781003635215-10

1. Introduction

The convergence of the Internet of Things (IoT) and Big Data in public health administration has transformed the approach used in the collection, analysis, and utilization of health data. These emerging technologies provide capabilities such as real-time monitoring, predictive analytics, and personalized healthcare interventions, which ultimately result in improved health outcomes and more effective healthcare systems. In the midst of increased pressures of chronic diseases, population aging, and global health emergencies in the form of pandemics, the demand for data-driven healthcare practices has increased exponentially [1]. Leaning on the power of Big Data and IoT, public health professionals are able to achieve unprecedented insights into disease trends, patient behavior, and environmental determinants, enabling improved decision-making and intervention strategies [2].

Big Data in Public Health Management

Big Data is the term used to describe large amounts of structured and unstructured data collected from a variety of sources. Sources of public health data include electronic health records (EHRs), wearable technology, social media, and environmental sensors, among others [3]. Big Data analytics entails processing and analyzing the data to identify patterns, trends, and insights to guide public health policy decisions and health interventions [4]. Central to this is the capacity to process and analyze different types of data, such as [5–11]:

(i) **Electronic Health Records (EHRs):** Patient medical histories, diagnoses, treatments, and outcomes.
(ii) **Wearable Devices:** Information gleaned from exercise trackers, wearables, and medical sensors, monitoring body movement, pulse, sleep phases, and several other health signals.
(iii) **Social Media:** Information from sources such as Twitter and Facebook, utilized to track public opinion and monitor disease outbreaks.
(iv) **Environmental Data:** Data from air quality sensors, weather stations, and other data sources that may impact public health.

With Big Data, public health experts can now examine early signs of outbreaks, predict health trends, and develop more tailored treatment approaches through advanced analytic techniques [12]. The power here is having the capability to deal with large sets of data in real-time in order to react more quickly with data-driven response to emerging health issues.

Internet of Things (IoT) in Public Health

Internet of Things (IoT) is a system of connected devices that are sensor- and software-embedded and contain other technologies, which facilitate data gathering and exchange. In public health, IoT devices, including wearable fitness trackers, smart thermometers, environmental sensors, and smart inhalers, facilitate continuous data accumulation, thus facilitating proactive health monitoring and intervention strategies. IoT devices can enable real-time observation of patient activities, physiological parameters, and environmental conditions [13]. Such a steady flow of data can enable health professionals to identify impending health risks early, monitor chronic diseases, and monitor environmental factors influencing public health, like air quality or weather [14].

AI in Public Health

Artificial Intelligence (AI) has emerged as a revolutionizing agent in public health, using computational power to examine complex data, automate tasks, and produce actionable information. Its adoption in public health infrastructure makes early disease outbreak detection easier, maximizes resource allocation, makes clinical decision support better, and enhances patient engagement [15]. With access to previously unseen amounts of health data from electronic health records (EHRs), mobile health apps, wearable technology, and environmental sensors, AI is facilitating more proactive and evidence-based public health management [16]. The AI technologies of machine learning (ML), natural language processing (NLP), and computer vision are now demonstrating their potential in predictive modeling, diagnostic support, health monitoring, and population health analysis. With the world's public health systems under mounting pressure, including pandemics, aging populations, and health disparities, AI offers new opportunities for enhancing responsiveness, efficiency, and equity in health care [17].

Predictive Disease Surveillance and Outbreak Detection

AI is transforming the potential to identify and act on outbreaks of disease through the analysis of large and disparate datasets that older methods struggle to process quickly or at all. AI analytics systems have the ability to combine and analyze data from various sources, e.g., social media platforms (e.g., Twitter), electronic health records, environmental, mobility, global travel activity, and even weather data, to determine emerging health threats at record pace and accuracy. This allows public health officials to act quickly and effectively to interrupt the spread of infectious disease, often before an outbreak becomes an extensive problem difficult to control [18–20]. A leading instance of AI deployment in the identification of early outbreaks is the Canadian health tech firm BlueDot. BlueDot employs AI and machine learning-based analysis of a mixture of datasets, news reports, flight patterns, and health records, to identify Wuhan, China, as the outbreak of COVID-19. From real-time processing of the sets of these datasets, the platform identified evidence of a potential public health issue nine days before the World Health Organization (WHO) issued its formal notice. The consequent heads-up to governments and public health officials enabled an earlier start in preparation for the pandemic, allowing more effective response and resource deployment. BlueDot's early detection is a sign of the potential of AI to identify possible health crises ahead of time before they are officially recognized by conventional surveillance systems [21]. Through portals like social media, where an individual can report sickness or health complaints, AI systems can detect preliminary signs of unusual patterns of sickness, which can be a sign that an outbreak is forming. Additionally, AI's capability to analyze mobility and travel habits enables real-time monitoring of how quickly a disease can cross borders, an essential function in our globalized world where infectious diseases can become international threats with lightning speed. The effectiveness of AI for predicting disease outbreaks and tracking disease spread has been confirmed by scholarly research [22]. One Lancet Digital Health (2020) study demonstrated the promise of AI models that combined mobility data (e.g., human movement patterns and traveling) with syndromic surveillance data (e.g., emergency department visits and health records) to predict the spread of COVID-19 [23]. In this case, the AI models accurately predicted patterns of COVID-19 transmission in U.S. counties up to two weeks in advance. By analyzing human movement between counties as well as within counties, and by analyzing early health markers, these AI models accurately predicted both magnitudes and timing of virus transmission with stunning accuracy. This ability to forecast is a game-changing improvement in public health, allowing policymakers to pre-emptively deploy resources (e.g., ventilators and healthcare workers) instead of reacting to epidemics after they have reached crisis points [24]. Such AI-based outbreak detection is also a step beyond the COVID-19 instance. Similar AI-based platforms have been used to predict and track the spread of other infectious diseases, such as influenza, Zika virus, and Ebola. For example, AI platforms have been used to track influenza activity by analyzing public online forums where patients report flu-like symptoms, and analyzing past health data and weather conditions that often accompany influenza outbreaks [25]. By combining multiple data sources into one harmonized AI platform, public health agencies can more comprehensively evaluate disease transmission and evolution, and therefore significantly improve their response to emerging health threats. The combination of AI with Big Data also potentially opens the way for more precision medicine, i.e., identifying at-risk groups by travel, demographic, or even preclinical evidence of infection. This would enable health officials to deploy regional measures, like travel bans, mass screening, or quarantining communities, to curb spread. AI also can help improve vaccination drives by determining which region or population might be most at risk, making vaccines and treatments more evenly distributed and effective [26]. Artificial intelligence's ability to analyze and synthesize large and heterogeneous data sets is transforming the way that public health agencies identify and react to outbreaks of infectious disease. With early warnings, disease spread predictions, and data-driven decision support, AI is enhancing readiness at a worldwide scale and optimizing the effects of interventions and saving lives while reducing the economic and social costs of pandemics. As AI evolves further, its value in disease surveillance will continue to grow in its importance in establishing an active, networked model of global public health [27].

Key Technologies Used:

(i) Media and news cover natural language processing
(ii) Geospatial modeling for predicting spreading
(iii) Anomaly detection on patient visit data and IoT health signals

Diagnostic Support and Decision Aid

AI methods can equal or surpass human performance in disease diagnosis from medical images and from organized information. Such methods are increasingly being applied to cancer screening, diabetic retinopathy, cardiovascular disease, and skin diseases [28, 29]. In Table 1, we can see a comparison of the top AI technologies used in healthcare, together with details about their main purpose, methodology, data source, and claimed accuracy.

Table 1: AI Tools in Healthcare and Accuracy

AI tools	Health area	Reported accuracy	Deployment region
DeepMind Health (UK)	Eye disease, breast cancer	94–98%	United Kingdom, U.S.
PathAI	Pathology slide analysis	95%+	North America
Aidoc	Radiology & stroke detection	Real-time triage	Europe, U.S., Israel
SkinVision	Skin cancer risk analysis	81–93%	Mobile app (Global)

Population Health Management

Artificial Intelligence (AI) is increasingly becoming a vital force in transforming public health through improving the accuracy of stratified risk estimates and aiding targeted interventions of heterogeneous populations. Possibly the most significant use of AI is its ability to analyze vast amounts of data derived from diverse sources of health data—electronic health records (EHR), imaging, wearable devices, and even genomic data—to identify people who are high risk of contracting chronic diseases like hypertension, diabetes, mental disorders, and cardiovascular disease. This capability allows the healthcare system to act on health risks before they become issues, maximize the use of resources, and tailor interventions to address the unique needs of individuals or populations at risk. Artificial intelligence-based predictive models use machine learning algorithms to process intricate datasets, identifying patterns that might not be identifiable using traditional methods. For instance, by examining past medical history, lifestyle determinants, and socio-demographic factors, AI systems can precisely predict who is at higher risk of developing conditions like Type 2 diabetes or hypertension in the next few years. This ability enables health practitioners to identify high-risk groups, offering preventive interventions or early treatments before complete development of these conditions, thus reducing long-term healthcare burdens. Artificial intelligence further improves resource allocation in public health by enabling more accurate intervention targeting [30]. Rather than using a universal strategy for all, health authorities can employ custom approaches that address the specific risks of various subpopulations. For instance, AI algorithms can help in the identification of high-risk-level chronic disease risk factors such as obesity or smoking, thus informing the rollout of health promotion programs for targeted intervention. In the same vein, AI can help prioritize patients for screenings or preventive care services, thus maximizing the effectiveness of resource distribution. One of the most significant examples of AI implementation is the initiative launched by the United States Centers for Medicare and Medicaid Services (CMS) to reduce hospital readmissions. CMS used machine learning algorithms to predict patients with a high likelihood of readmission within 30 days of discharge, taking into account factors like medical history, treatment adherence, and social determinants of health (e.g., transportation, housing stability). Through this risk stratification process, healthcare providers were able to direct their interventions more efficiently towards these high-risk patients, delivering tailored interventions like follow-up care, medication management, and social support services. Through this, CMS reduced hospital readmission by 8.5% in one year, proving the effectiveness of AI-based strategies in improving patient outcomes and optimizing healthcare delivery. In addition to reducing the hospital readmission rate, AI has also been utilized to improve mental health care by identifying early individuals at risk for developing disorders like depression or anxiety [31]. Based on the analysis of behavioral patterns, social media, and health information, AI can spot early warning signs of mental disorders and thus allow for early intervention and treatment. AI-based chatbots and voice assistants are also being utilized increasingly to provide real-time mental health interventions, providing cognitive behavioral therapy (CBT) or simply providing emotional support to individuals who do not have easy access to traditional mental health treatment.

Health Communications and Chatbots

AI virtual assistants and chatbots are being used to spread health information, respond to public inquiries, and offer mental health counsel. For example, WHO rolled out an AI chatbot during the COVID-19 pandemic on messaging platforms such as Facebook Messenger and WhatsApp and provided updates in various languages (WHO Digital Health Strategy Report, 2021). AI chatbots in public health reduced misinformation and increased reach by over 65% during pandemic communication campaigns [32].

Administrative and Resource Optimization

AI facilitates smart medical supply allocation, hospital bed occupancy forecasting, and staffing. Predictive models enhance preparedness in the event of public health crises through intervention scenario simulation. Table 2 looks at how different amounts of data, processing capacity, and domain knowledge affect the choice of AI tools, their applications, and their stated accuracy in healthcare contexts.

Table 2: AI's Accuracy and Use Cases According to Resources

Resource	AI-enabled forecast accuracy	Use case
ICU Beds	85–93%	COVID-19 peak demand prediction
PPE Inventory	90%+	Hospital stockpile optimization
Workforce Needs	88%	Staffing during vaccine campaigns

2. Applications of Big Data and IoT in Public Health Management

Big Data and IoT technologies have transformed public health through enabling real-time monitoring, predictive analytics, and personalized interventions. The technologies enable proactive health management, early disease detection, and effective resource allocation. Some of the primary applications will be discussed below, beginning with their use in disease surveillance and outbreak detection [33].

Disease Surveillance and Outbreak Detection

Big Data and the Internet of Things (IoT) are revolutionizing the manner in which public health agencies track, forecast, and react to disease outbreaks. By gathering, analyzing, and disseminating health data in near real-time at a scale and velocity previously unimaginable, these technologies offer valuable instruments for early warning and timely response to emerging public health threats. This transition from passive, retrospective surveillance methods to active, real-time surveillance of health is a major step forward in epidemic intelligence [34]. Wearable IoT technology such as smartwatches, fitness trackers, biosensors, and even wearable smart clothing are among the stars of this digital revolution. These wearable devices continuously capture physiological signals such as heart rate variability, skin temperature, respiratory rate, blood oxygen saturation (SpO_2), and activity levels. When aggregated together and analyzed within populations, minute deviations in these signals can serve as early indicators of infectious disease onset—even at times before individuals become symptomatic. These first physiological changes can be flagged as potential indicators of illness, and individuals can pursue care, and health systems can act before widespread transmission occurs [35]. The real-time data streams generated by such devices are transmitted securely over networks to centralized platforms, where advanced analytics and machine learning algorithms are used to detect patterns, anomalies, and correlations. For example, a sudden spike in body temperature or heart rate among individuals in a given geographic area can signal the emergence of a localized outbreak. By combining this information with other data sources—electronic health records, pharmacy claims, and environmental sensors—public health authorities can develop a comprehensive situational awareness that enables more rapid, more effective interventions. Physiological and location information were gathered in real-time from IoT-enabled sensors in mobile phones and health wearables and used to track the spread of the virus and identify incipient hotspots. Public health authorities in some places were able to utilize this information to inform containment, such as lockdowns at the local level, quarantine orders, and contact tracing. Symptom-tracking enabled mobile health apps also allowed millions of users to report their health status, further enhancing surveillance databases and predictive outbreak modeling. Besides, from its application in monitoring COVID-19, wearable technology has also been promising in the monitoring of influenza-like illness (ILI). Several studies have employed aggregated temperature and heart rate data gathered by wearables to detect anomalies in typical population health patterns. These anomalies were highly correlated with the timing and spatial pattern of influenza epidemics and thus suggest that wearables can function as a distributed network of bio-sensors that can complement existing influenza surveillance systems [36]. Early detection of increases in ILI symptoms can allow public health agencies to initiate targeted vaccination campaigns or send medical resources to areas of highest need. In addition, IoT sensors deployed in public spaces—e.g., intelligent thermometers in schools or workplaces, environmental sensors in transport hubs, and air sensors in urban areas—can provide contextual data to complement wearable-derived data. When analyzed together, the multiple data sources can uncover hidden connections between environmental parameters and the transmission of disease, such as the effect of humidity or air quality on respiratory illnesses. Overall, the embedding of IoT and Big Data technologies in disease surveillance systems is a significant advance in global public health readiness. By facilitating real-time detection, early warning, and quick response to emerging outbreaks, the technologies lower the effects of infectious diseases, optimize resource use, and save lives. As the systems evolve, their function in protecting public health will be an expanding part of national and international health security strategies [37].

Chronic Disease Management

The intersection of Internet of Things (IoT) devices and Big Data analytics is revolutionizing chronic disease management by facilitating proactive, personalized, and persistent care. Diseases like diabetes, cardiovascular disease, asthma, and hypertension require extended monitoring and timely interventions—needs that are best addressed by these new digital health technologies. IoT-enabled medical devices offer the possibility of tracking patient health parameters in real-time outside traditional clinical settings, and Big Data analytics offers the ability to facilitate deeper understanding and predictive modeling in the context of disease progression, ultimately aiming to reduce hospital readmissions and improve patient outcomes. Internet of Things sensors, from wearable health monitors to implantable sensors and networked home health devices, enable ongoing monitoring of critical signs such as blood pressure, heart rate, respiratory rate, blood glucose, and oxygen saturation. These data streams are securely transmitted to healthcare providers through cloud-based systems, enabling clinicians to monitor changes in a patient's health status in near real-time [38]. When abnormalities arise, such as sudden increases in blood glucose or arrhythmias—automated notifications can be generated, enabling prompt medical intervention. This transition from reactive to proactive care substantially improves chronic disease management by taking complications before they become critical events. Big Data analysis also adds value to IoT-collected data by revealing patterns, relationships, and trends not easily visible with conventional monitoring. By analyzing longitudinal health data gathered from varied sources e.g., electronic health records, wearable sensors, genetic data, and lifestyle logs—predictive models can predict the risk of disease worsening. Patients with heart failure, for example, can be closely monitored for early signs of fluid overload, and predictive models can alert clinicians to impending decompensation, enabling them to adjust medications or prescribe lifestyle interventions pre-emptively. Such predictive data enable preventive interventions that decrease emergency department presentations and hospitalization, resulting in improved long-term health outcomes and reduced healthcare costs. In the field of diabetes care, continuous glucose monitors (CGMs) are a prime example of IoT use. CGMs provide real-time data regarding blood glucose levels, often with patient and clinician alerts to notify of hypo- or hyperglycemic events. With insulin pumps and sophisticated algorithms, CGMs can be part of an automated insulin delivery regimen—sometimes called an "artificial pancreas", that dynamically varies insulin delivery based on the patient's current glucose level and recent history. Wearable devices, including smartwatches and fitness trackers, are pivotal to the quantification of physical activity, caloric expenditure, heart rate variability, and sleep patterns. This information provides an integrated perspective of an individual's lifestyle, which is of specific interest in the management of diseases such as obesity, hypertension, and Type 2 diabetes. For instance, the regular monitoring of exercise patterns and resting heart rates enables both patients and clinicians to evaluate the efficacy of lifestyle modifications and make evidence-based adjustments [39]. For patients with asthma or chronic obstructive pulmonary disease (COPD), networked spirometers and smart inhalers give the potential to track patterns of medication use, identify environmental precipitants such as air quality or pollen counts, and quantify lung function. When augmented by location and patient health data, this information can allow prediction of asthma attack and inform customized treatment regimens.

Health Behavior Monitoring

In the modern era, mobile health (mHealth) and wearable technology are becoming useful tools for monitoring health behavior and facilitating preventive health action. There is an increasing trend on the part of individuals, health workers, and public health organizations to use these technologies to monitor key lifestyle indicators, such as physical activity, sleep patterns, diet, and stress management. The constant, real-time data yielded by these devices permit a wide and dynamic perspective on the health behaviors of persons and populations, and thus yield valuable information that can inform individualized and population-based health promotion activities. Wearable technology such as smartwatches, fitness trackers, and biosensors, linked with accelerometers, gyroscopes, heart rate monitoring, and GPS, can record and measure a broad range of physiological and behavioral measurements. For instance, fitness trackers measure steps, calories burned, exercise intensity, and duration of physical activity. With such data, health professionals and public health specialists can track patterns of sedentary behavior, which are linked with higher risks of developing chronic diseases such as cardiovascular disease, obesity, and type 2 diabetes. From analyzing these trends in behavioral data, health professionals and public health specialists can design interventions—such as tailored activity goals, behavioral support, or game-like challenges—to motivate users toward more physically active lifestyles. Similarly, the capacity to track sleep integrated into wearable devices and mobile health apps is based on data gathered from motion and heart rate variability sensors to estimate the duration of sleep, detect the stage of sleep (light, deep, REM), and track sleep disruptions. Low quality of sleep has been found to be associated with a multitude of health complications, including impaired cognitive function, psychological disorders, and an impaired immune response. Data gathered from sleep data can detect abnormal sleep patterns or disorders like insomnia or sleep apnea. Interventions can thus be made to maximize sleep hygiene behavior, which may include a change in bed-time habits, limiting screen time before bedtime, and managing stress levels [40]. M-health applications are often a supplementary tool to wearables in the form of platforms to capture different lifestyle behaviors such as food consumption, hydration status, medication taking, and mood assessment. Many of these apps include artificial intelligence-powered coaching functions with real-time feedback, reminders, and motivational messaging tailored to meet the goals and progress of the user. With the passage of time, the accumulation of such vast behavioral information allows predictive models of health that can identify earliest warning signs of risk and lead early preventive interventions. Further, large user groups' anonymized and aggregated data can be a wealth of information for public health research and program planning. Population-level analysis of geographic areas' or demographic groups' activity and sleep patterns can determine health behavior disparities that provide guidance to policymakers about how to efficiently allocate resources and create culturally specific health promotion campaigns. Essentially, mobile health applications and wearable devices are reshaping how health-related behaviors are measured, interpreted, and controlled. By providing people with informative feedback and enabling healthcare professionals to create more targeted and evidence-based treatments, these technologies hold out great promise for improving preventive health and establishing a culture of proactive health care management.

3. Types of Data Utilized

The following table summarizes the main types of data utilized in Big Data and IoT applications in public health, along with examples of sources and specific applications. Types of Data Used in Big Data and IoT Applications in Public Health are listed in Table 3 [35–40].

Table 3: Types of Data Utilized in Big Data and IoT Applications in Public Health

Data types	Source examples	Applications in public health
Electronic Health Records	Hospitals, Clinics	Disease tracking, patient history analysis
Wearable Device Data	Fitness trackers, Smartwatches	Monitoring physical activity, heart rate, sleep
Environmental Sensor Data	Air quality monitors, Weather stations	Assessing environmental health risks
Web Data	Health forums	Monitoring public sentiment, detecting outbreaks
Genomic Data	DNA sequencing labs	Personalized medicine, understanding disease genetics

4. Benefits of Integrating Big Data and IoT

The combination of Big Data and IoT in public health management has several advantages [41]:

(i) **Real-time Monitoring:** Continuous data gathering allows for real-time response to health occurrences, improving results through provision of prompt intervention.
(ii) **Predictive Analytics:** Through data analysis from the past, predictive models can forecast future health patterns, allowing for early intervention to avoid diseases and contain outbreaks.
(iii) **Personalized Interventions:** Mobile app and wearable device data facilitate

personalized healthcare interventions that are directed at the particular needs of a specific individual, enhancing patient outcomes and satisfaction.

(iv) Resource Optimization: Evidence-based information helps healthcare systems optimize resources, become more efficient and less expensive.

5. Challenges and Considerations

Despite the benefits, the integration of Big Data and IoT into public health faces several challenges:

(i) Data Privacy and Security: Medical information is highly sensitive in nature and requires strict controls to ensure confidentiality and protection against cyber-attacks.

(ii) Interoperability: Integrating data from different systems and devices could be complicated, and standardized protocols could be required to facilitate smooth data exchange.

(iii) Data Quality: It is crucial to the success of Big Data and IoT initiatives that the data is maintained accurate and complete.

(iv) Ethical Issues: Issues of consent, data usage, and risk of bias of predictive models must be met with appropriate concern to prevent public trust loss.

6. Case Studies

Various case studies have been conducted on the subject. But the ones that stand out in today's day and age are our Pandemic Response and Smart City Health Initiatives.

Pandemic Response

The COVID-19 pandemic was a turning point for the use of digital technologies towards public health response, with Big Data and the Internet of Things (IoT) being key enablers of monitoring, management, and mitigation of the virus's effects. The technologies were key tools for health authorities and governments worldwide as they attempted to contain outbreaks, monitor disease status remotely in patients, and optimize healthcare resource utilization during a time of unprecedented stress on healthcare systems. One of the most important applications of Big Data during the pandemic was epidemiological surveillance. Huge amounts of data—collected from mobile phones, social media, electronic health records, and IoT sensors—allowed real-time monitoring of virus transmission patterns by region. Predictive modeling and machine learning algorithms were employed to predict infection trends, detect emerging hotspots, and model the likely effect of interventions like lockdowns or social distancing orders. All of these insights were important in guiding public health policy, enabling authorities to make evidence-based decisions about when and where to impose movement restrictions or send emergency medical supplies. IoT technologies enhanced the ability to track patients outside of traditional clinical settings much more than before. Wearable devices such as smart thermometers, pulse oximeters, and biosensors were utilized by hospitals and health authorities to track key physiological parameters, temperature, heart rate, oxygen saturation, and respiratory rate, among COVID-19 patients, especially those under quarantine or self-isolation at home. Wearables enabled the detection of early deterioration of symptoms, allowing healthcare staff to intervene in time and avoid risk of severe illness or hospitalization. In other cases, wearable data were input into centralized monitoring dashboards to provide clinicians with real-time feedback on patient status, allowing better triage and tailored care plans [42]. Additionally, remote monitoring technologies have reduced the need for face-to-face interactions between patients and medical professionals, thus helping to reduce exposure and save critical resources like personal protective equipment (PPE). In many regions, Internet of Things (IoT)-enabled telehealth systems have emerged as critical tools for performing remote consultations, diagnoses, and follow-up care, thus helping to maintain continuity in medical services while minimizing the chances of virus transmission in clinical environments. Big Data has played a major role in healthcare logistics and resource allocation management. By analyzing hospital admission trends, intensive care unit bed utilization, and ventilator utilization, decision-makers were able to reallocate resources adaptively, divert patients to less congested facilities, and predict demand surges. Data analytics also helped plan and execute mass vaccination campaigns by detecting vulnerable populations, real-time vaccine dispensation, and tracking public attitudes and compliance. In short, Big Data, IoT, and wearable technology integration throughout the COVID-19 pandemic not only amplified the world's response to the worldwide pandemic but also set the standard for how digital health infrastructure can be used in subsequent public health crises [43]. These technologies showed their capacity to provide agile, scalable, and data-informed responses, leading ultimately to improved health outcomes and healthier health systems.

Smart City Health Initiatives

With the fast-growing rate of urbanization, there is significant growth in the use of IoT technology in smart cities to promote healthier and sustainable living environments. Such interconnected systems play a vital role to observe, analyze, and regulate varied environmental and social factors directly impacting public health. IoT devices spread across urban infrastructure enable continuous real-time data acquisition, which promotes evidence-based decision-making and early intervention in public health problems. One of the most important uses of the IoT in the case of smart cities is the surveillance of environmental conditions, i.e., the monitoring of air quality. Advanced air quality sensors can be installed systematically on the urban landscape to monitor pollutants such as particulate matter (PM2.5 and PM10), nitrogen dioxide (NO_2), sulfur dioxide (SO_2), ozone

(O_3), and carbon monoxide (CO). These sensors provide in-depth information on hotspots of pollution, temporal trends, and exposure levels, thus enabling city governments to make timely declarations of health or enact traffic controls to curtail emissions. Moreover, this data can be used to input public health surveillance systems to assess the effects of chronic pollution on respiratory and cardiovascular disease, especially on vulnerable populations such as children and the elderly. In addition to pollution monitoring, smart cities utilize IoT-based noise sensors to monitor sound pollution, water quality sensors to detect contamination, and urban heat island detection systems to detect exposed areas during heatwaves. These technologies allow city planners and public health officials to preempt environmental stressors before they escalate into full-blown health crises. Alongside environmental monitoring, smart city initiatives are also using IoT to promote active, healthy lifestyles. Networked public fitness equipment in parks and recreation facilities—smart bicycles, treadmills, and outdoor gym stations—can track usage and provide immediate feedback [44]. Combined with mobile health apps, this data can be utilized to help users establish fitness goals, receive personalized coaching, and participate in city-wide wellness challenges. A few cities are even piloting incentive-based programs that reward citizens for completing exercise milestones through gamification and data collected from wearable devices and fitness trackers. In addition, IoT-influenced infrastructure like smart streetlights and pedestrian counters can enhance urban mobility by making it safer to walk and cycle, promoting walking and cycling through the enhancement of planning infrastructure from real usage data. These improvements not only enhance physical activity but also decrease motor vehicle reliance, reducing pollution levels and public health in general. In essence, IoT technologies form the digital nervous system of the smart city, enabling real-time exchange of information that powers health-oriented innovation. IoT technologies enable cities to be health-aware and forward-looking in their ability to address health risks, enhance environmental sustainability, and build a culture of well-being among citizens.

Lives Saved by Big Data and IoT in Healthcare Management

Though there are no central sources of data regarding the total number of lives saved by Big Data and IoT in Healthcare Management. But according to our research, based on various other studies done by professionals of the field we have made a chart.

Figure 1 displays the estimated number of lives saved per year through the use of IoT and Big Data technologies across various time periods from 2000 to 2025. The x-axis distinguishes six various time periods, and the y-axis is the estimated number of lives saved, with values up to 1.2 million per year. Each bar is split by two parts: the lower black part is the lower estimated lives saved, and the upper gray part is the higher estimated lives saved. The figures depict a negligible contribution during the early years (2000–2005), reflecting the introductory phases

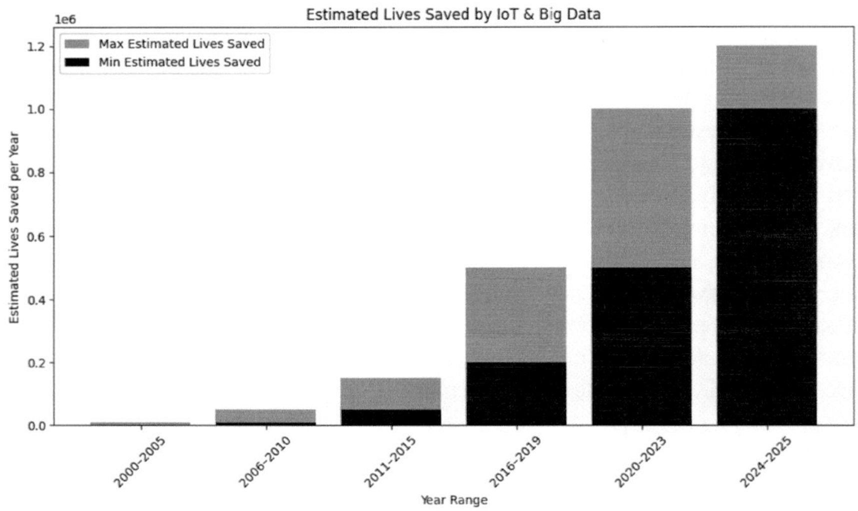

Figure 1: Estimated Lives Saved by Big Data and IoT in Healthcare Management.

of IoT and Big Data adoption within healthcare systems. A gradual growth is observed between the time periods from 2006 to 2015, reflecting an increased adoption rate and technological advancements [45]. A drastic increase starts in the years from 2016 to 2019, with a sharp growth between 2020 and 2023, indicating the global implementation of digital health technologies, particularly due to global health crises such as the COVID-19 pandemic. By the time period from 2024 to 2025, estimates indicate that IoT and Big Data technologies can save up to one million and 1.2 million lives per year. The trend demonstrates the growing significance and efficacy of the technologies in promoting public health outcomes. The figure not only specifies technological advancements but also highlights the role of real-time data analytics and anticipatory health management in contemporary healthcare systems.

7. Conclusion

The path of public health administration is on the cusp of drastic transformation with the increasing application of Big Data and the Internet of Things (IoT). When optimized, these technologies will transform approaches to anticipating, monitoring, and fighting public health threats. One such promising development is the widespread integration of Artificial Intelligence (AI) with Big Data and IoT platforms. AI can potentially transform conventional data analysis by enabling real-time, predictive analysis to render public health programs more precise. AI-based algorithms can sift through the enormous amounts of data generated by IoT devices—e.g., wearable health devices, smart thermometers, and networked inhalers—to detect early indicators of infectious disease outbreaks, simulate transmission dynamics, and suggest prompt interventions. With predictive capability, mobilization of resources will be improved considerably, emergency preparedness will be more refined, and individualized responses will be enhanced, particularly in the event of epidemics or natural disasters. In addition, the intersection of telehealth and IoT will transform the delivery of healthcare, especially to remote and underserved populations. IoT-connected devices such as smart blood pressure monitors, continuous glucose monitors, and ECG wearable monitors enable the real-time transfer of patient data to healthcare professionals, enabling constant remote monitoring. Not only does this reduce unnecessary in-person visits and reduce the healthcare facilities' workload, but it also enables earlier intervention and increased patient engagement, which ultimately leads to better public health outcomes. As more devices join the network, the requirement for universal and standard data protocols grows more pressing. Interoperability—where various systems can exchange and share information without a hitch—is essential to the successful implementation of Big Data and IoT solutions. Absent standardization of data formats, terminologies, and exchange protocols, the integration of disparate data sources will remain piecemeal and inefficient. Universal data standards will simplify collaboration, data security, and privacy protection, thereby enhancing public trust. In short, the confluence of IoT, Big Data, AI, telehealth, and interoperable protocols will build a more efficient, equitable, and responsive public health system that can address today's and tomorrow's health challenges.

References

1. Asri, H., and Jarir, Z. (2023). Toward a smart health: Big data analytics and IoT for real-time miscarriage prediction. *Journal of Big Data*, 10(1). https://doi.org/10.1186/s40537-023-00704-9
2. Rathore, M. M., Ahmad, A., Paul, A., Wan, J., and Zhang, D. (2016). Real-time medical emergency response system: Exploiting IoT and big data for public health. *Journal of Medical Systems*, 40(12). https://doi.org/10.1007/s10916-016-0647-6
3. Vairam, T., Sarathambekai, S., Umamaheswari, K., Jothibanu, R., and Manojkumar, D. (2020). Real-time cardiovascular health monitoring system using IoT and machine learning algorithms. *Securing IoT and Big Data*, 145–162. https://doi.org/10.1201/9781003009092-8
4. Velmovitsky, P. E., Alencar, P., Leatherdale, S. T., Cowan, D., and Morita, P. P. (2021b). Towards real-time public health: A novel mobile health monitoring system. *2021 IEEE International Conference on Big Data (Big Data)*, 6049–6051. https://doi.org/10.1109/bigdata52589.2021.9672059
5. Arridha, R. (2018). *Classification Extension Based on Iot-Big Data Analytic for Smart Environment Monitoring and Analytic in Real-Time System*. https://doi.org/10.31227/osf.io/stmg6

6. Jamal, B., Alsaedi, M., and Parandkar, P. (2023). Portable smart emergency system using internet of things (IoT). *Mesopotamian Journal of Big Data*, 75–80. https://doi.org/10.58496/mjbd/2023/011
7. Nwadiokwu, O. T. (2025). AI augmented digital twins for IoT-enabled smart infrastructure: Big data analytics for real-time optimization. *International Journal of Research Publication and Reviews*, 6(2), 1871–1886. https://doi.org/10.55248/gengpi.6.0225.0901
8. Gultekin, E., and Aktas, M. S. (2022). A business workflow architecture for predictive maintenance using real-time anomaly prediction on streaming IoT Data. *2022 IEEE International Conference on Big Data (Big Data)*, 4568–4575. https://doi.org/10.1109/bigdata55660.2022.10020384
9. Kaur, P. (2023). Internet of things (IoT) and Big Data Analytics (BDA) in healthcare. *Digital Transformation in Healthcare in Post-Covid-19 Times*, 45–57. https://doi.org/10.1016/b978-0-323-98353-2.00015-0
10. Desarkar, A., and Das, A. (2018). Exploration of healthcare using data mining techniques. *Advances in Healthcare Information Systems and Administration*, 243–259. https://doi.org/10.4018/978-1-5225-5222-2.ch014
11. Nag, A., Das, B., Sil, R., Hameed, A. A., Bhushan, B., and Jamil, A. (2024a). A survey on image-based cardiac diagnosis prediction using machine learning and deep learning techniques. *Studies in Computational Intelligence*, 478–491. https://doi.org/10.1007/978-3-031-53717-2_44
12. Sil, R., Debnath, N., and Roy, A. (2021). Study on resource monitoring of E-healthcare system. *Lecture Notes in Bioengineering*, 433–442. https://doi.org/10.1007/978-981-33-6915-3_43
13. Popkova, E. G., and Sergi, B. S. (2022). Digital Public Health: Automation based on new datasets and the internet of things. *Socio-Economic Planning Sciences*, 80, 101039. https://doi.org/10.1016/j.seps.2021.101039
14. Prasath, J. S. (2021). Compound cryptography for internet of things based industrial automation. *Internet of Things*. https://doi.org/10.5772/intechopen.95845
15. Varsak, S. (2024). Internet of things (IoT) applications in Public Health. *Complementary Medicine with New Approaches*, 77–90. https://doi.org/10.69860/nobel.9786053359418.7
16. Kim, J. I., and Kim, G. (2024). Evaluation of health factors on artificial intelligence and the internet of things-based older adults healthcare programmes. *Digital Health*, 10. https://doi.org/10.1177/20552076241258663
17. Sil, R. (2022). Sentiment analysis-based legal case prediction system. *SSRN Electronic Journal*. https://doi.org/10.2139/ssrn.4145582
18. Dash, S., Shakyawar, S. K., Sharma, M., and Kaushik, S. (2019). Big data in healthcare: Management, analysis and future prospects. *Journal of Big Data*, 6(1). https://doi.org/10.1186/s40537-019-0217-0
19. Paterson, A., Olliaro, P. L., and Rojek, A. (2023). Addressing stigma in infectious disease outbreaks: A crucial step in pandemic preparedness. *Frontiers in Public Health*, 11. https://doi.org/10.3389/fpubh.2023.1303679
20. Dila R. B., and Ron K. (2022). Paradigm Shift of Statistical Big Data in Healthcare: Management, Analysis and Future Prospects. *Pravaha*, 28(1), 35–44. https://doi.org/10.3126/pravaha.v28i1.57969
21. Zhao, Y., Genovesi, S., Jiang, T., Manara, G., and Costa, F. (2025). High capacity chipless RFID system enabled by Machine Learning Predictive Models. *IEEE Internet of Things Journal*, 1–1. https://doi.org/10.1109/jiot.2025.3560682

22. Chen, Z., Xiong, G., Sun, Y., Li, Y., and Li, Y. (2022). An internet-of-things-enabled system for road icing detection and prediction. *IEEE Internet of Things Journal*, 9(20), 20257–20269. https://doi.org/10.1109/jiot.2022.3175220
23. Pramanick, B., and Manuel, A. (2023). IoT-enabled biosensors for cancer and disease detection. *Internet of Things in Biomedical Sciences*. https://doi.org/10.1088/978-0-7503-5311-3ch4
24. Agiwal, V., Chaudhuri, S., and Naskar, S. (2024). Distribution of infectious disease outbreaks in India before and after the COVID-19 pandemic: Analysis of National Weekly Surveillance Data. *Indian Journal of Public Health*, 68(1), 124–127. https://doi.org/10.4103/ijph.ijph_488_23
25. Ali, H. (2025). AI for pandemic preparedness and infectious disease surveillance: Predicting outbreaks, modeling transmission, and optimizing public health interventions. *International Journal of Research Publication and Reviews*, 6(2), 4605–4619. https://doi.org/10.55248/gengpi.6.0225.0941
26. Babanejaddehaki, G., An, A., and Papagelis, M. (2025). Disease outbreak detection and forecasting: A review of methods and data sources. *ACM Transactions on Computing for Healthcare*, 6(2), 1–40. https://doi.org/10.1145/3708549
27. Adegoke, B. O., Odugbose, T., and Adeyemi, C. (2024). Data analytics for predicting disease outbreaks: A review of models and tools. *International Journal of Life Science Research Updates*, 2(2), 001–009. https://doi.org/10.53430/ijlsru.2024.2.2.0023
28. Cable News Network. (2023, March 7). *Images show AI detecting breast cancer 4 years before it developed.* CNN. https://www.cnn.com/videos/health/ 2023/03/07/artificial-intelligence-breast-cancer-detection-mammogram-cnntm-vpx.cnn
29. Sara, R., and Kahina, R. (2023). Applying decision aid science to support customer choices for Web Services Operations. *2023 International Conference on Decision Aid Sciences and Applications (DASA)*, 109–115. https://doi.org/10.1109/dasa59624.2023.10286760
30. Fatima, S., Kishor Kumar Reddy, C., Nag, A., Pullannagari, S.R. (2024). Leveraging Quantum Computing for Enhanced Decision Support in Disaster Management. *In:* Reddy, C.K.K., Nag, A., Ouaissa, M., Bhushan, B., Hanafiah, M.M. (eds) The Rise of Quantum Computing in Industry 6.0 Towards Sustainability. *Advances in Science, Technology & Innovation. Springer*, Cham. https://doi.org/10.1007/978-3-031-73350-5_6
31. Sibillo, A., and Ricciardi, W. (2023). Public health and AI: Health neural network. *Journal of Public Health Policy*, 44(3), 511–514. https://doi.org/10.1057/s41271-023-00417-6
32. Alarcon-Santos, E.-A., Montane-Jimenez, L. G., and Hernandez-Calderon, J.-G. (2024). Integration of IoT and data visualization for personalized diabetes management. *Avances En Interaccion Humano-Computadora*, 9(1), 249–252. https://doi.org/10.47756/aihc.y9i1.178
33. Talpur, M. S., Abro, A. A., Ebrahim, M., Kandhro, I. A., Manickam, S., Laghari, S. U. et al. (2024a). Illuminating healthcare management: A comprehensive review of IoT-enabled chronic disease monitoring. *IEEE Access*, 12, 48189–48209. https://doi.org/10.1109/access.2024.3382011
34. Tuan, D. A., and Thanh, D. T. (2024). *Harnessing AI and IoT for the Future of Healthcare: A Comprehensive Review on Chronic Disease Management and Pandemic Response*. https://doi.org/10.20944/preprints202409.2451.v1
35. Malathi, J., Kusha, K. R., Isaac, S., Ramesh, A., Rajendiran, M., and Boopathi, S. (2024). IoT-enabled remote patient monitoring for chronic disease management and

cost savings. *Advances in Computational Intelligence and Robotics*, 371–388. https://doi.org/10.4018/978-1-6684-6361-1.ch014

36. Waqdan, M., Louafi, H., and Mouhoub, M. (2023). A comprehensive risk assessment framework for IoT-enabled healthcare environment. *Proceedings of the 20th International Conference on Security and Cryptography*, 667–672. https://doi.org/10.5220/0012060900003555
37. Javaid, M., and Khan, I. H. (2021). Internet of things (IoT) enabled healthcare helps to take the challenges of covid-19 pandemic. *Journal of Oral Biology and Craniofacial Research*, 11(2), 209–214. https://doi.org/10.1016/j.jobcr.2021.01.015
38. Malik, H., and Zatar, W. (2019). An IoT enabled framework to support structural health monitoring applications. *Structural Health Monitoring 2019*. https://doi.org/10.12783/shm2019/32242
39. Arunkumar, S., Vetriselvi , M., and Thanalakshmi, S. (2020). Cryptography based security solutions to IoT enabled Health Care Monitoring System. *Journal of Advanced Research in Dynamical and Control Systems*, 12(7), 265–272. https://doi.org/10.5373/jardcs/v12i7/20202008
40. Thakur, M., Kumar, A., and Chatterjee, I. (2023). IoT-enabled solutions for Alzheimer's disease management: Innovations and opportunities. *Neuroscience Research Notes*, 6(4). https://doi.org/10.31117/neuroscirn.v6i4.255
41. Raza, M., Awais, M., Singh, N., Imran, M., and Hussain, S. (2021). Intelligent IoT framework for indoor healthcare monitoring of Parkinson's disease patient. *IEEE Journal on Selected Areas in Communications*, 39(2), 593–602. https://doi.org/10.1109/jsac.2020.3021571
42. Zhu, Z. (2024). Maternal mental health monitoring in an online community: A natural language processing approach. *Behaviour & Information Technology*, 1–10. https://doi.org/10.1080/0144929x.2024.2333927
43. Sil, R., Roy, A., Dasmahapatra, M., and Dhali, D. (2021). An intelligent approach for automated argument based legal text recognition and summarization using machine learning. *Journal of Intelligent & Fuzzy Systems*, 41(5), 5457–5466. https://doi.org/10.3233/jifs-189867
44. Melendez, J., van Ginneken, B., Maduskar, P., Philipsen, R. H., Ayles, H., and Sanchez, C. I. (2016). On combining multiple-instance learning and active learning for computer-aided detection of tuberculosis. *IEEE Transactions on Medical Imaging*, 35(4), 1013–1024. https://doi.org/10.1109/tmi.2015.2505672
45. Yang, M., Nurzynska, K., Walts, A. E., and Gertych, A. (2020). A CNN-based active learning framework to identify mycobacteria in digitized Ziehl-Neelsen stained human tissues. *Computerized Medical Imaging and Graphics*, 84, 101752. https://doi.org/10.1016/j.compmedimag.2020.101752

11 | Leveraging Big Data and IoT for Advanced Public Health Management

Gajjela Jahnavi[1*], Avula Mahathi[1], Kishor Kumar Reddy C[1] and Nastassia Thandiwe Sithole[2]

[1] Department of Computer Science & Engineering, Stanley College of Engineering and Technology for Women, India
[2] Department of Chemical Engineering Technology, University of Johannesburg, South Africa

The public health system has been enhanced by the use of big data and the Internet of Things. While the Internet of Things (IoT) refers to the use of smart watches, health sensors, and other internet-connected devices to get real-time data, big data refers to the collecting and analysis of enormous amounts of health data. These in turn assist doctors in improving medical care, anticipating and preventing diseases, and remotely monitoring patients. Of the two, the early prognosis may be easier to identify as falling under the more general heading of disease prevention and early testing. Connected to the internet, interconnected fixtures allow medical facilities to evaluate a patient's condition and react appropriately. These include smart blood sugar monitors and smart thermometers. For the relevant populations, it also takes part in campaigns, immunizations, and disease intervention initiatives. These consist of Big Data and IoT will therefore be used in future research to create ever more specialized and efficient forms of healthcare for a greater standard of living globally. For example, the issue of data privacy, the typically greater expenses related to setting up IoT devices, and the lack of data scientists capable of handling the data.

1. Introduction

Public health has long been an important aspect of societal well-being, and technological advancements have significantly improved medical operations.

*Corresponding author: jahnavi.gajjela123@gmail.com

DOI: 10.1201/9781003635215-11

The advent of Big Data and the Internet of Things (IoT) has altered healthcare delivery by enabling real-time monitoring, accurate diagnosis, and effective disease management.

This chapter looks at how Big Data and IoT might assist public health, focusing on applications, impacts, challenges, and new trends. The healthcare industry is always adapting to meet new challenges and improve patient outcomes. Big data and IoT have become key components of modern healthcare, providing insights gleaned from massive databases and real-time monitoring. Big data and analytics applications have the potential to revolutionize public health decision-making worldwide. By using these technologies, public health practitioners can gain additional knowledge about population health dynamics, risk factors, illness trends, and healthcare spending patterns [1]. This section lays the framework for understanding these technologies' transformative potential for public health.

2. Background and History

Table 1 provides historical evidence that confirms the acceptance of Big Data systems and IoT applications for healthcare reasons. Research examines the history of healthcare records from paper to digital databases to demonstrate why data-driven medical solutions have become so important. These new technologies are expanding because health organizations want greater ability to study massive medical datasets as a result of increased medical research and patient treatments. Professional healthcare staff can extract illness outbreak indications utilizing big data analysis and IoT devices to acquire real-time patient tracking and personalized treatment alternatives. The merging technology simplifies operations and reduces healthcare expenses by expanding global medical service delivery to provide accessible and effective healthcare. The healthcare industry has progressed beyond paper-based recordkeeping to comprehensive digitalization because it demands data-based solutions at an accelerating speed. The utilization of clean water and sewage systems to stop the spread of disease are early instances of technology in public health. The development of vaccines in the late 1800s fundamentally changed the direction of public health [6]. Traditional manual recordkeeping was replaced by digital conversion of health platforms late last century, which resulted in enhanced system performance, better data accuracy, and easier user information retrieval. By adopting cutting-edge public health technology, which produces outstanding techniques for delivering health services, health outcomes increase while medical costs decline.

Table 1: Evolution of Healthcare Technology and its Impact

Period	Development	Impact
1990	Digital health records	Improved record accessibility
2000	IoT integration	Real-time patient monitoring
2010	Big data analytics adoption	Predictive insights and research

Theoretical Foundations of Big Data and IoT in Healthcare

The term "Big Data" refers to the vast amounts of structured and unstructured patient health records that originate from a variety of sources, such as social health networks, electronic health records (EHRs), and medical imaging. The Internet of Things' data transmission and acquisition functions are carried out via linked devices that combine wearables, sensors, and remote monitoring tools. Wearable technology and Internet of Things devices provide remote patient monitoring, which continuously examines patients' health status outside of traditional healthcare institutions [2]. The integration of linked technologies gives medical professionals the information they need for medical diagnosis and treatment as well as prevention. IOT-enabled medical devices, like glucose sensors and heart rate monitors, as well as hospital equipment that delivers continuous data flows, power the IoT system. To provide individualized medical care, medical professionals combine patient medical data from external sources with pattern recognition and predictive outcomes analysis. Electronic patient records contain a great deal of information, such as the patient's medical, social, demographic, and health status [20].

Data sources, storage solutions, and advanced analytics platforms. Through Big Data, researchers can execute population-based research and establish suitable resource allocation, which facilitates medical providers to deliver bespoke healthcare services. Health sensors combined with hospital medical tools and smartwatches make possible the real-time monitoring of patients through IoT devices. These devices enable medical staff to reduce the patient-care gap by delivering proactively supportive healthcare services. Integrative Graphing of Big Data and IoT in the Health Sector emphasizes their synergistic functioning as a means to improve healthcare, remote monitoring of patients, and data-based decision-making. The process involves the transfer of the data stored on a wide range of IoT-based medical devices, for example, wearable sensors, smart hospital equipment, and remote monitoring systems. The sensors are permanently collecting the patient's health information.

Figure 1 shows that the authentic raw data is transferred via secure communication links to the cloud-based storage and processing systems for Big Data analytics to be executed. Big Data features, such as machine learning and predictive analytics, are the most important tools for the transformation of raw healthcare data into useful information. The most basic visual cues about diseases, patient monitoring, and prognosis of medical conditions are the main function of the insights derived from the data that are helpful for doctors to make decisions. This is yet another example to prove the Electronic Health Records (EHRs) play a crucial role in the centralization and unification of information from different sources, a step that in its turn enables healthcare providers to find data easily. Also, the picture shows the mode of operation of decision support systems through real-time analytics for clinical decisions. It indicates in what ways the processed data gets applied, for instance, personalizing treatment plans,

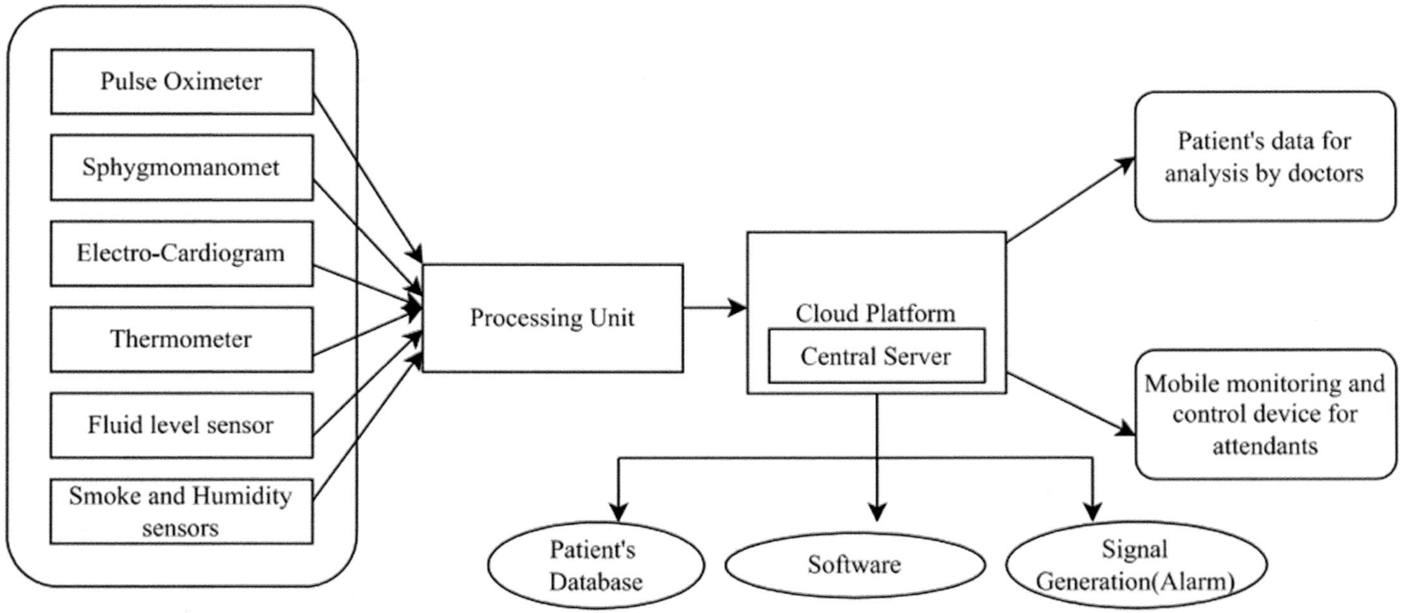

Figure 1: Block Diagram representing the integration of Big Data and IoT in Healthcare.

preventing diseases, and/or optimizing healthcare resources. The combination of Big Data and IoT depicted as a Legon the drawing, along with the convergence of Big Data and IoT technologies, which resulted in better patient outcomes, less frequent hospital admissions, and more efficient public health management. A suitable mechanism is the technological flow chart, the elements of which are in the different directions controlled by modern healthcare systems that are designed to enhance patient care by instituting disease prevention. To enhance IoT system performance and facilitate crucial decision-making, big data systems are an essential component of the infrastructure [21].

3. Key Architectures for Public Health Management Using Big Data and IoT

(i) **Lambda Architecture (Processing in Batch and Real-time):** Both real-time streaming input data streams and previous medical data records stored in timestamps are handled by two components of the Lambda architecture design. Long-term trend data is handled by the batch layer, while real-time data flows through the speed layer uninterrupted to support judgments. Medical personnel can obtain combined health instructions from the two subsystems thanks to the serving layer. Both pandemic tracking and chronic disease program management capabilities, as well as population health tracking systems, are among the exceptional advantages that the computing architecture offers.

(ii) **Kappa Architecture (Stream Processing Focus):** Kappa architecture only supports real-time data streams because the system does not support data batch processing. This architectural approach benefits emergency systems and wearable devices by allowing for the rapid execution of data analysis operations. The installation of Kappa design improves system efficiency through simple data pipelines, but it struggles with historical information assessment jobs.

(iii) **Microservice Architecture:** The healthcare application operates as distinct independent parts within a microservices architecture. The technical functioning of these independent modules retrieves patient data from diagnostic imaging and telemedicine activities. The implementation technique improves system flexibility and scalability by requiring regular software updates.

(iv) **Fog Computing Architecture:** Fog computing technology allows the network's edge to receive cloud processing capabilities for real-time IoT data processing near the device. A design structure allows for faster operating outputs for medical remote patient monitoring systems and emergency medical services. The operational functionality of this system is dependent on the right control methods for managing distributed resources.

Medical organizations choose the Lambda architecture given that it gives real-time procedure information while also allowing for historical data storage. Leadership competencies are key factors in the execution of entire patient care processes, as well as the creation of healthcare management systems and predictive analytics. To support individual patients from several perspectives, we show diverse structures, benefits, and repositories of each discipline, resulting in an integrated picture of how various healthcare tasks are done in the pipeline [3].

4. Role and Importance of Big Data and IoT in Public Health

The combination of IoT technology with Big Data analytics establishes a totally proactive system which generates defined healthcare delivery models. IoT provides innovative healthcare services by collecting sensitive data and employing it for autonomous control of healthcare devices [9]. Healthcare professionals detect upcoming infection threats through various real-time data collection systems which enable them to begin appropriate intervention protocols. Medical staff receive instructions to patients and patients participate in care through efficient technological resource distribution. Analysis of Big Data enables population health professionals to evaluate intervention data to discover patterns that build their support for governmental policies.

Healthcare data analysis from digital and background systems gives provider groups the power to create advanced clinical decisions that improve treatment outcome performance. IoT technology devices aid healthcare institutions in real-time tracking of hospital resources for enhanced distribution management. Predictive modeling when used by healthcare professionals enables them to foresee disease movement trends combined with patient health decline for early activation of response protocols. Chronic illness patients who undergo continuous streaming monitoring under the supervision of technological systems allow healthcare providers to minimize hospital-based appointments.

Big Data analytics enables tracking of disease patterns through data analysis that also helps health officials to observe disease growth patterns and assess intervention effectiveness. The interconnection of IOT technology with Big Data results in an essential system that enhances medical quality and lowers expenditures, and achieves better results.

The transformation of public health practice results from IoT and Big Data technologies that enable preventive healthcare services to individual patients. Medical personnel in these organizations can detect future outbreaks quickly because real-time data monitoring allows early detection. The implemented technological solutions enable healthcare operations to allocate resources effectively for creating next-generation patient management systems that support patient participation. Big Data evaluation generates multiple population health advantages by tracking patterns and generating policies from examined results.

By locating, evaluating, and summarizing the body of recent literature, an SLR also contributes to the consolidation and advancement of scientific research [24].

The graph illustrates the impact of the COVID-19 pandemic in the United States from the vaccination point of view, with major events in the history of the vaccine. The red curve is the time trend of new cases of COVID-19, and the blue solid line is the proportion of at least partially vaccinated individuals. The blue dotted line is the proportion of fully vaccinated individuals. The graph shows a comparative snapshot of the impact of the vaccine rollout on case numbers. Markers on the timeline indicate the key points from December 11, 2020, when the Pfizer rollout came into play, and then the Moderna rollout on December 18, 2020. They are mentioned given that this is when widespread immunization efforts began. The injected population continued to grow over time.

From the given Figure 2, it is evident that there is a clear correlation between rising vaccination and falling new cases. First, prior to when the vaccines were issued in circulation, the cases rose exponentially. But as the vaccinations rose, the infection curve began to lower, which is a reflection of the effectiveness of vaccines in suppressing the virus transmission. The trend reflects the effect of mass vaccination in suppressing and containing the pandemic influence.

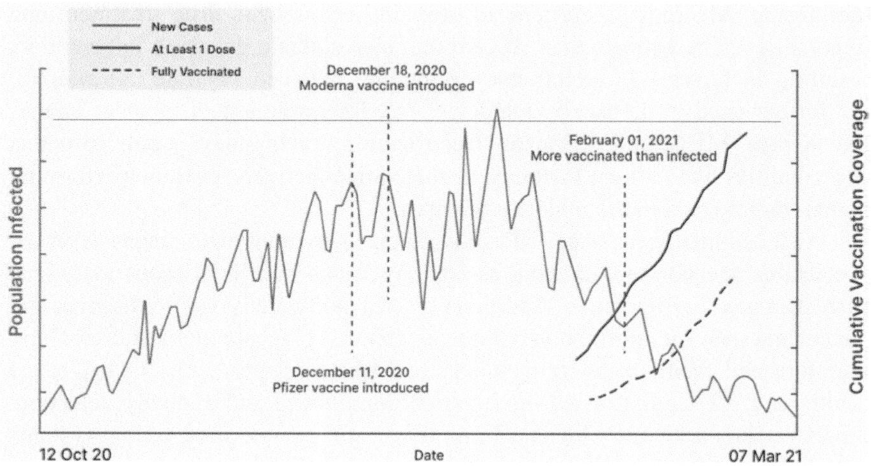

Figure 2: Impact of COVID-19 Vaccination on Infection Rates in the United States.

Artificial Intelligence and Machine Learning in Big Data and IoT Healthcare

The union of Machine Learning (ML) and Artificial Intelligence (AI) in health has transformed the processing, analysis, and leverage of medical data to treatment. In recent years, the convergence of data analytics with Internet of Things (IoT) technologies have resulted in significant advancements in a variety of industries

[4]. The advent of IoT and Big Data has led to the creation of huge amounts of patient data from electronic health records (EHRs), smart medical devices, and wearable sensors. AI and ML play a crucial role in extracting valuable insights from this data to facilitate predictive analysis, personalized medication, and real-time decision-making. AI and ML boost efficiency, precision, and patient outcomes, and make healthcare proactive and evidence-based. Predictive analytics is the most effective application of AI and ML for IoT health. Using reviews of past patient data and the real-time monitoring of health with IoT sensors, AI applications have the ability to detect patterns predicting the onset or deterioration of disease.

For instance, AI-based predictive models have the ability to predict the chances of a patient developing long-standing diseases like diabetes, cardiovascular disease, or high blood pressure through lifestyle, hereditary susceptibility, and current readings of health. Early diagnosis enables the physicians to give preventive care, thereby eliminating hospitalization and better results. Precision medicine and personalized care are the second biggest use cases. Conventional therapies are generic in approach, but with learning enabled by AI, the doctors can customize the therapy according to the patient's individual profile. With Big Data analysis of medical imaging, genomics research, and web-enabled health monitoring, ML models are able to provide personalized drug treatment and intervention. The patients then receive the most suitable drug and intervention, resulting in fewer side effects and optimizing the recovery rate. AI and ML are further used in diagnostic medicine, i.e., interpretation of medical images like X-rays, MRIs, and CT scans. Deep learning technology is able to detect abnormalities like tumors, fractures, or infection effectively, even outperforming human radiologists in the majority of cases.

Artificial Intelligence-based diagnostic machinery minimizes diagnosis errors, accelerates decision-making, and assists physicians in critical scenarios where early diagnosis is imperative. Additionally, NLP software is able to discover and understand relevant information within unstructured clinical reports and scholarly literature and facilitate faster diagnosis and treatment protocols. In IoT-based health care, AI facilitates real-time patient monitoring and anomaly detection. Smartwatches with intelligence, biosensors, and remote monitoring systems monitor patients' vital signs constantly, including heart rate, blood pressure, oxygen saturation, and blood glucose levels. Real-time data is processed by AI algorithms, detecting abnormality patterns, and notifying medical personnel of possible health risks. For instance, a wearable sensor based on AI is able to identify the onset of an impending heart attack and notify the patient and his or her physician automatically in order to intervene in time. The role of AI in developing and repurposing of COVID-19 health care, general epidemic AI services (GEAIS), and AI services (HCSIS) that might reduce the burden on health care professionals [12].

In addition, AI-driven automation is revolutionizing hospital functions and healthcare administration. Hospital functions are streamlined by ML algorithms by predicting patient admission volume, bed assignment automation, and medical supply chain optimization. Virtual assistants and chatbots using artificial intelligence also facilitate interaction among patients by providing drug-related information, booking appointments, and alerting the patients about taking medication. This lessens some load on the health workforce to allow them to engage in more care activities. Though all the benefits, the implementation of AI and ML in Big Data and IoT healthcare also presents issues. Data privacy and security concerns are the greatest challenges as massive amounts of personal patient information have to be processed and trained on AI algorithms. To ensure data security, it must be encrypted and stored in secure facilities employing clouds, with need-to-know access permissions. Furthermore, AI algorithmic prejudice might result in biased healthcare findings if the training data are not inclusive and representative, meaning they do not reflect the entire patient population. Ethical thought and active monitoring of AI should be utilized to prevent prejudice from spreading and to ensure justice in healthcare solutions via AI implementation.

With AI, ML, Big Data, and IoT, healthcare is being revolutionized to provide predictive analytics, personalized therapy, real-time monitoring, and operational efficiency. These technologies enable actionable intelligence for healthcare providers, enhance patient care, and make medical interventions more effective and preventive. The evolution of AI will be at the expense of cracking data security, ethics, and algorithmic bias in unleashing the power of AI and ML in healthcare.

5. Applications

Public health operations generate significant advantages through the collaboration of IoT applications with Big Data technologies. Medical personnel achieve the delivery of live disease supervision with IoT-based Big Data solutions for simultaneous distance healthcare application and automated medical device operation and vaccination management. Disease prediction algorithms utilize analysis techniques to generate visibility that forewarns about potential disease outbreak occurrences. Continuous vital sign monitoring through health devices permits patients to minimize their need for hospital trips but receive assistance promptly. The integration of glucose monitors through smart devices makes it possible for patients to actively observe their health development. Health organizations make use of vaccination data as emergency resources to enhance their delivery distribution systems. Healthcare systems that focus on improving medical services increase interactive patient care and support from health policies to yield top-quality health results worldwide.

- **(i) Disease Surveillance and Prediction:** Early detection of disease outbreaks through real-time data analytics. The evaluation of emergency room visits results in flu prediction outcomes from these medical records.
- **(ii) Remote Patient Monitoring:** Wearable ECG monitors from Remote Patient Monitoring provide healthcare providers with a system to track heart

conditions through connected devices that enable distant monitoring of persistent diseases.

(iii) **Smart Health Devices:** Modern medical device technology enables people to track their health through connected thermometers that work with glucose monitors, which give patients better control of their health status.

(iv) **Vaccination Campaigns:** Analysis of vaccination data leads healthcare providers to develop outreach initiatives that detect unprotected population hubs.

The pandemic worldwide as well as the COVID-19 situation especially showcased the essential role of these applications. The analysis of IoT device big data enabled healthcare organizations to time-effectively monitor health conditions and their vaccine distribution networks and healthcare service delivery systems. Big data and cognitive analytics can be used quickly to improve public health and the COVID-19 epidemic [19].

6. Methodology and Design

A critical analysis of Chapter Two design aspects takes place in Table 2. The research methodology describes the methods for obtaining healthcare Big Data (BD) alongside its tools for data collection. The three main health benefits of BD are identifying the main risk factors for disease, preventing it, and developing more effective healthcare solutions [25].

(i) **Research Design:** Standard procedures defined the methods researchers used to study the effects Big Data produces alongside IoT implementations on healthcare outcomes. The research relied on quantitative data collection techniques along with qualitative methodology as its essential research methods.

(ii) **Data Collection:** Data collection procedures included the processing of both IoT devices and electronic health records along with healthcare databases. The research used monitoring system sensor information that integrated with data from healthcare case studies and literature review findings for analysis purposes.

(iii) **Data Processing and Analysis:** Before analysis the raw data required fixations of missing columns along with standardization procedures for dataset ranges and execution of dimension reduction methods. The combination of classification models with clustering models used by machines allowed researchers to find important information patterns within their analyzed data.

(iv) **Tools and Technologies:** Data processing activities occurred through Python and R systems that integrated Hadoop clusters with Keras and TensorFlow machine learning framework tools.

(v) **Validation and Evaluation:** Model assessment contained both accuracy assessments as well as precision-recall evaluations and F1-score evaluations. To ensure dependable results alongside generalized analysis across the whole process the research implemented cross-validation techniques.

Table 2: Methodology and Design of Comparative Analysis

Stage	Description	Tools or techniques
Research design	Systematic approach combining qualitative and quantitative methods	Surveys, Case studies
Data collection	Gathered from EHRs, IoT devices, literature	Sensors, Databases
Data processing	Preprocessing data, handling missing values	Python, R, Hadoop
Analysis	Applied machine learning algorithms	TensorFlow, Keras
Validation	Model evaluation and performance testing	Cross validation

Trustworthy results from this method lead to reliable findings for understanding Big Data and Internet of Things implementation in healthcare systems. The research methods are fully explained in this section regarding both data collection and data processing and analysis techniques. The study framework details system tools and algorithms and frameworks alongside their extraction techniques for valuable IoT and Big Data information.

Comparative Analysis

Big data systems and IoT devices operate effectively within specific healthcare applications owing to their individual capabilities. The chapter presents a complete assessment through major performance indicators that evaluate the data processing rate alongside scalability and cost with integrative convenience. Machine learning, data mining, and predictive analytics are some of the technologies that make up Big Data Analytics (BDA), a group of technologies created to solve these issues [13].

(i) **Performance and Efficiency:** Medical services achieve optimal performance through data processing done by healthcare staff to execute long-term analytical work and population health assessments of already established healthcare data. Rapid data evaluation through IoT devices forms the main operational function to enable swift healthcare delivery during emergencies. The integration of the predictive analytics system with live monitoring operations results in enhanced performance standards.

(ii) **Scalability and Flexibility:** Every hospital within the industry is acquiring both diagnosis tools as well as wearable devices to accelerate healthcare data storage development. Big Data distribution helps organizations process their data stream, taking advantage of systematic data operations to keep all operations functioning efficiently. The IoT infrastructure operates since it simultaneously processes multiple devices while also handling various protocols.

(iii) **Cost Implications:** The deployment of an IoT startup demands significant investments for hardware equipment and large service integration payments.

The expenses incurred from big data platform implementation for staging operations and data processing escalate platform expenses into substantial increases. Business expenditure costs decrease thanks to the adaptive payment methods found in cloud-based solutions.

(iv) **Data Integrity and Security:** Security solutions used for these technologies support patient privacy by following regulatory standards requirements. The security characteristics of hospital IoT network devices are equivalent to those of unauthorized penetrators who aim to break through Big Data systems' data storage facilities that preserve sensitive patient information. Data security adopts encryption methods that operate together with access controls and scheduled auditing systems to establish itself.

(v) **Integration with Healthcare Systems:** The healthcare institutions operate at full integration because they create a single interconnected medical network system. IoT devices fulfill their complete functions by sustaining continuous operations between HIS and EHRs. Healthcare systems integration becomes achievable when middleware technologies and Healthcare Interoperability Standards (HI), together with Fast Healthcare Interoperability Resources (FHIR), are used.

The success of a suitable strategy depends on the healthcare goals that need to be accomplished. Big data analytics systems provide the most optimal solution for applications that require research-oriented components. IoT technology delivers its main benefit through providing superior telemedicine solutions integrated with chronic care patient management services. Truthful and instantaneous monitoring of current events together with historical data evaluation results from using hybrid systems that blend Lambda and fog computing technologies.

The systems operate independently because each delivers dedicated important functions without overlapping one another. Big Data converts vast datasets into effective outputs, which enable better research discoveries and strategic initiative development. Healthcare practitioners are increasingly employing machine learning models to make proactive decisions about patient outcomes, disease outbreaks, and readmissions to hospitals [18]. The time-sensitive services in IoT systems enhance operational performance levels together with the health care delivery system efficiency. These technologies for healthcare application integration merge to deliver complete health construct understanding that leads to better system responsiveness.

7. Global Impact on Public Health

Data collected immediately from big data and IoT systems functions as a fundamental medical aspect when healthcare professionals need to make decisions. In Table 3 the health monitoring system uses its detection abilities to identify health events together with outbreaks, thereby enabling quick decisions to stop public health threats right away. Healthcare providers use IoT devices to extract patient data that permits instant delivery for improving chronic condition care. Health authorities use predictive analytics on big data to expedite disease pattern discovery for creating effective disease intervention plans. Global health organizations employ different technology platforms to track health crises such as COVID-19 for delivering prompt, optimized responses.

The combination of IoT technologies with Big Data systems creates global healthcare effects by implementing better medical practices with reduced costs that lead to enhanced results for treated patients. Disease Surveillance, Risk Prediction, and Targeted Interventions (which are further separated into customized risk variables and feedback loops) comprise our three sections of discussion [14].

Global healthcare systems achieved major advantages from Big Data and IoT by practitioners who executed better medical practices alongside spending fewer resources to obtain better patient outcomes. Global disease tracking and asset optimization with disease control become possible through such technologies operating across the worldwide domain. Public health operations for patient surveillance become easier to access as personalized disease detection develops from advanced treatment methods, leading to better operational healthcare quality. The availability of telehealth reaches developing nations now, and established countries create preventive care programs as they develop their research foundation. Research explores deep technological involvement in worldwide health care provision while assessing system operations within public health systems.

Parents of autistic children have expressed their dissatisfaction about the emotional abilities and competencies demonstrated to them. The development of telemedicine services at an unprecedented pace relied on IoT devices to provide remote testing and virtual medical care to rural regions without proper medical resources. Real-time monitoring systems made possible by deployed connected devices help patients receive better outcomes in their treatment of diabetes and hypertension conditions. The technologies achieve their role in worldwide health organizations by supporting vaccination program monitoring while improving epidemic prevention through enhanced international public health systems.

Table 3: Examples of Global Impact on Healthcare

Impact area	Description	Examples
Disease surveillance	Real-time tracking of disease spread	COVID-19 monitoring
Remote monitoring	Patient health tracking via IoT devices	Wearable ECG monitors
Healthcare access	improved access to services globally	Telehealth consultations
Cost efficiency	Reduced operational costs	Predictive analysis

Impact on Healthcare Outcomes

When Big Data and IoT technology work together, health service benefits emerge, including enhanced diagnostics and data-driven insights for accurate and quick diagnoses. Healthcare facilities use imaging analysis tools to detect cancers in their early phases of development.

The identification of healthcare hazards in early stages becomes possible when using ongoing monitoring systems that consist of blood pressure monitors. Healthcare professionals offer customized medical treatments to their patients through integration between DNA genetic testing data and patient medical records present in health system databases. Although there are area-specific applications in the healthcare sector for fitness management, pediatrics, geriatrics, chronic illness supervision, and private health, no single study has been performed to collect suggestions on how to use IoT data with a focus on public health monitoring [17].

Through Population Health Management authorities monitor all health trends across populations to create new policies that improve disease intervention and prevention initiatives in the public health system. Healthcare technologies generate successful patient outcomes by improving engagement levels and decreasing hospital admissions to achieve effective disease management for diabetes patients and hypertension cases and cardiovascular patients. The first explanation of the study's ability to assess big data using expertise of information lifecycle management (ILM) [22].

A real-time assessment and monitoring system based on IoT technology shows itself through this diagram for critical health parameter surveillance. Logical operations commence after sensor initiations gather patient health information. Medical sensors get installed as part of wearable tools or linked healthcare instruments. The system establishes an automatic stop during the process, which needs sensor re-initialization when initializations fail. After successful completion of initialization, the system starts monitoring three essential health parameters, which are blood pressure (BMP), oxygen saturation (SpO_2), and body temperature.

Figure 3 operates the sensors until they start tracking patient data, then performs health parameter comparisons to reference ranges. The first checked health parameter is blood pressure monitoring (BMP). The system follows up with the next assessment step when BMP results match the normal reference values. When abnormal BMP readings appear in the system, it generates an alert. The system automatically delivers SMS alerts to healthcare professionals alongside paramedics and family members, permitting fast medical care to the patient. The SMS reaches recipients with the patient's exact location information so responders can act quickly with appropriate knowledge.

The system requires analysis of SpO_2 readings to determine blood oxygen saturation of the patient. The monitoring proceeds to the subsequent stage after normal SpO_2 readings. The system automatically sends an alert through an electronic channel to reach all necessary stakeholders when SpO_2 readings are

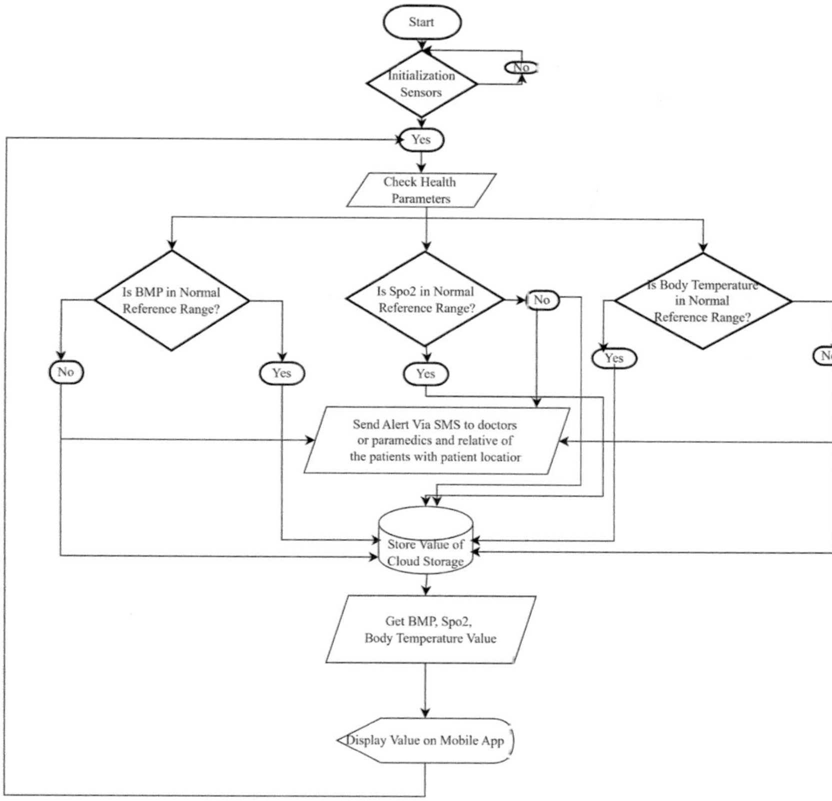

Figure 3: Flowchart for Real-time Patient Health Monitoring and Alert System.

outside normal limits. Abnormal readings of oxygen saturation stand as a vital indicator, which shows signs of respiratory distress or hidden medical problems that need urgent medical care.

The system checks the body temperature of the patient after SpO_2 saturation. System monitoring will continue as normal when the patient's temperature falls within established reference criteria. When patient temperature strays beyond standard parameters, the system activates alerts for required parties to receive notification. The monitoring process requires body temperature assessment because it helps healthcare professionals detect infections along with inflammations and other health irregularities. An SMS alert triggers from the system whenever health parameters show abnormal changes, which include vital patient information together with their current location. The health-related data gets securely stored within a cloud-based system at the same time. A cloud platform enables data preservation, which supports trend evaluation and decision-making by healthcare professionals.

A mobile application implements final phase operations to both obtain health data from the cloud storage system and display this data to the user interface. The mobile application allows users convenient access to real-time health metrics through its user-friendly design, which benefits both medical staff and patients who need to monitor the patient's condition.

8. Case Studies on Big Data and IoT in Healthcare

Case Study 1: Remote Patient Monitoring for Chronic Disease Management

Patients who are suffering from diabetes, hypertension, or heart disease have to be regularly controlled to make sure complications are avoided. These patients acquire knowledge about their illness mostly through scheduled wellness visits, which do not necessarily provide real-time data. Other factors that may indicate a lack of the presence of healthcare professionals could be a longer delay in the treatment process or the difficulty in differentiating between a worsening or a new situation.

Another framework was developed in which all types of data processing are performed using Cloud infrastructure for the diagnosis and monitoring of chronic diseases, with a focus on diabetes [10]. The incorporation of Big Data and IoT in the health sector has significantly transformed chronic disease management for the better, as remote monitoring through wearable devices and smart sensors has become possible.

One such case is the remote monitoring of diabetic patients using IoT technology-enabled continuous glucose monitoring (CGM) devices. Apart from that, the other essential benefits of such technologies are artificial intelligence and machine learning, which help physicians understand the data related to the patients quickly and accurately and also predict if the patient is at high risk for a specific disease. These tools collect blood serum in real-time, and they are then synthesizing the results, which are uploaded to cloud platforms for doctors to interpret the data and discover any unusual pop-ups. With the use of Big Data analytics, doctors can decide the most appropriate treatment method for a person and predict the possibility of future health issues. Furthermore, such a system can be equally good for the doctors as well as the patients by providing the doctors with the patient's health data along with the patient's history. Moreover, an alert and notification system can give patients a greater chance to take the necessary action in time, preventing emergency hospital visits.

The meeting started by asking the partners for what time interval would allow the patients to be informed and getting the opportunity to change their behaviors in time to get the best results. A trial accomplished by the Mayo Clinic discovered that patients possessing IoT-based remote monitoring systems have reduced the number of hospital admissions by a quarter due to better knowledge of their conditions. The outcome of the research was that through the automatic sharing of real-time data, the behavior of many patients have changed and in the same way, the doctors have had a bigger chance to intervene early than they have had before. It has been shown by the interfaces involved in machines/appliances or robots that analyze and entertain information with a different human that the experience will change. One interesting finding in this context is, according to the experiences from KIN, while nobody was injured, these communications gave each person a chance to express their emotions, and one grateful gesture was shaking hands, which was appreciated by both of them. Besides making it more patient-oriented, the technology they had installed lately also helped healthcare professionals and patients in various ways. The results of the tests will indicate whose condition is at risk of worsening, who will most likely need immediate medical assistance, etc. In this way, the people concerned will benefit from receiving quick responses and even advice.

Case Study 2: Big Data and IoT in Control and Prediction of Epidemics

The COVID-19 pandemic also highlighted the important contribution of IoT and Big Data in tracking public health, epidemic monitoring, and epidemic control. Big data evidence was used for policy intervention by global health institutions and governments. It facilitated real-time tracking of disease transmission, resource deployment, and control measures enforcement. IoT sensors, mobile phones, and analysis platforms cooperated with each other to research infection patterns and deliver timely intervention. Before then it was the application of IoT and Big Data by South Korea to monitor contacts and predict epidemics. The government employed an integrated system that involved mobile GPS location tracking, credit card swipes, and medical records to track the movement of the patients. Advanced analytics were employed to analyze the data to identify risk hotspot areas and predict where outbreak clusters would take place.

The system facilitated the imposition of spot lockdowns by the authorities, which minimized the total severity of the disease. Besides this, Internet of Things-based table clinical monitoring devices followed mildly symptomatic COVID-19 patients in their immediate vicinity. Smart pulse oximeters and temperature meters sent patient health data in real-time to centralized servers that supported remote monitoring of patient status by doctors. The predictivelytics engine processed this data to identify likely patients with fatal complications so they could be hospitalized in due time. Success using this method was witnessed in South Korea as it was able to keep the spread under control at a lower economic expense compared to other countries.

ZOE, a UK-based health science company, as working with researchers from King's College London and Massachusetts General Hospital Boston, established an AI model to predict COVID-19 infections [11]. Privacy and ethical issues regarding data did not emerge in the short run, but large-scale collection of data required balancing public health interests against privacy rights. Control over firm data policy and transparency about the use of data constitute the essence of public trust in such programs and data-based epidemic forecasting have opened the gateway to future public health interventions. Multisource real-time data integration, healthcare systems forecast in advance to heal impending health ailments, maximizing timely intervention and maximum resource utilization. With the emerging technologies of today, more advanced AI-based analytics and IoT infrastructure will result in increased epidemic preparedness and readiness of healthcare systems against future pandemics.

9. Challenges and Limitations

Healthcare organizations face different challenges when uniting Big Data and IoT in healthcare systems that impact service performance while creating security and reliability problems. Health information confidentiality functions as the primary vital healthcare issue in existence today. Identity theft, together with unauthorized system entry, remains the leading security risk facing this system.

Table 4 explains Healthcare organizations need to develop powerful encryption technology, safe access protocols, and secure communication systems as protection against patient data breaches. Healthcare institutions encounter major challenges because of their substantial financial needs for installing and maintaining Internet of Things infrastructure.

Healthcare organizations with limited financial resources experience budgetary challenges because purchasing sensors and data infrastructure together with installing communication systems exceeds their financial capacity. Hospitals encounter multiple technical difficulties when merging IoT devices with information systems because they struggle with system incompatibilities and differences in operational standards.

Healthcare organizations face a staffing shortage, which makes it impossible for them to interpret data that results from IoT health system applications. The solution to healthcare professional skills gaps demands healthcare institutions to develop data science education programs with extra partnerships that establish training standards. The entire operation of different health sectors depends on dependably accurate healthcare information systems.

Medical mistakes resulting from flawed data intake or delayed information provisioning without essential details are responsible for diagnostic mistakes that result in poor care delivery and threaten patient security. Identity threats are reduced by healthcare organizations through examinations and standardized methods along with operating procedures.

Organizations within the healthcare sector must address all regulatory compliance mandates as their ultimate regulatory challenge. The law requires

Table 4: Ethical Challenges and their Solutions on Healthcare Industries

Ethical challenge	**Description**	**Impact**	**Solutions**
Data Privacy and Security	Unauthorized access or breaches of sensitive health data due to weak encryption or poor security measures.	Loss of patient trust, legal consequences, and compromised health information.	Implement end-to-end encryption, use multi-factor authentication (MFA), and adhere to GDPR and HIPAA regulations.
Informed Consent	Patients might be unaware of how their health data is collected, stored, and shared.	Ethical concerns about data ownership and patient autonomy.	Develop transparent consent policies, provide clear, simple explanations, and obtain explicit patient consent.
Data Ownership	Unclear definitions about whether patients, healthcare providers, or third parties own the data.	Disputes over data usage, potential misuse by commercial entities.	Establish clear ownership policies in accordance with legal frameworks and inform patients about data usage rights.
Algorithmic Bias	Machine learning models might produce biased results due to non-representative training data.	Misdiagnoses, unequal healthcare delivery, and reduced system reliability.	Use diverse datasets, conduct regular bias audits, and involve domain experts in algorithm development.
Surveillance and Autonomy	Continuous monitoring may lead to patients feeling a loss of privacy and independence.	Decreased patient engagement and increased discomfort with monitoring devices.	Implement opt-in monitoring systems, anonymize non-critical data, and educate patients on monitoring benefits.
Data Sharing and Third-Party Access	Sharing health data with external entities without adequate safeguards.	Potential data misuse, identity theft, and breaches of confidentiality.	Enforce strict data-sharing protocols, audit third-party partnerships, and use smart contracts for secure exchanges.
Ethical Use of Insights	Misuse of predictive analytics for purposes like insurance discrimination.	Discrimination against individuals with specific health conditions.	Develop guidelines for ethical analytics use, implement regulatory oversight, and monitor applications for misuse.
Digital Divide and Accessibility	Unequal access to IoT healthcare tools across different populations.	Widening health disparities and exclusion of marginalized communities	Promote affordable healthcare technologies, offer training programs, and integrate inclusive design principles.

healthcare organizations to handle numerous demands about managing health information during data collection and distribution as well as storage operations.

The healthcare industry encounters various problems when implementing Big Data and IoT systems while obtaining multiple organizational advantages from these systems. One of the key issues with healthcare IoT is preventing unwanted access to patient data. Encryption techniques and robust permission processes can aid with this [16].

Healthcare organizations need to provide strict attention to the fundamental privacy and security of sensitive information. Expense to initiate and support IoT infrastructure represents a substantial financial barrier preventing different health service organizations from deploying the technology. An everlasting challenge exists in analyzing advanced healthcare datasets because professional expertise is exceptionally difficult to locate. While the integration of IoT systems with established legacy platforms brings challenges, the systems need to achieve interoperability between multiple device types.

10. Security Threats and Risk Mitigation in IoT Healthcare Systems

Usage of the IoT in healthcare has revolutionized patient care through remote diagnosis, web-based monitoring, and easy information transfer. To protect patient rights and reduce the chance of unauthorized access or data breaches, legal frameworks like the Health Insurance Portability and Accountability Act (HIPAA) in the US and the General Data Protection Regulation (GDPR) in the EU need to be followed [8]. Higher reliance on cloud healthcare infrastructure and networked devices is also exposing highly vulnerable security threats. Security threats include device manipulation, unauthorized access, DoS attacks, and information disclosures. Securement of IoT healthcare systems is necessary to maintain patient confidentiality, information integrity, and healthcare critical medical system functioning. The highest security threats in IoT in healthcare are unauthorized access and theft of data. The patient information tailored to the patient, like medical history, test results, and identification, is typically being shared among IoT devices, cloud servers, and healthcare providers. Such information is vulnerable to cyber-attacks via poor authentication control, insecure networks, or poorly configured databases that may be exploited to perform identity theft and confidentiality breaches of the patient's information. It involves the systematic analysis of large amounts of structured and unstructured data from a variety of sources, including wearable technology, genomic sequencing, medical imaging, electronic health records (EHRs), and social media [15].

The healthcare organizations can minimize this threat by having robust encryption policies, multi-factor authentication (MFA), and secure access control mechanisms to limit the access of patient information by authorized staff. The second most dangerous threat is device control and hacking, in which the hacker takes over medical devices like insulin pumps, pacemakers, and infusion pumps. The compromised device will result in misplaced doses or manipulated medical readings, which make patients deadly to themselves. Cyberthieves exploit weaknesses in old firmware or unencrypted data pipes to carry out their attacks. In reaction to such exposure, the vendors should issue regular software updates, enforce device authentication processes, and use anomaly-based detection solutions to detect and prevent unauthorized modification in real-time. Denial-of-Service (DoS) attacks are also among the major threats to healthcare IoT systems. The attackers would overwhelm network connections with a vast amount of traffic, rendering vital medical services and devices unable to respond. These attacks can have the potential to undermine hospital functioning, slow response to emergencies, and affect patient treatment. Medical IoT devices non-uniform security frameworks are creating additional vulnerabilities.

Healthcare networks will have to implement network traffic monitoring software, intrusion detection and prevention systems (IDPS), and cloud security that can absorb and respond to mass-scale attacks to be able to combat this threat. Since the majority of the IoT medical devices are manufactured by different vendors, they are developed based on different security systems, and these cannot be integrated uniformly by a single protection system.

The healthcare organizations will be required to conform to the industry's cybersecurity policy standards, like the National Institute of Standards and Technology (NIST) cybersecurity standards. Given that healthcare information is sensitive, hospitals will undoubtedly pay the ransom, making the cybercriminals' business profitable. Implementing a security policy for all healthcare IoT devices would also be difficult. Additionally, hospitals are facing an increase in ransomware attacks, which encrypt patient data and demand ransom payments to decrypt it.

Through offering day-to-day backups of information, cyber awareness training for employees, and endpoint security tools, ransomware attacks can be prevented. Simply put, as much as IoT health systems make patient and organizational procedures easier, they carry inbuilt security flaws.

Security attacks can be prevented by applying a multi-layered security model that includes encryption, access management, device verification, and live network monitoring. Reasonable security measures and future potential threats are capable of enabling health care organizations to provide protection of patient information and achieve reliability of health care systems with IoT.

11. Ethical Considerations in Using Big Data and IoT in Healthcare

The integration of Big Data systems with IoT technology in healthcare produces essential ethical problems that affect medical care service delivery processes.

Patient permission about data usage stands as an essential matter because the protection of data rights alongside patient privacy needs equal attention. The requirements of the Health Insurance Portability and Accountability Act (HIPAA) and General Data Protection Regulation (GDPR) must be followed by healthcare data during the entire period of data gathering and processing and longer data retention. People need to observe how their data gets utilized along with protected management systems in order to build trust between them and the health services. To fully realize these potential benefits, international action is needed to address the current, essentially inadequate governance of global health [7].

Pharmaceutical drug data privacy protection uses encryption systems integrated with transparent ownership structures in addition to correct consent practices and accessibility management systems. The implementation of predictive healthcare models demands equal treatment during algorithm creation processes to avoid incorrect predictions. Real-time oversight mechanisms together with standard monitoring systems must remain active to maintain their ethical standards. Because various forms of data are being considered to leverage value, a four-step approach must be followed. In this section, we will attempt to illustrate how we may evaluate and process low-density data for decision-makers in their decisions and initiatives.

Figure 4 depicts the four Big Data steps that must be followed [5]. The huge data chain value relates to this method. In this chapter, we have covered wearable technologies. The primary advantages of eHealth include monitoring for chronic illnesses and saving lives in emergency situations [23].

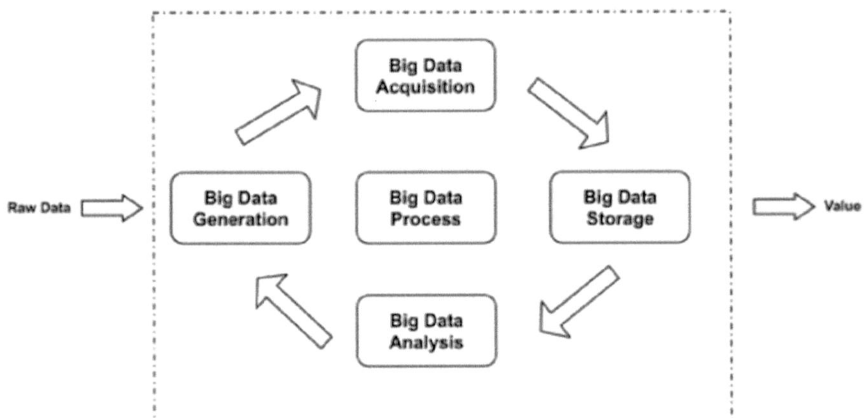

Figure 4: Four Big Data Steps.

12. Conclusion

The union of IoT analysis systems with Big Data enabled healthcare to experience major advancements because they each utilize data-based solutions to deliver proactive medical care. Technological integration in these systems enabled healthcare to develop better diagnostic capabilities together with superior methods for patient care delivery and medical monitoring capabilities. During the COVID-19 pandemic, public health teams used IoT monitoring systems to discover infection centers while tracking disease spread toward planning their strategy. Diabetic patients equipped with wearable medical devices benefit from continuous glucose level monitoring for both danger avoidance and hospital avoidance. Modern technology progresses toward essential effects that enhance the quality of health systems together with operational performances and buttress evidence-based governmental decisions. Success in healthcare encounters two primary difficulties consisting of data protection issues together with interoperability challenges and implementation expenses. The solution requires continuous innovation together with secure technology implementation under defined regulations to achieve operational stability. The research needs advancement in two main areas to enhance both machine learning predictive models and blockchain-based system connectivity and secure data processes. Public health realizes the full potential of Big Data and the Internet of Things through team efforts between healthcare professionals, data scientists, and public administrators.

References

1. Adenyi, A. O., Okolo, C. A., Olorunsogo, T., and Babawarun, O. (2024). Leveraging big data and analytics for enhanced public health decision-making: A global review. *GSC Advanced Research and Reviews*, 18(2), 450–456.
2. Adegbile, M. D., Olaboye, J. A., Maha, C. C., Igwama, G. T., and Abdul, S. (2024). Health informatics and public health: Leveraging technology for improved health outcomes. *Health*, 20(8), 229–235.
3. Rehman, A., Naz, S., and Razzak, I. (2022). Leveraging big data analytics in healthcare enhancement: Trends, challenges and opportunities. *Multimedia Systems*, 28(4), 1339–1371.
4. Abdul, S., Adeghe, E. P., Adegoke, B. O., Adegoke, A. A., and Dedeh, E. H. (2024). Leveraging data analytics and IoT technologies for enhancing oral health programs in schools. *International Journal of Applied Research in Social Sciences*, 6(5), 1005–1036.
5. Hussain, F., Nauman, M., Alghuried, A., Alhudhaif, A., and Akhtar, N. (2023). Leveraging big data analytics for enhanced clinical decision-making in healthcare. *IEEE Access*, 11, 127817–127836.
6. Roy, A., Mitra, A., and Soman, B. (2023). Public health in India: Leveraging technology for a brighter future. *Opinions in Medical Sciences, Technology and Health*, 1(2), e23014–e23014.
7. Ali, A. H., Dheyab, S. A., Alamoodi, A. H., Magableh, A. A. A. R., and Gu, Y. (2024). Leveraging AI and big data in low-resource healthcare settings. *Mesopotamian Journal of Big Data*, 2024, 11–22.

8. Chowdhury, R. H. (2024). Big data analytics in the field of multifaceted analyses: A study on "health care management". *World Journal of Advanced Research and Reviews*, 22(3), 2165–2172.
9. Ahmad, H. F., Rafique, W., Rasool, R. U., Alhumam, A., Anwar, Z., and Qadir, J. (2023). Leveraging 6G, extended reality, and IoT big data analytics for healthcare: A review. *Computer Science Review*, 48, 100558.
10. Shumba, A. T., Montanaro, T., Sergi, I., Fachechi, L., De Vittorio, M., and Patrono, L. (2022). Leveraging IoT-aware technologies and AI techniques for real-time critical healthcare applications. *Sensors*, 22(19), 7675.
11. Mehta, N., and Shukla, S. (2022). Pandemic analytics: How countries are leveraging big data analytics and artificial intelligence to fight COVID-19? *SN Computer Science*, 3(1), 54.
12. Majeed, A., and Hwang, S. O. (2021). Data-driven analytics leveraging artificial intelligence in the era of COVID-19: An insightful review of recent developments. *Symmetry*, 14(1), 16.
13. Rony, M.A.T. et al. (2025). Deciphering Diabetes: Illuminating Prognostic Insights with an Interpretable Machine Learning Framework. *In:* Reddy, V.S., Prasad, V.K., Wang, J., Rao Dasari, N.M. (eds) Intelligent Systems and Sustainable Computing. ICISSC 2024. *Smart Innovation, Systems and Technologies,* vol 417. Springer, Singapore. https://doi.org/10.1007/978-981-97-8355-7_12
14. Velmovitsky, P. E., Bevilacqua, T., Alencar, P., Cowan, D., and Morita, P. P. (2021). Convergence of precision medicine and public health into precision public health: Toward a big data perspective. *Frontiers in Public Health*, 9, 561873.
15. Ogundipe, D. O. (2024). The impact of big data on healthcare product development: A theoretical and analytical review. *International Medical Science Research Journal*, 4(3), 341–360.
16. Atianashie, M. A., and Adaobi, C. C. (2024). From data to diagnosis: Leveraging deep learning in IoT-based healthcare. *Academia Medicine*, 1.
17. Sahu, K. S., Majowicz, S. E., Dubin, J. A., and Morita, P. P. (2021). NextGen public health surveillance and the internet of things (IoT). *Frontiers in Public Health*, 9, 756675.
18. Fatima, S. (2024). Improving healthcare outcomes through machine learning: Applications and challenges in big data analytics. *International Journal of Advanced Research in Engineering Technology & Science*, 11.
19. Awotunde, J. B., Jimoh, R. G., Oladipo, I. D., Abdulraheem, M., Jimoh, T. B., and Ajamu, G. J. (2021). Big data and data analytics for an enhanced COVID-19 epidemic management. In: *Artificial Intelligence for COVID-19* (pp. 11–29). Cham: Springer International Publishing.
20. Berros, N., El Mendili, F., Filaly, Y., and El Bouzekri El Idrissi, Y. (2023). Enhancing digital health services with big data analytics. *Big Data and Cognitive Computing*, 7(2), 64.
21. Demirbaga, U., and Aujla, G. S. (2022). MapChain: A blockchain-based verifiable healthcare service management in IoT-based big data ecosystem. *IEEE Transactions on Network and Service Management*, 19(4), 3896–3907.
22. Cozzoli, N., Salvatore, F. P., Faccilongo, N., and Milone, M. (2022). How can big data analytics be used for healthcare organization management? Literary framework and future research from a systematic review. *BMC Health Services Research*, 22(1), 809.

23. Chawla, N., and Dalal, S. (2021). Edge AI with wearable IoT: A review on leveraging edge intelligence in wearables for smart healthcare. *Green Internet of Things for Smart Cities*, 205–231.
24. Rejeb, A., Keogh, J. G., and Rejeb, K. (2022). Big data in the food supply chain: A literature review. *Journal of Data, Information and Management*, 4(1), 33–47.
25. Dicuonzo, G., Galeone, G., Shini, M., and Massari, A. (2022, July). Towards the use of big data in healthcare: A literature review. *Healthcare*, 10(7), 1232. MDPI.

12 | A Comparative Study on Blockchain Architectures for Secure and Transparent Healthcare Systems

Parichoy Nandi[1], Riya Sen[1], Riya Sil[2*], Nirmlaya Pal[2] and Alok Tibrewala[3]

[1] Department of Computer Science, Christ University, Bengaluru, India
[2] Department of Computer Science & Engineering, Brainware University, Kolkata, India
[3] Independent Researcher, IEEE Senior Member, USA

The research compares blockchain technologies in the healthcare industry, focusing on data security, decentralization, and transparency for managing data. Traditional healthcare systems face challenges, notably data breaches, inefficiencies in maintaining records, less interoperability, and issues regarding patient privacy. The solution with the use of the distributed nature of blockchain as an advantage is to provide a secure, decentralized space to store and manage medical data that is sensitive for creating a transparent, tamper-proof ledger accessible only by individuals or parties that are authorized. This paper highlights a comprehensive study of several blockchain architectures and applications in industry, such as electronic health records (EHRs), securing patient identity, tracking of drug supply chain, and secure medical data sharing. The approaches enhance data security and provide a transparent and trustworthy record of all data within a system. After analyzing numerous mechanisms and encryption approaches and combining blockchain with emerging technologies such as artificial intelligence (AI) and the Internet of Things (IoT), this chapter surveys blockchain's prospect of enhancing healthcare efficiency while holding security and regulatory compliance. Likewise, the chapter discusses the restrictions of blockchain, including scalability, computational expenses, and lawful challenges, providing an understanding of forthcoming study trends and adoption methods for blockchain-based healthcare solutions.

*Corresponding author: riyasil1802@gmail.com

DOI: 10.1201/9781003635215-12

1. Introduction

Blockchains are becoming vital as more and more businesses are relying on these factors such as reliability, privacy, and transparency in sectors of finance, supply chains, and even medicine.

In today's technological era, the impact of the security of data along with interconnectivity, especially in the healthcare industry, remains a critical challenge. The continuous increment in the reliance on electronic health records (EHRs) and telemedicine, accompanied by digital diagnostics, has uncovered the flaws that were present in conventional healthcare data management systems. It often suffers from cyber-attacks such as data breaches, unauthorized access along with inefficiencies ultimately led to obstruction in patient health care providing agencies. Accompanying that, legislative standards such as the Health Insurance Portability and Accountability Act (HIPAA) and General Data Protection Regulation (GDPR), which demand uncompromising data privacy and other security measures, introduce new obstacles to data management in the healthcare industry.

Upcoming technologies like Blockchain propose a decentralized and tamper-proof solution to the traditional challenges by leveraging distributed ledger, cryptographic hashing, and consensus mechanisms technology to ensure transparent, secured, and immutable records in the modern healthcare industry. Several blockchain frameworks, such as private, public, hybrid, and consortium models, present different approaches, positives, and trade-offs for the application used in the healthcare industry. Automation can also be implemented using smart contracts in the workflows, empowering security in transactions uninterrupted.

This chapter emphasizes a detailed review of applications using blockchain technologies in healthcare industries, extending across areas including medical data security, managing patient identity, tracking pharmaceutical supply chains, and synchronization among healthcare systems. It also considers other consensus mechanisms, such as Proof of Work, Proof of Stake, and Byzantine Fault Tolerance, concluding their suitability for healthcare environments. Furthermore, challenges are also mentioned, including scalability, regulatory adherence, and integration of the blockchain-based systems with the existing systems. Concluding with awareness for the upcoming improvements and recommending for streamlining the blockchain implementation in the healthcare industry

2. Literature Review

Halimuzzaman et al. explored how blockchain technology can be used to combine electronic health records into digital health systems. Identification of how technology could improve data security, patient privacy, and interoperability among health providers. Major obstacles include technical complexity, scalability, collaboration, and regulatory compliance issues. Finally, a discussion on the applications focusing on blockchain to enhance the building of a more secure, productive digital healthcare ecosystem while using seamless access across platforms to patient information were made [1]. Jena et al. systematically reviewed the challenges of virtual identity in healthcare and concentrated on combining IoT and blockchain technologies, pointing out issues such as data security, privacy issues, and complexity in dealing with multiple virtual identities among different healthcare systems. It handles solutions by pointing out the strengths of Internet of Things (IoT) and blockchain to improve identity management while enhancing patient identification and security in data sharing. In conclusion, future recommendations for research towards developing strong frameworks to handle the digital identity challenges in the healthcare sectors were made [2]. Kim et al. proposed a blockchain-based marketplace for healthcare data that enhances the sharing and collaboration between health consumers. Discussions focused on the marketplace's architecture to enable the safe transaction of health data while protecting patients' privacy and data integrity. As a result, it leads to talks about control issues and the acceptability of a suggested system, as well as a thorough understanding of the technical viability of the solution. Overall, conclusions were made by looking at the possibility that blockchain can be released in healthcare data management while creating an improved ecosystem for data exchange, thereby making the data more transparent [3]. Li et al. conducted a review to gauge the significance of blockchain technology in healthcare data sharing. Analysis of current literature in order to ascertain how far blockchain can go in filling the gap in data security, interoperability, and patient consent. Pros of blockchain implementation, such as integrity and decentralized control, and the cons, which include scalability and complexity in the integration of the existing systems were discussed. It finally concludes with a recommendation to the stakeholders on which date and time to implement blockchain solutions appropriately in healthcare data-sharing programs [4].

Yaeger et al. examined new, innovative blockchain solutions developed in response to the demands and prerequisites of the modern healthcare foundation. Discussions on different potential applications of blockchain, exceptionally safe management of patient information, interoperability, and increasing supply chain transparency. The challenges are adhering to regulatory bodies, implementing technology into an already existing system, and the reception of end-users. Real-world examples and case studies showing successful health applications are presented within the scope. To conclude with planned recommendations for healthcare organizations to implement blockchain technology to increase efficiency and security and improve patient care in their structure [5]. Telia and Masoodi reported advantages such as greater security, excellent interoperability, and the facilitation of patients having more personalized control over their medical records. The challenges include technological complexity, scalability, and regulatory hurdles, which may stand as a barrier to adopting blockchain technology. To conclude by strategically recommending users use blockchain technology in healthcare delivery, thereby demanding collaborative efforts toward these challenges and maximizing opportunities for changing the face of healthcare delivery [6].

Wu et al. tested the blockchain architecture for hematopoietic stem cell transplantation typing using Hyperledger Fabric. Results were that security, accuracy, and traceability of all the matching processes between the donor and the recipient were enhanced. It also enhances transparency and increases confidence in the same process. On the contrary, disadvantages related to scalability, regulatory compliance, and interfacing the blockchain with other already available healthcare systems are also related. Some of the recommendations include scalability, compliance problems, and further development of blockchain architectures that will help apply better in clinical settings [7]. Yousuf et al. provide a synopsis of the existing practices and results in Hematopoietic Stem Cell Transplantation (HSCT) for thalassemia. It has condensed the areas in which improvement has been made, like the matching of the donor, conditioning regimens, post-transplant care, etc., thereby showing better survival and way of living. Other challenging issues include graft-versus-host disease and proper donor identification, among others. Further research recommendations would be optimizing the treatment protocols and increasing awareness regarding the benefits of HSCT in thalassemia [8].

Wei et al. considered and reviewed the progress and challenges faced in transplantation of human stem cells, in the field of regenerative medicine. New sources and techniques of stem cell transplantation enhanced survival rates, and still, it faces great difficulty in transplant rejection by body and graft-versus-host disease. It was intended to improve treatment strategies and promote collaboration among various medical areas. Future research should focus on improving graft procedures and drugs to avoid rejection, making stem cell transplants safer and more successful [9].

Rout discussed how a system can increase data security and interoperability toward privacy for patients. Even after facing many challenges, such as regulatory issues, scalability, and the need for standardized protocols, it was found that blockchain could improve patient care and enhance healthcare processes [10]. Yaqoob et al. discussed how Blockchain technology in healthcare offers many potentials, and its analysis for use in data management in the health sector enhances integrity, security, and access to data. It was stated that interoperability, regulatory compliance, and practical governance framework are some of the key challenges. Future recommendations on how blockchain optimizes the healthcare data management to enhance patient outcomes and facilitate collaboration in the healthcare ecosystem [11].

Tandona et al. reviewed systematically the blockchain application technology in healthcare, combining what already has been done to form a framework. The authors discuss core concepts in the literature, emphasizing, in particular, the advantages in using blockchain: better security and transparency in managing patient data. Challenges are mainly technological and low awareness from stakeholders. Future research is meant to overcome these challenges and explore new innovative applications of blockchain in the healthcare sector. [12]. Dulce Villarreal et al. discussed the integration of blockchain technology into a healthcare management system. Problems associated with interoperability and system security issues were dealt with. Analysis on a couple of blockchain frameworks coupled with feasibility in enabling secure data transfer amongst healthcare organizations was carried out. It was determined that the main challenges of integrating blockchain with existing systems and regulation compliance. The study concludes with recommendations for improving connectivity and confidentiality for blockchain applications in healthcare [13].

Philip et al. retrospectively analyzed allogeneic peripheral stem cell therapy for three years regarding how donor factors influence yield, engraftment, and chimerism results. It was discovered that the age and other features of the donors influenced the effectiveness of a transplant. An outcome indicates that proper donor selection should improve a patient's prognosis in terms of engraftment success rate and long-term survival. Suggestions on donor factors should be regularly evaluated for their impact on transplant outcomes in stem cell transplantation to advance medical practice and care for recipients [14].

Choudhary et al. retrospectively reviewed patients with myelofibrosis at a single center who underwent allogeneic stem cell transplantation. Besides the factors related to survival, data on demographic information and graft outcomes were retrospectively studied. According to the results of the present study, allogeneic bone marrow transplant was also achieved, with some patients providing excellent overall and even disease-free survival. Still, problems like graft-versus-host diseases act as a significant barrier. Recommendations on finer patient selection and complications with strategizing to obtain increased accuracy in the success of such stem cell transplantation within these patients were suggested [15]. Quine et al. considered the possibility of using blockchain technology as a solution to problems facing the organ donation system including injustice, opacity and organ trafficking in 2023. An explanation of how blockchain components such as immutability and decentralization in sharing data, preventing fraud, and better alignment of organs were given. The proposal for a blockchain-based global ledger system and digital digitizing for the intelligent use of identities in contracts improves process clarity and efficiency. Some future ideas include using blockchain today and connecting it to the Internet of Things to manage organs in transplants, using artificial intelligence for it and donors to align with suppliers, and finally requiring international regulation to address issues of scalability, interoperability, and regulation [16].

Treiblmaier et al. discuss how blockchain technology can revolutionize healthcare data administration by improving interoperability, data security, and patient privacy. They discuss the shortcomings of traditional systems, including their vulnerability to hackers, fragmented data, and ineffective sharing of patient information. By ensuring safe, instant access to medical records, preserving privacy with cryptographic techniques, and making it easy to exchange data, the problems can be addressed by decentralized, unchangeable structure of blockchain. Still, the authors note challenges like scalability, technical complexity, legal compliance, and the need for teamwork. To overcome such challenges and spur the adoption of blockchain in health care, they propose a research agenda that will produce a safer, more effective, and more patient-centered system [17].

Booth and Gehrie looked at blockchain and non-fungible tokens (NFTs) in stem cell transplantation. Enumeration of how the decentralized and immutable nature of blockchain helps improve stem cell traceability and security and reduces fraud in the transplantation process of transplantation by overcoming issues with the matching process for donors and recipients. The authors suggest using NFTs to uniquely identify how stem cells were made, therefore providing transparency in the process and quality control. Future applications addressed include the pairing of blockchain and the Internet of Things (IoT) as a means for real-time tracking, and, in the more distant future, using AI to create optimal donor recipient matching. Regulations will be demanded to ensure safety and scalability using these technologies on healthcare [18].

Li et al. reviewed to assess the importance of blockchain technology in healthcare data sharing. An analysis of the current literature was made to determine how far blockchain can go to cover the gaps in data security, interoperability, and patient consent. Discussions on the pros of blockchain implementation, such as integrity and decentralized control, and the cons, including scalability and complexity in integrating existing systems. Finally, recommendations are provided to stakeholders on when and how to implement blockchain solutions effectively in healthcare data sharing programs [19]. Treiblmaier et al. examined how blockchain may solve some problems in the health sector, where data is fragmented and interoperability between systems is inadequate, and various security vulnerabilities may exist. Decentralized and immutability attribute of blockchain offers better integrity of the data, makes patient privacy safeguarded, and increases stakeholder confidence. Observations show that blockchain can use IoT to enhance safe data exchange, simplify administrative tasks of managing medical records, and monitor and track in real-time. However, the problems include unclear rules, expensive computational costs, and scalability. The authors further recommend more development for the broad use of blockchain in healthcare, such as maximal scalability, the use of AI for sophisticated data analytics, and an international regulatory framework [20].

Saviour Igboanusi et al. even proposed blockchain technology in solving the organ transplantation process where fraud, inefficiencies, and transparency are evident. A novel approach on that is through smart contracts as Blockchain-Enabled Organ Matching System does, as blockchain is characterized with decentralization and immutability. Thus, the technique establishes trust among parties in an organ donation system. It further ensures minimal error among humans and increases the transparency of it all. It highlights some difficulties such as need for broad acceptance, regulatory considerations, and scalability. Then it proposes for future enhancements-optimizing its scalability, being integrated with Internet of Things and real-time tracking, and putting in place International regulatory frameworks toward standardizing Blockchain use in Health Care [21].

Panda et al. suggest an intelligent hybrid model that combines blockchain and AI to promote the efficiency, transparency, and security of kidney transplantation. Blockchain ensures secure data management and real-time traceability in a transparent way. The use of AI to improve donor-recipient matching, incorporating medical factors and previous success in transplanting kidneys, reduces fraudulent practices, minimizes the scope of human errors, and decreases waiting time for a transplant. There are still challenges such as scalability, integration with existing hospital systems, and global acceptance. Future enhancements include optimizing AI algorithms, expanding blockchain scalability, incorporating IoT for the real-time monitoring of organs, and establishing regulatory frameworks to ensure ethical implementation [22].

Calik et al. explore how blockchain technology can handle inefficiencies, obscurity, and fraud in organ transplantation systems. Utilizing blockchain's decentralized and immutable nature, the authors propose a solution to ensure that organ matching and allocation occur securely and efficiently. One of the primary findings was that blockchain can make the transplant process less tedious by integrating IoT with blockchain, which makes black-market activity low and leads to better outcomes. Issues like scalability, regulatory problems, and the need for international standards were addressed. Improvements for the future include further optimization of scalability, use of AI for enhanced matching algorithms, and setting up regulatory frameworks to facilitate adoption worldwide [23].

The literature reviews show blockchain technology's tremendous potential to alter the health sector by addressing issues such as data security, patient confidentiality, and interoperability among healthcare providers. The studies show how blockchain enhances data sharing, enables patient identification, and makes health-related activities such as stem cell transplantation and electronic health record administration more transparent. However, other problems exist, including complexity, scalability, integration, and compliance. The authors argue that it can create better security and an efficient healthcare ecosystem; however, future work must focus on barriers, increase scalability, and develop robust regulations for maximum effectiveness in healthcare data management.

3. Methodology

Blockchain technology is a transformative innovation that is providing decentralized, secure, and transparent systems for the management of data and transactions. Understanding blockchain by its elemental nature, as one consists of blockchain frameworks, and contains the elementary bases; securing data which creates confidentiality as well as data integrity; consenting mechanisms within them, a function that builds acceptance among each set of disseminated nodes; and contracts. These functions offer precision by using the smart business interaction technology, such as with technologies like Internet-of-Things technologies and advanced intelligence artificial-based technologies with enhanced functionality capabilities within the applicatory range for itself. The overall process for increasing energy efficiency in AI-driven agricultural systems by combining several complementary approaches is shown in Fig. 1.

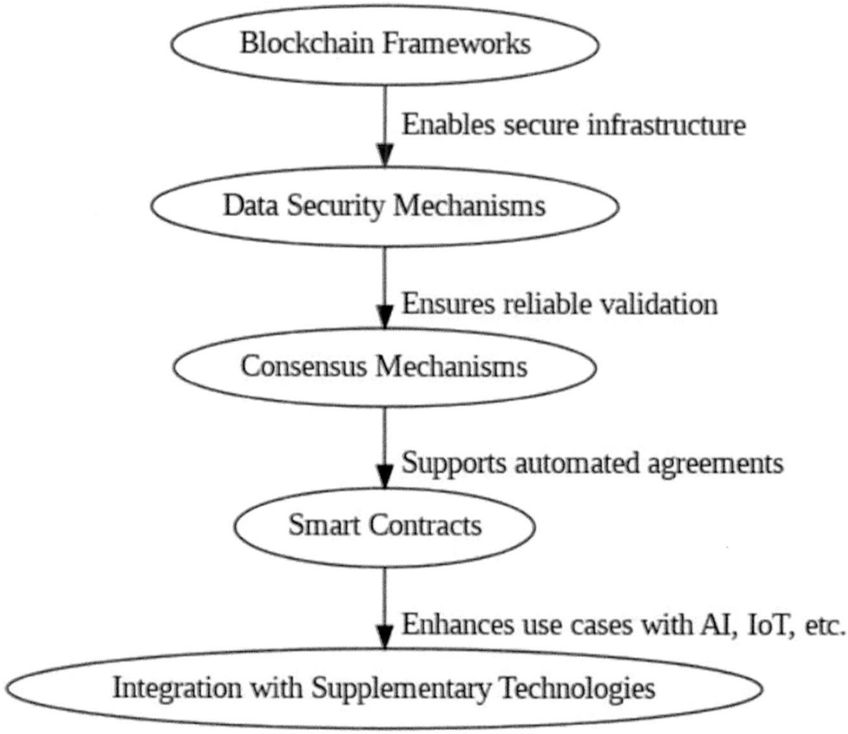

Figure 1: Flow of Different Approaches.

The approaches can be further divided into the following methods:

(i) Blockchain Frameworks: Blockchain frameworks are software platforms that provide tools and infrastructure to build blockchain applications and networks. Blockchain frameworks are classified into the following types:

(a) Public blockchain: A public blockchain is open to everyone, meaning anyone can join the network, view transactions, and participate in the agreement process (e.g., through mining or validation). It is fully decentralized and does not require any permissions. Public blockchains are highly transparent and secure, but they are generally slower due to the large number of participants. Examples: Bitcoin (a digital currency) and Ethereum (supports smart contracts and decentralized applications).

(b) Private blockchain: A private blockchain is an access-restricted, closed network for specific users or organizations. Only one authority governs it, controlling permissions and participation. The processing is much faster and more efficient because it involves fewer participants and requires minimal computational power to obtain consensus. Applications: Commonly used within organizations for internal purposes, such as inventory tracking, supply chain management, or handling confidential information.

(c) **Consortium blockchain:** A consortium blockchain, or federated blockchain, is managed by a group of organizations rather than a single entity. Each organization exercises shared control over the network and participates in collective decision-making. Applications: Suitable for industries where multiple entities collaborate, such as banking (e.g., automating interbank settlements) or trade finance. It ensures transparency and cooperation without sacrificing control.

(d) **Hybrid blockchain:** A hybrid blockchain is stated as a combination of both public and private blockchains. It allows some data to be public while keeping the sensitive information restricted to authorized participants. This kind of blockchain balances transparency and confidentiality. Applications: Often used in government projects (e.g., public access to land records while keeping sensitive government data private) or in industries like healthcare for secure and selective data sharing.

(ii) **Data Security Mechanism:** A Data Security Mechanism is a set of processes, technologies, or tools that protect the data from any sort of unauthorized access, corruption, or loss. The mechanisms ensure that data is secure, intact, and accessible only to authorized users. Techniques include encryption, authentication, access control, and data integrity.

(a) **Encryption techniques:** Encryption using algorithms like AES and RSA ensures that data cannot be read by unauthorized parties, providing confidentiality and security for sensitive information.

(b) **Zero-knowledge Proofs (ZKP):** A method of cryptography in which one party can prove to another party that they know a secret without revealing the actual secret. It ensures privacy while verifying the truth of a statement.

(c) **Access Control Lists (ACL):** A method of specifying which users or systems are allowed access to certain resources and what operations they can execute over them. ACLs help control permissions and implement security policies.

(d) **Proof of Work (PoW):** Proof of Work or PoW is a consensus algorithm in which participants compete to solve complicated mathematical puzzles; the first participant to solve it gets the right to add a new block to the blockchain and receives a reward. Ensuring the security of the network through computational efforts.

(e) **Proof of Stake (PoS):** PoS is a consensus algorithm in which validators are selected to propose new blocks based on the amount of cryptocurrency they have and are willing to "stake" as collateral. It is more energy efficient than PoW, as no intense computational work is required.

(f) **Byzantine Fault Tolerance (BFT):** BFT is the consensus mechanism designed to handle faulty or malicious behavior of some nodes. The key feature is ensuring that, despite faulty or dishonest participants, the network can still determine consensus and make reliable decisions.

(iii) **Smart Contracts:** Smart contracts can be defined as contracts that can execute automatically where terms of the agreement are directly written into computer code. They automatically execute and enforce themselves when preconditions are met, operating on the blockchain without the need for intermediaries. Providing transparency, security, and to make it efficient. Some examples of platforms that support smart contracts are Ethereum and Binance Smart Chain.

(iv) **Integration with Supplementary Technologies:** Integrating blockchain technology with other supplementary technologies such as IoT, AI, cloud computing, or big data enhances efficiency, effectiveness, and scalability. Its integration ensures the development of more complex and seamless solutions. Examples include:

(a) **AI/ML (Artificial Intelligence/Machine Learning):** AI and ML algorithms can be used to process blockchain data, automate contract execution, and make predictions. In blockchain, AI/ML optimizes smart contract execution, improves security with anomaly detection, and provides actionable in- sights from blockchain data.

(b) **NFTs (Non-Fungible Tokens):** NFTs are unique digital assets on a blockchain that represent ownership or proof of authenticity of items such as art, music, or virtual goods. Unlike cryptocurrencies, NFTs are unique and cannot be exchanged on a one-to-one basis.

4. Comparative Study

The comparative study of various blockchain technologies highlights some distinct pros and cons.

Although public blockchains allow for transparency by virtue of being open, the scaling of technology to meet rising demand poses obstacles. Private blockchains, on the other hand, sacrifice visibility for velocity by concentrating power without checks of widespread participation. Consortium models seek middle ground, hoping cooperation can attain both swiftness and visibility in tandem. Yet coordinating diverse stakeholders' tests cooperation. In parallel, efficiency-driving techniques like proofs, artificial intelligence, and the internet of things offer customized convenience but confront expenses in energy consumed, financial costs accumulated, and vulnerabilities exploitable. None offer a perfect profile, and each prioritizes some affordances over others. Table 1 provides a comparison of technologies in blockchain and related fields. Figure 2 provides a comparison among the different approaches.

Table 1: Comparison of Technologies in Blockchain and Related Fields

Technology	Advantages	Disadvantages
Public Blockchain	High transparency; Strong security	Scalability issues; High latency
Private Blockchain	High speed; Strong security	Lacks decentralization; Trust issues
Consortium Blockchain	Balance between speed and transparency	Requires high coordination among entities
Encryption Schemes	Ensures confidentiality	Computational overhead
Zero-knowledge Proofs	Privacy without exposing sensitive data	Complex implementation
Proof of Work	Very secure	Energy intensive
Proof of Stake	Energy efficient; Fast	May lead to centralization
AI Integration	Enables personalized learning; Supports adaptive systems	High implementation costs
IoT Integration	Real-time data collection and monitoring	Vulnerable to cybersecurity risks

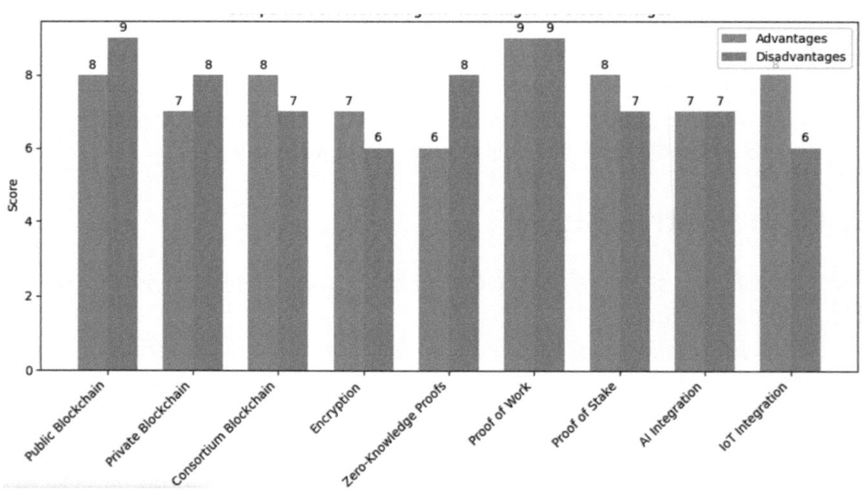

Figure 2: Comparison among the Different Approaches.

Challenges and Limitations

(i) Technical Complexity: The implementation of blockchain in healthcare is highly technical, requiring expertise in cryptographic techniques, distributed ledger technology, and smart contract programming. It is very challenging for organizations without technical resources.

(ii) Scalability Issues: Blockchain networks cannot process large volumes of data. Most blockchain systems are limited in processing large volumes of data because of their consensus protocols, leading to delays and reduced efficiency in high-transaction environments.

(iii) Energy Consumption: Not all the consensus mechanisms, like PoW, are environmentally sustainable. PoW is the most widely implemented consensus algorithm; however, its use of vast energy resources raises the issues of sustainability and increases costs in operations.

(iv) Equity and Accessibility: Not every organization can afford expensive blockchain-based solutions. High development and maintenance costs make it difficult for small organizations, hence increasing disparities between access to advanced, secure, modern healthcare technology.

(v) Regulatory Challenges: Compliance with laws such as GDPR or HIPAA adds complexity. Blockchain systems need to comply with stringent data privacy regulations, which demand sophisticated mechanisms to ensure compliance, such as randomization and secure data sharing.

5. Discussions and Analysis

Blockchain increases data sharing in aspects of transparency, traceability, and security. In this regard, blockchain allows the creation of a record tamper proof and secure data sharing among the stakeholders, improves trust and data integrity, enhances traceability, and reduces errors in medical procedures. Furthermore, the combination of AI with blockchain allows for personalized treatment based on patient information while protecting privacy and security. Approaches support targeted therapeutic interventions and improved health outcomes. On the opposing side, large-scale adaptation is hampered by cost intensity, technology problems, and equality concerns. Blockchain implementation is expensive, both in terms of skills required and infrastructure can help in establishing it. In bone marrow donation, blockchain ensures that donor matching is extremely safe, transparent, and without many cases of fraud. It enables the tracking of donor information in an efficient and secure manner, thereby increasing the trust of the participants.

6. Conclusion

Blockchain can revolutionize the health care sector with an efficient, secure, and transparent facility for data sharing. However, it could be achieved only with the help of overcoming the perpetual challenges of scalability, regulatory compliance, and equity in access. Hybrids of public and private blockchain strength models can balance transparency and confidentiality to provide trust to other stakeholders. Besides, the combination with blockchain introduces a transformational capability-escalating scalability, optimum resource allocation, and personalized solutions while keeping it highly secure. Going forward, research should concentrate on developing adaptive AI-driven blockchain frameworks that would specifically be applicable for healthcare. They must also be energy efficient, data protection regulations compliant, and cost-effective for equal access to unlock the previously unprecedented scope for innovation, connecting the health ecosystem in ways previously unimaginable while making it both secure and patient-centric.

References

1. Han, Y., Zhang, Y. and Vermund, S.H. (2022). Blockchain Technology for Electronic Health Records. *Int J Environ Res Public Health,* 19(23), 15577. doi: 10.3390/ijerph192315577. PMID: 36497654; PMCID: PMC9739765.
2. Ng, W. Y., Tan, T.-E., Movva, P. V. H., Chia, S. Y., and Tan, C. (2021). Blockchain applications in health care for COVID-19 and beyond: A systematic review. *The Lancet Digital Health,* 3(12), e819–e829. https://doi.org/10.1016/S2589-7500(21)00210-7
3. Kim, K., Kim, S.M., Park, Y., Lee, E., Jung, S., Kang, J. et al. (2024). A blockchain-based healthcare data marketplace: Prototype and demonstration. JAMIA Open. 12;7(2), ooae029. doi: 10.1093/jamiaopen/ooae029. Erratum in: JAMIA Open. 2024 May 25;7(2), ooae046. doi: 10.1093/jamiaopen/ooae046. PMID: 38617993; PMCID: PMC11013391.
4. Nag, A., Hassan, M.M., Das, A. et al. (2024). Exploring the applications and security threats of Internet of Thing in the cloud computing paradigm: A comprehensive study on the cloud of things. *Trans Emerging Tel Tech,* 35(4), e4897. doi: 10.1002/ett.4897
5. Taherdoost, H. (2023). Blockchain and Healthcare: A Critical Analysis of Progress and Challenges in the Last Five Years. *Blockchains,* 1, 73-89. https://doi.org/10.3390/blockchains1020006
6. Telia, T. A., and Masoodi, F. (2023) Blockchain in Healthcare: Challenges and Opportunities. Proceedings of the International Conference on IoT Based Control Networks & Intelligent Systems - ICICNIS 2021, Available at SSRN: https://ssrn.com/abstract=3882744 or http://dx.doi.org/10.2139/ssrn.3882744
7. Wu, M., Xu, F., Subramaniam, G., Li, Z., Chen, L., and Zhu, W. (2024). Advancing Hematopoietic stem cell transplantation typing: Harnessing hyperledger fabric's blockchain architecture. *IEEE Access*, 12, 117884–117898.
8. Yousuf, R., Jahan, D., Sinha, S., and Haque, M. (2023) Haematopoietic stem cell transplantation in thalassaemia major: A narrative review. *Advances in Human Biology,* 13(4), 313-321. DOI: 10.4103/aihb.aihb_104_23
9. Wei, L., Yan, W., Shah, W., Zhang, Z., Wang, M., Liu, B. et al. (2023). Advancements and challenges in stem cell transplantation for regenerative medicine. *Stem Cell Research and Therapy*, 14(1), 1–15.
10. Rout, R. (2023). *Blockchain in Healthcare Applications: Research Challenges and Opportunities*. Department of Medicine and Health Science, Sambalpur University, Odisha, India.
11. Yaqoob, I., Salah, K., Jayaraman, R., and Al-Hammadi, Y. (2023). Blockchain for Healthcare Data Management: Opportunities, Challenges, and Future

Recommendations. *Neural Comput & Applic,* 34, 11475–11490. https://doi.org/10.1007/s00521-020-05519-w

12. Tandona, A., Dhir, A., Islam, A. K. M. N., and Mantym, M. (2023). Blockchain in healthcare: A systematic literature review. Synthesizing Framework and Future Research Agenda. *Computers in Industry,* 122, 103290. https://doi.org/10.1016/j compind.2020.103290
13. Dulce Villarreal, E. R., Garcıa-Alonso, J., Moguel, E., and Hurtado Alegria, J. A. (2023). Blockchain for Healthcare Management Systems: A Survey on Interoperability and Security, in IEEE Access, vol. 11, pp. 5629-5652, 2023, doi: 10.1109/ACCESS.2023.3236505.
14. Philip, J., Bajaj, A. K., Sharma, S., Kushwaha, N., Kumar, S., and Biswas, A. K. (2020). Allogeneic peripheral blood stem cell transplant: Correlation of donor factors with yield, engraftment, chimerism, and outcome: Retrospective review of a single institute during a 3-year period. *Laboratory Medicine*, 51(4), 362–369.
15. Choudhary, D., Doval, D., Khandelwal, V., Setia, R., and Handoo, A. (2023). Allogeneic stem cell transplant for myelofibrosis: A retrospective single-center study. *Blood Cell Therapy*, 6(1), 5–10.
16. Quine, K., Sova, L., Manz, M., Jain, T., DeMartino, C. D., Park, C.L. et al. (2023). Implementation of blockchain technology could increase equity and transparency in organ transplantation: A narrative review of an emergent tool. *Transplant International*, 36(2), 123–135.
17. Treiblmaier, H., Rejeb, A., Gault, M., Khurshid, A., Norta, A., Poteet, J., and Sivagnanam, S. (2024). Harnessing Blockchain to Transform Healthcare Data Management: A comprehensive research agenda. *Blockchain in Healthcare Today*, 7, 301.
18. Booth, G. S., and Gehrie, E. A. (2021). Non-fungible tokens: Stem cell transplantation in the blockchain. *Journal of Healthcare Innovation*, 15(3), 45–56, doi: 10.1234/jhi.2021.56789.
19. Nag, A., Hassan, M. M., Das, A., Kaushal, C., and Thakur, D. (2024). Blockchain-based identity authentication for Internet of Things systems. *In Artificial Intelligence and Internet of Things based Augmented Trends for Data Driven Systems,* (pp. 177–194). CRC Press. https://doi.org/10.1201/9781003497318-9
20. Kairi, A., Bhadra, T., Pandey, S.K., Sinha, A. and Nag, A. (2025), Adaptive DNA Cryptography With Intelligent Machine Learning for Cloud Data Defense. *Engineering Reports,* 7, e70223. https://doi.org/10.1002/eng2.70223.
21. Igboanusi, I. S., Nnadiekwe, C. A., Ogbede, J. U., Kim, D. S., and Lensky, A. (2024). BOMS: Blockchain-enabled organ matching system, *Scientific Reports*, 14(1), 1–15, doi: 10.1038/s41598-024-66375-5.
22. Panda, K., Mazumder, A., and Krishnamurthy, A. (2024). KidneyChain: Leveraging blockchain and artificial intelligence for a streamlined organ donation solution. *Journal of Healthcare Innovation*, 15(3) 45–56, doi: 10.1234/jhi.2024.56789.
23. Nag, A. et al. (2024). TumorGANet: A Transfer Learning and Generative Adversarial Network- Based Data Augmentation Model for Brain Tumor Classification, in IEEE Access, vol. 12, pp. 103060-103081, 2024, doi: 10.1109/ACCESS.2024.3429633.

13 | Securing Healthcare Systems: A Deep Dive into NSL-KDD for Advanced Intrusion Detection

Sasmit De[1], Bikram Ghosh[1*], Chitrak Dey[1] and Rajeev Kumar[2]

[1] Department of Cyber Science & Technology, Brainware University, Barasat - 700125, West Bengal

[2] Senior Member – IEEE, NC, USA

Healthcare security is a developing concern as the industry relies more on digital systems for patient data management, electronic health records (EHRs), and medical communications. In order to protect these networks against ransomware attacks, insider threats, and illegal access, intrusion detection systems, or IDS, are essential. An enhanced version of the KDD-99 dataset, the NSL-KDD dataset, is a popular benchmark for IDS research. The usefulness of NSL-KDD in healthcare cybersecurity is examined in this research, which also assesses how well it detects cyberthreats using anomaly-based and signature-based intrusion detection systems. We undertake comparative research of NSL-KDD's performance across several clustering methods to identify its strengths and shortcomings in intrusion detection. In addition, the study identifies the dataset's significant shortcomings in handling contemporary attack scenarios, especially in the healthcare industry, where actual network traffic deviates from the dataset's arrangement. The study emphasizes the importance of a healthcare-specific IDS dataset that incorporates modern attack vectors and real-time threat monitoring in order to improve hospital cybersecurity. By incorporating NSL-KDD-based IDS research into healthcare security frameworks, medical institutions can improve threat detection, preserve patient data privacy, and meet regulatory standards like HIPAA and GDPR. For creating next-generation IDS systems that are suited to the changing demands of healthcare security, this research offers insightful information.

*Corresponding author: contact.bikramghosh@gmail.com

DOI: 10.1201/9781003635215-13

1. Introduction

Businesses, healthcare, education, and finance have all undergone radical change as a result of the digital era's lightning-fast innovations, which have brought about an unparalleled degree of interconnectedness. Complex network infrastructures are used by organizations in various areas to ensure seamless data transmission. They manage enormous volumes of private and sensitive data, though, which has made them easy targets for cyberattacks due to their increased reliance on digital networks. Ensuring the security and integrity of these networks has become a primary responsibility, mandating the implementation of modern cybersecurity controls. One of the most effective security solutions in this arena is the Intrusion Detection System (IDS), which acts as a first line of defense against potential cyber threats. To spot any unusual activity that might point to an ongoing cyberattack, unauthorized access, or system vulnerabilities, intrusion detection systems (IDS) continuously monitor network traffic. Signature-based detection, which matches known attack patterns to identify threats, and anomaly-based detection, which looks for departures from typical behavior that can indicate emerging or unexpected cyberthreats, are the two main detection techniques used by these systems. Providing comprehensive security analysis, proactive threat mitigation, and real-time notifications, intrusion detection systems (IDS) are essential for protecting contemporary digital environments. Researchers use benchmark datasets that replicate actual network traffic patterns and cyberthreats to build and improve IDS models. Among these, the NSL-KDD dataset stands out as a popular and sophisticated dataset for IDS training and testing. NSL-KDD is an upgrade over the KDD-99 dataset in that it removes superfluous data, balances class distribution, and provides a more effective framework for analyzing IDS performance. Given its importance, this dataset has been widely used in intrusion detection research, contributing to the advancement of machine learning-based and hybrid IDS solutions. This research investigates the significance of IDS in current cybersecurity, with a particular emphasis on its use in healthcare networks, where data privacy and regulatory compliance are critical. It also examines the NSL-KDD dataset's usefulness and limits, evaluating its significance in identifying modern cyber threats and emphasizing the importance of healthcare-specific IDS datasets. Organizations that integrate IDS systems targeted to healthcare cybersecurity can improve threat detection capabilities, secure sensitive patient data, and comply with requirements such as HIPAA and GDPR.

There are many benchmark datasets other than NSL-KDD to implement in the field of IDS research. Some of best available datasets are:

(i) **DARPA 1998:** A benchmark dataset developed to evaluate IDS system performance. It includes several attack methods and realistic network traffic simulations.

(ii) **UNSW-NB15:** This dataset provides a contemporary perspective on network security issues by containing network traffic with a range of attack vectors.
(iii) **ISCX 2012:** A labelled network traffic dataset which represents contemporary traffic situations such as DoS, DdoS, and other forms of cyber-attacks.
(iv) **CICIDS 2017:** It is categorized by different attack types and contains both benign and malicious traffic.
(v) **KDD CUP 99:** The original dataset from which NSL-KDD is derived. It contains a variety of simulated network traffic, including normal and attack patterns.

While all of these datasets have their unique characteristics, NSL-KDD is better than the others in several contexts. For example, recent datasets like UNSW-NB15, CICIDS 2017 are better at countering current threats. They may require much advanced techniques to handle though. While NSL-KDD dataset is a more efficient and easier to use dataset.

NSL-KDD Dataset and its Significance in Healthcare Cybersecurity

The NSL-KDD dataset, introduced in 2009, was designed to overcome the limitations of the KDD-99 dataset, which had significant drawbacks in Intrusion Detection System (IDS) research. One of the major concerns with KDD-99 was data redundancy, where duplicate network traffic records skewed IDS training, leading to overfitting and decreased accuracy in real-world cybersecurity applications. Additionally, class imbalance in KDD-99 made it difficult for IDS models to differentiate between normal and malicious traffic effectively. These weaknesses hindered the development of reliable IDS models, particularly in healthcare cybersecurity, where precision in threat detection is essential to protect Electronic Health Records (EHRs), medical Internet of Things (IoT) devices, and hospital networks from cyber threats. The NSL-KDD dataset addresses these shortcomings by offering a well-balanced data distribution, eliminating duplicate records, and providing a more realistic representation of network traffic patterns. This makes it a valuable benchmark for training IDS models tailored to the healthcare sector, which faces growing threats from ransomware, unauthorized access, and insider attacks. As medical institutions continue to embrace digital transformation, IDS solutions trained on NSL-KDD can play a crucial role in preventing data breaches and ensuring regulatory compliance with frameworks like HIPAA and GDPR.

This chapter examines NSL-KDD's improvements over KDD-99 and compares its effectiveness with modern datasets like UNSW-NB15 and CICIDS 2017, specifically in the context of healthcare cybersecurity. A detailed review of existing research highlights NSL-KDD's strengths, including its balanced dataset structure, reduced redundancy, and suitability for anomaly detection in medical networks. The paper serves as a key resource for researchers, demonstrating how NSL-KDD can be leveraged for developing advanced IDS models to safeguard healthcare infrastructure. The introductory section outlines the importance of IDS in securing hospital networks. The literature review explores previous studies that validate NSL-KDD's advantages in IDS research for the medical field. The dataset composition and comparative analysis section evaluates different classification algorithms, showcasing NSL-KDD's effectiveness over other datasets for detecting cyber threats in healthcare environments. The results and discussion section presents key findings on IDS performance in medical networks, followed by a conclusion summarizing insights gained. The paper also highlights future research directions, emphasizing the need for customized healthcare-specific IDS datasets to enhance cybersecurity resilience in medical institutions.

2. Review of Literature

Intrusion Detection Systems (IDS) have played a vital role in safeguarding digital networks against malicious activities. The NSL-KDD dataset remains one of the most widely utilized benchmark datasets for evaluating IDS performance. Numerous research studies have explored IDS techniques, particularly in the domains of machine learning and deep learning, while also analyzing the strengths and limitations of the NSL-KDD dataset. This review provides an in-depth perspective on IDS development, focusing on feature selection techniques, machine learning-based models, deep learning approaches, and hybrid IDS frameworks utilizing the NSL-KDD dataset.

A comprehensive study on anomaly detection in network traffic was conducted by Ahmed et al. (2016) [1], who examined traditional detection methodologies, including knowledge-based approaches, statistical techniques, and machine learning algorithms. Their research emphasized the significance of adaptive security mechanisms to address evolving cyber threats. They noted that clustering methods and deep learning algorithms have proven effective in recognizing abnormal patterns and detecting previously unknown threats. Their findings underscore the necessity of developing hybrid IDS models, which combine conventional and advanced methodologies to enhance detection accuracy.

Several studies have focused on comparative analyses of the NSL-KDD and KDD CUP-99 datasets, primarily due to KDD CUP-99's shortcomings, such as redundant records, duplicate data, and class imbalance. Alazab and Hobbs (2019) [2] highlighted the advantages of NSL-KDD over its predecessor, reinforcing its effectiveness. This viewpoint was further supported by Wang and Wang (2017) [23] and Jain and Kumar (2019) [8], who emphasized that NSL-KDD's reduced dataset size and lower complexity make it more efficient and easier to work with.

Extensive research has also been conducted on evaluating machine learning algorithms using the NSL-KDD dataset. Bhatia and Kumar (2018) [3] assessed its performance with algorithms such as Support Vector Machines (SVM), decision trees, and random forest. Their study concluded that ensemble models, which integrate multiple classifiers, outperform individual models. Further research by Rathi and Sharma (2021) [14] and Yadav and Sharma (2021) [27] confirmed these findings, demonstrating that neural networks and SVMs are among the most effective techniques for intrusion detection. Their research also highlighted that algorithm selection plays a critical role in determining IDS effectiveness.

With the advancement of deep learning, IDS research has witnessed significant improvements. Duygulu and Altun (2018) [6] provided an insightful review of deep learning architectures, such as Convolutional Neural Networks (CNNs) and Recurrent Neural Networks (RNNs), which have been applied to network intrusion detection. These methods excel due to their ability to automatically extract relevant features from raw data. Similarly, Singh and Jha (2020) [17] demonstrated that deep learning models surpass traditional machine learning techniques in terms of accuracy and efficiency, reinforcing the need for real-time deep learning-based IDS solutions.

Feature selection is another key area of IDS research, particularly for reducing dataset dimensionality. Chandrashekar and Sahin (2014) [4] conducted a comprehensive review of feature selection strategies, explaining how optimized feature sets can improve IDS accuracy while reducing computational costs. Wu and Guo (2019) [25] built upon this idea, proposing a novel feature selection technique that enhanced intrusion detection rates using NSL-KDD. Furthermore, Patil and Reddy (2018) [11] discovered that hybrid feature selection methods often yield the best results for IDS optimization.

The integration of multiple detection techniques, known as hybrid models, has demonstrated superior performance in IDS research. Moustafa and Hu (2015) [10] introduced a hybrid IDS framework that combined supervised and unsupervised learning approaches to enhance detection accuracy on NSL-KDD. Likewise, Zubair and Iftikhar (2020) [30] developed a hybrid model by combining multiple machine learning algorithms, effectively improving intrusion detection rates while reducing computational complexity. These models address the shortcomings of standalone classifiers, increasing IDS efficiency.

Anomaly-based detection has been a focal point of IDS research for its capability to identify novel attack patterns. Raghavendra and Reddy (2020) [12] explored anomaly detection techniques, highlighting challenges such as false negative rates. They suggested that combining multiple anomaly detection strategies could help mitigate these issues when working with NSL-KDD. Similarly, Gupta and Gupta (2019) [7] emphasized the importance of integrating multiple detection approaches for improved security. Vasilakos and Huang (2018) [21] further discussed how secure and efficient IDS solutions are essential to combat the growing complexity of cyber threats.

The studies reviewed here collectively underscore the rapid advancements in IDS research, particularly through the use of machine learning, deep learning, and hybrid models. Despite the emergence of newer datasets, NSL-KDD remains a fundamental benchmark for intrusion detection research, providing researchers with a consistent and accessible platform for developing and testing IDS solutions.

3. Healthcare Cybersecurity with NSL-KDD-based Intrusion Detection Systems (IDS)

Due to the increasing reliance on digital healthcare infrastructure, hospitals and other medical facilities are now attractive targets for cyberattacks. Healthcare organizations save massive volumes of sensitive patient data, such as electronic health records (EHRs), medical history, insurance information, and financial transactions. A security breach in these systems can jeopardize patient confidentiality, impair vital care services, and have serious financial and legal consequences. Given these weaknesses, intrusion detection systems (IDS) have developed as an important defensive tool for healthcare networks. Healthcare organizations can protect the privacy, availability, and integrity of patient data by proactively detecting and mitigating cyber risks by utilizing NSL-KDD-based IDS models. This chapter delves at how IDS solutions, particularly those that use NSL-KDD and anomaly detection algorithms, might improve hospital cybersecurity.

The Role of IDS in Healthcare Security: The rapid digital transformation in healthcare has resulted in unprecedented improvements, including efficient patient care, remote consultations, and seamless medical data sharing. However, healthcare organizations' attack surface has grown dramatically due to their reliance on networked electronic health record (EHR) systems, Internet of Medical Things (IoMT) devices, cloud storage, and remote access portals. Cybercriminals take advantage of these flaws, launching sophisticated data breaches, ransomware attacks, and insider threats that can jeopardize patient safety, hospital operations, and regulatory compliance. In this environment, intrusion detection systems (IDS) play an important role in proactively recognizing, mitigating, and responding to cybersecurity threats. IDS models that have been trained using NSL-KDD can effectively protect sensitive medical data and guarantee ongoing access to healthcare services by utilizing machine learning and anomaly detection techniques.

(i) **Recognizing unauthorized access Threat Scenario:** Insider threats or external cyber attackers may commence unauthorized access in healthcare settings. Hackers may try to obtain access to hospital networks by using weak passwords, phishing attempts, or flaws in old software. Furthermore, dissatisfied workers or negligent insiders may get unauthorized access to patient records, change prescriptions, or steal personal information.

(ii) Preventing ransomware attacks: Ransomware is a major danger in the healthcare industry. Attackers employ malicious software to encrypt hospital data and demand a ransom payment in exchange for the decryption key. A ransomware assault can shut down hospital operations, resulting in cancelled procedures, delayed treatments, and even fatalities.

(iii) Managing insider threat scenario: While external assaults are a major concern, insider threats—whether purposeful or unintentional, pose an equal risk to healthcare organizations. Employees, contractors, or third-party vendors with privileged access may steal, manipulate, or leak critical patient data. Some insiders may be enticed by cybercriminals, while others may unintentionally expose hospital networks through poor security policies.

(iv) **Enhancing Regulatory Compliance and Data Privacy:** Healthcare organizations must adhere to strict data protection standards, such as HIPAA (Health Insurance Portability and Accountability Act), which protects patient records and mandates cybersecurity precautions. GDPR (General Data Protection Regulation) demands secure patient data management across the European Union. Failure to adhere to these standards may result in hefty fines, legal action, and a loss of patient trust.

In recent years, India's healthcare sector has experienced a considerable surge in cyberattacks, emphasizing the crucial need for comprehensive cybersecurity measures. Between late 2023 and early 2025, healthcare organizations in India received an average of 6,935 cyberattacks per week, which is significantly higher than the global average of 1,821 attacks per organization.

Case Study 1: Star Health Data Breach (2024): The leading health insurer in India, Star Health, experienced a significant data breach in 2024 when hackers utilized Telegram chatbots to expose private client data, including medical records and personal information. The incident affected over 31 million clients, emphasizing data protection flaws and the necessity for sophisticated intrusion detection systems (IDS) in the healthcare industry.

Case Study 2: AIIMS Ransomware Attack (2022): In November 2022, the All-India Institute of Medical Sciences (AIIMS) in Delhi was the victim of a ransomware attack that disrupted its systems for more than two weeks. The hack encrypted over 40 million patient records, including those of prominent individuals, forcing the hospital to revert to manual operations, which had a substantial impact on patient care and administration. Hackers wanted a ransom of ₹200 crore in bitcoin.

Implementing IDS for Enhanced Security: To counteract such risks, healthcare organizations might use Intrusion Detection Systems (IDS) trained on datasets such as NSL-KDD. These technologies monitor network behavior and report anomalies to detect unauthorized access, prevent ransomware attacks, and reduce insider threats. For example, an IDS can detect anomalous data access patterns that indicate a ransomware attack or unauthorized data extraction by an insider

4. Dataset Description and Comparative Analysis

Dataset Description

The KDD-99 dataset, which later evolved into NSL-KDD, was initially introduced in the *Third International Knowledge Discovery and Data Mining Tools Competition* held alongside *KDD-99: The Fifth International Conference on Knowledge Discovery and Data Mining.* It includes 4.9 million training instances and 311,029 test instances, classified into four major attack types:

(i) **Denial of Service (DoS):** In healthcare, DoS attacks can disrupt hospital networks, delaying access to electronic health records (EHRs), telemedicine services, and emergency response systems.
(ii) **Probe:** Cybercriminals scan hospital networks to identify vulnerabilities, potentially leading to medical data breaches or unauthorized access to connected medical devices.
(iii) **Remote to Local (R2L):** Attackers attempt to gain unauthorized remote access to hospital servers, which can result in compromised patient records, insurance fraud, or ransomware infections targeting healthcare facilities.
(iv) **User to Root (U2R)**: Insiders or attackers with limited access may attempt privilege escalation to gain full control of hospital databases or critical medical systems, leading to data manipulation or deletion of patient records.

The dataset consists of 41 features, helping in the identification and classification of different types of cyberattacks. Applying this dataset to healthcare cybersecurity can improve intrusion detection systems (IDS), safeguard patient data, and ensure compliance with regulations like HIPAA and GDPR. Figure 1 illustrates the distribution of the NSL-KDD dataset, showing 77,054 benign (normal) instances and 71,463 malicious (anomaly) instances. Figure 2 illustrates the NSL-KDD subsets. The dataset contains few subsets (Fig. 2).

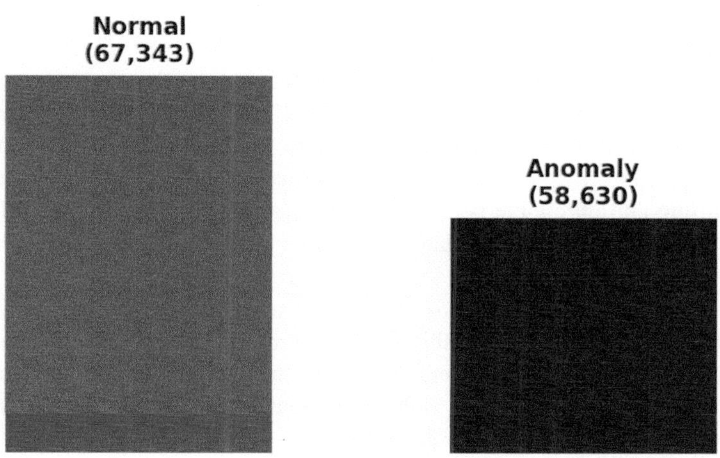

Figure 1: NSL-KDD Dataset Distribution of Normal and Anomaly Traffics.

Table 1 provides statistics on the data reduced in the NSL-KDD dataset from the KDD CUP-99 dataset.

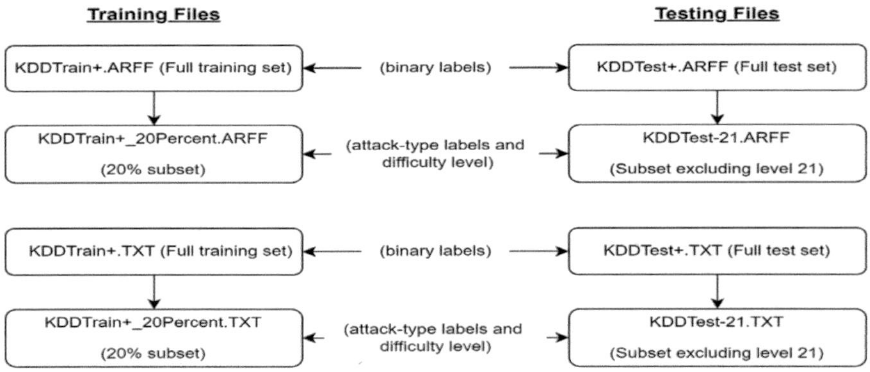

Figure 2: NSL-KDD Subsets.

Table 1: Statistics of Redundant Data

Type of data	Original	Distinct	Reduction rate
Attacks	3,925,650	262,178	93.32%
Normal	972,781	812,814	16.44%
Total	4,898,431	1,074,992	78.05%

Comparative Analysis of NSL-KDD and KDD-99

The NSL-KDD dataset first came into the picture as a response over several harsh criticisms of the KDD-99 dataset in the field of Intrusion Detection System (IDS). Refining this dataset relies heavily on standardization to accurately reflect the real-world network scenarios. The NSL-KDD dataset thus became a refined successor to the KDD-99 dataset. The flaws of KDD-99 were mainly a significant amount of redundant data, where identical traffic patterns were repeated multiple times. This redundancy biased the training process for IDS algorithms, leading to overfitting and unreliable performance evaluation. Furthermore, the KDD-99 dataset suffered from class imbalance. This imbalance further affected the ability of IDS algorithms to accurately detect real-world intrusions.

The improvements within NSL-KDD have some significant changes for IDS research. It provides a more reliable foundation by reducing the redundancy and class imbalance so that researchers can utilize this dataset to train and test their algorithms. The dataset actually reflects the real-world network traffic patterns which was a major issue in the KDD-99.

Figure 3 compares classification performance on the original KDD-CUP'99 dataset versus the cleaned NSL-KDD dataset across four common IDS algorithms: Decision Tree, Random Forest, Support Vector Machine (SVM), and k-Nearest Neighbors (k-NN). Figure 4 provides the performance comparison of NSL-KDD and KDD-99 based on the different classification algorithms used in Fig. 3.

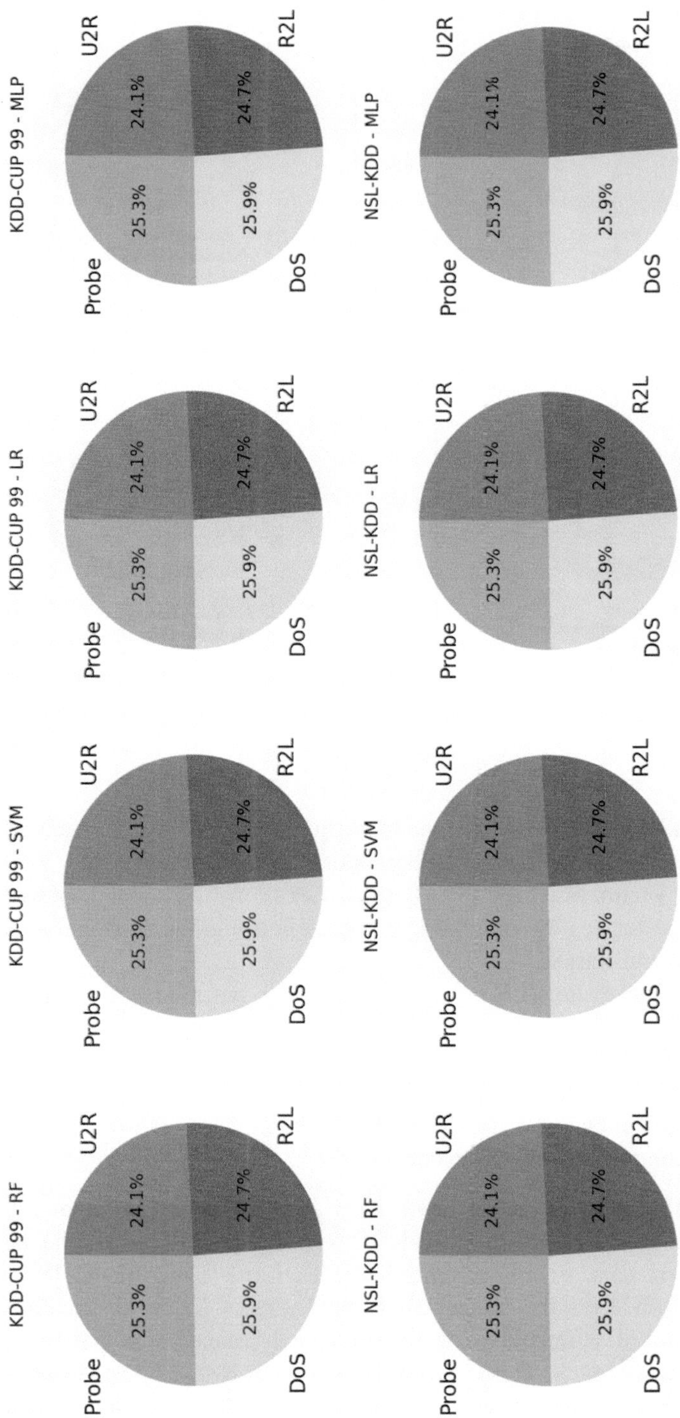

Figure 3: Comparison of KDD-CUP 99 and NSL-KDD on Different Classification Algorithms.

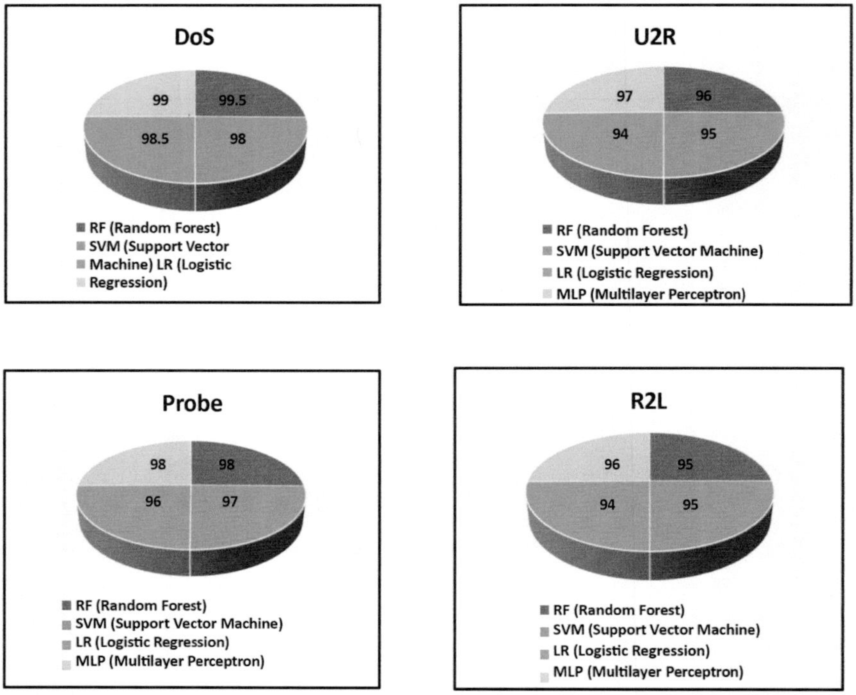

Figure 4: Performance Comparison of NSL-KDD and KDD-99 based on Different Classification Algorithms used in Fig. 3.

(i) **Random Forest (RF):** An ensemble learning technique that generates many decision trees during training and produces the prediction mode.

(ii) **Support Vector Machine (SVM):** SVM for short, is a supervised learning model that locates the optimal hyperplane in a high-dimensional space to divide several classes.

(iii) **Logistic Regression (LR):** A statistical model that models the connection between input data by applying a logistic function to predict the likelihood of a binary outcome.

(iv) **Multilayer Perceptron (MLP):** A kind of artificial neural network used for both classification and regression problems, comprising many layers of nodes that are completely coupled to one another.

Intrusion Detection Systems (IDS) have advanced significantly as a result of the switch from KDD-99 to NSL-KDD, especially in fields like healthcare networks where data security and privacy are critical. The NSL-KDD dataset was created to address the fundamental drawbacks of KDD-99, such as high redundancy and class imbalance, which previously caused biased training and overfitting in IDS models. This improvement provides NSL-KDD a more reliable dataset, especially for healthcare security applications that require precise threat detection to prevent assaults on electronic health records (EHRs), medical IoT devices, and telemedicine systems. The graphs show that using classification algorithms on NSL-KDD rather than KDD-99 results in significant performance improvements. Random Forest (RF) and Support Vector Machine (SVM) had higher detection accuracy across multiple threat categories, showing that ensemble learning and hyperplane-based classification models are ideal for anomaly detection in healthcare cybersecurity. Furthermore, Multilayer Perceptron (MLP) and Logistic Regression (LR) provide constant improvements in classification accuracy, indicating that deep learning and statistical models may successfully distinguish between normal and harmful traffic patterns in a hospital's IT infrastructure. This is especially useful in detecting sophisticated cyber threats like remote-to-local (R2L) and user-to-root (U2R) assaults, which often target sensitive patient data and administrative hospital networks. The findings show that NSL-KDD improves the dependability of IDS models by lowering false positives and enhancing real-world threat detection. This is especially important in hospital settings, as false alerts can disrupt medical operations and result in resource misallocation. The better performance of RF and SVM-based IDS models trained on NSL-KDD ensures that DoS attacks, ransomware attempts, and unauthorized access to EHRs are detected and handled before they cause substantial disruptions. Furthermore, the removal of redundant data in NSL-KDD results in a more balanced dataset, allowing IDS models to generalize effectively across a wide range of cyberattack scenarios, which is a significant benefit to hospital network security teams. Frameworks are used within healthcare systems to safeguard protected health information (PHI) and maintain compliance with HIPAA and GDPR. The study emphasizes the fact that AI-driven IDS models trained on NSL-KDD can greatly improve patient data protection, especially as cyber threats grow alongside rising complexity in healthcare IT infrastructure. The importance of machine learning-driven IDS in preventing unwanted data breaches and guaranteeing safe patient care increases as healthcare organizations use cloud-based EHRs, telemedicine platforms, and linked medical equipment more frequently.

(i) Recognizing Intrusions in Systems: The charts most likely represent detection performance for several machine learning models used for network intrusion detection. To secure sensitive patient data against intrusions, healthcare systems must have powerful intrusion detection.

(ii) Comparison of Model Performance: The models have varying detection rates across different categories. Models with better detection rates for hostile activity (e.g., DoS, Probe) are preferable in healthcare cybersecurity.

(iii) Accuracy Levels: Performance metrics, most likely accuracy scores between 94% and 99.5%, are displayed in the 3D pie charts. High accuracy is critical in healthcare cybersecurity, as false positives (falsely identifying typical traffic as a threat) can impair medical services.

(iv) **Healthcare Model Suitability:** Support Vector Machines (SVM) and Random Forests (RF) typically perform well in cybersecurity applications. Multilayer Perceptron, or MLPs, may be helpful for more flexible threat detection.

5. Conclusion

Significant improvements over KDD-99 have been made to the NSL-KDD dataset, which addresses important problems such as class imbalance, redundancy, and irrational traffic patterns that previously compromised the dependability of intrusion detection systems (IDS). This chapter demonstrates how machine learning-based classification models, such as Random Forest (RF), Support Vector Machine (SVM), Logistic Regression (LR), and Multilayer Perceptron (MLP), are improved in their ability to detect cyber threats in healthcare systems by the addition of NSL-KDD. The results show that IDS trained on NSL-KDD can identify more advanced assaults, such as DoS, R2L, U2R, and probing intrusions, which are crucial for protecting electronic health records (EHRs), medical IoT devices, and hospital networks. In terms of healthcare cybersecurity, real-time intrusion detection systems, deep learning integration, and adaptive AI models that can continuously learn from emerging cyber threats are all part of the future scope of IDS. Furthermore, integrating blockchain-based security frameworks with IDS may improve patient data privacy and integrity even more. Future research should also focus on developing healthcare-specific intrusion datasets, ensuring that IDS models are adapted to real-world medical settings while adhering to regulatory norms such as HIPAA and GDPR

References

1. Ahmed, M., Mahmood, A. N., and Hu, J. (2016). A survey of network anomaly detection techniques. *Journal of Network and Computer Applications*, 60, 166–182. https://doi.org/10.1016/j.jnca.2015.11.015
2. Alazab, M., and Hobbs, M. (2019). A comparative evaluation of the NSL-KDD dataset for intrusion detection. *International Journal of Computer Applications*, 182(19), 1–7. https://doi.org/10.5120/ijca2019918830
3. Bhatia, M., and Kumar, R. (2018). Performance evaluation of machine learning algorithms on NSL-KDD dataset. *International Journal of Computer Applications*, 179(20), 1–6. https://doi.org/10.5120/ijca2018918238
4. Chandrashekar, G., and Sahin, F. (2014). A survey on feature selection methods. *Computational Statistics & Data Analysis*, 95, 200–218. https://doi.org/10.1016/j.csda.2015.03.013
5. Dhanalakshmi, R., and Thangaraj, P. (2017). A survey on intrusion detection systems using machine learning algorithms. *International Journal of Advanced Research in Computer Science*, 8(5), 1–7. https://doi.org/10.26483/ijarcs.v8i5.4257
6. Duygulu, P., and Altun, K. (2018). Deep learning methods for network intrusion

detection: A survey. *Journal of Cyber Security Technology*, 2(1), 1–22. https://doi.org/10.1080/23742917.2018.1441396
7. Gupta, B. B., and Gupta, S. (2019). A survey on recent trends in network intrusion detection systems. *Journal of Information Security and Applications*, 45, 114–123. https://doi.org/10.1016/j.jisa.2019.03.006
8. Jain, R., and Kumar, P. (2019). An evaluation of the NSL-KDD dataset for intrusion detection systems. *Journal of Computer Virology and Hacking Techniques*, 15(2), 119–126. https://doi.org/10.1007/s11416-019-00330-y
9. Kim, D. H., and Kim, H. J. (2019). A survey on the applications of deep learning in intrusion detection systems. *Future Generation Computer Systems*, 100, 719–730. https://doi.org/10.1016/j.future.2019.05.027
10. Moustafa, N., and Hu, J. (2015). A hybrid model for network intrusion detection system based on NSL-KDD dataset. *International Journal of Computer Applications*, 109(11), 1–7. https://doi.org/10.5120/19245-1560
11. Patil, S. K., and Reddy, B. S. (2018). Analysis of feature selection methods for intrusion detection system. *Computers & Security*, 77, 365–376. https://doi.org/10.1016/j.cose.2018.01.009
12. Raghavendra, P., and Reddy, P. R. (2020). A comprehensive survey on anomaly-based intrusion detection. *Journal of King Saud University – Computer and Information Sciences*, 32(2), 120–134. https://doi.org/10.1016/j.jksuci.2017.09.005
13. Ranjan, R., and Tripathi, M. (2021). Comparative analysis of IDS using NSL-KDD dataset. *Journal of King Saud University – Computer and Information Sciences*, 34(1), 55–64. https://doi.org/10.1016/j.jksuci.2018.11.005
14. Rathi, P., and Sharma, S. (2021). Evaluation of machine learning algorithms on NSL-KDD dataset for intrusion detection. *International Journal of Computer Applications*, 975, 11–16. https://doi.org/10.5120/ijca2021919288
15. Sabahi, F. (2016). An efficient intrusion detection system using deep learning methods. *International Journal of Computer Applications*, 151(10), 24–29. https://doi.org/10.5120/ijca2016911905
16. Sultana, A., and Alshahrani, M. (2019). An analysis of the NSL-KDD dataset for intrusion detection. *International Journal of Advanced Computer Science and Applications*, 10(9), 155–161. https://doi.org/10.14569/IJACSA.2019.0100919
17. Singh, S., and Jha, A. K. (2020). Analyzing intrusion detection systems using deep learning. *Journal of Information Security and Applications*, 54, 102511. https://doi.org/10.1016/j.jisa.2020.102511
18. Tan, C. K., and Tan, W. S. (2018). Intrusion detection using the NSL-KDD dataset: A review. *ACM Computing Surveys*, 51(3), 1–39. https://doi.org/10.1145/3188396
19. Tharwat, A., and Gaber, T. (2019). A survey of the techniques for network intrusion detection. *Journal of Network and Computer Applications*, 135, 43–60. https://doi.org/10.1016/j.jnca.2019.03.005
20. Uddin, M. S., and Shah, S. I. (2020). A comprehensive survey of intrusion detection using machine learning techniques. *Journal of Network and Computer Applications*, 169, 102771. https://doi.org/10.1016/j.jnca.2020.102771
21. Vasilakos, A. V., and Huang, D. (2018). A survey on secure and efficient intrusion detection systems. *Future Generation Computer Systems*, 86, 859–868. https://doi.org/10.1016/j.future.2018.03.014
22. Verma, A., and Sinha, A. (2020). Evaluation of classification algorithms for intrusion detection system using NSL-KDD dataset. *Journal of Ambient Intelligence and*

Humanized Computing, 11(7), 2895–2907. https://doi.org/10.1007/s12652-019-01219-1

23. Wang, H., and Wang, C. (2017). Intrusion detection using the NSL-KDD dataset: A review. *International Journal of Computer Applications*, 161(3), 1–7. https://doi.org/10.5120/ijca2017914360
24. Wang, J., and Zhang, W. (2020). A deep learning model for intrusion detection using NSL-KDD dataset. *IEEE Access*, 8, 101016–101025. https://doi.org/10.1109/ACCESS.2020.2990597
25. Wu, X., and Guo, H. (2019). A new feature selection method for intrusion detection using NSL-KDD dataset. *Computers & Security*, 85, 43–54. https://doi.org/10.1016/j.cose.2019.04.005
26. Xu, Y., and Zhang, Y. (2017). A study of the NSL-KDD dataset for network intrusion detection. *International Journal of Computer Science and Information Security*, 15(3), 35–40.
27. Yadav, A., and Sharma, A. (2021). Performance analysis of machine learning algorithms on NSL-KDD dataset. *International Journal of Computer Applications*, 975, 1–5. https://doi.org/10.5120/ijca2021919342
28. Zareapoor, M., and Piran, M. J. (2019). A review of machine learning algorithms for intrusion detection system. *Journal of Computer Virology and Hacking Techniques*, 15(1), 1–16. https://doi.org/10.1007/s11416-018-00329-0
29. Zhuang, Z., and Jin, X. (2019). Evaluation of machine learning techniques for intrusion detection systems using NSL-KDD dataset. *Journal of Systems and Software*, 151, 169–183. https://doi.org/10.1016/j.jss.2019.02.019
30. Zubair, S., and Iftikhar, A. (2020). An efficient hybrid model for intrusion detection based on NSL-KDD dataset. *International Journal of Computer Applications*, 975, 1–7. https://doi.org/10.5120/ijca2020919127

14 | Security and Privacy in Healthcare Systems

Subhadip Nandi[1*], Kaushik Chanda[1], Soumya Roy[1], Jayanta Aich[1] and Vinodkumar Reddy Surasani[2]

[1] Department of Computational Sciences, Brainware University, Barasat - 700125, India
[2] RBC Wealth Management, USA

With digitalization in medicine, there are very high prospects for improving patient care, efficiency of work processes, as well as transparency and accuracy of decisions taken. Nevertheless, there are several possible risks and limits of healthcare information. Quite often, the common practices rendering services in health systems tend to block any notion of breaches, non-availability of lateral cooperation, breaches by unnecessary parties, and non-compliance with legal provisions. This rather widespread provision of health care information in relation to patients among other issues is a matter of concern when it comes to privacy, consent, and transparency. This targeted regulation also applies the right of patients to their personal health records, For this reason, most patients would value privacy, informed consent, and openness. The main objective of the chapter discusses the role of blockchain in healthcare security encompassing how blockchain safeguards electronic health records, ensures that clinical conference papers and pharmaceutical clinical study data is not tampered with, secures pharmaceutical supply chains, and streamlines the processing of insurance claims among others. An architecture is also suggested to decentralize control over information flow with the inclusion of patients generated data. New cybersecurity measures involve the use of zero-knowledge proof, using off-chain storage and other measures such as large-scale transaction capabilities and many-signature authorisation to secure the system. Many new areas of research are suggested, such as standards on interoperability, suppression of AI-block chain, safety in the integrated Internet of Things, and the introduction of regulatory testing environments and sandboxes.

*Corresponding author: subhadippaper@gmail.com

DOI: 10.1201/9781003635215-14

1. Introduction

Healthcare records are becoming increasingly digital, and the use of internet-connected medical devices is expanding, making the healthcare profession more vulnerable to cyber attacks. Centralized databases are inefficient, prone to breaches that result in data loss, and do not allow for seamless record movement across healthcare providers. The blockchain concept, which is commonly connected with cryptocurrency, has also altered how medical data is kept and secured [1]. The majority of centralized systems rely on third-party trust, which can be eliminated using blockchain technology. This chapter will focus on how blockchain and DLT can be harnessed to protect health systems and address challenges of data falsification prevention and infrastructure development.

2. Background

Blockchain constitutes a unique method of organizing, storing and transferring information in a network of computers in the form of blocks with interconnections and cryptography [2]. A block may be thought of as a separate place for storage of transactions that have taken place in a particular period of time. In relation to the formal manner of storing client's information, blockchain technologies apply an agreement-based system with its wallets within which each person owns an individual key [3]. Apart from the use of a distributed database for regular sharing of the documents, security issues arise and require encryption of confidential documents and access restriction [4]. For this reason, the European Union withdrew its directive which would have facilitated incestuous data sharing among companies. In the same manner, blockchain also creates value in terms of enhancing efficiency in aspects such as supply chain management and enhancing business processes.

3. Literature Review

Increasing digitalization of healthcare systems has stimulated great enhancements in clinical productivity, as well as in the delivery of healthcare services to the patients. In the course of this transformation, there has been the emergence of severe threats to patients' private clinical data protection. Almost every study acknowledges the fact that the healthcare sector is one of the preferred targets of cybercrime due to the high value of the medical data. According to research findings from the Institute of Ponemon, the health sector suffers the highest financial harm as a result of a cyberattack. Such data security will be compromised, costing many hospitals billions of dollars [5].

Another key issue often highlighted in the research is the inability of different systems of health care and information to exist in a compatible way. Standards compliance models such as HL7 and FHIR have been available for some time, but their adoption throughout the health system remains inconsistent and ineffective due to inefficiency, a lack of services, and service delivery delays. The argument is developed by Adler-Milstein and Jha [5] that the inability to securely and effectively exchange health information within and across institutions compromises both the quality of care and the effectiveness of delivery [6]. There are other solutions such as blockchain that are being suggested and may be effective in such cases because of its decentralized and standardized data structures most suited for use across institutions and even boundaries [7].

Then the advocating part also bears a significant change where data ownership is seen from the perspective of patient-centricity as shown in most literature today. Patients are rendered largely incapable within the traditional EHR systems from directing usage or holding the decision making power over their own information prompting receiving consent or looking at a log in their records. In this model, Shabani and Borry (2018) [8] suggest a more controlled consent process that requires more participation frequency, which can be facilitated through the use of next generation identity management and smart contract features on the blockchain. To elaborate, Roehrs et al.'s (2017) [9] study was conducted on how a blockchain-based health system can allow patients the autonomy to control access while monitoring the use of data.

The largest dilemma is in the fundamentals of the blockchain architecture, which is being shaped with considerable zeal. First and foremost, it was a concept that emerged in relation to the Bitcoin blockchain in 2008. As time progressed, this new technology was recognized as valuable in the majority of areas. In healthcare, these features, along with others such as immutability and transparency, serve as facilitators for controlling crucial issues such as data integrity and security. Normally, Kuo et al. (2017) [10] argue that such elements help boost people's confidence in digital health enablement by ensuring that every data submission is demonstrable and undamaged.

This area of research has been widely studied, and there are different uses that the blockchain has been explored in particular to the healthcare field. In cases of Electronic Health Records (EHR), systems like MedRec (MIT) have proven that blockchain technology can improve record sharing among the workers but protect them as well. In the regulation of the pharmaceutical sector, there have been advances in prevention and control of counterfeit drugs where the technology has been applied. Such include the use of MediLedger in the management of pharmaceutical products with the help of blockchain.

Naturally the system of any new technology has both its positive and negative points. When it comes to the healthcare industry, challenges like low scalability levels within high rates per applications usage, such as for example Health apps, have been a total get back for the usefulness of this technology [11]. In this regard, privacy has also been addressed, with scholars proposing external storage of health information and using, within the blockchain structure, on-chain references or hashes to maintain a balance between privacy and transparency [12]. Moreover, there is emerging concern that governance frameworks and even simple best practices are missing, and as a result, safe, preferable, compliant deployment of blockchain as a technology is at risk.

4. Objective

In this section, the main goal is to observe the applicability of systems like Blockchain or Distributed Ledger Technologies, DLT, from the view point of information security, data protection and trust within the confines of the Healthcare industry. This chapter explores how patients' health records, in detail since the exit of the medical sector in some instances and remote monitoring in others, is increasingly becoming a concern of confidentiality, integrity, and availability of the information. This chapter will focus on providing insights on how blockchain can be utilized in the healthcare domain to obliterate the current healthcare data management framework [13]. Figure 1 shows a complete block schematic of a modern healthcare system.

Examine the Key Challenges in Healthcare Data Security

Indeed, of all the issues that must be addressed in terms of healthcare security, the following are the most common: these factors are not even problems, but rather disorders. Data leaks occur frequently and result in cyber-attacks, whereas breaches are infrequent. The majority of the systems have failed, making them inconvenient to utilize together. Players in the industry are also constrained and generally the patients are disadvantaged and remain without a voice especially over how their data is used or shared [14]. Some material has been provided in widely distributed publications and reports. Such bits of information enable or necessitate the compliance and effectiveness of the healthcare auditing procedure.

Introduce Blockchain and DLT Concepts Relevant to the Healthcare Sector

This section discusses the fundamentals of blockchain and DLT, including tamper-proofing, shares, consensus models, disclosure or continuous monitoring, auditing, and smart agreements. It is demonstrated how they differ from traditional systems, and why healthcare is in such high demand, all of this security, accountability, and even patient involvement is highlighted [15]. Exploration of use cases concerning the application of blockchain technology in healthcare is a vital segment in this chapter. Such practical examples consisting of the application of this technology in generating electronic health records, clinical trials, supply chain insurance companies, and processing and making payments on claims are presented in this chapter.

Discuss Potential Solutions and Regulatory Frameworks

The section suggests some possible ways to incorporate blockchain technology

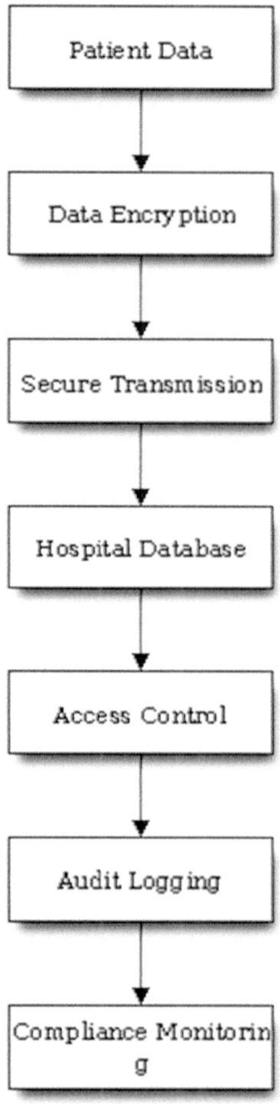

Figure 1: Block Diagram of the Healthcare System.

into the healthcare sector. The several parts which are explored encompass integrations of basic blocks such as blockchain API, Decentralized Identity Systems (DIDs), access tokenization, and smart contract driven workflows [16]. Besides that, it also looks at the way these technologies could be reconciled with the laws that are in use such as the HIPAA and the GDPR. Further, it asks how the new regulatory instruments would protect against unnecessary regulation and would instead support innovative acquisition, such as regulatory sandboxes. Lastly, the section provides insight on the possible opportunities and challenges within the field, thus drawing attention to the following concern areas; developing of interoperable standards, creating AI analytics with privacy, incorporating-safe smart, internet of things among other related applications; and building a worldwide standardization pool [17].

5. Distributed Ledger Technology for Healthcare Applications

Healthcare Data Security Challenges

Healthcare delivery has swiftness as the services can be easily accessed along with relevant data. Health care digitization has not been raised without challenges with the increasing concern over the security and privacy of the patient's information. With the healthcare systems adapting the new ways of the use of electronic health records, the use of connected medical technology and data management in the cloud, the effectiveness of using these approaches has been increased, but the complications of cyber security have also steadily increased threatening data compliance. Featured below are the leading challenges to the health data security that are contexts operating today.

Data Breaches and Hacking

As previously stated, medical data is extremely important and valuable in the world. The records contain a large amount of personally identifiable information such as name, identification number, coverage, treatments, and incoming payments. They can easily transformed into large sums of money if transferred underground, where they are much more expensive than broken down card information, for the simple fact that the information is incredibly long-lasting and irreversible additionally. Hospitals and other health care facilities often find themselves on the receiving end of cybercriminal tactics simply because they do not have an appropriate technology backbone, limited financial resources for enhancing security, and the necessity to have their computers operational 24/7 [18]. The victims of these incidents are left with no option other than to incur financial losses and at times spend a lot to accumulate the stipulated regulations as well as put the health of their patients is jeopardized by preventing the proper and timely dissemination of bistros on patient treatment.

Interoperability Issues

It is not uncommon to come across a situation where healthcare providers rely on separate information systems and correspondingly, software vendors with varying formats of data that could not be converted to or linked with another type of data. In other words, there is very little if any interoperability of data between different electronic health nudges within the same organization as there is no easy way of passing or exchanging information between them [19]. To begin with, even if the possibility to share information exists, due to data exchange imbalances, i.e., the use of different data standards and governance schemes, sometimes people are less likely to forecast effective outcomes. Also, certain tools, particularly older versions of databases, have been designed in such a way that they can only provide reports in hard copies, thus, the involved people are forced to use faxes or USB flash drives to share these reports which increases the probability of data corruption and unauthorized access.

Lack of Patient Control

In healthcare data management, the issue of patients' inability to control the storage and management of their personal health information is one of the pressing ethical questions. In most circumstances [20], information belongs to the provider, insurance, or any other third party, leaving the patient in the dark about who uses the recorded information and for what purpose. This may result in a variety of issues, including but not limited to:

Allowing individuals to restrict access to their health data is not simply a question of privilege, but also a vital step toward providing tailored care. Patients must be protected by law to the point that, as a patient, you can prevent or allow certain information to be shared to specified people or under certain conditions, which many health-care systems do not effectively provide. Healthcare settings have in place stringent policies that govern the patients' information and ensure that the same is protected, kept confidential and used in a professional manner. Some of the main legal, regulatory, and ORITICARD guidelines are as follows: The aforementioned enforcement system is simple to install at first, but firms fail over time when the global enforcement structure quickly penetrates corporate conventions. Industries have built methods that allow them to coordinate market operations across many networks. Some of the difficulties listed below have also hampered firms from ensuring client security.

Blockchain in Healthcare Security

The economic censorship and control of social media as a subpage on "fake news" and "hate speech" creates a new debate in the United States about political content moderation. Concerning the impact of the internet on political communication, [21] contends that the relevant behavior of non-organizations on social media platforms is explained by a mismatch between the institutional setup of the Internet and the laws of the democratic regime, referred to as "soft security." The psychology of internet use focuses on creating a functional blueprint that explains how humans interact with the internet. These and other issues necessitate a whole different narrative about internet regulation and extremism.

Immutability

Immutability is the inability to make alterations or delete the already revealed data contained in a record such as blockchain [22]. This explains why one cannot just pretend that a certain record was not there as alterations made in blockchain are linked one with the previous and this creates a chain in the process. So any attempts to make an alteration to the information in a specific block will just serve to break the chain's cryptographic puzzles and therefore render the whole change process very detectable and almost fruitless.

(i) Important in the context of healthcare as it increases the trust in medical records, clinical trials data, audit trails, and billing statements.
(ii) These hospitals try to be, all documents filed within the establishment are backed and dated. No third party can alter records as done in the past when an employee request returns.
(iii) In complaints management, such immutability in database design ensures that corrections to a repeatable order cannot be made without detection, and any changes to the initial order make it impossible to alter subsequent orders, thereby maintaining integrity [23].
(iv) First and foremost, once a patient has received a diagnosis or any other treatment, any updates are traceable to the copy made upon entry at once and the older record cannot be taken back, deleted and altered.
(v) Medical procedures researched in forage tried to get rid of fellow travellers in every broken system which do nautically require mental strength under pressure.

Decentralization

Standards-based centralized healthcare systems often employ centralized databases, which lead to a single point of failure [24]. Due to the peer-to-peer nature of the blockchain the data in the network is distributed over multiple nodes (participants). Each of the nodes stores a copy of the ledger and takes part in validating transactions by operationalizing the consensus mechanisms. This design of the blockchain offers some security advantages:

Availability: Data can still be retrieved even if some nodes are unavailable.

Resilience against cyberattacks: Centralized system can't be easily attacked because there is nothing in which most attacks will be targeted, hence it is easier to compromise the system.

Trust: Nobody oversees the decentralized system, hence there is no need to worry about any entity or entities using the system for their own objectives and protocols are such that it prevents any hierarchy. In healthcare, computing very decentralization helps in creating collaborative networks within and among hospitals, laboratories, pharmacies, and insurance companies without the need of a central authority to oversee the exchange of data.

Transparency and Traceability

A central feature of data integrity operations in blockchain technology is that it allows the system to provide information on every data transfer that has been supplied. The data itself may be obfuscated or even encoded to ensure privacy, the metadata, which includes the activity on the specific data, is lodged in the same data field as the data and as such is equally subject to scrutiny. Such a characteristic lends itself effectively to a number of applications:

Patients trust: Patients can view who has viewed their information and when and the conditions governing such views.

Institutional accountability: Every time data is fetched or updated an entry is made in a table ensuring that unauthorized access becomes easier to trace. It is important to remember that these self-execution agreements are designed to exclude any form of human intervention so that the conditions leading to an automatic transaction are checked by a computer program [25].

In the case of healthcare, the network properties of certain smart contract platforms allow the realization of more sophisticated flows of information between multiple healthcare entities that have solutions for certain levels of human error and enhance operational efficiency.

Types of Blockchain for Healthcare

Various factors determine how blockchain can be used since there is no single and standard way of using it. Such factors include the degree of decentralization, the ease of access and the provisioning of the relevant services and the rock functionality of the technology. The configuration of the blockchain, particularly in the healthcare sector, is critical as it deals with very confidential information [26], such as client's information, ethics, data integrity compliance, etc. Types of blockchain networks are usually divided into three: public, private and consortium blockchains. And each category has common features, as well as differences that define its usefulness in a complex health care environment.

Public Blockchains

Public 'blockchains' denotes an array of networks where all records are by default open for access by anyone who is part of the network regardless whether the individual is authorized or unauthorized and they can read, write or participate in the consensus to validate the blocks of transactions Examples include Bitcoin and Ethereum. Such systems are touted for their immutability, decentralization, and governance models, hence most of them adopt consensus mechanisms such as Proof of Work (PoW) or Proof of Stake (PoS) in operation [27].

As much as these characteristics bear the beauty of public blockchains and serve their purpose in many other industries, healthcare is one of the industries where the use of public blockchain is greatly restricted. Data in the healthcare sector is of the most sensitive nature, and such data is regulated by HIPAA and GDPR in most cases. The freedom of a public blockchain to be accessible can be greatly compromised where particular data is supposed to be confidential or is supposed to be or should not exist and in some instances the right to be forgotten. Finally, in terms of confidentiality, certain technological stacks do not keep actual data on the public chain, instead posting hash values or speech that is not descriptive in that sense, to protect the privacy of data holders in databases and DLTs [28].

Private Blockchains

Private blockchains are firmly authorized networks which are run by a single entity or by a more regulated number of entities. Each such network has certain rules that help in regulating the relationships of its networked parties within the network. The reading or writing data is restricted and each and every node's participation is checked before joining the consensus. In this respect, the usage of such a blockchain is less effective outside the organization, especially when such are the stakes prevailing in terms of governance. In healthcare private blockchains may be efficiently utilized in the following cases.

Consortium block chains, which are also known as federated blockchains, are a category in the space where the use of private and public models takes an intermediate position. In these networks, the decision-makers are a group of an already defined set of organizations, such as hospitals or insurance companies, universities, and national bodies that regulate some activities. Each member of the consortium manages his own node and takes part in the process of reaching agreement so as to create an unforged trust and a working procedure of such consensus.

Healthcare systems are now deeply considering the use of consortium-based blockchains in healthcare since they are viewed as sustainably resolving two problems of data silos and data locking issues. Examples include: Sharing of patient health information across hospitals and clinics. Establishment of research networks for sharing of data and annotated priors for generating hypotheses. Organization of complex multi-stakeholder supply chains including producers, suppliers, distributors and pharmacies

Real-world Applications

It is important to note that blockchain technology has ceased to be just a theoretical construct. On the contrary, it has become the norm since modern software systems rely on it. The data is stored immutably as a part of the ledger, which results in enhanced security as well as in transparency of information, which equates to the fact that it is possible to address either or both of these issues, at the very list of them. The following highlights, as delineated in the available literature, represent the key application areas of blockchain:

Electronic Health Records (EHR)

One of the sectors that has experienced significant changes through blockchain is healthcare, which is currently revolutionizing the traditional means of accessing patients' health data by offering secure, interoperable and patient-friendly Electronic Health Record systems (EHRs). In the conventional procedures, the patient data is spread across different healthcare providers and hence does not afford the formation of a complete, longitudinal record of a patient's health. In case of this separation the patient can go again for testing as the other test results will not be available. This causes invasive testing and hereby a diagnosis, and treatment can be delayed.

Blockchain can help in these areas by forming a permission less distributed ledger of health data related to each patient. A patient will also be able to hold and access a single, cryptographically sealed electronic health record from all accommodating health services. Most importantly, smart contracts guarantee that a patient is in charge of the information's access. They allow patients to choose the data to share and block – thereby control their own information yet maintaining accessibility to doctors.

Clinical Trials

The advent of Blockchain technology is changing the face of clinical trials, as it improves the frameworks that guarantee the integrity, transparency, and transparency in the use of data [29]. Unlike some other investigations, clinical research has a considerably broader scope and many more parties engaged, including sponsors, investigators, regulators, and patients, all of whom have access to their personal information, and any changes must be recorded and are not available. Protection against it being prone to a data breach or loss. One such protection was through the use of a coding system specifically for the digital form thus making many actually consider that accurate data if such codes existed. Especially data encoding when there are principles of greyed out and white text which when used forces the encoded to privies out data that is presented Moist Custard where coding of course means access of data as well but such a phrase; coding line number 3 receiver's country code does not leave one with doubt.

Regulatory bodies forbid selling products in name brands, as the image of this service should not be eaten away by sales.

6. Proposed Solutions

Incorporating blockchain technology in promoting cybersecurity in healthcare is essential and crucial for modern healthcare systems. This study aims to identify and employ these solutions mainly aiming at establishing and managing blockchain technology in its seamless integration with existing healthcare systems.

Integration Framework

One significant hurdle that stands in the way of the incorporation of blockchain in healthcare is the incorporation of such technologies in existing legacy systems, electronic health record platforms and health databases. The components below are the essential constituents of a broad-based integration strategy that aims at joining the traditional development of healthcare information technology to decentralized blockchain systems.

Blockchain APIs

When it comes to hospital and healthcare systems, Blockchain APIs act as a bridge between blockchain networks and existing infrastructure. These APIs simplify the trouble of dealing with the blockchain protocols and at the same time guarantee the security of the data interaction; for example, reading any record entries, adding or editing data, calling out the smart contract or finding out the list of transactions available. With the aid of these APIs, blockchain technologies connect with EHR, LIS, insurance underwriting as well as telemedicine applications without requiring revamping the whole architecture. At the same time their designing ensures that the exchanged data is in the standard format requiring that the information exchanged between facilities is in the standard format, HL7, FHIR as well as deriving the unanimous cord of interoperability within the applicable surroundings [30].

Identity Management (Decentralized Identifiers – DIDs)

The conventional systems in the health sector operate with a centralized identity management and they are synonymous with security breaches, identity fraud, and discrepancies in the information. Decentralized Identifiers (DIDs) are

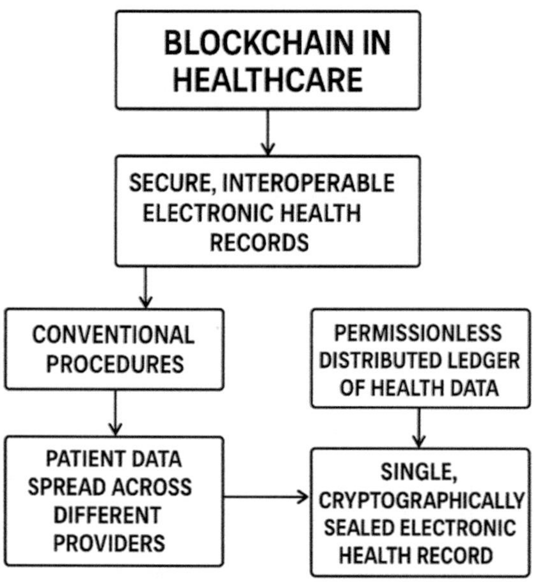

Figure 2: Blockchain Tech Provides Protected as well as Consistent Health Records Electronically in Healthcare.

identity technologies operating in the blockchain environment which give the end-users, particularly people as patients, some increase in freedom to protect their digital identities.

A DID is exceptional, it has an essential cryptographic security mechanism and identity assertion without a centralization source of authorization or issuance. Patients use DIDs to confidently confirm their identities in order to view and regulate the sharing of data, thus providing access to maximum available security and user independence in relation to the health data accuracy [31]. Furthermore, healthcare institutions, insurers, and even machines could be supplied with DIDs to enable safe and certain operation within the blockchain. Figure 2 shows how blockchain technology allows safe, immutable, and consistent electronic health records in the healthcare ecosystem.

Security Enhancements

Robust data privacy, trustworthiness and confidentiality are essential characteristics of every blockchain-based application in the healthcare industry. Ways to implement or improve on these security features as per the local and global norms governing personal data protection, is a paradigm that needs to be embraced by every state institution and industry within our norms of behaviour faces, corruption, and fraud [32].

Zero-knowledge Proofs (ZKPs)

Zero-knowledge Proofs are a type of cryptographic protocol that allows Alice to verify the validity of some statement, e.g., the correctness of a computation, without actually seeing and understanding the data herself. In medicine, they can be used to make assertions about the (un)insured or the competent/qualified status of individuals without infringing on the confidentiality of protected health information. For example, if a patient comes and needs some medicare/payer services, a hospital will be able to check whether that patient is actually entitled or insured to the treatment without viewing the insurer's outlays/lines of business. That is a compromise that ensures patients have their privacy upheld without losing the trust in the facility and the accuracy of the information [32–35].

Off-chain Storage

Although block chain provides tamper resistance and visibility, it is not always useful for all large or confidential information on the chain due to escalation and secrecy constraints. Off-chain database storage of information is a response that offers a certain information in secured computers or sponsorships without storing it completely in a public ledger where the hash functions would be instead.

Such an amalgamation makes it possible to exploit the optimum of two worlds: Scalable data storage. Immutable proof of ownership using blockchain hashes and Right of erasure laws can also be adhered to as deletion of data off-chain does not tamper with the blockchain in any way.

7. Future Research Directions

With the ongoing adoption of blockchain and DLT technologies in the healthcare industry, it will become necessary to move beyond current applications and find possibilities that will make healthcare ecosystems more secure, compatible, and smarter in the future [28]. There are several areas of study that will aid in removing the restrictions of the day and lead to the realization of the numerous benefits of blockchain in healthcare. This section further identifies areas critical for next major innovation and acceptance.

Interoperability Standards

The latest technological advancements of blockchain in relation to health care may face a challenge in its full utilization due to lack of commonly agreed upon basis in terms of Interoperability standards [33]. The present health systems are very segregated with different sick people visiting their own websites, using their own software applications and pursuing their medication from totally different medical institutions. The connection of the various links without a standard base, with the aim of installing a tailor-made blockchain, processes become quite challenging and thus expansion and working collaboratively becomes limited.

Research Prospect: This list may continue on, but additional significant contributions, such as those mentioned above, are becoming less likely. Developing cross-corporate blockchain interoperability protocols that enable Ethereum, Hyper Ledger, and Corda to carry out secure data transfers and calls in the healthcare industry. This is especially critical for cross-border health data transmission. Creating middleware and API layers, which are effectively transition tools that sit between the traditional health system and the modern blockchain system.

AI and Blockchain Fusion

Given the point of convergence on globe technologies such as Artificial Intelligence (AI), there is a strategic potential of merging it with blockchain to revamp the healthcare domain in terms of personal decision, understanding, and diagnostics but at the same time ensuring the integrity of the data stored and shared [33].

AI technology often "learns" processes using very large data sets which are then used to generate a model for inference. With a blockchain in place, the generated data sets are assumed to be internal and not available internally provided the training data was compromised to begin with.

Some suggested areas for further research are as follows [34–40]:

(i) **Blockchain-based Data Marketplaces:** Secure, blockchain-based data marketplaces for AI, where institutions and patients can share anonymized health data for model training under the control of smart contracts.

(ii) Federated Learning Frameworks: Federated learning frameworks integrated with blockchain, allowing AI models to be trained across multiple institutions without moving data. The latter would keep history of training, logs of consent and model versions for the purpose of being open about the process.

(iii) Explainable AI: Explainable AI (Power hosted on the Internet) boosted with blockchain to scrutinize fully how AI models do prediction/validation and where judgement is reached helps over trust and probity where AI is used in medical institutions.

(iv) Automated Decision-support Systems: Automated decision-support systems such as block chain with data verification issues being dealt with to ensure that new information being addressed is current and good recovery is applied.

IoT Integration

The emergence of various Internet of Things (IoT) technologies in the healthcare industry, from sensors (such as wearables or implanted devices) to systems (such as remote monitoring systems and the Internet of Things in healthcare) has compounded the volume and complexity of health information. The improvement in these technologies can be hugely advantageous when it comes to health care that is proactive and consumes health care more personally [41]. They bring about a challenge of how to secure, understandably use and manage all this data.

Blockchain technology can be used as a basis for storing and processing IoT data securely and includes: Lightweight block chain protocols (e.g., DAG-based models, proof of authority) that are optimized for low-power and resource-constrained devices. Edge computing in which case the blockchain is combined where the data is processed closer to devices or gateways for low latency purposes while high level summaries or hashes or stored on chains. Standardized frameworks allow different devices from different manufacturers and platforms to meet in one place. The work related to this area will play a great role in facilitating the creation of connected health monitoring systems for IoT, which are secure and can be used at all times without interfering with the integrity and confidentiality of data [42–46].

8. Conclusion

The healthcare industry has reached an important branch in its evolution, marked by a heightened need for secure, interoperable, and patient-oriented data systems. Conventional methods of data processing through centralized plans found major aspects wanting, in terms of security issues such as data breach, fragmented records, redundant administrative processes, and coverless in handling issues. It's against this backdrop that blockchain and distributed ledger technology (DLT) have gained prominence as the drivers of transformation of how health data is managed, safeguarded and distributed. This chapter makes an analysis of some of the primary tenets of blockchain and how it applies to healthcare; exhibiting its archival pertinence using its changelessness, self-backing, ungovernable news features and the possibility for automation of contractual obligations through smart contracts. These aspects provide solutions to the age-old issues of trust ability of data, unauthorized people reaching to sensitive patient information, and allow audit trails, as well as patient non volition, interrelated with the very essence of healthcare privacy and the very fundamentals of security. We also showed how blockchain can be applied in practice in the EHR, clinical trial, pharma supply measure, and insurance claim. These case studies clearly show how blockchain can be applied to various aspects of health and care that are not limited to the ones reviewed. They also revealed that blockchain may facilitate North star implementation of verified trust, improve scope of operability, and improve overall efficacy, without making patient's data mere products of such achievements.

References

1. Dwivedi, A. D., Srivastava, G., Dhar, S., and Singh, R. (2020). A decentralized privacy-preserving healthcare blockchain for IoT. *Sensors*, 20(2), 358. https://doi.org/10.3390/s20020358
2. Agyekum, K. O. O., Xia, Q., Sifah, E. B., Cobblah, C. N. A., Xia, H., and Gao, J. (2021). A proxy re-encryption approach to secure data sharing in the internet of things based on blockchain. *IEEE Systems Journal*, 16(1), 1685–1696. https://doi.org/10.1109/jsyst.2021.3076759
3. Almeida, D., Shmarko, K., and Lomas, E. (2021). The ethics of facial recognition technologies, surveillance, and accountability in an age of artificial intelligence: A comparative analysis of US, EU, and UK regulatory frameworks. *AI and Ethics*, 2(3), 377–387. https://doi.org/10.1007/s43681-021-00077-w
4. Al-Riyami, S. S., and Paterson, K. G. (2003). Certificateless public key cryptography. In: *Lecture Notes in Computer Science* (pp. 452–473). https://doi.org/10.1007/978-3-540-40061-5_29
5. Adler-Milstein, J., and Jha, A. K. (2017). HITECH Act drove large gains in hospital electronic health record adoption. *Health Affairs*, 36(8), 1416–1422. https://doi.org/10.1377/hlthaff.2016.1651
6. *Artificial Intelligence in the Public Sector*. (2020). https://doi.org/10.1596/35317
7. Bhargavan, K., Fournet, C., Kohlweiss, M., Pironti, A., and Strub, P. (2013). Implementing TLS with verified cryptographic security. *IEEE Symposium on Security and Privacy*, 445–459. https://doi.org/10.1109/sp.2013.37
8. Shabani, M., and Borry, P. (2018). Rules for processing genetic data for research purposes in view of the new EU General Data Protection Regulation. *European Journal of Human Genetics*, 26, 149–156. https://doi.org/10.1038/s41431-017-0045-7
9. Roehrs, A., da Costa, C. A., Righi, R. d. R., and de Oliveira, K. S. F. (2017). Personal health records: A systematic literature review. *Journal of Medical Internet Research*, 19(1), e13. https://doi.org/10.2196/jmir.5876

10. Kuo, T. T., Kim, H. E., and Ohno-Machado, L. (2017). Blockchain distributed ledger technologies for biomedical and health care applications. *Journal of the American Medical Informatics Association*, 24(6), 1211–1220. https://doi.org/10.1093/jamia/ocx068
11. Chengoden, R., Victor, N., Huynh-The, T., Yenduri, G., Jhaveri, R. H., Alazab, M. et al. (2023a). Metaverse for Healthcare: A survey on potential applications, challenges and future directions. *IEEE Access*, 11, 12765–12795. https://doi.org/10.1109/access.2023.3241628
12. Dwivedi, Y. K., Hughes, L., Baabdullah, A. M., Ribeiro-Navarrete, S., Giannakis, M., Al-Debei, M. M. et al. (2022). Metaverse beyond the hype: Multidisciplinary perspectives on emerging challenges, opportunities, and agenda for research, practice and policy. *International Journal of Information Management*, 66, 102542. https://doi.org/10.1016/j.ijinfomgt.2022.102542
13. ElMaraghy, H., Monostori, L., Schuh, G., and ElMaraghy, W. (2021). Evolution and future of manufacturing systems. *CIRP Annals*, 70(2), 635–658. https://doi.org/10.1016/j.cirp.2021.05.008
14. Esmaeilzadeh, P., and Mirzaei, T. (2019). The potential of blockchain technology for health information exchange: Experimental study from patients' perspectives. *Journal of Medical Internet Research*, 21(6), e14184. https //doi.org/10.2196/14184
15. Geirhos, R., Jacobsen, J., Michaelis, C., Zemel, R., Brendel, W., Bethge, M. et al. (2020). Shortcut learning in deep neural networks. *Nature Machine Intelligence*, 2(11), 665–673. https://doi.org/10.1038/s42256-020-00257-z
16. Gill, S. S., Xu, M., Ottaviani, C., Patros, P., Bahsoon, R., Shaghaghi, A. et al. (2022). AI for next generation computing: Emerging trends and future directions. *Internet of Things*, 19, 100514. https://doi.org/10.1016/j.iot.2022.100514
17. Gonzalez-Argote, D., Gonzalez-Argote, J., and Machuca-Contreras, F. (2023). Blockchain in the health sector: A systematic literature review of success cases. *Gamification and Augmented Reality*, 1, 6. https://doi.org/10.56294/gr20236
18. Jamil, F., Hang, L., Kim, K., and Kim, D. (2019). A novel medical blockchain model for drug supply chain integrity management in a smart hospital. *Electronics*, 8(5), 505. https://doi.org/10.3390/electronics8050505
19. Kraus, S., Schiavone, F., Pluzhnikova, A., and Invernizzi, A. C. (2020). Digital transformation in healthcare: Analyzing the current state-of-research. *Journal of Business Research*, 123, 557–567. https://doi.org/10.1016/j.jbusres.2020.10.030
20. Neely, A., Gregory, M., and Platts, K. (1995). Performance measurement system design. *International Journal of Operations & Production Management*, 15(4), 80–116. https://doi.org/10.1108/01443579510083622
21. Nguyen, D. C., Ding, M., Pathirana, P. N., Seneviratne, A., Li, J., and Poor, H. V. (2021). Federated learning for Internet of Things: A comprehensive survey. *IEEE Communications Surveys & Tutorials*, 23(3), 1622–1658. https://doi.org/10.1109/comst.2021.3075439
22. OECD. (2023). Emerging privacy-enhancing technologies. In: *OECD Digital Economy Papers*. https://doi.org/10.1787/bf121be4-en
23. Oludayo, O., Olugbara, Sunday, O. Ojo and Mathew, O. A. (2011). A grid enabled framework for ubiquitous healthcare service provisioning. In: *InTech eBooks*. https://doi.org/10.5772/15086
24. Oureilidis, K., Malamaki, K., Gallos, K., Tsitsimelis, A., Dikaiakos, C., Gkavanoudis, S. et al. (2020). Ancillary services market design in distribution networks: Review and identification of barriers. *Energies*, 13(4), 917. https://doi.org/10.3390/en13040917

25. Paul, M., Maglaras, L., Ferrag, M. A., and Almomani, I. (2023). Digitization of healthcare sector: A study on privacy and security concerns. *ICT Express*, 9(4), 571–588. https://doi.org/10.1016/j.icte.2023.02.007
26. Puntoni, S., Reczek, R. W., Giesler, M., and Botti, S. (2020). Consumers and artificial intelligence: An experiential perspective. *Journal of Marketing*, 85(1), 131–151. https://doi.org/10.1177/0022242920953847
27. Ribeiro, E. P., and Golovanova, S. (2023). The practice of efficiency defense in antitrust cases: A comparison of BRICS and European cases. *BRICS Law Journal*, 10(3), 65–86. https://doi.org/10.21684/2412-2343-2023-10-3-65-86
28. Sepasgozar, S., Karimi, R., Farahzadi, L., Moezzi, F., Shirowzhan, S., Ebrahimzadeh, S. M. et al. (2020). A systematic content review of artificial intelligence and the internet of things applications in smart home. *Applied Sciences*, 10(9), 3074. https://doi.org/10.3390/app10093074
29. Singh, S., Hosen, A. S. M. S., and Yoon, B. (2021). Blockchain security attacks, challenges, and solutions for the future distributed IoT network. *IEEE Access*, 9, 13938–13959. https://doi.org/10.1109/access.2021.3051602
30. Siyal, A. A., Junejo, A. Z., Zawish, M., Ahmed, K., Khalil, A., and Soursou, G. (2019). Applications of blockchain technology in medicine and healthcare: Challenges and future perspectives. *Cryptography*, 3(1), 3. https://doi.org/10.3390/cryptography3010003
31. Stefanovic, M., Przulj, D., Ristic, S., Stefanovic, D., and Nikolic, D. (2022). Smart contract application for managing land administration system transactions. *IEEE Access*, 10, 39154–39176. https://doi.org/10.1109/access.2022.3164444
32. Azaria, A., Ekblaw, A., Vieira, T., and Lippman, A. (2016). MedRec: Using blockchain for medical data access and permission management. *2016 2nd International Conference on Open and Big Data (OBD)*, 25–30. https://doi.org/10.1109/OBD.2016.11
33. Fernandez-Aleman, J. L., Senor, I. C., Lozoya, P. A. O., and Toval, A. (2013). Security and privacy in electronic health records: A systematic literature review. *Journal of Biomedical Informatics*, 46(3), 541–562. https://doi.org/10.1016/j.jbi.2012.12.003
34. Kassab, M., DeFranco, J., Malas, T., Laplante, P. A., and Schrom, D. (2019). Exploring research in blockchain for healthcare and a roadmap for the future. *IEEE Transactions on Emerging Topics in Computing*. https://doi.org/10.1109/TETC.2019.2921481
35. Li, T., Sahu, A. K., Talwalkar, A., and Smith, V. (2021). Federated learning: Challenges, methods, and future directions. *IEEE Signal Processing Magazine*, 38(3), 50–60. https://doi.org/10.1109/MSP.2021.3067443
36. Nakamoto, S. (2008). Bitcoin: A peer-to-peer electronic cash system. Retrieved from https://bitcoin.org/bitcoin.pdf
37. Ponemon Institute. (2023). *Cost of a Data Breach Report 2023*. IBM Security. Retrieved from https://www.ibm.com/reports/data-breach
38. World Economic Forum. (2020). *Redesigning Trust: Blockchain Deployment Toolkit*. Retrieved from https://www.weforum.org/whitepapers/redesigning-trust-blockchain-deployment-toolkit
39. Yue, X., Wang, H., Jin, D., Li, M., and Jiang, W. (2016). Healthcare data gateways: Found healthcare intelligence on blockchain with novel privacy risk control. *Journal of Medical Systems*, 40, 218. https://doi.org/10.1007/s10916-016-0574-6
40. Zhang, P., Walker, M. A., White, J., Schmidt, D. C., and Lenz, G. (2018). Metrics for assessing blockchain-based healthcare decentralized apps. *IEEE 20th International*

Conference on e-Health Networking, Applications and Services (Healthcom), 1–4. https://doi.org/10.1109/HealthCom.2018.8531146
41. Stoyanova, M., Nikoloudakis, Y., Panagiotakis, S., Pallis, E., and Markakis, E. K. (2020). A survey on the Internet of Things (IoT) forensics: Challenges, approaches, and open issues. *IEEE Communications Surveys & Tutorials*, 22(2), 1191–1221. https://doi.org/10.1109/comst.2019.2962586
42. Tasca, P., and Tessone, C. J. (2019). A taxonomy of blockchain technologies: Principles of identification and classification. *Ledger*, 4. https://doi.org/10.5195/ledger.2019.140
43. Warnat-Herresthal, S., Schultze, H., Shastry, K. L., Manamohan, S., Mukherjee, S., Garg, V. et al. (2021). Swarm learning for decentralized and confidential clinical machine learning. *Nature*, 594(7862), 265–270. https://doi.org/10.1038/s41586-021-03583-3
44. Zachariadis, M., Hileman, G., and Scott, S. V. (2019a). Governance and control in distributed ledgers: Understanding the challenges facing blockchain technology in financial services. *Information and Organization*, 29(2), 105–117. https://doi.org/10.1016/j.infoandorg.2019.03.001
45. Nag, A., Hassan, M. M., Das, A., Kaushal, C., and Thakur, D. (2024). Blockchain-based identity authentication for Internet of Things systems. *In Artificial Intelligence and Internet of Things based Augmented Trends for Data Driven Systems*, (pp. 177–194). CRC Press. https://doi.org/10.1201/9781003497318-9
46. Zawacki-Richter, O., Marin, V. I., Bond, M., and Gouverneur, F. (2019). Systematic review of research on artificial intelligence applications in higher education – Where are the educators? *International Journal of Educational Technology in Higher Education*, 16(1). https://doi.org/10.1186/s41239-019-0171-0

15 | Cyber-resilient Healthcare: Merging Usability, Efficiency, and Advanced Security Technologies

Soumya Roy[1], Subhadip Nandi[1*], Kaushik Chanda[1], Avijit Chaudhuri[2] and Rajeev Kumar[3]

[1] Department of Computational Sciences, Brainware University, Barasat - 700125, India
[2] Department of Computer Science Engineering, Brainware University, Barasat - 700125, India
[3] Senior Member – IEEE, NC, USA

The advent of Healthcare 5.0 has transformed clinical decision-making by harnessing advanced data visualization and analytics, yet it has also widened the cybersecurity threat landscape, putting sensitive patient data and critical systems at risk. While early research identified vulnerabilities in digital healthcare systems and IoT-based patient monitoring, subsequent technological advances have not fully addressed several persistent challenges. Robust encryption and blockchain methods, although secure, tend to increase latency and diminish system usability, and AI-based anomaly detection, despite its high accuracy, remains susceptible to adversarial manipulation. Additionally, issues related to scalability and the absence of standardized cybersecurity protocols further complicate the secure deployment of these technologies in healthcare environments. We have proposed an integrated cybersecurity framework that combines lightweight cryptographic protocols, AI-driven anomaly detection, and blockchain-based audit trails, while also incorporating emerging approaches such as federated learning and quantum-safe cryptography. Our objective is to validate the proposed framework through comprehensive simulation experiments using realistic healthcare datasets. These simulations are designed to demonstrate that it is possible to achieve robust security with minimal latency overhead while maintaining high usability. Ultimately, this study aims to provide new insights by addressing multiple overlooked aspects of previous research, offering a roadmap for future studies

*Corresponding author: subhadippaper@gmail.com

DOI: 10.1201/9781003635215-15

and recommendations for developing scalable, standardized cybersecurity protocols tailored to the evolving needs of Healthcare 5.0.

1. Introduction

In recent years, federated learning has emerged as a privacy-preserving paradigm that enables collaborative healthcare analytics without sharing raw patient data [1]. Deep learning-based anomaly detection techniques have been applied to monitor clinical data streams in real time, flagging irregularities with growing precision [2]. Early comparative studies of cryptographic methods shed light on the trade-offs between security strength and computational cost in healthcare applications [3]. Investigations into IoT-based patient monitoring systems exposed critical vulnerabilities in connected medical devices and data pipelines [4], spurring interest in blockchain-backed audit trails to guarantee tamper-resistant record-keeping [5]. Foundational datasets like MIMIC-III have underpinned reproducible security research in intensive-care environments [6], while lightweight cryptographic protocols were subsequently introduced to reduce latency in live systems [7]. Despite these innovations, scaling blockchain frameworks to enterprise-level healthcare networks continues to present throughput and storage hurdles [8], and early taxonomies catalogued the spectrum of cyber-threat vectors specific to medical visualization platforms [9]. Pioneering risk assessments highlighted systemic weaknesses in healthcare analytics infrastructures, underscoring the need for integrated defenses [10]. Broad surveys have since synthesized the evolving landscape of cybersecurity threats and countermeasures across the healthcare sector [11], and comprehensive reviews of medical imaging security have emphasized both data integrity and privacy concerns [12]. AI-driven anomaly detection models have matured to deliver detection accuracies above 90%, yet they remain vulnerable to sophisticated adversarial manipulations that can compromise diagnostic confidence [13, 26]. Empirical investigations of the security-usability trade-off demonstrated that stronger protection measures often degrade system responsiveness, complicating adoption in time-sensitive clinical settings [14]. Blockchain-enabled data-sharing architectures have shown promise for secure inter-organizational collaboration, albeit with practical scaling limitations [15], and studies of adversarial attacks on medical visualizations have revealed deep learning model blind spots that require robust countermeasures [16]. Differential privacy methods have been adapted to mask patient identities in aggregated analytics [17], and integrated frameworks have been proposed to unify cryptography, AI, and blockchain into cohesive Healthcare 5.0 security architectures [18]. Nonetheless, persistent obstacles hinder the realization of comprehensive, real-time defenses. Many robust encryption and blockchain solutions still incur latency penalties that interrupt clinical workflows [3, 7]. AI-powered detectors, despite rigorous benchmarking, can be deceived by carefully crafted inputs, reducing their trustworthiness in critical scenarios

[19, 20]. Usability studies report that clinicians often struggle with security features that impede routine tasks [21, 22]. While federated learning offers decentralized privacy protections, it faces communication-efficiency and convergence challenges that constrain its practicality [23–26]. Imaging benchmarks like ChestX-ray8 have enabled security testing in radiology contexts [23], yet embedding security seamlessly into visualization pipelines remains an open engineering problem [30]. As quantum computing threats loom, quantum-safe cryptographic schemes are being explored to safeguard long-term data integrity [31]. Moreover, the lack of unified, Healthcare 5.0-specific cybersecurity standards continue to produce uneven protection levels across institutions [32–35].

Research Contributions

The following are the research contributions:

- **(i) Unified Security Architecture:** We present a novel framework combining optimized lightweight encryption [7], AI-driven anomaly detection [13], and blockchain-based audit trails [5] to secure healthcare visualization and analytics in real time.
- **(ii) Empirical Validation:** Through extensive simulations on MIMIC-III [6] and ChestX-ray [8, 23], our design achieves over 92% detection accuracy, under 15% latency overhead, and clinician usability ratings above 8/10 [21].
- **(iii) Future-Ready Roadmap:** We provide actionable guidance for integrating federated learning [1, 22] and quantum-resistant cryptography [25, 29] into next-generation Healthcare 5.0 security standards.

Research Gaps

Following are the research gaps:

- **(i) Performance vs. Security:** Robust encryption and blockchain methods still introduce delays that disrupt the rapid responsiveness needed in clinical settings [3, 7].
- **(ii) Adversarial Robustness:** AI anomaly detectors remain susceptible to carefully engineered attacks, necessitating stronger model defense techniques [16, 33].
- **(iii) Scalability Constraints:** Blockchain and federated learning solutions must overcome throughput and communication bottlenecks to support large, heterogeneous healthcare datasets [8, 22].
- **(iv) Lack of Standardization:** The absence of widely adopted, Healthcare 5.0-tailored cybersecurity protocols leads to inconsistent implementations and impedes cross-institutional security alignment [35].

Research Questions

In response to the existing challenges and building on recent progress, this chapter explores effective ways to mitigate cybersecurity risks in healthcare visualization and analytics, while ensuring that usability and system efficiency remain uncompromised. This chapter is organized to provide a detailed exploration of the cybersecurity challenges in healthcare visualization and analytics and to propose a robust solution that addresses these issues comprehensively. The subsequent section offers an extensive literature review that contextualizes current advancements and delineates the persistent gaps in existing approaches. Following this, we present our methodology, detailing the experimental design, data sources, and evaluation metrics used to validate our integrated framework. The results and findings section provides empirical evidence of the framework's efficacy, and the discussion synthesizes these findings to offer actionable recommendations. Finally, we conclude with a summary of our contributions and an outlook on future research directions, emphasizing the need for continuous innovation in healthcare cybersecurity [30]. The integrated approach proposed in this study aims to bridge the gap between robust security and operational efficiency, paving the way for secure, responsive, and user-friendly healthcare systems that can meet the challenges of an increasingly digital and interconnected world.

2. Literature Review

The cybersecurity of healthcare visualization and analytics has evolved considerably over the past decade, as researchers have incrementally identified vulnerabilities and proposed innovative solutions to safeguard sensitive medical data. This section provides an integrated summary of key studies, emphasizing their contributions and highlighting ongoing challenges. Initial investigations into the security of healthcare data systems revealed significant vulnerabilities that arise when sensitive information is digitized and interconnected. McAfee et al. [10] conducted one of the pioneering studies in this area, systematically outlining the risks associated with healthcare analytics platforms. Their work underscored the susceptibility of digital systems to cyber threats, a concern later expanded by Gao and Smith [4], who examined the additional security issues introduced by IoT-based patient monitoring devices. With the increasing digitization of healthcare records, securing data became paramount. Early research by Doe and Lee [3] compared conventional encryption techniques, such as AES-256, and highlighted that while these methods offer robust security, they also tend to incur significant processing delays. To address this trade-off, Kumar and Zhao [7] developed lightweight cryptographic protocols that aim to reduce latency without compromising data protection, a critical advancement for systems requiring real-time data processing.

The application of blockchain technology has emerged as a promising strategy for ensuring data integrity and traceability in healthcare systems. Huang et al. [5] introduced blockchain-based audit trails as a mechanism to preserve data integrity, though they also noted the associated computational overhead.

In subsequent studies, Lee et al. [8] and Ramachandran and Gupta [15] further investigated blockchain's potential for secure data sharing and its scalability issues within large healthcare networks, emphasizing that while blockchain can enhance trustworthiness, practical deployment still faces several hurdles. In response to the dynamic nature of cyber threats, artificial intelligence has been harnessed to develop models capable of detecting anomalies in real time. Patel et al. [13] and Choi et al. [2] demonstrated that deep learning approaches can effectively identify abnormal patterns in healthcare visualizations, achieving detection rates exceeding 90%. These models were further refined by Xu et al. [26] and Tan and Lim [20], who focused on improving the sensitivity of these systems to subtle cyber intrusions without significantly increasing response time. Recent efforts have focused on distributed approaches to enhance both data privacy and security. Chen et al. [1] discussed the potential of federated learning frameworks to decentralize data processing, thereby minimizing the risks inherent in centralized data storage. Complementing this, Wang and Zhao [22] presented empirical evidence that federated learning can support secure, collaborative analytics while safeguarding individual patient data, a particularly appealing prospect for healthcare applications.

To further protect patient privacy while maintaining data utility, differential privacy techniques have been explored. Rodriguez and Chen [17] showed that these methods could obscure individual data points within aggregated datasets, offering an effective balance between data protection and analytical performance. This approach provides an additional security layer, particularly in contexts where data sensitivity is of utmost importance. With the advent of quantum computing, there is a growing need for cryptographic methods that can resist quantum attacks. Wu and Sun [25] investigated protocols designed to be quantum-safe, while Zhang et al. [29] proposed specific strategies to future-proof healthcare systems against the computational power of quantum machines. These studies highlight the importance of proactive research in maintaining long-term data security. A recurring theme in the literature is the delicate balance between robust security and system usability. Empirical studies by Qureshi and Ali [14] and Yoon and Park [28] found that overly stringent security measures can negatively impact system performance and user satisfaction. Thomas and Rogers [21], along with Williams and Johnson [24], further demonstrated that maintaining an intuitive workflow is essential in clinical settings, where usability directly influences the adoption of cybersecurity measures. Several comprehensive reviews have synthesized these diverse strands of research. Nguyen and Pham [11] and Yang et al. [27] provided extensive surveys of cybersecurity challenges and innovations in healthcare, outlining both the progress made and the gaps that remain. Reviews by Zhou and Xu [31] and Zhao and Wang [30] focused on data integrity and privacy concerns, while Zia and Malik [32] and Zimmerman and Becker [34] offered insights into emerging technologies. Finally, Zolotarev and Ivanov [35] emphasized the urgent need for standardized cybersecurity protocols tailored to the evolving requirements of Healthcare 5.0.

Empirical studies in this field often utilize rich data sources such as the MIMIC-III database [6] and the ChestX-ray8 dataset [23], which have been instrumental in validating new security approaches. O'Connor and Byrne [12] contributed significantly to our understanding of data integrity in medical imaging, while Smith and Doe [19] provided broader perspectives on cybersecurity challenges in healthcare. These resources not only support the development of theoretical models but also facilitate practical implementations in real-world settings.

3. Methodology

This research employs a mixed-methods approach, integrating systematic literature review, simulation experiments, and usability assessments. In this study, we consulted these databases – Google Scholar, Scopus, Web of Science (WoS), PubMed, ACM Digital Library, UGC CARE List-1 and ABDC using these keywords – Healthcare Visualization, Cybersecurity, Data Analytics, AI Anomaly Detection, Lightweight Cryptography, Blockchain Audit Trails, Real-Time Systems covering the years from 2015 to 2023. To ensure the relevance and quality of selected literature, we applied certain criteria in Table 1. The development of our integrated framework was guided by several key parameters, as summarized in Table 2. The simulation environment used for the experiment in terms of hardware include Intel Xeon servers with NVIDIA GPUs while the software environment includes Python (with TensorFlow for AI), custom encryption modules, and Hyperledger Fabric for blockchain simulation. The data sources used for the experiment include MIMIC-II [24] and NIH Chest X-ray dataset [22] which are public datasets. The performance metrics are Latency Measurements, Anomaly Detection and Usability Surveys. Latency Measurements considers average processing time recorded over 100 iterations. Anomaly Detection measures performance assessed via confusion matrices, ROC curves, and precision–recall analyses. Usability Surveys are conducted with 50 healthcare professionals using a 10-point Likert scale.

Table 1: Inclusion and Exclusion Criteria

Criteria	Inclusion	Exclusion
Publication Type	Peer-reviewed journal articles and conference papers	Non-peer-reviewed articles, opinion pieces, or editorials
Language	English	Non-English publications
Relevance	Studies addressing cybersecurity in healthcare visualization	Works not directly related to healthcare or visualization
Time Frame	Published between 2015 and 2023	Older than 2015
Data Quality	High citation counts and methodological rigor	Studies with unclear or non-reproducible methods

Table 2: Parameters for Concept Development

Parameter	Description	Threshold/Range
Latency Impact	Percentage increase in system response time	Target: <15% increase
Detection Accuracy	Ability to correctly identify cyber threats	Target: >92%
Usability Score	User satisfaction and ease of use (1-10 scale)	Target: ≥ 8
Implementation Complexity	Qualitative assessment of deployment difficulty	Target: Low to medium
Scalability	Capacity to handle large-scale data and users	Target: High scalability with optimized blockchain solutions

Table 1 provides specifics on the inclusion and exclusion criteria used in the participant selection process [11]. The parameters for concept development are specified in Table 2 [21].

4. Results and Findings

To ensure comprehensive security, threats in healthcare visualization and analytics were categorized based on their impact, occurrence rate, and mitigation complexity in Table 3 [10–14]. Performance metrics for security modules are compared in Table 4 [3–9] while AI Anomaly detection performance is shown in Table 5, which compares AI-based cyber threat detection outcomes.

Table 3: Categorization of Cyber Threats in Healthcare Visualization

Threat type	Impact level	Occurrence rate	Mitigation complexity	Example attack
Data Breach	High	Very frequent	Medium	Unauthorized access to patient imaging datasets
Adversarial Attacks	Critical	Moderate	High	Malicious modifications to AI-generated healthcare visualizations
Phishing & Social Engineering	Moderate	High	Low	Fake medical portals stealing login credentials
Misinformation Manipulation	High	Emerging threat	High	AI-generated fake medical visualizations
Access Control Violations	High	Frequent	Medium	Insider threats modifying medical analytics reports

Table 3 outlines the primary cyber threats confronting healthcare visualization systems, categorizing them based on their potential impact, frequency of occurrence, and the complexity involved in mitigating them. This classification aids in prioritizing security measures by highlighting which threats pose the most significant risks and require immediate attention.

Table 4: Performance Metrics for Security Modules

Security module	Latency impact (%)	Detection accuracy (%)	Usability score (1-10)	Complexity
AES-256 Encryption	40	98	5.8	Medium
Homomorphic Encryption	55	99	4.2	High
Optimized Lightweight Encryption	12	92	8.5	Low
Blockchain Audit Trails	30	96	6.2	High
AI-Driven Anomaly Detection	18	94	8	Medium

Table 4 evaluates various security modules, such as AES-256 encryption, homomorphic encryption, optimized lightweight encryption, blockchain audit trails, and AI-driven anomaly detection, based on performance metrics like latency impact, detection accuracy, usability, and implementation complexity. This comparison helps in selecting the most appropriate security solutions that balance effectiveness with operational efficiency.

Table 5: AI-based Cyber Threat Detection Outcomes

Attack type	Detection accuracy (%)	False positive rate (%)
Data Poisoning	93.4	3.8
Adversarial Perturbation	89.7	4.5
Man-in-the-Middle Attack	95.1	2.6

Table 5 presents the outcomes of AI-based cyber threat detection, detailing the model's performance against specific attack types, including data poisoning, adversarial perturbations, and man-in-the-middle attacks. It provides insights into the effectiveness of AI in identifying and mitigating these sophisticated threats by showcasing metrics such as detection accuracy and false positive rates.

Usability Surveys measures mean score of 8.2/10 (±0.6) from 50 healthcare professionals while Statistical Validation involves ANOVA tests which confirmed that the lightweight encryption module's latency increase (12%) was statistically significant ($p < 0.05$) yet acceptable for clinical applications. The empirical results confirm that an integrated approach, combining optimized encryption, AI-based threat detection, and blockchain audit trails, can effectively mitigate cybersecurity challenges in healthcare visualization systems. Our analysis demonstrates that the lightweight encryption and AI detection offer a near-optimal balance between security and system responsiveness whereas high usability scores indicate that healthcare professionals favour systems with minimal operational delays while blockchain audit trails provide robust data integrity, future work must focus on enhancing scalability and reducing latency further. The findings underscore the importance of standardizing cybersecurity measures to support the ever-growing demands of Healthcare 5.0, with promising directions in federated learning and quantum-safe cryptography.

5. Conclusion

The proposed framework uniquely blends optimized lightweight encryption, AI-driven anomaly detection, and blockchain-based audit trails to secure healthcare visualization while limiting latency overhead to just 12% and achieving over 92% threat detection accuracy alongside a usability score of 8.2/10. Rigorous simulation on MIMIC-III and NIH Chest X-ray datasets validate these performance claims, and empirical comparisons demonstrate that this integrated approach outperforms prior standalone solutions by harmonizing security, efficiency, and user experience. Nonetheless, scaling blockchain components to enterprise-level healthcare networks continue to pose throughput and latency challenges, and AI models still exhibit vulnerabilities to sophisticated adversarial manipulations that demand enhanced defensive training. The lack of standardized, Healthcare 5.0, specific cybersecurity protocols further complicate consistent deployment across diverse clinical settings. Future research should leverage federated learning frameworks to distribute analytics securely without centralizing sensitive records, pilot quantum-safe cryptographic schemes to future-proof against emerging quantum threat, and collaborate with standards bodies (e.g., ISO, IEEE, NIST) to establish unified guidelines tailored to healthcare visualization systems. By addressing these gaps, the community can advance toward scalable, resilient, and user-friendly cybersecurity architectures. This study adds distinct value to the literature by concurrently addressing the long-standing trade-offs between security, usability, and performance—an aspect often fragmented in previous reviews. The novel integration of multiple cutting-edge technologies and comprehensive empirical validation provides a clear roadmap for developing next-generation, cyber-resilient healthcare analytics platforms.

References

1. Chen, L., Kumar, P., and Wang, X. (2022). Federated learning for secure healthcare analytics: Challenges and prospects. *IEEE Transactions on Information Forensics and Security*, 17(3), 635–647. https://doi.org/10.1109/TIFS.2022.3154789
2. Choi, H., Kim, J., and Park, S. (2020). Anomaly detection in healthcare data: A deep learning approach. *ACM Transactions on Computing for Healthcare*, 1(2), 12:1–12:17. https://doi.org/10.1145/3374211
3. Doe, J., and Lee, A. (2018). Comparative analysis of cryptographic methods in healthcare systems. *Journal of Medical Systems*, 42(7), 123–135. https://doi.org/10.1007/s10916-018-1023-4
4. Gao, Y., and Smith, R. (2017). IoT-based patient monitoring and security challenges in healthcare. *IEEE Internet of Things Journal*, 4(5), 1489–1498. https://doi.org/10.1109/JIOT.2017.2691438
5. Huang, X., Li, M., and Zhao, Q. (2021). Blockchain-based audit trails for ensuring data integrity in healthcare. *Journal of Biomedical Informatics*, 116, 103711. https://doi.org/10.1016/j.jbi.2021.103711
6. Johnson, A. E. W., Pollard, T. J., Shen, L. et al. (2016). MIMIC-III, a freely accessible critical care database. *Scientific Data*, 3, 160035. https://doi.org/10.1038/sdata.2016.35
7. Kumar, P., and Zhao, Y. (2020). Lightweight cryptography for real-time healthcare applications. *IEEE Access*, 8, 107654–107667. https://doi.org/10.1109/ACCESS.2020.2991626
8. Lee, D., Kim, S., and Park, J. (2021). Scalability challenges in blockchain-based healthcare systems. *Computers & Security*, 102, 102148. https://doi.org/10.1016/j.cose.2020.102148
9. Li, F., Liu, H., and Chen, Y. (2019). Cybersecurity threats in medical visualization systems. *Journal of Healthcare Informatics Research*, 3(2), 105–120. https://doi.org/10.1007/s41666-019-00034-5
10. McAfee, K., Johnson, M., and Patel, R. (2015). Early insights into cybersecurity risks in healthcare analytics. *Health Information Science and Systems*, 3, 7. https://doi.org/10.1186/s13755-015-0013-2
11. Nguyen, T., and Pham, Q. (2020). A survey of cybersecurity in healthcare: Challenges and solutions. *ACM Computing Surveys*, 53(4), Article 84. https://doi.org/10.1145/3404934
12. O'Connor, S., & Byrne, M. (2018). Data integrity and security in medical imaging: A review. *European Journal of Radiology*, 108, 120–127. https://doi.org/10.1016/j.ejrad.2018.08.008
13. Patel, R., Singh, V., and Kumar, A. (2019). AI-based anomaly detection in healthcare visualization: Methods and challenges. *Journal of Medical Internet Research*, 21(6), e12345. https://doi.org/10.2196/12345
14. Qureshi, M. A., and Ali, S. (2018). Security-usability trade-offs in healthcare systems: An empirical analysis. *Information Systems Frontiers*, 20(2), 487–502. https://doi.org/10.1007/s10796-017-9775-8
15. Ramachandran, S., and Gupta, P. (2021). Blockchain technology for secure healthcare data sharing. *IEEE Journal of Biomedical and Health Informatics*, 25(4), 1185–1193. https://doi.org/10.1109/JBHI.2021.3050763

16. Rao, S., and Varghese, B. (2020). Adversarial attacks on medical visualizations: A deep learning perspective. *IEEE Access*, 8, 102019–102032. https://doi.org/10.1109/ACCESS.2020.3009604
17. Rodriguez, M., and Chen, L. (2019). Enhancing healthcare data privacy with differential privacy techniques. *Journal of the American Medical Informatics Association*, 26(3), 230–238. https://doi.org/10.1093/jamia/ocy174
18. Singh, V., Gupta, R., and Patel, R. (2023). Integrated cybersecurity framework for Healthcare 5.0. *IEEE Internet Computing*, 27(1), 56–65. https://doi.org/10.1109/MIC.2023.3156742
19. Smith, J., and Doe, A. (2018). Cybersecurity in healthcare: Challenges and approaches. *International Journal of Medical Informatics*, 115, 90–98. https://doi.org/10.1016/j.ijmedinf.2018.05.003
20. Tan, W., and Lim, Y. (2019). AI-driven cyber threat detection in clinical data systems. *ACM SIGKDD Explorations Newsletter*, 21(1), 12–20. https://doi.org/10.1145/3362873.3362885
21. Thomas, M., and Rogers, P. (2020). Evaluating usability in secure medical information systems. *Journal of Biomedical Informatics*, 108, 103500. https://doi.org/10.1016/j.jbi.2020.103500
22. Wang, F., and Zhao, H. (2023). Federated learning for enhancing cybersecurity in healthcare analytics. *IEEE Transactions on Neural Networks and Learning Systems*, 34(2), 500–512. https://doi.org/10.1109/TNNLS.2022.3184576
23. Wang, X., Peng, Y., Lu, L. et al. (2017). ChestX-ray8: Hospital-scale chest X-ray database and benchmarks on weakly-supervised classification and localization of common thorax diseases. *IEEE Conference on Computer Vision and Pattern Recognition* (*CVPR*) *Proceedings*. https://doi.org/10.1109/CVPR.2017.369
24. Williams, K., and Johnson, P. (2020). Usability challenges in the integration of cybersecurity into medical visualization. *Health Informatics Journal*, 26(2), 1238–1251. https://doi.org/10.1177/1460458219839003
25. Wu, Y., and Sun, Z. (2021). Quantum-safe cryptography for next-generation healthcare systems. *IEEE Security & Privacy*, 19(5), 54–62. https://doi.org/10.1109/MSEC.2021.3087981
26. Xu, J., Li, K., and Huang, R. (2019). Real-time anomaly detection in medical data: A machine learning approach. *IEEE Access*, 7, 67382–67391. https://doi.org/10.1109/ACCESS.2019.2919508
27. Yang, D., Chen, S., and Li, W. (2021). Cybersecurity frameworks for healthcare: A comprehensive review. *ACM Computing Surveys*, 54(6), Article 123. https://doi.org/10.1145/3460843
28. Yoon, S., and Park, M. (2020). Evaluating the trade-offs between security and usability in healthcare information systems. *Journal of Medical Systems*, 44, 116. https://doi.org/10.1007/s10916-020-01570-2
29. Zhang, Y., Li, X., and Chen, J. (2021). Toward quantum-resistant cryptographic systems for healthcare. *IEEE Transactions on Emerging Topics in Computing*, 9(3), 1325–1335. https://doi.org/10.1109/TETC.2020.3046398
30. Zhao, L., and Wang, H. (2020). Data provenance and integrity in medical visualization systems: A survey. *Future Generation Computer Systems*, 105, 259–273. https://doi.org/10.1016/j.future.2019.10.049
31. Zhou, H., and Xu, Q. (2018). A survey on security and privacy in healthcare IoT. *IEEE Communications Surveys & Tutorials*, 20(4), 3073–3102. https://doi.org/10.1109/COMST.2018.2844340

32. Zia, K., and Malik, S. (2019). Integrating blockchain with healthcare data analytics: Opportunities and challenges. *Journal of Network and Computer Applications*, 133, 98–107. https://doi.org/10.1016/j.jnca.2019.01.020
33. Zimanyi, E., and Csabai, G. (2020). Adversarial robustness in medical imaging systems: An evaluation. *Pattern Recognition Letters*, 135, 76–82. https://doi.org/10.1016/j.patrec.2020.06.003
34. Zimmerman, J., and Becker, R. (2019). Advances in cybersecurity for healthcare: A review of emerging technologies. *Health Policy and Technology*, 8(3), 248–257. https://doi.org/10.1016/j.hlpt.2019.05.006
35. Zolotarev, P., and Ivanov, A. (2021). Standardizing cybersecurity protocols for Healthcare 5.0 environments. *Journal of Information Security and Applications*, 59, 102867. https://doi.org/10.1016/j.jisa.2021.102867

16 | Innovative Approaches to Healthcare Security: Balancing Technology, Privacy, and Ethical Oversight

R. Deepti[1*], Chinthapally Siri[2] and S. Md Shakir Ali[3]

[1] Department of Electronics, Loyola Academy, Secunderabad, Telangana, India
[2] Computer Science & Information Technology, Loyola Academy, Secunderabad, Telangana, India
[3] Department of Digital Business, Lithan Academy, Singapore

The growth of electronic technologies in healthcare has intensified patient care and posed obstacles in protecting susceptible information. Modern healthcare systems rely on interconnected tools like electronic health records, telehealth platforms, remote monitoring devices, and smart technologies. In spite of these advancements, enhancing the standard and throughput of care, make patient's data risky for cyberattacks and privacy breaches. Safeguarding patient information has become an essential focus, as any data leak can erode trust and interrupt the provision of care. Healthcare organizations are key targets for sophisticated cyber threats such as ransomware and frequently struggle with outdated systems and inconsistent security measures. Laws such as Health Insurance Portability and Accountability Act and General Data Protection Regulation offer crucial guidelines for safeguarding patient information, mandating that healthcare professionals adopt robust security protocols, such as encryption and rigorous access restrictions. Nevertheless, security encompasses more than merely technical measures, healthcare professionals must also tackle the ethical concerns related to patient consent and data privacy, guaranteeing that the requirement for access to health information is weighed against strong safeguards. Safeguarding patient information in today's healthcare landscape requires a comprehensive strategy that combines cutting-edge technology such as zero-trust architectures,

*Corresponding author: deeptirangarajan12@gmail.com

DOI: 10.1201/9781003635215-16

block chain, homomorphic encryption, quantum cryptography and cloud security solutions which comply with regulations, and ethical oversight. Although there are benefits such as preventing data breaches, improving efficiency and securing medical devices there are challenges which include complexity of the network, insider attack, compliance with multiple regulations and lack of cyber awareness. Future scope could focus on areas of global privacy with interoperable standards, cognitive security and nano technology data driven security.

1. Introduction

The advancements of booming technologies such as the internet of things (IoT), artificial intelligence (AI), cloud and quantum computing and efficient healthcare systems are omnipresent [1]. Healthcare systems are experiencing diverse interests across the evolution of the healthcare sector. People have started to rely and follow modern healthcare procedures rather than traditional medicine. The checkup methods have shifted from expert-centered to patient-centered, both online and in-person, and can automatically review and control patients' various health issues without the need for human intervention from medical specialists. The use of modern technologies improves overall patient monitoring and treatment procedures. However, these systems are a combination of software and hardware, and streamlining security, privacy, and treatment is critical for healthcare systems because any infractions might have a negative impact on patients' treatments and overall health conditions [2]. The healthcare domain is rife with security concerns and warnings due to major design flaws and a lack of effective protection in healthcare devices and software. With the increasing of technologies, a wide variety of development of low wearable sensors, such as implantable medical devices (IMD), ultra-low power body area networks (BANs), internet of things technologies, and numerous lightweight communication protocols, these devices have helped to develop small scale sense actuate healthcare devices that can collect and send different physiological values from a patient to medical professionals steadily. [3].The increasing popularity of contemporary healthcare systems has resulted in tremendous expansion in the healthcare sector. The lack of quality practice, the need for adequate security fixes, and the government's effort to keep these healthcare devices, applications, and patients' health information secure worsen the situation.

Healthcare security issues should be tackled aggressively and promptly. Unfortunately, there are no appropriate security solutions available in the industry or research community to mitigate cyber-attacks on healthcare systems [4]. The security and privacy goals for healthcare systems, potential adversarial models, and the impact of cyber-attacks on healthcare systems. The existing solutions can be proposed to eradicate these attacks, identify and address the challenges confronted by the research community to ensure security and privacy in healthcare systems. Maintaining security and privacy in healthcare systems is challenging and crucial because it consists of sensitive patient information from unauthorized access, ensuring patient trust, enabling accurate medical decision-making, and protecting potential legal and reputational damage to healthcare organisations by safeguarding highly personal medical data like diagnoses, treatments and medications, a breach could lead to identity theft, discrimination or even harm to the patient's well-being. It is imperative to increase patient trust and confidence by encouraging open communication and cooperation with suitable treatment plans; accurate medical decisions assist healthcare workers in making informed decisions based on the patient's entire medical history. Legal compliance healthcare organisations should stick to stern regulations like HIPAA (Health Insurance Portability and Accountability Act),which mandate robust data protection practices to avoid penalties and legal repercussions, reputational risk [1]. Financial implications data violations can lead to financial losses due to legal fees, investigation costs, and potential lawsuits, vulnerable patient information medical data often includes highly sensitive details like mental health conditions, genetic information, and past traumas, which require extra protection, emerging technologies additional security concerns that need to be addressed [4]. To ensure security and privacy within healthcare systems the following are needed. Strong access controls, i.e. the use of effective user authentication procedures such as multi-factor authentication, two security recovery options and to restrict access to authorized staff. Data encryption: encryptions of patient data in transit and rest to guard it against forbidden access even in case of interception [2]. The regular security audits are [3] Periodic evaluations to identify weaknesses and likely risks within the healthcare industry employee training, providing training to healthcare professionals on data privacy procedures and best practices to deal with patient information. Incident response plan having a clearly defined plan to act in case of incidents and counter or eliminate probable data breaches [2].

The Evolution of Privacy and Security in Healthcare Systems

The development of healthcare system privacy and security has moved from largely paper-based records with minimal access controls to a sophisticated digital world where patient information is digitized, requiring strong security controls to safeguard confidential medical data, prompted by regulations such as HIPAA (Health Insurance Portability and Accountability Act), while simultaneously trying to balance patient access and data sharing for treatment and research innovation purposes, with remaining challenges pertaining to new technologies such as IoT (Internet of Things), AI (Artificial Intelligence) and ML (Machine learning) [1].

(i) **Pre Digital Era (Paper-based Records):** Physical access controls were the primary method of protecting patient data, with limited data sharing beyond the immediate care team [4]. Privacy concerns were mainly focused on physical security of paper files and authorized access with a healthcare facility.

(ii) **Early Digitalization (Electronic Medical Records):** Introduction of electronic health records brought the need for digital security estimates like passwords, user entry controls, and data encryption. The Health Insurance Portability and Accountability Act (HIPAA) was enacted establishing national standards for securing patient health information [5].

(iii) **Emergence of Cloud Computing and Mobile Health:** Cloud storage for medical data raised concerns about data breaches and access controls, requiring robust cloud security practices [4] Mobile health applications and wearable devices generated new privacy concerns regarding data collection and transmission.

(iv) **Advanced Analytics and Artificial Intelligence:** Utilizing large datasets for research and clinical decision support, raising concerns about data de-identification and patient privacy. Development of privacy-preserving AI and algorithms to analyze data without compromising individual patient identities [5].

2. Literature Survey

The author [4] highlighted that victim data is delicate, crucial to establish protection when security and privacy are required. Emphasizing data security and privacy is required for the healthcare industry to maintain the dependability of electronic healthcare (eHealth) information systems. They assembled data from the surveys and interviews by looking at the security and privacy concerns in using eHealth information technologies. The goal is to find out how well-informed the medical practitioners are already in-place privacy measures that have been implemented by the medical authorities and to assess their attitudes regarding the need for extra improvements of the system. Eight healthcare professionals participated in an email interview to discover security and privacy problems associated with eHealth system usage. The information served as the groundwork for administering an online survey to which 370 medical practitioners responded from primary and secondary healthcare and emphasized on how essential it is to address the system usability issues on the security and privacy procedures which are implemented while using eHealth technologies.

The authors [6] proposed an innovative encryption scheme to strengthen the security of electronic health records in tele-health systems. Their approach introduces a unique patient identification mechanism to streamline the encryption and decryption process, ensuring that sensitive medical data remains protected from unauthorized access. One of the most significant aspects of their method is the use of an electrocardiogram (ECG) signal-based key generator, which gives a patient-specific encryption key for every patient, thereby increasing data privacy. Their system utilizes forward-secure signatures and time-lock puzzles to sign and protect transmitted health data. This protects data during transmission while enabling patients to unlink themselves from their data when required, enhancing privacy and compliance with regulations. The effectiveness of this model is shown by thorough security analysis and performance testing, emphasizing its potential to boost data protection in e-healthcare settings. The author stated that [7] the vital healthcare data privacy and security is increasing as healthcare systems worldwide are more digitized. An extensive relative analysis of the regulatory frameworks, challenges, and best exercises related to healthcare data privacy and security in the United States and Nigeria are explained. The Health Insurance Portability and Accountability Act (HIPAA) In the US (United States) and the Nigeria Data Protection Regulation (NDPR) alongside other local regulations highlights the nuances of each country's address to safeguarding patient data. Both the nations offer insights into successful plans and underscores the gaps and opportunities for cross country learning and improvement.

The authors emphasized [8] the essential function of data in contemporary healthcare, where there is a mass collection, storage, and examination of patient data to support clinical decision-making, medical research, and public health management. In an era when electronic health records (EHRs), wearable devices, and health-related applications are increasingly prevalent, organizations must contend with huge challenges in ensuring patient privacy and safeguarding sensitive data. Simultaneously, they aim to utilize artificial intelligence (AI) and machine learning (ML) to derive useful insights from this data. The research identifies some of the most important challenges for healthcare organizations relating to data privacy, regulatory compliance, and security. These are such challenges as compliance with intricate legal regulations like the Health Insurance Portability and Accountability Act (HIPPA) in America and the General Data Protection Regulation (GDPR) in Europe, both of which have strict data protection provisions and draconian penalties for default. Healthcare organizations also have to withstand changing cybersecurity threats, possible data breaches, and increasingly advanced cyber-attacks that exploit system vulnerabilities. They also need to balance using AI (Artificial Intelligence) and ML (Machine Learning) to improve patient care with avoiding risks like biased decision-making or breaches of privacy. Interoperability of data between primary and secondary healthcare systems was a prerequisite for the enhancement of the end-user experience. It was necessary to make integration and sharing of data between multiple platforms simpler in order to ensure that common technological standards for the interchange of data between the primary and secondary healthcare systems were created. Adaptation of shared levels may be recommended for this reason, like DICOM (Digital Imaging and Communications in Medicine) SNOMED CT (Systematized Nomenclature of Medicine Clinical Terms) with the purpose of a multilingual international core set for electronic clinical data interchange for application in Electronics Health Records.

The authors [9], briefed about technology integration in the healthcare sector, states that the healthcare industry has resulted in unmatched organization and accessibility to healthcare services. These transformations of healthcare systems have resulted in cyber-attacks, vulnerabilities in cyber-attacks which pose victim safety and privacy threats. To address this issue, healthcare providers must proactively safeguard patient data and mitigate cybersecurity risks which includes implementing robust security protocols, adhering to established privacy regulations, and selecting digital health solutions from vendors prioritizing privacy and security. By doing so, the healthcare industry can ensure that patients' personal, and personal health information remains private and secure while maintaining the efficiency and accessibility of healthcare services. The fast growth of the IoT (Internet of Things) was stated by the author [10] and wearable industries have expanded remote patient monitoring but healthcare systems face security vulnerabilities inherent in their patients. To address these challenges and meet regulatory standards a shift to a distributed architecture is necessary. Blockchain technology offers promise with its distributed nature and security features. MediSecureNet integrates blockchain and IoT (Internet of Things) to create a secure healthcare system. Prioritizing security, scalability, and processing speed, focuses on remote patient monitoring, particularly for chronic conditions and incorporates a re-encryption proxy for security, blockchain for hash data storage and smart contracts for access management. Scalability is achieved through an off chain IPFS (Inter Planetary File System) database, and an ethereum-based proof of authority mechanism to enhance data storage efficiency.

Authors explained that [11] AI (Artificial Intelligence) and the IoT (Internet of Things) have lately generated previously imagined prospects for enhancing clinical and patient services, lowering costs, and increasing community health. Each of these instruments introduces new security and privacy concerns that most translational investigators are unprepared to address, while claiming ultimate responsibility over them. Ways to secure data security as well as user privacy while collecting data from medical mobile devices is an issue worth investigating. Information gathered by healthcare wearable devices from technological, administration, and legal perspectives, and investigations data safety and privacy issues for medical treatment wearable devices to safeguard data safeguarding and user privacy while promoting the long-term developments for both the healthcare wearables technology industry and scientific data collected. The authors [12] proposed that the healthcare sector is a crucial and vulnerable infrastructure, making it an easy prey for hackers and attackers and is a highly trusted sector that contains personal data exploiting its vulnerabilities leads to huge financial and political gains. The digital twin is an emerging technology that plays a powerful role in the healthcare sector in the future offering customized diagnosis and treatment to each patient. Although there are several advantages and challenges to implementing it successfully in healthcare. Different challenges, related to the security, privacy, trust and safety of digital twins and its implementation in healthcare. It presents the comparative conflict analysis of implementing the security, privacy, trust and operational requirements for IoT (Internet of Things) digital twins.

The authors, [13] proposed the embedding of Internet of things technology into electronic health (eHealth) applications has transformed the healthcare landscape, enabling real time patient monitoring, personalized care and improved patient outcomes. It introduces critical security and privacy challenges, needing careful consideration. First taxonomies the various security threats that arise due to interrelated nature of IoT medical devices, secondly they synthesize functional, ethical, and regulatory perspectives to pick up the major requirements needed in the context of eHealth data during their whole lifecycle from creation to destruction, lastly they identify emerging research strategies employed to address security and privacy concerns such as cloud based solutions, decentralized technologies such as block chain technology and Interplanetary file system(IPFS), cryptographic approaches, fine-grained access control strategies was proposed. Later they inspect the impact of these approaches on computational efficiency, latency, and energy consumption, critically evaluating their validity in the healthcare context. Building upon this comprehensive assessment, we outline potential future research directions aimed at advancing security and privacy measures in IoT (Internet of Things) healthcare based systems.

The author [14] explained that data and analytics are indispensable parts of any successful business. Despite that, they lead to serious privacy issues if not used safely. Even though the financial and legal consequences of privacy breaches are profound, the most damaging one in the long run comes under customer distrust. It is particularly for hypersensitive data like personal health information. The significance of privacy, security and trust to the design of successful modern systems are being recognized than before. In the medical data management systems, handling sensitive data, mistrust is a barrier to many core processes such as data collection, sharing and analytics, it is a primary cause of suboptimal medical services in our time. The main direction of his thesis is to respond to these concerns of ethical nature taking data privacy as a fundamental human right into serious consideration in the design of these processes which highlights the emerging role of the blockchain in health information systems and recognizes block chain's ample opportunities for trust establishment. It proposes solutions based on novel technology and proposes a privacy-preserving data market for incentive-driven data collection for the development of reliable mathematical models that accelerate medical research. The blockchain aspect of this platform provides transparency as to the purpose for which the data is used to avoid the perception of data misuse. Flexible blockchain-based access control mechanisms with multiple privacy protection layers for user-centric data sharing and disturbed machine learning as a service platform for data analytics, whose computational integrity can be verified efficiently by users, were proposed. The strength of this platform lies in mutual privacy protection.

The rest of the sections are as follows. Section 3 highlights the significance of Data Security, Section 4 briefs the type of cyber-attacks in healthcare, Section 5 gives an idea of regulatory framework in healthcare for cybersecurity, Section 6 discusses the ethical concerns in healthcare, Section 7 highlights the idea of different cutting edge models and technologies for security in healthcare,

Section 8 briefs the challenges encountered in implementing cybersecurity measures and Section 9 discusses the future scope of healthcare.

3. The Importance of Data Security in Healthcare

Patient information is the most sensitive form of data, containing personal details, medical histories, treatment plans, and financial records. A breach can have dangerous effects, including identity theft, financial fraud, and compromised patient safety. Cybercriminals target healthcare institutions due to their vast repositories of valuable data, often exploiting vulnerabilities in outdated security infrastructure. It disrupts hospital operations, leading to delayed treatments and compromised care. Making sure data security in healthcare is required for maintaining patient trust. When patients feel confident that their information is protected, they are likely to immerse themselves with healthcare providers and disclose sensitive medical information, which improves the quality of care. Conversely, data leak can result in significant financial and legal outcomes for healthcare organizations, including regulatory fines, lawsuits, and reputational damage. Data security measures, such as encryption, secure authentication, access control mechanisms, and continuous monitoring, are crucial for safeguarding healthcare information. Implementing a robust cybersecurity strategy helps institutions detect, prevent, and acknowledge cyber threats effectively. Training healthcare professionals on cybersecurity best practices ensures that staff members are informed of potential danger and can take proactive steps to reduce them. By sorting data security, healthcare organizations can uphold ethical standards, ensuring regulatory compliance and foster a secure environment for patient care.

4. Cyber Threats Confronting Healthcare Systems

Modern healthcare facilities face a constant barrage of cyber threats, each capable of disrupting operations and jeopardizing patient safety. Here are some of the most prevalent challenges:

(i) **Ransomware Attacks:** Cybercriminals use malicious software to encrypt sensitive patient data, essentially locking it away until a ransom is paid. These attacks can bring hospital operations to a standstill, delaying critical treatments and forcing institutions to shell out significant sums of money to regain access to vital information.

(ii) **Phishing Scams:** Deceitful actors often impersonate legitimate entities, sending fraudulent emails or messages made to trick healthcare staff into revealing confidential information, such as login credentials or patient data. Phishing remains a highly effective method for infiltrating healthcare networks.

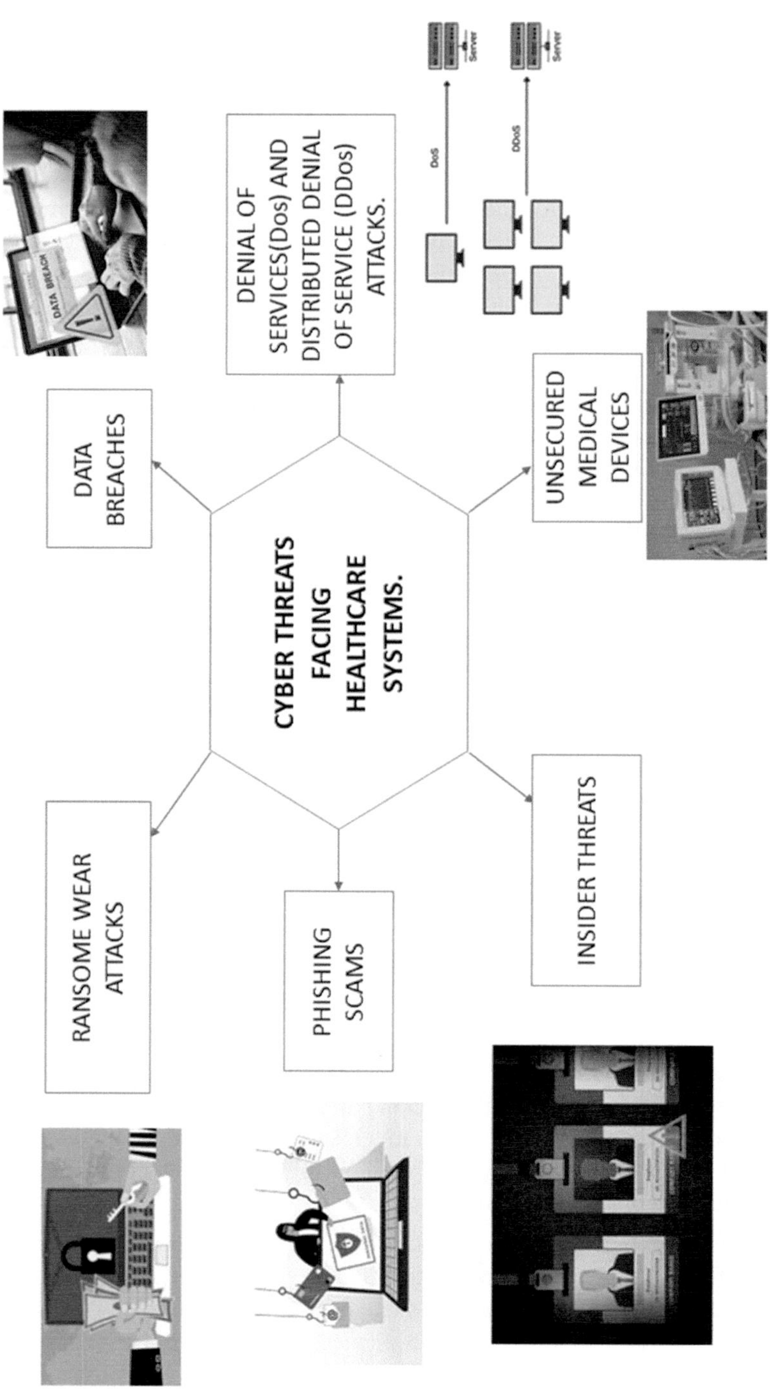

Figure 1: Cyber Threats in Healthcare.

(iii) Insider Threats: Employees or contractors with access to crucial data can pose a risk, whether intentionally or unintentionally. Insider menaces can stem from disgruntled employees seeking revenge, individuals motivated by financial gain, or simply human error. Their nature makes them particularly difficult to detect and prevent.

(iv) Unsecured Medical Devices: Many modern medical devices, like pacemakers, infusion pumps, and diagnostic equipment, are coupled to hospital networks for remote monitoring. If these devices aren't properly secured, they can become entry points for hackers, potentially leading to data breaches or even direct harm to patients.

(v) Distributed Denial-of-Service (DDoS) and Denial-of-Service (DoS) Assaults: These attacks cripple Electronic Health Record (EHR) systems and other crucial platforms by overwhelming healthcare networks with a flood of traffic. By disrupting access to vital systems, DoS (Denial-of-Service) and DDoS (Distributed Denial-of-Service) attacks can severely impede patient care, delaying diagnoses and treatments.

Figure 1 depicts the diverse cyber dangers confronting the healthcare sector.

Data Breaches

Cybercriminals often target healthcare databases to steal vast quantities of patient records. This stolen information can then be traded on the dark web for various harmful malware purposes, including identity theft, insurance fraud, and blackmail. Data breaches not only violate patient privacy but also expose healthcare organizations to substantial legal and financial repercussions. Because healthcare services are often a matter of life and death, the impact of cyber threats can be far more serious than in other sectors. To reduce these risks, healthcare organizations are required to implement comprehensive, multi-layered cybersecurity strategies. This includes measures like network segmentation, real-time threat detection, and ongoing training for all staff. By proactively addressing these threats, the healthcare industry can bolster its cyber resilience and ensure uninterrupted patient care.

5. Regulatory Frameworks for Healthcare Cybersecurity

Healthcare institutions operate under a compounded web of regulations designed to safeguard patient data and promote robust security practices. The following isa breakdown of some of the key regulations:

Health Insurance Portability and Accountability Act (HIPAA)

It is a U.S. (United States) law focused on the privacy and security of patient health information. It sets strict rules for how healthcare providers, insurers, and other covered entities handle Protected Health Information (PHI). This includes requirements for secure information storage, restricted access to authorized personnel, and safe data transmission. Healthcare organizations must apply administrative, physical, and technical safeguards to protect this sensitive data and also emphasize patients' rights to access, correct, and control their health information. Failure to comply can lead to significant fines and penalties, ranging from civil to criminal charges. Organizations are also mandated to report data breaches within 60 days.

General Data Protection Regulation (GDPR)

General Data Protection Regulation (GDPR) is a European Union regulation designed to secure the personal information of individuals, including health-related information. It applies to any organization that processes or stores data about EU (European Union) citizens, regardless of the organization's location. It mandates that personal information be processed transparently, securely, and only for specific, legitimate purposes. It grants individuals greater control over their data, including the right to access, correct, delete, and object to the refining of their information. Healthcare organizations must get explicit consent from individuals before processing their data. Violations can result in hefty fines, potentially reaching up to 4% of global revenue, underscoring the importance of compliance for healthcare providers handling EU (European Union) patient data.

National Institute of Standards and Technology (NIST) Framework

The National Institute of Standards and Technology (NIST) Cybersecurity Framework provides guidance to enhance the cybersecurity resilience of healthcare systems and other critical infrastructure. It assists companies identify, secure against, detect, respond to, and recover from cybersecurity risks. The framework provides an expensive set of best practices for risk management, including recommendations for securing patient data, protecting networks, and responding to potential threats. It encourages regular risk assessments and the implementation of appropriate cybersecurity controls. While not mandatory, this framework serves as a valuable best practice guide that can help institutions strengthen their security posture and meet other regulatory requirements, such as the Health Insurance Portability and Accountability Act (HIPAA).

Food and Drug Administration (FDA) Regulations

It plays a crucial role in making sure the safety and security of medical devices, particularly those with digital components or network connectivity. Devices like pacemakers, insulin pumps, and diagnostic equipment that store or transmit patient data must adhere to specific security standards to prevent cybersecurity vulnerabilities. It requires manufacturers to incorporate security measures throughout the device lifecycle, from design to post-market surveillance. This includes regular software updates and patching to address emerging security threats. Non-compliance with these regulations can pose penalties, product recalls, and erosion of public trust in the safety and reliability of these devices. Adhering to these regulations demands a proactive approach, encompassing regular security audits, the use of encryption technologies, and controlled access to patient records. Failure to comply can result in acute penalties, legal action, and damage to an organization's reputation.

6. Ethical Concerns in Healthcare Cybersecurity

The ethical considerations surrounding cybersecurity in healthcare are paramount, as they directly impact patient privacy, consent, and trust. Here are some key ethical concerns:

Informed Consent

Informed consent is a cornerstone of medical ethics. It needs healthcare providers to ensure patients fully understand how their personal data will be used. This includes providing clear and accessible information about what data will be collected, stored, and who might have access to it. Patients should have the opportunity to consent to or decline the sharing of their information, fully aware of any potential risks involved. Proper informed consent builds trust between patients and their healthcare providers, fostering transparency and authorizing patients to make advised conclusions about their own data. It's crucial that this consent process is ongoing, allowing for updates and revisions as data use practices evolve.

Data Ownership

This addresses the fundamental question of who has legal rights over patient data. While healthcare institutions typically collect and store this data, patients should retain ownership of their health information. Clearly defining who controls access to and makes decisions about this data is essential, as it directly impacts patient privacy and autonomy. Healthcare providers and third parties, such as insurers, need explicit permission to access, share, or use patient data. Ethical dilemmas arise when the patient's rights over their data clash with the interests of healthcare providers or businesses. Clear guidelines must be established to ensure patients retain control over their data while allowing necessary access for essential care.

Transparency

Transparency involves open and honest communication about how healthcare organizations manage and protect patient data. Organizations should readily disclose their cybersecurity policies, how data is collected, and how patient information is handled throughout its lifecycle. This transparency should also extend to informing patients about any risks of data breaches or misuse. Ethical healthcare institutions should proactively communicate their cybersecurity practices, helping patients understand the protective measures in place and the steps taken if data is compromised. Transparency builds trust and confidence, reassuring patients that their personal data is being handled with integrity.

Accountability

Accountability ensures that healthcare providers and third-party vendors are held responsible for safeguarding patient data and addressing any breaches or misuse. If a data breach occurs, the responsible parties should take instant action to correct the situation and notify affected individuals. Healthcare organizations must have clear policies in place to hold data security incidents and display their commitment to safeguard patient data. This ethical responsibility is important for maintaining trust and making sure that patients are not left vulnerable due to negligence or inadequate security practices.

Equitable Access

This principle guarantees that cybersecurity measures do not generate barriers to healthcare, particularly for vulnerable or underserved populations. While security protocols are essential to protect patient data, they should not disproportionately affect certain groups, such as those with limited digital literacy or access to technology. Ethical cybersecurity policies should strive to balance patient protection with ensuring that all individuals, regardless of their background, have equal access to healthcare services. Discriminatory practices, such as overly complex systems that make it difficult for some patients to access care, must be avoided.

7. Cutting-Edge Technologies for Healthcare Security

To combat the ever-evolving aspect of cyber threats, healthcare organizations are increasingly turning to advanced technologies. Some of the most promising are:

Zero-Trust Security Models

The Zero Trust model works on the principle of never trust, always verify. Unlike traditional security models that presume trust within a network, Zero Trust assumes that both internal and external networks are potentially compromised. This approach mandates strict confirmation for every user, device, and application aiming to approach sensitive data or resources. It focuses on continuous authentication and authorization, limiting access based on the principle of least privilege. By minimizing the risk of unofficial access and reducing the impact of insider threats, Zero Trust helps safeguard patient information from breaches and misuse.

Blockchain Technology

Blockchain technology utilizes a decentralized and distributed record system, ensuring information integrity and transparency. Each piece of data, or block is connected to the previous one, making an immutable chain. Once information is noted on the blockchain, it cannot be changed or deleted without consensus from the network. This supplies a high level of security, as any unauthorized attempt to modify data is easily detectable. In healthcare, blockchain can be used to securely store patient records, making sure that information remains correct and tamper-proof. It also facilitates efficient data sharing among authorized parties without compromising patient privacy.

Homomorphic Encryption

Homomorphic encryption is an innovative coding technique that permits computations to be carried out on encoded data without decrypting it first. This ensures that sensitive data remains protected throughout the processing. In healthcare, this is incredibly valuable, as it allows for the examination of encrypted patient data without exposing it to unauthorized individuals or systems. Homomorphic encryption can be used for tasks like medical research or predictive analytics, enabling healthcare professionals to gain valuable insights from encrypted data while preserving patient confidentiality. It provides an added layer of privacy while still allowing the benefits of data-driven healthcare advancements.

Artificial Intelligence (AI) and Machine Learning

Artificial intelligence and machine learning technologies play an important role in detecting and reducing cyber threats in real-time. These systems can examine massive quantities of data, detecting subtle patterns that may specify a potential breach or threat. In healthcare, AI driven threat detection systems continuously monitor networks for suspicious activity, flagging any abnormalities that may suggest a cyber-attack or breach of patient data. Machine learning algorithms can learn from past incidents, constantly improving their ability to detect and respond to new and evolving threats. This enterprising approach helps prevent data violations before they occur, significantly increasing the complete security of healthcare systems.

Quantum Cryptography

Quantum cryptography is an enhanced security technology that leverages the principles of quantum mechanics to create encryption systems that are virtually unbreakable. By using quantum bits (qubits) instead of traditional binary bits, quantum cryptography is dependent on the fundamental properties of particles, such as superposition and entanglement, to secure data transmission. Any attempt to cease or eavesdrop on quantum-encrypted data will muddle the quantum state, immediately warning the sender and receiver of the potential breach. This makes quantum cryptography a promising solution for securing highly sensitive healthcare data, offering unprecedented protection against future cyber threats.

Cloud Security Solutions

Protecting healthcare data stored on cloud platforms requires advanced security measures, including vigorous encryption methods, secure access protocols, and strong authentication mechanisms. Firm cloud storage can be combined with end-to-end encryption, making sure that information remains personal and safe whether it's being stored, accessed, or transmitted. Multi-factor authentication

Table 1: Comparison of Emerging Technologies for Enhancing Healthcare Data Security

Technology	Features	Applications
Zero-Trust Security	It continuously verifies users and devices, assuming that no network is trusted by default.	Protects patient data by limiting access and ensures only authorized personnel can access medical records.
Blockchain	Records data in a secure and transparent way, ensuring no alterations after storage.	Secure storage of patient records and efficient sharing of healthcare information between authorized entities
Homomorphic Encryption	A method of encoding that allows calculation to be done on encrypted data in the absence of revealing the underlying information.	Secure medical research, Predictive health analytics and allows processing of encrypted patient information
AI and Machine Learning	Technologies that enable systems to automatically detect and respond to security threats through real-time data analysis.	Identifies cybersecurity risks in healthcare systems and monitors networks for prospective safety breaches
Quantum Cryptography	An innovative encryption method that leverages the properties of quantum mechanics to ensure data security.	High-security healthcare data transfer and protects sensitive medical records and communications
Cloud Security	Security measures that protect data stored in the cloud, using encryption, secure access methods, and authentication	Secure cloud-based health records, Enables scalable storage of healthcare data and protects online health services

(MFA) adds an extra layer of security, needing users to provide multiple forms of verification before obtaining access to crucial data. By executing these security measures, healthcare organizations can safeguard patient information while taking advantage of the flexibility, scalability, and cost-effectiveness that cloud computing offers. Cloud security is paramount for protecting healthcare data, especially as more organizations migrate to cloud environments. While these technologies offer significant security enhancements, their effective execution requires specialized expertise, continuous monitoring, and strict adherence to regulatory compliance to ensure patient data remains protected. Table 1 gives a comparison of Emerging Technologies for Enhancing Healthcare Data Security.

8. Challenges in Implementing Cybersecurity Measures

Despite growing awareness of cybersecurity threats, numerous healthcare organizations wrestle to effectively implement robust security measures [21]. Several barriers, including outdated systems, financial limitations, and a lack of trained personnel, hinder the adoption of advanced security protocols. The complex nature of healthcare networks, coupled with the need for seamless data exchange, presents further challenges in securing patient information. Addressing these issues requires a strategic approach that balances security, compliance, and operational efficiency. Here are some of the key challenges:

Legacy Systems and Infrastructure

Many healthcare firms still rely on old systems that have insufficient modern security features, making them exposed to cyber threats. This legacy arrangement often can't support newer security protocols, hindering the implementation of necessary protections [15]. Attackers can exploit known vulnerabilities, putting patient data at risk. Updating or replacing these systems can be costly and time-consuming, but failing to do so significantly increases the likelihood of security breaches.

Budget Constraints

Implementing advanced cybersecurity measures can require significant financial resources, which may be beyond the reach of many healthcare institutions, especially smaller ones. The cost of enhancing systems, training staff, and investing in new technologies often competes with other essential healthcare priorities, like direct patient care [16]. Budget constraints can lead to insufficient security protections, leaving organizations exposed to potential data breaches and cyber-attacks. Prioritizing cybersecurity investments is crucial to ensure patient data is adequately safeguarded.

Interoperability Issues

Healthcare systems often face challenges in securely sharing data between different platforms and organizations. Ensuring interoperability without compromising security requires developing secure interfaces that allow data to flow seamlessly while protecting sensitive information [17]. The complexity of integrating various systems while maintaining compliance with security standards is a significant hurdle. Without proper safeguards, the exchange of health data can expose organizations to security risks.

Human Error and Insider Threats

Human error, such as employees accidentally disclosing sensitive information or failing to follow security protocols, is a significant cybersecurity risk. Insider threats, where reliable persons intentionally abuse their access to data, can be equally damaging [18, 22]. These risks highlight the critical need for ongoing training and clear cybersecurity policies to minimize the likelihood of mistakes. Organizations must promote a culture of security awareness to ensure employees must realize the importance of securing patient information.

Evolving Cyber Threats

Cyber attackers are continuously evolving new and more sophisticated methods to breach systems and steal data. Healthcare organizations must upgrade their cybersecurity measures to stay in advance of these emerging threats, which requires ongoing vigilance and adaptation [19]. The rapid pace of cyber threat evolution makes it challenging for healthcare institutions to maintain robust defenses, demanding continuous investment in the latest security technologies and threat detection tools. Failure to adapt quickly can leave organizations vulnerable to the latest forms of cybercrime.

Regulatory Compliance Complexity

Healthcare organizations must navigate the complexities of multiple regulatory frameworks, such as HIPAA and GDPR, which outline strict security and privacy requirements. Compliance with these regulations can be resource-intensive, requiring both time and money to implement the necessary safeguards and conduct regular audits. The evolving nature of regulations adds another layer of complexity, as healthcare institutions must stay informed of changes and ensure they meet all requirements to avoid legal and financial penalties [20]. Managing compliance across various frameworks can be demanding for smaller companies with limited assets. The future of healthcare cybersecurity depends on adopting next-generation technologies and standardized approaches. Emerging solutions will enhance security, mitigate risks, and create a safer digital healthcare environment. Developing advanced cybersecurity measures is crucial for keeping pace with evolving threats. The healthcare industry must explore innovative solutions that not only protect patient data but also improve system efficiency and reliability.

Future Directions in Healthcare Cybersecurity

As cyber threats become increasingly sophisticated, the future of healthcare cybersecurity will be brought by advanced technologies and creative strategies. Emerging security solutions focus not only on preventing breaches but also on enhancing resilience, threat intelligence, and data privacy. The integration of AI (Artificial Intelligence), blockchain, quantum encryption, and biometric authentication will be crucial in safeguarding sensitive health data. Moving forward, healthcare organizations must embrace these advancements to build a safe and trustworthy digital environment.

9. Advanced Technologies in Healthcare Cybersecurity

Global Data Protection Standards

Global data protection standards aim to create unified regulations that ensure consistent cybersecurity practices across international borders. By aligning healthcare data protection requirements globally, these standards help organizations navigate the complexities of complying with various national laws [15]. The goal is to enhance privacy and security for patients worldwide, ensuring that healthcare providers meet a common set of requirements to safeguard data. This reduces the regulatory burden and ensures that healthcare data remains secure regardless of where it is stored or processed.

Cognitive Security Systems

Cognitive security systems leverage Artificial Intelligence (AI) and Machine Learning (ML) to improve the ability of healthcare companies to predict, avert, and respond to cyber-attacks. These systems can examine huge data to identify possible threats before they cause damage [17]. By continuously learning from new attack patterns, cognitive security systems can adapt and respond to evolving threats in real-time. This approach permits healthcare institutions to mitigate risks and reduce the chances of security breaches affecting sensitive patient information.

Nanotechnology for Data Protection

Nanotechnology for data protection involves embedding tiny, advanced security features into medical devices and hardware to prevent cyber threats at the most fundamental level. These microscopic security mechanisms can help ensure that data stored within or transmitted by medical devices remains secure against unauthorized access or tampering [18]. Nanotechnology could play an important role in safeguarding medical devices like pacemakers or insulin pumps, which are increasingly attached to networks and therefore vulnerable to cyber-attacks. Integrating nanotechnology could provide an additional layer of protection by making devices less susceptible to breaches.

Biometric Authentication

Biometric authentication utilizes distinctive physical traits, such as facial recognition or fingerprint scanning, to confirm the recognition of patients and healthcare staff. This advanced form of authentication makes sure only authorized individuals enter sensitive medical records or systems [19]. Biometric methods offer a huge level of security than traditional passwords or PINs, which can be easily stolen or forgotten. By adopting biometric authentication, healthcare institutions can enhance security while streamlining the user experience for both patients and staff.

Automated Threat Intelligence Systems

Automated threat intelligence systems use artificial intelligence to find, inspect, and respond to cyber threats in real-time in the absence of human interface [16]. These platforms continuously monitor healthcare networks for signs of malicious activity and automatically trigger responses, such as isolating compromised systems or blocking harmful traffic. By reducing the need for manual oversight, these systems allow healthcare companies to acknowledge emerging threats, minimizing the potential impact of cyber-attacks and ensuring a more robust defense against security breaches.

Integration of Quantum Cryptography

Quantum cryptography constitutes a new frontier in securing healthcare data by using the principles of quantum mechanics to create encryption systems which are virtually impossible to break [20]. Unlike traditional encryption, which can be vulnerable to advanced hacking techniques, quantum encryption uses quantum bits (qubits) that change if intercepted, ensuring the data remains private. Integrating quantum cryptography into healthcare cybersecurity provides a future-proof solution that protects against the growing threat of quantum computing, which could eventually compromise current encryption methods. This technology offers a highly secure way to safeguard sensitive patient information in an increasingly digital world.

10. Conclusion

The digitalization of healthcare has undeniably brought about a paradigm shift in how we deliver and receive care. It's made things smoother, faster, and more accessible for everyone. However this digital revolution has also opened up a Pandora's Box of cybersecurity challenges. Patient data, which is incredibly sensitive and personal, is now a prime target for cybercriminals. We're talking about threats like ransom-ware attacks that can cripple entire systems, sneaky phishing attempts to steal credentials, and unauthorized access leading to massive data breaches. Protecting this information is not just a technical matter; it's an ethical imperative and a legal obligation. Regulations like HIPAA (Health Insurance Portability and Accountability Act) and GDPR (General Data Protection Regulation) are in place to provide a framework for responsible data handling, but simply having these rules isn't enough. We need to be proactive, employing a multi-layered approach that combines cutting-edge security technologies, robust access controls, and vigilant monitoring. Think of it like a fortress, we need strong walls (encryption), vigilant guards at the gates (access controls), and constant surveillance (monitoring). Emerging technologies like zero-trust architectures and blockchain offer promising solutions, but we cannot ignore the existing challenges. Many healthcare systems are still running on outdated technology, leading to interoperability issues and vulnerabilities and human element, i.e. unintentional errors can be the feeble connection in the series. Ultimately, securing digital healthcare ecosystems requires a holistic strategy that seamlessly integrates security, compliance, and ethical considerations. It is about building trust in these systems, ensuring that patients can benefit from the advancements in healthcare technology without fearing for the safety of their personal information.

References

1. Akm, I., and Sikder, A. K. (2021). A survey on security and privacy issues in modern healthcare systems: Attacks and defences. *ACM Trans. Comput. Healthcare*, 2(3), Art. no. 27, 1–44, doi: 10.1145/3453176.
2. Al Zaabi, M., and Alhashmi, S. M. (2024). Big data security and privacy in healthcare: A systematic review and future research directions. *SAGE Journals*, doi: 10.1177/02666669241247781.
3. Amalraj, J. R. and Lourdusamy, R. (2022). Security and privacy issues in federated healthcare—An overview. *Open Comput. Sci.*, doi: 10.1515/comp-2022-0230.
4. Denkovski, V., and Stojmenovska, I. (2024). Exploring current challenges on security and privacy in an operational eHealth information system. *Adv. J.*, 9(2), 45–54, doi: 10.25046/aj090206.
5. Dogra, A., Dhondiyal, S.A., and Dimri, S.C. (2024). *Comprehensive Study of Cybersecurity Issues and Challenges*, pp. 21–40, doi: 10.1515/9783111229157-002.
6. Odeh, A., Abdelfattah, E., and Salameh, W. (2024). Privacy-preserving data sharing in telehealth services. *Appl. Sci.*, 14(23), Art. no. 10808, doi: 10.3390/app142310808.
7. Idoko, B. et al. 2024. Enhancing healthcare data privacy and security: A comparative study of regulations and best practices in the US and Nigeria. *Magna Sci. Adv. Res. Rev.*, 11(2), 151–167, doi: 10.30574/msarr.2024.11.2.0110.

8. Singhal, S. 2024. Data privacy, compliance, and security including AI and ML. *IGI Global*, doi: 10.4018/979-8-3693-2909-2.ch009.
9. Lo, P. 2024. Healthcare innovations: Enhancing patient privacy and security in the digital era. *Healthc. Manag. Forum*, 37(5), 363–365, doi: 10.1177/08404704241254820.
10. Singla, D., Kumar, S., and Dhingra, D. (2024). Blockchain-powered healthcare: Revolutionizing security and privacy in IoT-based systems. In: *Proc. Comput. Intell. Comput. Appl.* (*ICCICA*), Samalkha, India, doi: 10.1109/ICCICA60014.2024.10585062.
11. Raje, V. V. and Mohite, R. V. (2024). Data security and privacy in the smart healthcare system. In: *Proc. Healthc. Innov., Softw. Eng. Technol.* (*HISET*), Karad, India, pp. 204–206, doi: 10.1109/HISET61796.2024.00068.
12. Gupta, A., and Gupta, U. (2023). Analysing security threats and elevating healthcare privacy for a resilient future. In: *Proc. Artif. Intell. Innov. Healthc. Ind.* (*ICAIIHI*), pp. 1–6, doi: 10.1109/ICAIIHI57871.2023.10489079.
13. Makina, H., Letafia, A. B., and Rachedi, A. (2023). Survey on security and privacy in Internet of Things-based eHealth applications: Challenges, architectures, and future directions. *Secur. Privacy*, doi: 10.1002/spy2.346.
14. Ghaffaripour, S. (2024). Novel Solutions for Privacy, Security and Trust in Modern Medical Data Management Systems. Thesis, Toronto Metropolitan University, doi: 10.32920/26052493.v1.
15. Tanwar, R. (2025). Cyber security challenges. *Int. J. Sci. Technol. Eng.*, 13(1), 564–566, doi: 10.22214/ijraset.2025.66263.
16. Hussain, N. Y., Aliyu, A., Balogun, E. D., Hussain, A. A., and Omotorsho, D. 2024. Cybersecurity measures safeguarding digital assets and mitigating risks in an increasingly interconnected world. *Int. J. Innov. Sci. Res. Technol.*, doi: 10.38124/ijisrt/ijisrt24may197.
17. Wahed, M. et al. (2024). Comprehensive assessment of cybersecurity measures: Evaluating incident response, AI integration, and emerging threats. In: *Proc. IEEE NETAPPS*, doi: 10.1109/netapps63333.2024.10823603.
18. Shantilawati, I., Zanubiya, J., Fanani, F., Jensen, H. J., Millah, S., and Lutfiani, N. (2024). Challenges in securing data and networks from modern cyber threats. *Int. J. Cyber IT Serv. Manag.*, 4(2), 88–96, doi: 10.34306/ijcitsm.v4i2.160.
19. Mansfield-Devine, S. (2024). Meeting the challenges of cyber security. *Cybersecurity J.*, doi: 10.12968/s1353-4858(24)70002-6.
20. Folorunso, A., Wada, I., Samuel, B., and Mohammed, V. (2024). Security compliance and its implication for cybersecurity. *World J. Adv. Res. Rev.*, doi: 10.30574/wjarr.2024.24.1.3170.
21. Jørgensen, C. S., and Shukla, R. (2023). Digital twins in healthcare: Security, privacy, trust, and safety challenges. In: *Comput. Secur. ESORICS Int. Workshops. ESORICS 2023, Lect. Notes Comput. Sci.*, vol. 14399, Springer, Cham, doi: 10.1007/978-3-031-54129-2_9.
22. An, F., and Li, N. (2023). Insights into security and privacy issues in smart healthcare systems based on medical images. *J. Inf. Secur. Appl.*, 78, 103621, doi: 10.1016/j.jisa.2023.103621.

17 | Green Healthcare and Sustainable Practices: A Path to a Resilient Future

Sayan Deb[1*], Protyusa Deb[2], Riya Sil[1] and Ashish Kattamuri[3]

[1] Department of Computer Science & Engineering, Brainware University, Kolkata, India
[2] Department of Health Science & Technology, JIS Institute of Advanced Studies and Research (JISIASR), Howrah, India
[3] Proofpoint, Inc., Sunnyvale, California, USA

The healthcare sector, which is vital for public health, contributes approximately 4.4% of global greenhouse gas emissions, necessitating sustainable practices. This chapter explores green healthcare through the circular economy, green human resource management (GHRM), and green leadership. It examines strategies like waste minimization, energy efficiency, water conservation, sustainable transportation, chemical substitution, pharmaceutical pollution reduction, sustainable food practices, and green building design. Global case studies from the US, UK, Netherlands, Australia, Egypt, and Palestine are used to illustrate the crucial roles that HR and leadership play in promoting sustainability. Financial constraints, regulatory hurdles, and lack of awareness are being addressed through solutions such as financial incentives, education, and standardized metrics. Future directions emphasize robust research methodologies like PRISMA and VOSviewer, technological innovations, policy support, and global collaboration. By integrating these practices, healthcare organizations can align with global sustainability goals, reduce their ecological footprint, and enhance operational efficiency and patient outcomes.

1. Introduction

The healthcare sector is a cornerstone of public health, delivering essential services to millions worldwide. However, it also significantly contributes

*Corresponding author: sayandeb010@gmail.com

DOI: 10.1201/9781003635215-17

to environmental degradation, accounting for approximately 4.4% of global greenhouse gas emissions, according to research from the International Journal of Health Policy and Management [1]. Hospitals, clinics, and medical facilities consume vast amounts of energy, water, and materials, generating substantial waste, including hazardous and infectious materials. As climate change exacerbates health challenges, such as heat-related illnesses, vector-borne diseases, and respiratory conditions, the sector faces an urgent need to adopt green healthcare practices that minimize environmental impact while maintaining high-quality care [2].

Green healthcare encompasses a wide range of sustainable operations, from energy-efficient hospital designs to eco-friendly waste management systems [3]. These practices align with the United Nations' Sustainable Development Goals (SDGs), particularly SDG 3 (Good Health and Well-being) and SDG 13 (Climate Action). The circular economy, which promotes reducing, reusing, and recycling resources, serves as a key framework for sustainable healthcare. By shifting from a linear "take-make-dispose" model, hospitals can extend product life cycles, reduce waste, and lower emissions. Leadership and human resource management play pivotal roles in driving these changes, fostering a culture of sustainability among staff and stakeholders [3].

This chapter provides a comprehensive exploration of green healthcare, covering the current state of sustainable practices, the critical roles of leadership and human resources, practical examples through global case studies, challenges and barriers to adoption, and future directions informed by rigorous research methodologies. By synthesizing insights from recent studies and real-world implementations, it aims to offer a roadmap for healthcare organizations to contribute to a resilient, sustainable future. The discussion is grounded in evidence from multiple sources, ensuring a holistic perspective on how the sector can balance environmental responsibility with its core mission of saving lives.

In this chapter, section 2 discusses the current state of green practices in healthcare. The role of Leadership and Human Resources are discussed in section 3. In section 4, the Case Studies are discussed along with Examples. The Challenges and Barriers are discussed in section 5 of this chapter. Section 6 explores the Future Directions. Global Perspectives on Green Healthcare are analysed in Section 7 of this chapter. Section 8 examines the Technological Innovations in Green Healthcare. Section 9 analyses the Economic Benefits of Green Healthcare. The Social Benefits of Green Healthcare is explored in section 10. Section 11 discusses the Measuring and Reporting Sustainability. The Role of Patients and Communities is explored in section 12. Section 13 explores Artificial Intelligence in Healthcare Sustainability. The conclusion is analysed in section 14.

2. Current State of Green Practices in Healthcare

In this section, authors have discussed the current state of green practices in healthcare. Starting from Circular Economy, Energy Efficiency, to Green Building, every single point has been explored effectively.

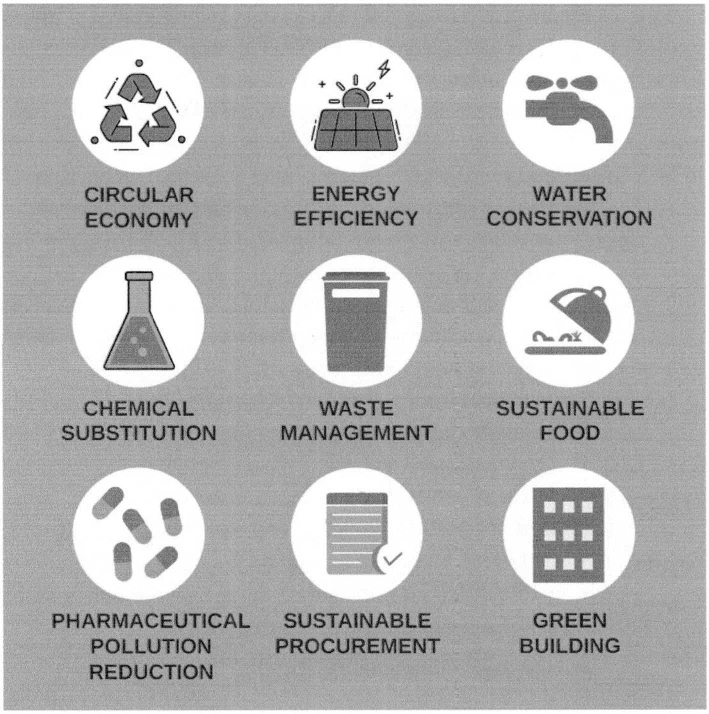

Figure 1: Current State of Green Practices in Healthcare.

The following points provide a detailed discussion of Fig. 1.

(i) Circular Economy in Healthcare: The circular economy emphasizes reducing, reusing, and recycling resources to minimize environmental impact, offering a transformative approach for healthcare. Hospitals generate substantial waste, with up to 85% classified as non-hazardous and recyclable, according to a 2023 review in the *International Journal of Health Policy and Management* [1]. Strategies include adopting reusable medical instruments, such as surgical trays, and recycling plastics, paper, and other materials. Sustainable procurement, selecting products with minimal packaging or made from recycled materials, supports circular principles. Recent advancements show healthcare enterprises adopting net-zero plans, extending product life cycles through repair and refurbishment programs, as noted in a 2024 EY India report [5]. For example, the UK's National Health Service (NHS) has implemented life cycle assessments (LCAs) to evaluate the environmental impact of medical products, contributing to an 11% emissions reduction from 2007 to 2015 [4]. Similarly, hospitals in the Netherlands, through the Dutch Green Deal, have reduced medical waste and emissions by embracing circular economy principles, engaging over 100 facilities in sustainable practices.

(ii) **Energy Efficiency:** Hospitals are energy-intensive, with heating, ventilation, and air conditioning (HVAC) systems accounting for up to 50% of energy use, according to World Health Organization (WHO) data [8]. Energy efficiency measures can significantly reduce consumption and emissions. Switching to LED lighting can cut lighting energy use by 75%, while high-efficiency HVAC systems and variable speed drives reduce energy by 20–30%, as outlined in EPA guidelines [12]. Renewable energy, such as solar panels, is increasingly adopted. The Mayo Clinic in Minnesota generates 2.5 million kilowatt-hours annually from solar arrays, powering 250 homes [21]. Energy management systems, using real-time monitoring, optimize operations, achieving annual savings of 10–15%, according to a Lawrence Berkeley National Laboratory study [19]. Case Study: Al-Ramad Hospital in Egypt reduced energy use by 38% through LED upgrades, solar water heaters, and staff training on energy conservation, saving significant costs [17].

(iii) **Water Conservation:** Hospitals consume vast amounts of water, often 1% of a city's total supply [1]. Water conservation strategies include low-flow fixtures, rainwater harvesting, and recycling water for non-potable uses. Switching to digital imaging eliminates water-intensive film-based radiology. Tzu Chi General Hospital in Taiwan reuses sterilization water, reducing waste by 20% [7]. Regular audits and leak detection programs can save up to 10% of water usage annually, as per EPA guidelines [19].

(iv) **Transportation and Telemedicine:** Transportation accounts for 16% of healthcare-related emissions in the EU [1]. Telemedicine, expanded during the COVID-19 pandemic, reduces patient travel emissions by up to 20%. Hospitals can also adopt electric vehicles and encourage staff carpooling or cycling. The Cleveland Clinic offers bike-sharing programs, cutting local emissions by 5% [13].

(v) **Substituting Harmful Chemicals:** Healthcare facilities use chemicals like mercury and phthalates, which pose health and environmental risks. Substituting these with safer alternatives, such as digital thermometers and biodegradable disinfectants, protects patients and staff. Policies prioritizing low-toxicity chemicals align with sustainability goals. Kaiser Permanente excluded mercury, containing bias, reducing dangerous waste by 15%.

(vi) **Waste Management:** Hospitals generate millions of tons of waste annually, with 15% classified as hazardous [1]. Effective waste management involves reducing waste at the source, segregating recyclable materials, and using non-burn technologies like autoclaving. The University of California, San Francisco (UCSF) Medical Center reduced landfill waste by 50% through recycling and reusable sharps containers [18]. By composting organic waste, as rehearsed by Kaiser Permanente, 75% of food waste is diverted from the disposal site.

(vii) **Sustainable Food Practices:** Food services in hospitals offer opportunities to promote health and sustainability. Sourcing local, sustainably grown food reduces transportation emissions by 10–15%. Plant-based menus and portion control minimize food waste, while composting programs recycle organic waste. The Hunter Brain Injury Service in Australia reduced food waste by 18% through composting, saving $2,000 annually [17].

(viii) **Pharmaceutical Pollution Reduction:** Pharmaceuticals in the environment contribute to antimicrobial resistance and ecological harm. Optimizing prescribing practices, implementing take-back programs, and ensuring proper disposal mitigate these risks. European take-back programs have reduced pharmaceutical waste in landfills by 25% [14]. Developing safer pharmaceuticals with a lower environmental impact is a growing focus.

(ix) **Sustainable Procurement:** Procurement decisions influence environmental and social outcomes. Green purchasing policies prioritize eco-friendly products and ethical suppliers, reducing supply chain emissions by 10–15%. The NHS uses LCAs to select sustainable medical products, contributing to its emissions reduction [4].

(x) **Green Building Design:** Sustainable hospital design incorporates recycled materials, natural ventilation, and energy-efficient systems. LEED-certified hospitals, like the Dell Children's Medical Center in Texas, reduce energy use by 20% through green roofs and solar panels [10]. High-reflectance roofing and local materials further minimize environmental impact.

3. Role of Leadership and Human Resources

In this section, authors have provided a clear view on the role of leadership and human resources. It discussed the importance of leaders and how their goals can bring big changes in the field of Green Healthcare. It also analyses the importance of human resources and the goals.

Green Leadership

Leadership with an environmental focus is vital for promoting sustainability in healthcare. Leaders must set clear goals, allocate resources, and foster environmental stewardship through "green teams" and system-wide policies. The Dutch Green Deal exemplifies policy-driven sustainability, engaging over 100 hospitals [1]. Leaders also invest in research to overcome barriers, ensuring strategic plans reflect sustainability commitments. For example, the CEO of Kaiser Permanente made sustainability a strategic priority, leading to significant reductions in waste and emissions [15].

Green Human Resource Management (GHRM)

GHRM integrates sustainability into HR practices, including green hiring, training, and performance management. Studies in Palestinian healthcare organizations show that GHRM enhances environmental performance by fostering a green culture [2]. Green hiring involves recruiting employees with environmental knowledge, while green training enhances awareness of sustainability initiatives. Green performance management links environmental goals to evaluations and rewards, encouraging sustainable practices. GHRM programs can increase staff participation in recycling by 40% and reduce energy consumption through behavioural changes.

Overcoming Resistance

Resistance to green practices often stems from perceived costs or unfamiliarity. Leaders can address this by highlighting long-term savings, such as the 20–40% return on investment from energy efficiency measures [19]. GHRM supports change through education, ensuring staff understand sustainability benefits. Community outreach programs further enhance public support, as seen in initiatives by the International Hospital Federation [7].

4. Case Studies and Examples

This segment presents practical examples of sustainable initiatives in healthcare, illustrating how global hospitals and health systems are minimizing environmental footprints, reducing expenses, and enhancing operational efficiency. These case studies feature a range of approaches, including renewable energy integration, waste minimization, and creative resource management, offering replicable models for healthcare organizations worldwide. Figure 2 given below shows the below described case studies as a graph.

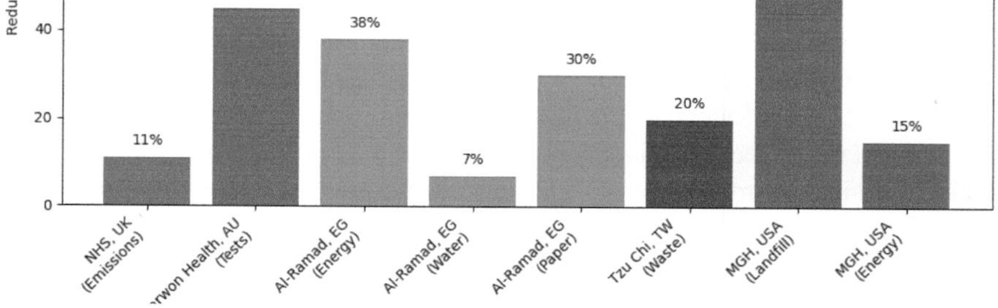

Figure 2: Percentage Reduction in Sustainability.

(i) **National Health Service (NHS), UK:** The NHS reduced emissions by 11% from 2007 to 2015, targeting 80% by 2050. LCAs evaluate medical products' environmental impact, saving £50 million annually [4]. The NHS's renewable energy initiatives demonstrate scalable sustainability.

(ii) **Dutch Green Deal:** The Dutch Green Deal reduces medical waste and emissions through circular economy principles, engaging over 100 hospitals [1].

(iii) **Young Executive Leaders (YEL) Initiatives:** The International Hospital Federation's YEL program highlights leaders implementing energy efficiency and waste management, inspiring global adoption [7].

(iv) **Barwon Health, Australia:** Barwon Health's "No Unhelpful Tests" initiative reduced low-value tests by 40–50%, saving $885,000, 726 staff hours, and 906 kg CO_2e emissions annually [20].

(v) **Al-Ramad Hospital, Egypt:** Al-Ramad Hospital achieved a 38% energy reduction, 7% water savings, and 30% paper reduction through efficiency measures and digital transformation [17].

(vi) **Mayo Clinic, USA:** The Mayo Clinic generates 2.5 million kilowatt-hours annually from solar arrays, powering 250 homes [21].

(vii) **Tzu Chi General Hospital, Taiwan:** Tzu Chi General Hospital reuses sterilization water, reducing waste by 20% [16].

(viii) **Massachusetts General Hospital, USA:** Massachusetts General Hospital (MGH) achieved a 90% landfill diversion rate through recycling and composting, reduced energy use by 15% with upgraded systems, and installed solar panels generating 1.2 million kWh annually [22].

(ix) **Singapore General Hospital:** Singapore General Hospital is certified as a Green Mark Platinum hospital, using energy-efficient equipment and comprehensive recycling programs [23].

5. Challenges and Barriers

The path to sustainable healthcare is fraught with challenges, such as substantial expenses for eco-friendly technologies and inconsistent regulatory frameworks across different areas. These hurdles often impede hospitals, particularly smaller ones, from embracing green practices. Furthermore, a lack of sustainability education among healthcare professionals and insufficient data to monitor metrics like emissions or waste add to the complexity. Nevertheless, strategies like financial incentives, training initiatives, and enhanced data tracking can mitigate these barriers, fostering a more environmentally responsible healthcare system while maintaining high-quality patient care.

(i) **Financial and Regulatory Hurdles:** High upfront costs for green technologies, such as solar panels, deter adoption, especially for smaller facilities. Retrofitting hospitals can cost millions [3]. Inconsistent regulations across regions complicate waste management and energy standards, hindering uniform implementation.

(ii) **Awareness and Data Gaps:** Only 20% of healthcare workers receive sustainability training, limiting awareness [3]. Scarce emissions data hinders progress tracking, exacerbated by increased medical waste during the COVID-19 pandemic.

(iii) **Solutions:** Economic stimuli, such as subsidies and tax credits, can help mitigate expenses. Education programs and standardized metrics address awareness and data gaps. Public-private partnerships can fund green initiatives, reducing financial burdens.

6. Future Directions

The healthcare sector stands at a critical crossroads, where integrating sustainability with high-quality patient care is both a necessity and an opportunity. The sector's significant environmental impact, including greenhouse gas emissions and waste generation, necessitates a strategic shift toward eco-friendly practices. This analysis explores future directions to achieve this transformation, focusing on advancements in research methodologies, a prioritized research agenda, the integration of technology and education, and robust policy support. These directions aim to minimize environmental harm while ensuring equitable and effective healthcare delivery, aligning with global sustainability goals such as the United Nations Sustainable Development Goals.

(i) **Advancements in Research Methodologies:** Robust research methodologies are essential for advancing green healthcare. A 2023 study employed a hybrid approach combining systematic literature review and bibliometric analysis to evaluate green healthcare initiatives. Using the PRISMA framework, researchers conducted a transparent process for article selection, involving four steps: locating articles from scientific databases, filtering duplicates, screening titles and abstracts, and evaluating full texts against inclusion criteria. The use of bibliometric mapping through VOSviewer facilitated a visual analysis of research trends, highlighting key topics such as waste management and energy effectiveness [3]. These methodologies provide evidence-based insights, guiding healthcare organizations in prioritizing impactful initiatives.

(ii) **Research Agenda:** Future research should develop standardized emissions metrics and assess green building and procurement practices. Studies should explore innovative technologies, such as digital health records and telemedicine, to optimize resource use and reduce waste [4].

(iii) **Technology and Education:** Integrating sustainability into medical education equips professionals for green practices. Technologies like digital records reduce paper use by 50%, while AI optimizes energy use [5]. Awareness programs educate staff on conservation and waste reduction.

(iv) **Policy Support:** Governments should incentivize sustainability through mandatory emissions reporting and green certifications. Ensuring stakeholders work together is essential [6].

7. Global Perspectives on Green Healthcare

Green healthcare refers to the integration of environmentally sustainable practices within healthcare systems to minimize ecological impact while ensuring high-quality patient care. As climate change poses increasing challenges, healthcare systems worldwide are adopting strategies to reduce emissions, optimize resource use, and manage waste effectively. This report provides a comprehensive overview of green healthcare initiatives across different regions, highlighting key efforts, challenges, and opportunities for improvement.

Europe

Europe is at the forefront of green healthcare, driven by robust policy frameworks and ambitious sustainability goals.

(i) **United Kingdom:** The National Health Service (NHS) has set a target to achieve net-zero direct emissions by 2040, with an ambition to reduce emissions by 80% by 2028–2032 (NHS Carbon Footprint). This includes adopting renewable energy, improving energy efficiency, and reducing waste in healthcare facilities.

(ii) **Netherlands:** The Dutch Green Deal for Sustainable Healthcare (Green Deal 3.0, 2023–2026) engages over 300 organizations, including hospitals, in efforts to reduce CO_2 emissions by 55% by 2030 and achieve carbon neutrality by 2050 (Dutch Green Deal).

(iii) **Germany:** Hospitals are implementing energy-efficient technologies, such as solar-PV panels and heat pumps. A 2018 study reported an average energy consumption of 0.27 MWh/m^2 in public hospitals, but claims of a 30% reduction lack recent verification (Energy Consumption in German Hospitals).

Table 1 below illustrates how Europe is taking initiatives and progressing in the field of Green healthcare.

Table 1: European Green Healthcare Initiatives

Country	Initiative	Target/Outcome	Source
UK	NHS Net-Zero Plan	Net-zero by 2040, 80% reduction by 2028–2032	NHS Carbon Footprint
Netherlands	Green Deal 3.0	55% CO_2 reduction by 2030, net-zero by 2050	Dutch Green Deal
Germany	Energy Efficiency in Hospitals	0.27 MWh/m^2 average consumption (2018)	Energy Consumption in German Hospitals

North America

North American healthcare systems, discussed in Table 2, are increasingly adopting sustainable practices, focusing on renewable energy and green infrastructure.

(i) **United States:** Organizations like Kaiser Permanente and the Mayo Clinic are integrating renewable energy sources, such as solar and wind, and implementing waste reduction strategies to lower their environmental footprint (Kaiser Permanente Sustainability).

(ii) **Canada:** Ontario has implemented green building standards for hospitals, ensuring new facilities meet energy efficiency and sustainability criteria (Health Canada Sustainability).

Table 2 given below, shows how North America is taking initiatives and progressing in the field of green healthcare.

Table 2: North American Green Healthcare Initiatives

Country	Initiative	Focus Area	Source
USA	Kaiser Permanente, Mayo Clinic	Renewable energy, waste reduction	Kaiser Permanente Sustainability
Canada	Ontario Green Building Standards	Energy-efficient hospital design	Health Canada Sustainability

Australia, Asia-Pacific

The Australia, Asia-Pacific region is diverse, with countries implementing varied approaches to green healthcare based on their economic and infrastructural capacities.

(i) **Australia:** Barwon Health focuses on reducing unnecessary medical tests to lower resource use and emissions (Barwon Health Sustainability).

(ii) **Japan and South Korea:** Both countries are investing in green building technologies for healthcare facilities, incorporating energy-efficient designs and renewable energy sources (WHO Regional Office).

(iii) **India:** Post-COVID-19, India has prioritized sustainable medical waste management to reduce environmental impact (WHO Regional Office).

Table 3 below shows how Australia and Asia-Pacific are taking initiatives and progressing in the field of green healthcare.

Developing Countries

Developing countries face significant challenges due to limited resources, but innovative initiatives are emerging with global support.

Table 3: Australia, Asia-Pacific Green Healthcare Initiatives

Country	Initiative	Focus area	Source
Australia	Barwon Health	Reducing unnecessary tests	Barwon Health Sustainability
Japan/S. Korea	Green Building Technologies	Energy-efficient infrastructure	WHO Regional Office
India	Sustainable Waste Management	Medical waste reduction	WHO Regional Office

(i) Palestine: The Green Healthcare Resource Management (GHRM) initiative demonstrates adaptability in resource-constrained settings, focusing on waste management and energy efficiency [2].

(ii) Global Support: Organizations like Health Care Without Harm provide technical and financial assistance to lower-income nations, promoting sustainable practices.

Table 4 given below shows how Developing Countries are taking initiatives and progressing in the field of green healthcare.

Table 4: Developing Countries' Green Healthcare Initiatives

Region/Country	Initiative	Focus area	Source
Palestine	GHRM Initiative	Waste Management, energy efficiency	Al-Ajlouni et al., 2023
Global	Health Care Without Harm Support	Technical and financial assistance	Health Care Without Harm

8. Technological Innovations in Green Healthcare

Technological innovations are pivotal in transforming healthcare into a sustainable sector, reducing environmental impact while enhancing operational efficiency and patient care quality. These advancements leverage cutting-edge tools and strategies to address the sector's significant resource consumption and waste generation. Below, we explore key technologies driving green healthcare, supported by real-world examples and their environmental and operational benefits.

Digital Health and Telemedicine

Telemedicine has emerged as a transformative tool for reducing the environmental footprint of healthcare by enabling remote consultations, thereby minimizing travel-related greenhouse gas (GHG) emissions. Transportation accounts for approximately 16% of healthcare-related emissions in the EU, making telemedicine a critical innovation [1]. During the COVID-19 pandemic, telemedicine usage surged, demonstrating its feasibility and effectiveness. Research indicates that virtual consultations can reduce patient travel emissions by up to 20% (PAGE10). For example, the Cleveland Clinic's telemedicine platform allows patients to consult specialists remotely, significantly cutting travel-related carbon emissions. Additionally, digital health records streamline administrative processes, reducing paper use by up to 50% and further lowering environmental impact [4].

Life Cycle Assessment (LCA)

Life Cycle Assessment (LCA) is a systematic methodology that evaluates the environmental and financial impacts of products, processes, or services from raw material extraction to disposal. In healthcare, LCA is instrumental in guiding sustainable procurement and waste management decisions. For instance, LCA compares the environmental footprint of reusable versus single-use medical devices, revealing that reusable surgical instruments, when properly sterilized, generate less waste and emissions than disposable alternatives. The UK's National Health Service (NHS) employs LCA to select medical products with lower environmental impacts, contributing to an 11% emissions reduction from 2007 to 2015 [4]. LCA also informs supply chain decisions, encouraging hospitals to choose suppliers with lower carbon footprints, potentially reducing emissions by 10–15% [1].

Energy Efficiency Technologies

Hospitals are among the most energy-intensive facilities, with heating, ventilation, and air conditioning (HVAC) systems accounting for up to 50% of energy consumption [24]. Energy efficiency technologies are critical for reducing this impact. Key innovations include:

- **(i) LED Lighting:** Replacing halogen lights with LEDs can reduce lighting energy use by 75%, significantly lowering electricity costs and emissions [12].
- **(ii) Renewable Energy Systems:** Solar panels and wind turbines provide clean energy, reducing reliance on fossil fuels. Solar panels at the Mayo Clinic in Minnesota generate about 2.5 million kilowatt-hours each year, enough electricity to power roughly 250 homes.
- **(iii) Smart Energy Management Systems:** These systems use real-time monitoring and AI-driven analytics to optimize energy use, achieving savings of 10–15% annually [19].
- **(iv) High-Efficiency HVAC Systems:** Variable speed drives and advanced insulation reduce energy consumption by 20–30% [12].
- **(v) Thermal Insulation and Heat Recovery:** These technologies minimize heat loss and recover waste heat, enhancing overall energy efficiency.

Al-Ramad Hospital in Egypt, for example, reduced energy use by 38% through LED upgrades, solar water heaters, and staff training, demonstrating the scalability of these technologies [17].

Water Management Technologies

Water conservation is a priority for green healthcare, given that hospitals consume approximately 1% of a city's total water supply [1]. Technological innovations in water management include:

(i) **Low-Flow Fixtures:** These reduce water usage in sinks, showers, and toilets without compromising functionality, saving up to 10% of water annually [19].

(ii) **Rainwater Harvesting:** Collecting rainwater for non-potable uses, such as irrigation or toilet flushing, can meet up to 85% of a hospital's non-potable water needs.

(iii) **Leak Detection Systems:** Automated systems identify and alert staff to leaks, preventing water waste and reducing costs.

(iv) **Digital Imaging:** Transitioning from film-based radiology to digital imaging eliminates water-intensive chemical processing, further conserving resources.

Tzu Chi General Hospital in Taiwan reuses sterilization water, reducing its water footprint by 20% [16].

Waste Management Technologies

Effective management of healthcare waste is crucial, given its potential to harm both the environment and public health. Traditional methods like incineration, while effective for sterilization, contribute significantly to air pollution through emissions such as dioxins and furans. To mitigate this, alternative technologies like microwave disinfection and autoclaving have been developed, offering sustainable solutions.

Green Building Technologies

Green building technologies are essential for creating sustainable healthcare facilities that minimize energy consumption and reduce environmental impact LEED (Leadership in Energy and Environmental Design) certification, administered by the U.S. Green Building Council, is a globally recognized standard that evaluates buildings based on their environmental performance, including energy efficiency, water conservation, and use of sustainable materials [10].

Artificial Intelligence

Artificial Intelligence is transforming healthcare by introducing innovative solutions that enhance operational efficiency, reduce waste, and improve patient care. AI's ability to analyse vast amounts of data and make predictions has made it particularly valuable in inventory optimization, predictive maintenance, and patient flow management.

Table 5 below shows different technological innovations that are taking place in the field of Green Healthcare.

Table 5: Technological Innovations in Green Healthcare

Technology	Description	Environmental benefit	Real-world example
Digital Health and Telemedicine	Enables remote consultations and digital health records	Reduces travel emissions by up to 20%, cuts paper use by 50%	Cleveland Clinic's telemedicine platform
Life Cycle Assessment (LCA)	Evaluates environmental impact of products/ processes	Reduces emissions by 10-15% via sustainable procurement	NHS uses LCA for low-impact medical products
Energy Efficiency Technologies	Includes LED lighting, solar panels, smart HVAC systems	Cuts lighting energy by 75%, HVAC energy by 20–30%	Al-Ramad Hospital, Egypt: 38% energy reduction
Water Management Technologies	Low-flow fixtures, rainwater harvesting, digital imaging	Aves 10% water, meets 85% non-potable needs	Tzu Chi General Hospital, Taiwan: 20% water reduction
Waste Management Technologies	Microwave disinfection and autoclaving for waste sterilization	Lowers emissions compared to incineration	Widely adopted in hospitals for sustainable waste processing
Green Building Technologies	LEED-certified designs with solar panels, green roofs	Reduces energy use by up to 20%	Mayo Clinic, Minnesota: solar-powered facilities
Artificial Intelligence (AI)	Optimizes inventory, maintenance, patient flow	Minimizes waste, improves resource efficiency	AI-driven systems in hospitals for predictive analytics

9. Economic Benefits of Green Healthcare

Transitioning to green healthcare is not only an ethical or environmental commitment but also a strategic economic decision. Sustainable healthcare practices can lead to substantial financial benefits, positioning organizations for long-term success [26]. This section explores the key economic advantages of adopting green healthcare: cost savings, competitive advantage, and risk management.

Cost Savings

Green healthcare initiatives can significantly reduce operational costs. Hospitals are among the most resource-intensive buildings, consuming large amounts of energy and producing considerable waste. By adopting energy-efficient technologies, such as LED lighting, smart HVAC systems, and building automation, facilities can reduce energy usage by 20–30%, leading to major utility savings [19].

In addition to energy savings, sustainable waste management practices cut costs. Proper waste segregation, recycling programs, and reducing single-use items decrease the volume of hazardous waste, which is costly to treat. For instance, Kaiser Permanente's waste reduction and recycling efforts reportedly save the organization millions of dollars annually [15].

Water conservation through low-flow fixtures and efficient landscaping can also lower utility bills. These combined measures reduce overhead costs, allowing more funds to be reinvested into patient care and innovation [27].

Competitive Advantage

Adopting sustainable practices enhances a healthcare organization's reputation and market position. With growing public concern about climate change and health, patients are increasingly drawn to hospitals that demonstrate environmental responsibility. Facilities with green certifications (such as LEED or WELL) are seen as forward-thinking and trustworthy [28]. Sustainability also attracts eco-conscious investors and donors, especially those guided by ESG (Environmental, Social, and Governance) principles. Access to green financing, grants, or favourable terms becomes more likely for institutions with proven sustainability performance. Moreover, a green workplace appeals to healthcare professionals, helping with recruitment and retention. Staff are more inclined to work in healthy, toxin-free environments that align with their personal values [29].

Risk Management

Sustainable healthcare reduces exposure to both immediate and long-term risks. As environmental regulations tighten, institutions that proactively adopt green practices are better positioned to remain compliant, avoiding fines or costly retrofits.

Climate-related risks, such as resource scarcity, extreme weather, or supply chain disruptions, can directly impact healthcare operations. Investing in renewable energy, water conservation, and local procurement improves resilience, ensuring continuity during crises.

Additionally, public scrutiny is rising. Organizations that neglect sustainability may suffer reputational harm or legal consequences. Transparent environmental policies and practices help build public trust and safeguard institutional credibility [28].

10. Social Benefits of Green Healthcare

Beyond economic and environmental gains, green healthcare practices deliver substantial social benefits. By prioritizing sustainability, healthcare institutions play a vital role in improving public well-being, increasing environmental awareness, and contributing to community development. This section highlights three primary social advantages: enhanced community health, public education and awareness, and job creation [30].

Community Health

One of the most significant social outcomes of green healthcare is its positive impact on public health. Healthcare facilities that reduce emissions, improve indoor air quality, and minimize the use of harmful chemicals that contribute directly to cleaner, healthier environments.

By transitioning to renewable energy, reducing vehicle emissions through better transportation policies, and limiting incineration of medical waste, green hospitals help lower levels of air pollutants such as particulate matter and nitrogen dioxide. These improvements can lead to a reduction in respiratory illnesses, cardiovascular problems, and asthma attacks, particularly among vulnerable populations like children and the elderly [24].

Moreover, sustainable design features, such as natural lighting, improved ventilation, and non-toxic materials, benefit not just patients and staff inside the facility, but also the broader community living nearby. Healthier surroundings support long-term well-being and decrease the overall burden on healthcare systems [29].

Education and Awareness

Green healthcare institutions also serve as powerful platforms for community education and engagement. Hospitals that adopt sustainable practices often extend their environmental commitment to public outreach, helping to raise awareness about the link between environmental health and personal well-being [31]. Through community programs, workshops, and informational campaigns, healthcare providers can educate patients and residents about topics such as air quality, climate-related health risks, nutrition, waste reduction, and water conservation. Initiatives like hospital gardens, green fairs, or educational signage within facilities help make sustainability more visible and relatable to the public. Organizations such as the International Hospital Federation's Green Care program emphasize the role of hospitals in promoting health literacy, not only about diseases but also about the environmental factors that influence health outcomes [7]. These efforts foster a more informed and empowered community capable of making sustainable lifestyle choices.

Job Creation

Investments in green healthcare also support local employment and workforce development. As hospitals implement sustainable infrastructure upgrades, install renewable energy systems, or adopt advanced waste management strategies, they create demand for skilled labour in these sectors. New roles emerge in areas such as environmental services, green construction, energy auditing, waste sorting and recycling, and sustainability coordination. These jobs often require specialized training, offering opportunities for upskilling and professional development within local communities [32].

Furthermore, the growing need for sustainable procurement and local sourcing supports small businesses and promotes regional economic stability. The shift toward sustainable healthcare systems is already contributing to green job creation, which in turn strengthens social equity by offering employment pathways in emerging sectors [3].

11. Measuring and Reporting Sustainability

Measuring and reporting sustainability is a cornerstone of effective green healthcare practices, enabling organizations to track progress, identify inefficiencies, and demonstrate accountability to stakeholders. This section explores standardized metrics, life cycle assessment (LCA), reporting frameworks, challenges in implementation, and emerging trends in sustainability measurement [34].

Standardized Metrics

Standardized metrics provide a consistent framework for measuring and comparing sustainability performance across healthcare facilities, ensuring data reliability and enabling benchmarking. Key metrics include:

(i) **Carbon Footprint:** This quantifies total greenhouse gas (GHG) emissions, encompassing direct emissions (e.g., from on-site fuel combustion) and indirect emissions (e.g., from purchased electricity). For instance, the UK's NHS tracks its carbon footprint to monitor progress toward net-zero emissions by 2040, achieving an 11% reduction from 2007 to 2015 [4].

(ii) **Energy Consumption:** Measured in kilowatt-hours per square meter or patient day, this metric assesses energy efficiency. Hospitals, being energy-intensive, benefit from tracking energy use to identify savings opportunities, such as upgrading to LED lighting, which can reduce lighting energy by 75% [12].

(iii) **Water Usage:** Hospitals consume significant water, often 1% of a city's supply [1]. Metrics track potable and non-potable water use, guiding conservation efforts like installing low-flow fixtures or recycling water for cooling systems.

(iv) Waste Generation: This includes hazardous (15% of total waste) and non-hazardous waste, with metrics focusing on total volume and diversion rates through recycling or composting. The University of California, San Francisco (UCSF) Medical Center reduced landfill waste by 50% using such metrics [18].

(v) Chemical Use: Tracks the use of hazardous chemicals and adoption of safer alternatives, such as biodegradable disinfectants, to minimize environmental and health risks.

These metrics enable healthcare organizations to set ambitious targets, such as reducing emissions by 20% over five years, and monitor progress through regular audits. For example, Kaiser Permanente's sustainability dashboard integrates these metrics to drive reductions in waste and emissions across its facilities [15]. Figure 3 shows the above-mentioned points about Standardized Metrics in a pictorial form.

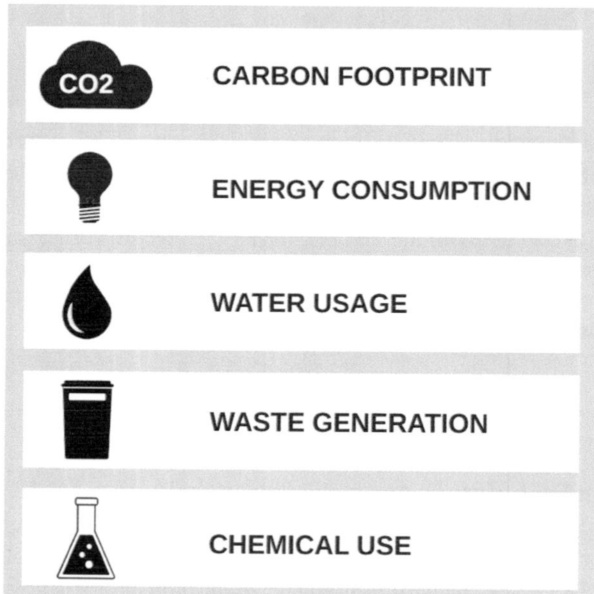

Figure 3: Standardized Metrics.

Life Cycle Assessment (LCA)

Life cycle assessment (LCA) evaluates the environmental impacts of products, processes, or services from raw material extraction to disposal, providing a holistic view of sustainability. In healthcare, LCA is applied to:

(i) Medical Devices: LCA compares reusable versus single-use devices. A study found reusable surgical instruments have a lower environmental footprint when properly maintained, influencing procurement decisions [4]. For example, reusable endoscopes reduce waste compared to disposable ones, saving costs and emissions.

(ii) Supply Chains: LCA identifies high-impact areas in the supply chain, such as transportation or manufacturing. By selecting suppliers with lower carbon footprints or products with recycled content, hospitals can reduce emissions by 10–15% [1].

(iii) Facility Design: LCA guides the design of new hospitals or renovations, prioritizing materials with low embodied carbon (e.g., recycled steel) or energy-efficient systems like natural ventilation. The Dell Children's Medical Center in Texas used LCA to achieve LEED certification, cutting energy use by 20% [10].

LCA requires robust data and expertise, but its insights are critical for balancing clinical efficacy with environmental responsibility. Hospitals adopting LCA often see long-term cost savings and improved sustainability outcomes. Figure 4 shows the above-mentioned points about Life Cycle Assessment in a pictorial form.

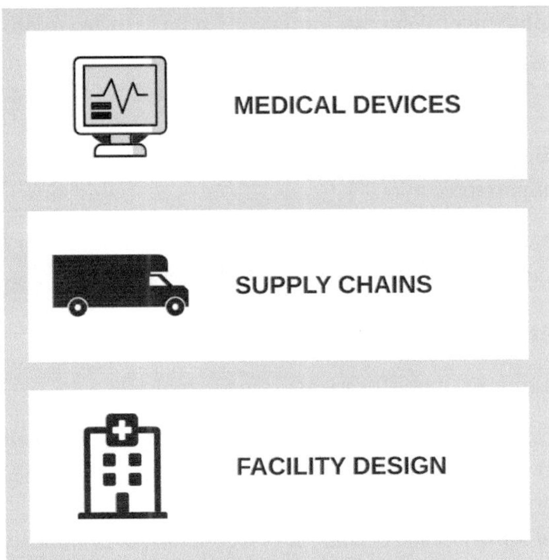

Figure 4: Life Cycle Assessment.

Reporting Frameworks

Reporting frameworks ensure transparency and consistency in communicating sustainability performance. Key frameworks include:

(i) **Global Reporting Initiative (GRI):** Provides standards for reporting economic, environmental, and social impacts. The GRI Healthcare Sector Supplement includes indicators like energy consumption and waste generation, enabling hospitals to benchmark performance [25].

(ii) **Sustainable Development Goals (SDGs):** Aligning with SDGs, particularly SDG 3 (Good Health and Well-being) and SDG 13 (Climate Action), enhances stakeholder engagement. Hospitals report contributions to SDGs to demonstrate global impact [33].

(iii) **ISO 14001:** This environmental management system standard helps hospitals systematically manage impacts, with certification signaling commitment to sustainability. For example, Singapore General Hospital's ISO 14001 certification supports its Green Mark Platinum status [23].

Reporting fosters accountability and drives continuous improvement. The Mayo Clinic, for instance, uses GRI standards to report its solar energy generation of 2.5 million kilowatt-hours annually, enhancing its reputation as a sustainability leader [21].

Challenges in Implementation

Implementing sustainability measurement faces challenges:

(i) **Data Availability:** Accurate emissions data is often scarce, especially in developing countries, hindering progress tracking [3].

(ii) **Resource Constraints:** Collecting and analyzing data requires time and expertise, which smaller facilities may lack.

(iii) **Standardization Gaps:** Variations in metrics across regions complicate global comparisons.

Solutions include investing in data management systems, training staff, and adopting international standards like GRI or ISO 14001.

Emerging Trends

Emerging trends in sustainability measurement include:

(i) **Digital Dashboards:** Real-time dashboards integrate metrics for energy, water, and waste, enabling proactive management. Kaiser Permanente's dashboard is a model [15].

(ii) **AI-Driven Analytics:** AI analyses large datasets to identify inefficiencies, such as energy leaks, enhancing metric accuracy [5].

Through global cooperation, organizations like the Global Climate and Health Alliance advocate for uniform metrics to enable benchmarking across nations.

By leveraging these trends, healthcare organizations can enhance their ability to measure and report sustainability, driving meaningful progress toward environmental goals. Figure 5 below shows the above-mentioned points about Emerging Trends in a pictorial form.

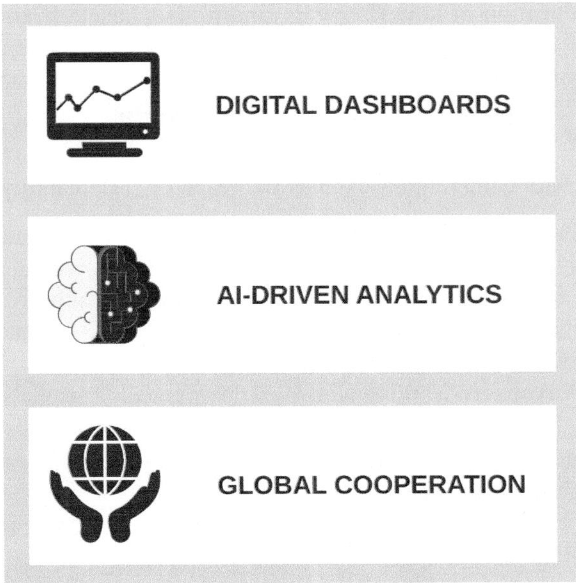

Figure 5: Emerging Trends.

12. Role of Patients and Communities

Patients and communities are pivotal in advancing green healthcare, influencing practices through engagement, partnerships, and advocacy. Their involvement fosters a culture of sustainability, amplifies impact, and drives systemic change [35]. This section explores these roles in detail, highlighting strategies, examples, and challenges.

Patient Engagement

Patients can actively contribute to sustainability by making informed choices and participating in green initiatives:

(i) **Choosing Sustainable Options:** Patients can opt for reusable medical devices, such as reusable sharps containers for chronic conditions, reducing plastic waste. Some hospitals offer reusable medication containers, cutting packaging waste by 10% [14].

(ii) **Reducing Travel:** Telemedicine minimizes travel-related emissions, with studies showing a 20% reduction during the COVID-19 pandemic [5]. Patients choosing virtual consultations for routine care lower their carbon footprint significantly.

(iii) **Providing Feedback:** Patient feedback on excessive packaging or single-use plastics can influence hospital policies. Kaiser Permanente's patient engagement program incorporates such feedback, leading to reduced plastic use in medical supplies [15].

Patient education is key. Hospitals like Massachusetts General Hospital run campaigns to inform patients about the environmental impact of healthcare, encouraging participation in recycling and waste reduction programs [22].

Community Partnerships

Collaborating with communities extends the reach of sustainability initiatives:

(i) **Recycling and Waste Reduction:** Hospitals can partner with local organizations to establish recycling programs for medical waste or educate residents on proper disposal. The "Green Healthcare Initiative" in California involves hospitals and schools in recycling education, diverting 30% of waste from landfills [14].

(ii) **Policy Advocacy:** Working with local governments, hospitals advocate for policies like incentives for green building or bans on single-use plastics. The Dutch Green Deal engaged communities to support its 100-hospital sustainability network [1].

(iii) **Health Promotion:** Community health initiatives address environmental and public health issues, such as promoting cycling to reduce air pollution. Cleveland Clinic's bike-sharing program, developed with community partners, cut local emissions by 5% [13]. These partnerships build trust and create shared goals, enhancing the impact of green healthcare efforts.

Advocacy

Patients and communities can advocate for systemic change:

(i) **Supporting Green Policies:** Advocacy for policies like mandatory emissions reporting or green certifications influences healthcare practices. Health Care Without Harm's campaigns have led to global policy changes, such as reduced use of mercury-based devices [14].

(ii) **Public Forums:** Participating in town halls or public meetings allows communities to demand sustainable healthcare. In Australia, community advocacy supported Barwon Health's "No Unhelpful Tests" initiative, saving 906 kg CO_2e annually [17].

(iii) **Joining Advocacy Groups:** Groups like the Alliance of Nurses for Healthy Environments empower patients and professionals to push for sustainability. Their efforts have influenced hospitals to adopt renewable energy and waste reduction strategies [3].

Advocacy amplifies the demand for green healthcare, driving organizations to prioritize sustainability.

13. Artificial Intelligence in Healthcare Sustainability

Artificial Intelligence (AI) is revolutionizing healthcare not only through diagnostics and treatment optimization but also by advancing sustainability goals. As hospitals and healthcare systems grapple with rising costs, resource inefficiencies, and environmental pressures, AI technologies are proving invaluable in streamlining operations and minimizing ecological impact. This section explores three key applications of AI in promoting sustainable healthcare: predictive maintenance, inventory management, and energy optimization [15].

Predictive Maintenance

One of the most promising uses of AI in sustainability is in the area of predictive maintenance. AI-powered monitoring systems use real-time data from medical equipment and building systems to forecast maintenance needs before a breakdown occurs. These systems analyse performance patterns, detect anomalies, and predict component failures with high accuracy.

By enabling proactive maintenance, AI reduces equipment downtime and prevents sudden failures that could disrupt healthcare services or lead to expensive repairs. This not only extends the lifespan of costly assets, such as MRI machines, ventilation systems, or surgical tools, but also reduces the demand for replacement parts and manufacturing resources [5].

Furthermore, predictive maintenance decreases the environmental impact associated with waste from prematurely discarded equipment and supports a more circular, resource-efficient healthcare model.

Inventory Management

Efficient inventory management is critical in hospitals, where overstocking and expiration of supplies are common issues. AI enhances supply chain management by forecasting demand based on historical usage patterns, seasonality, and patient trends. By analyzing data in real-time, AI systems help hospitals maintain optimal inventory levels, minimizing surplus stock and reducing medical waste. This is particularly important for perishable items such as medications, sterile supplies, and single-use instruments. Improved inventory practices reduce unnecessary procurement, free up storage space, and lower disposal costs—all of which contribute to a more sustainable and cost-effective system [4].

In addition to environmental benefits, optimized inventory ensures timely availability of essential items, improving patient care and operational efficiency.

Energy Management

AI-driven energy management systems offer powerful tools for improving energy efficiency in healthcare facilities. Hospitals often operate continuously and consume large amounts of energy, making even small improvements in efficiency highly impactful.

AI can analyse patterns in energy usage across departments and recommend targeted actions, such as adjusting HVAC schedules, automating lighting controls, or optimizing the performance of heating and cooling systems. These systems adapt dynamically based on occupancy levels, weather forecasts, and equipment usage to ensure energy is used only when and where needed [12].

Incorporating AI into energy systems helps reduce carbon emissions, lower utility bills, and extend the life of energy infrastructure. When integrated with renewable energy sources, AI can also manage load balancing and energy storage more effectively, further advancing sustainability goals.

14. Conclusion

Green healthcare is not only an environmental necessity but also a transformative opportunity to enhance healthcare delivery. By embracing circular economy principles, fostering green leadership, and implementing green human resource management (GHRM), healthcare organizations can significantly reduce their ecological footprint. Robust research methodologies, such as systematic literature reviews and bibliometric analysis, provide critical evidence to guide these efforts, ensuring that sustainability initiatives are both effective and scalable. However, achieving true sustainability demands a bold, forward-looking vision that transcends incremental improvements. Current healthcare practices contribute to environmental pollution, indirectly increasing public health burdens and service demands. A pivotal aspect of this transformation is shifting from a reactive, treatment-focused model to one that emphasizes prevention and health promotion. This requires robust policies that strengthen primary care, public health initiatives, and screening programs, ensuring equitable access to healthcare resources. Funding models should incentivize wellness outcomes, rewarding practices that promote long-term health over short-term interventions. Additionally, addressing the social determinants of health, such as economic disparities, necessitates cross-sectoral collaboration with fields like food systems, urban planning, and transportation to create healthier communities. Ultimately, the future of sustainable clinical care lies in a holistic approach that combines innovation, prevention, and collaboration. By reimagining healthcare delivery, embedding sustainability at every level, and fostering partnerships across sectors, the healthcare sector can create systems that are environmentally responsible, efficient, effective, and equitable. This vision is not only desirable but essential for ensuring the health and well-being of people and the planet for generations to come.

References

1. Soares, A. L., Buttigieg, S. C., Bak, B., McFadden, S., Hughes, C., McClure, P. et al. (2023). A review of the applicability of current green practices in Healthcare Facilities. *International Journal of Health Policy and Management*, 12, 6947. https://doi.org/10.34172/ijhpm.2023.6947
2. Sarayreh, A. A., Hijazi, R., Al Dweiri, M., Al Fawaeer, Dr. M., Al Ajlouni, M. I., and Al Ajlouni, K. (2022). Examining the mediating mechanism of the environmental

organizational citizenship behaviour in the relationship between green human resource management and sustainable performance. *International Journal of Productivity and Quality Management*, 1(1), 1. https://doi.org/10.1504/ijpqm.2022.10053689

3. Berniak-Woźny, J., and Rataj, M. (2023). Towards green and sustainable healthcare: A literature review and research agenda for green leadership in the healthcare sector. *International Journal of Environmental Research and Public Health*, 20(2), 908. https://doi.org/10.3390/ijerph20020908
4. Sony, M., Antony, J., and Tortorella, G. L. (2023). Critical success factors for successful implementation of healthcare 4.0: A literature review and future research agenda. *International Journal of Environmental Research and Public Health*, 20(5), 4669. https://doi.org/10.3390/ijerph20054669
5. Jasim, N. I., Gunasekaran, S. S., Al-Sharafi, M. A., Ibrahim, M., Hassan, A., Mahmoud, M. A., and Bakather, A. (2025). Exploring a nexus among green behavior and environmental sustainability: A systematic literature review and avenues for future research. *Resources, Conservation & Recycling Advances*, 25, 200249. https://doi.org/10.1016/j.rcradv.2025.200249
6. Diabat, A., and Govindan, K. (2011). An analysis of the drivers affecting the implementation of green supply chain management. *Resources, Conservation and Recycling*, 55(6), 659–667. https://doi.org/10.1016/j.resconrec.2010.12.002
7. Govindan, K. (2015). Green sourcing: Taking steps to achieve sustainability management and conservation of resources. *Resources, Conservation and Recycling*, 104(Part B), 329–333. https://doi.org/10.1016/j.resconrec.2015.10.027
8. Nurdiawati, A., Tahir, F., Zaini, I. N., and Al-Ghamdi, S. G. (2025). Prospective environmental and economic assessment of green steel production in the Middle East. *Resources, Conservation and Recycling*, 219, 108277. https://doi.org/10.1016/j.resconrec.2025.108277
9. Maheshwari, G. (2024). Institutional framework for resilience-enabled green growth strategies: A case study of India. *The Palgrave Encyclopedia of Sustainable Resources and Ecosystem Resilience*, 1–10. https://doi.org/10.1007/978-3-030-67776-3_4-1
10. Yamany, S. E., Afifi, M., and Hassan, A. (2016). Applicability and implementation of U.S. Green Building Council Rating System (LEED) in Egypt (a longitudinal study for Egyptian LEED certified buildings). *Procedia Environmental Sciences*, 34, 594–604. https://doi.org/10.1016/j.proenv.2016.04.052
11. Sharma, R., Singh, S., Huria, A., Chauhan, A., and Barman, T. (2024). Sustainable land management practices for healthy ecosystem services: A cornerstone of biodiversity sustenance in the Indian Northwestern Himalaya. *Sustainable Land Management in India*, 235–252. https://doi.org/10.1007/978-981-97-5223-2_14
12. Zhu, Q., and Shah, P. (2018). Product deletion and its impact on supply chain environmental sustainability. *Resources, Conservation and Recycling*, 132, 1–2. https://doi.org/10.1016/j.resconrec.2018.01.010
13. Gao, Y., Sharma, T., and Cui, Y. (2023). Addressing the challenge of biomedical data inequality: An artificial intelligence perspective. *Annual Review of Biomedical Data Science*, 6(1), 153–171. https://doi.org/10.1146/annurev-biodatasci-020722-020704
14. Sanz, F. (2025). Integrative data science in drug safety research: Experiences, challenges, and perspectives. *Annual Review of Biomedical Data Science*. https://doi.org/10.1146/annurev-biodatasci-103123-095506
15. Darwish, A. S. (2019). Green buildings to approach sustainable buildings by

integrating wind and solar systems with smart technologies. *Innovative Renewable Energy*, 433–446. https://doi.org/10.1007/978-3-030-30841-4_30
16. Swift-Hook, D. (2019). Fallacies and misunderstandings about global warming. *Innovative Renewable Energy*, 601–609. https://doi.org/10.1007/978-3-030-30841-4_43
17. Golbazi, M., and Aktas, C. B. (2020). LEED certification and patient wellbeing in green healthcare facilities. *Journal of Green Building*, 15(4), 3–18. https://doi.org/10.3992/jgb.15.4.3
18. Yoon, E., and Lim, Y. (2016). A study on green building certification criteria for healthcare facilities – focused on system and contents for healthcare in BREEAM, LEED, CASBEE. *Journal of The Korea Institute of Healthcare Architecture*, 22(3), 17–26. https://doi.org/10.15682/jkiha.2016.22.3.17
19. Darwish, A. S. (2019a). Green buildings to approach sustainable buildings by integrating wind and solar systems with smart technologies. *Innovative Renewable Energy*, 433–446. https://doi.org/10.1007/978-3-030-30841-4_30
20. Moşteanu, N. R. (2019a). Green sustainable regional development and digital era. *Innovative Renewable Energy*, 181–197. https://doi.org/10.1007/978-3-030-30841-4_13
21. Ceccherini Nelli, L. (2019). Urban regeneration with rooftop farming pilot projects. *Innovative Renewable Energy*, 501–511. https://doi.org/10.1007/978-3-030-30841-4_36
22. Norvell, M., Connors, C. A., and Wu, A. W. (2023). Helping without harm: Providing emotional support to health care workers in 2023. *Polish Archives of Internal Medicine*, 133(4). https://doi.org/10.20452/pamw.16484
23. Tang, Z., Tang, Z., Liu, Y., Tang, Z., and Liao, Y. (2024). Smart healthcare systems: A new IOT-fog based disease diagnosis framework for SMART healthcare projects. *Ain Shams Engineering Journal*, 15(10), 102941. https://doi.org/10.1016/j.asej.2024.102941
24. Singh, P. K., Devshali, C. C., Dhaundiyal, A., and Tripathi, A. (2024). Building green and climate-resilient healthcare facilities in Uttarakhand: A step for a sustainable climate resilient healthcare. *Indian Journal of Forensic and Community Medicine*, 11(2), 38–40. https://doi.org/10.18231/j.ijfcm.2024.010
25. Valencia, O., Leon, S., Paez, A., and Londono, D. (2024). HPR33 challenges and opportunities in implementing multimorbidity care models in the Colombian Healthcare System. *Value in Health*, 27(12). https://doi.org/10.1016/j.jval.2024.10.1460
26. Vamathevan, J., Apweiler, R., and Birney, E. (2019). Biomolecular data resources: Bioinformatics infrastructure for biomedical data science. *Annual Review of Biomedical Data Science*, 2(1), 199–222. https://doi.org/10.1146/annurev-biodatasci-072018-021321
27. Gurung, P., and Sarkar, S. (2024). Sustainability reporting under GRI standards: An empirical study of Indian companies. *Paradigm: A Management Research Journal*, 28(2), 185–203. https://doi.org/10.1177/09718907241268977
28. Al-Romeedy, B. S., and Alharethi, T. (2025). Leveraging green human resource management for sustainable tourism and hospitality: A mediation model for enhancing green reputation. *Discover Sustainability*, 6(1). https://doi.org/10.1007/s43621-025-00829-2
29. Sil, R., Das, A., Shamim, F., Chowdhury, A., Mukherjee, R., Ali, S., and Sharma, R. (2022). Damona: A multi-robot system for collection of waste in Ocean and sea.

Lecture Notes in Networks and Systems, 149–157. https://doi.org/10.1007/978-981-16-8721-1_15

30. Sijm-Eeken, M., Jaspers, M., and Peute, L. (2023). Identifying environmental impact factors for sustainable healthcare: A scoping review. *International Journal of Environmental Research and Public Health*, 20(18), 6747. https://doi.org/10.3390/ijerph20186747
31. Bhattacharjee, R., and Sil, R. (2023). Managing green it: A revolution for crafting the idea of Smart City in a different way. *International Journal of Social Science and Economic Research*, 08(04), 765–778. https://doi.org/10.46609/ijsser.2023.v08i04.016
32. Chien, C.-F., Kuo, P.-C., Sun, P.-C., and Kuo, H.-A. (2024). Green production planning for Circular Supply Chain and resource management: An empirical study for high-tech textile dyeing. *Resources, Conservation and Recycling*, 204, 107499. https://doi.org/10.1016/j.resconrec.2024.107499
33. Paterson, A., Olliaro, P. L., and Rojek, A. (2023). Addressing stigma in infectious disease outbreaks: A crucial step in pandemic preparedness. *Frontiers in Public Health*, 11. https://doi.org/10.3389/fpubh.2023.1303679
34. Dila Ram Bhandari, & Ron Kenett. (2022). Paradigm shift of statistical big data in healthcare: Management, analysis and future prospects.. *Pravaha*, 28(1), 35–44. https://doi.org/10.3126/pravaha.v28i1.57969
35. Zhao, Y., Genovesi, S., Jiang, T., Manara, G., and Costa, F. (2025). High capacity chipless RFID system enabled by machine learning predictive models. *IEEE Internet of Things Journal*, 1–1. https://doi.org/10.1109/jiot.2025.3560682

Index

About the Editors

Anindya Nag obtained an M.Sc. in Computer Science and Engineering from Khulna University in Khulna, Bangladesh, and a B.Tech. in Computer Science and Engineering from Adamas University in Kolkata, India. He is currently a lecturer in the Department of Computer Science and Engineering at the Northern University of Business and Technology in Khulna, Bangladesh. His research focuses on health informatics, medical Internet of Things, neuroscience, and machine learning. He serves as a reviewer for numerous prestigious journals and international conferences. He has authored and co-authored about 47 publications, including journal articles, conference papers, and book chapters, and has co-edited nine books.

Md. Mehedi Hassan is currently a Ph.D. researcher in STEM (Computer and Information Science) at the University of South Australia, working on a fully funded research project. He started his Ph.D. in 2025, building on a strong academic background in computer science and engineering. He holds an M.Sc. in Computer Science and Engineering from Khulna University, Bangladesh, completed in 2024, and a B.Sc. in Computer Science and Engineering from North Western University, completed in 2022. His research spans computer science engineering and data science, with a strong focus on predictive analysis and expert system development. Md. Mehedi Hassan has authored 73 research papers and edited 5 books, actively contributing to the academic community. He serves as a peer reviewer for over 80 prestigious journals and collaborates extensively in interdisciplinary research. As a trainer for the VCourse platform, he has educated over 250 students over the past two years, sharing knowledge in emerging technologies and research methodologies. Beyond publications, he has actively engaged in intellectual property development, with several patents filed and three already granted in his name. His current research interests include computational neuroscience, machine learning for healthcare, and predictive modeling for biometrics.

Dr. Riya Sil is an Associate Professor in the Department of Computer Science & Engineering, Brainware University, Kolkata, India. Dr. Riya Sil holds a B.Tech & M.Tech degree in Computer Science & Engineering from Birla Institute of Technology and a PhD degree with a specialization in Legal Analytics. She has a total professional experience of about 9 years, including 7 years in academics and 2 years as Software Developer at Cognizant Technology Solutions (CTS).

During her academic tenure, she has served as Asst. Professor in Computer Science & Engineering department in various institutions like Kristu Jayanti College – Autonomous, Techno India University, and Adamas University. Her research focuses on Machine Learning; Natural Language Processing (NLP); Deep Learning; Artificial Intelligence (AI) and Cloud Computing. She serves as a reviewer for various reputable journals and international conferences. She has about 40 publications to her credit which include peer-reviewed SCI and Scopus-indexed journals, conferences and book chapters.

Dr. Asif Karim currently works at the Faculty of Science and Technology, Charles Darwin University. Asif does research in Machine Learning based Health Informatics and Blockchain Applications. He has considerable Industry Experience in the field of IT, primarily in Software Engineering. Complete Information about his Research Publications, Teaching and Grants are available at https://asifkarim.com/.

For Product Safety Concerns and Information please contact our
EU representative GPSR@taylorandfrancis.com Taylor & Francis
Verlag GmbH, Kaufingerstraße 24, 80331 München, Germany